Get the eBook FREE!
(PDF, ePub, Kindle, and liveBook all included)

We believe that once you buy a book from us, you should be able to read it in any format we have available. To get electronic versions of this book at no additional cost to you, purchase and then register this book at the Manning website.

Go to https://www.manning.com/freebook and follow the instructions to complete your pBook registration.

That's it!
Thanks from Manning!

.NET in Action

SECOND EDITION

DUSTIN METZGAR

FOREWORD BY SCOTT HANSELMAN

MANNING
SHELTER ISLAND

For online information and ordering of this and other Manning books, please visit www.manning.com. The publisher offers discounts on this book when ordered in quantity. For more information, please contact

Special Sales Department
Manning Publications Co.
20 Baldwin Road
PO Box 761
Shelter Island, NY 11964
Email: orders@manning.com

Manning Publications Co.
20 Baldwin Road
PO Box 761
Shelter Island, NY 11964

Development editor: Dustin Archibald
Technical editor: Gerald Versluis
Review editors: Adriana Sabo and Dunja Nikitović
Production editor: Kathy Rossland
Copy editor: Keir Simpson
Proofreader: Jason Everett
Technical proofreader: Ricardo Peres
Typesetter: Gordan Salinovic
Cover designer: Marija Tudor

ISBN 9781633439313
Printed in the United States of America

brief contents

contents

foreword

Six years have passed since I wrote the foreword for the first edition of what was then *.NET Core in Action*. You're holding in your hands (or digitally) the massively revised and improved second edition, now titled *.NET in Action*. The word *Core* has gone from the branding, as cross-platform .NET is no longer thought of as a less-than-full version, but today, .NET is recognized as a robust, full-featured, incredibly powerful ecosystem. Today, we're shipping and enjoying .NET 8, with .NET 9 coming reliably at the end of 2024. The community enjoys long-term support versions, and millions of developers and enterprises trust .NET to run their software every day. Modern .NET is in action every day, and it's fast, it's portable, and it's awesome.

As Dustin called out in the first edition of his book, you'll be able to use a host of open source libraries to test your code, access databases, build microservices, and go live, either on your own hardware or in the cloud. Cross-platform GUI apps? .NET can make them happen for you. WebAssembly (WASM)? Check. Today, .NET powers games on your Xbox and Steam Deck, runs massive distributed applications in containers or orchestrated with Kubernetes, but also powers Internet of Things (IoT) devices and microcontrollers with technologies such as Wilderness Labs Meadow and .NET nanoFramework. You'd be hard-pressed to find a computer or system that doesn't run today's .NET.

This improved second edition includes a ton of new samples, chapters, and revisions with more than 300 pages of goodness! Dustin is sure to shout out many of the amazing open source libraries that make the .NET community successful. Whether they're games and graphics, databases and testing utilities, distributed systems, build tools, or workflows, a ton of fantastic projects out there are pushing .NET to the edges and beyond.

Finally, I want to call out the fact that you could hardly find a better guide to the .NET space than Dustin Metzgar. With more than 20 years of experience shipping software, he not only offers deep expertise on .NET, but also provides an inside look with important historical context as someone who worked on the .NET team at Microsoft. I appreciate Dustin as an open source advocate, community member, technologist, and writer. I hope you enjoy reading, exploring, and learning from this fantastic *.NET in Action, Second Edition* as much as I did!

—Scott Hanselman, Vice President,
Developer Community, Microsoft

preface

Software developers learn throughout their entire careers, which is part of the appeal. The more I learn, the more I discover how much I don't know (the known unknown). The times when I learned most were the times when an unknown became a known unknown, such as when a whole category of development that I'd never heard of was revealed to me. Subjects such as performance profiling and localization never occurred to me when I started, yet they play important roles in professional software development.

With so much information available through blogs, tweets, Stack Overflow, conferences, and online documentation, you might wonder whether physical books can still be relevant, especially books about a subject like .NET that might be outdated by the time they reach print. Learning a new software environment is like being dropped into an unfamiliar landscape. You can wander around certain parts that interest you and never see the whole area. A book is like a map and travel guide; it can give you a sense of the whole area and introduce places you may not have explored on your own. By the end of the book, you should feel confident in this new area.

I've spent a significant portion of my career on .NET. My introduction to .NET happened in Framework 1.0, thanks to a salesperson who didn't know (or care) that our product was written in Java when the customer wanted .NET. The project to convert to .NET and implement it at the customer site turned out to be my favorite consulting job. Years later, I was fortunate enough to be hired by Microsoft, where I worked on the .NET Framework and .NET Core. I got to work with many talented developers and write code that's now used by countless applications. I still use .NET today even after leaving Microsoft, which has further enriched my understanding.

My goal for this book is to provide an overview of the .NET environment so that you'll feel confident enough about .NET to write and maintain real-world applications. You'll get more out of this book if you write the code from the chapters and try the exercises. In this second edition, I've endeavored to make a book that's not only a great learning resource, but also a handy text to keep on your desk for quick reference.

acknowledgments

Thanks to the editors at Manning who kept the bar high and helped me write the book I wanted to write. Thanks to Dustin Archibald for guiding me through the whole process. Also, thanks to Melissa Ice for making sure that everything was delivered and to Ivan Martinović and Benjamin Berg for fixing all my AsciiDoc mistakes.

A big thanks goes to Scott Hanselman. Scott is a great developer, blogger, and speaker who has worked for many years to advance and evangelize .NET. I'm honored that he wrote the foreword for this book.

I'm also grateful to technical editor Gerald Versluis for helping make the manuscript what it is today. Gerald is a senior software engineer at Microsoft, working on .NET MAUI. Since 2009, he's worked on a variety of projects, ranging from frontend to backend and anything in between that involves C#, .NET, Azure, ASP.NET, and all kinds of other .NET technologies. At some point, he fell in love with cross-platform and mobile development with Xamarin, now .NET MAUI. Since then, he has become an active community member, producing content online and presenting about all things tech at conferences around the world.

I'd also like to thank Samer Alameer for his help with the localization chapter. He helped me with the Arabic and also taught me some important points about localization.

Finally, thank you to everyone who bought the early-access version of this book and to all the reviewers who provided invaluable feedback along the way: Adhir Ramjiawan, Andrei Tarutin, Barry L. Wallis, Cesar Aguirre, Chad Miars, Chris H. Shin, Dan Sheikh, Daniel McAlister, Daniel Vásquez, Dmitrii Slabko, Ernesto Cardenas, Georg Piwonka, George Onofrei, Jason Hales, Jonathan Reeves, Joe Cuevas, Krishna Chaitanya

Anipindi, Lakshminarayanan Sampath, Luigi Zambetti, Marios Solomou, Michael Williams, Mitchell Fox, Nikos Kanakaris, Oliver Korten, Renato Gentile, Tom Madden, Viktoria Dolzhenko, and Vladislav Bilay. Your suggestions helped make this book better.

about this book

.NET in Action was written to help you build applications and services in .NET. It takes you through many important aspects of developing high-quality software for release. Concepts and language features are introduced in action, with examples to show their practical application.

Who should read this book

Whether you're new to .NET and C# or a seasoned .NET Framework developer, this book has plenty of useful information for you. Although all this information may be available online through documentation, blogs, and the like, this book compiles and organizes everything in a format that's clear and easy to follow. The book assumes that you have working knowledge of imperative, object-oriented programming languages such as C++ and Java. Although the book isn't an instructional guide to C#, it explains key concepts of C# to aid the reader. This book also assumes that you have some proficiency with terminals or command lines and text editors.

How this book is organized: A road map

This book has 13 chapters:

- Chapter 1 introduces .NET—what it is and why you want to learn it.
- Chapter 2 gets you started creating .NET console applications.
- Chapter 3 expands to building web services and applications.
- Chapter 4 acquaints you with input/output (I/O) fundamentals such as files and HTTP requests.

- Chapter 5 introduces Entity Framework Core (EF Core), a popular way to access databases.
- Chapter 6 covers how to unit-test.
- Chapter 7 further enhances your unit-testing prowess by showing you how to use substitutes.
- Chapter 8 expands into integration testing, which is particularly useful for testing web services.
- Chapter 9 helps you secure your .NET applications.
- Chapter 10 looks at how to detect and understand performance issues.
- Chapter 11 shows various ways to recover from failures.
- Chapter 12 covers the internationalization process and shows you how to make applications world-ready.
- Chapter 13 walks you through putting your application in containers and handling configuration.

About the code

This book contains many examples of source code, both in numbered listings and inline with normal text. In both cases, source code is formatted in a `fixed-width font` `like this` to separate it from ordinary text. Sometimes, code is also in **bold** to highlight code that has changed from previous steps in the chapter, such as when a new feature adds to an existing line of code.

In many cases, the original source code has been reformatted; we've added line breaks and reworked indentation to accommodate the available page space in the book. In rare cases, even this was not enough, and listings include line-continuation markers (➥). Additionally, comments in the source code have been removed from the listings when the code is described in the text. Code annotations accompany many of the listings, highlighting important concepts.

The source code for the book is located at https://github.com/dmetzgar/dotnet-in-action-code. This GitHub repository contains all the source code from the book. The complete code for the examples in the book is also available for download from the Manning website at https://www.manning.com/books/dotnet-in-action-second-edition. You can get executable snippets of code from the liveBook (online) version of this book at https://livebook.manning.com/book/dotnet-in-action-second-edition.

liveBook discussion forum

Purchase of .NET in Action, Second Edition, includes free access to liveBook, Manning's online reading platform. Using liveBook's exclusive discussion features, you can attach comments to the book globally or to specific sections or paragraphs. It's a snap to make notes for yourself, ask and answer technical questions, and receive help from the author and other users. To access the forum, go to https://livebook.manning.com/book/dotnet-in-action-second-edition/discussion. You can also learn more about Manning's forums and the rules of conduct at https://livebook.manning.com/discussion.

Manning's commitment to our readers is to provide a venue where meaningful dialogue between individual readers and between readers and the author can take place. It is not a commitment to any specific amount of participation on the part of the author, whose contribution to the forum remains voluntary (and unpaid). We suggest that you try asking the author some challenging questions lest their interest stray! The forum and the archives of previous discussions will be accessible on the publisher's website as long as the book is in print.

about the author

DUSTIN METZGAR has been developing software professionally since 2003. He has worked in both startups and large enterprises including Microsoft, Uber, and UiPath. He has built many .NET services and applications and is active in the .NET open source community.

about the cover illustration

The caption for the illustration on the cover of *.NET in Action, Second Edition,* is "A Turk in a pelise," taken from a collection published in 1802 by William Miller.

In those days, it was easy to identify where people lived and what their trade or station in life was by their dress alone. Manning celebrates the inventiveness and initiative of the computer business with book covers based on the rich diversity of regional cultures centuries ago, brought back to life by pictures from collections such as this one.

Part 1

The basics

Welcome to the start of your .NET journey! This part establishes the basics of .NET programming.

In chapter 1, you'll learn what .NET is, what kinds of applications you can build with it, and the key features of the .NET runtime.

In chapter 2, you'll start building console applications and writing code. Chapter 2 also covers some important fundamentals, such as namespaces, classes, records, properties, command-line arguments, packages, and top-level statements. You'll build a command-line application that turns input strings into ASCII art.

In chapter 3, you'll expand on the skills you acquired in chapter 2 and learn to build web services and applications. This chapter creates a solid foundation for the rest of the book because most chapters involve web services.

This part is essential for newcomers to .NET, and it also has useful information for those who used .NET in the past but haven't kept up with the latest versions. Let's get started!

Why .NET?

This chapter covers

- What .NET is
- Where .NET is used
- What is in the .NET runtime

There has never been a better time to be a .NET developer. .NET runs on almost everything: from embedded devices and sensors to game engines such as Unity and Godot, from mobile devices to all major clouds. The skills you'll learn from this book apply across the broad .NET ecosystem. This book covers the necessary foundation and gets you building production-ready applications.

.NET looks a lot different now compared to 2002, when I started working with it professionally. Features were introduced, improved, and sometimes replaced or deprecated but still supported. Microsoft maintained backward compatibility with each version of the .NET Framework to prevent breaking existing applications, which was great for customers but resulted in the accumulation of some baggage over the past 20 years.

The first edition of this book, *.NET Core in Action*, explored how Microsoft decided to hit refresh and begin anew. It mixed the best parts of .NET with some new ideas and modern techniques to create .NET Core. The existence of different

.NETs, such as Framework and Core, caused some confusion, but it was clear that Core was the future. So Microsoft decided to drop the Core moniker and go with .NET alone when it released .NET 5 (5 being greater than .NET Core 3.0 and .NET Framework 4.8). In .NET 6, 7, 8, and beyond, we're seeing an evolution of what was once .NET Core. Whether you're new to .NET or an experienced veteran, now is an exciting time to be a .NET developer.

> ### What happened to Core, Framework, and Standard?
>
> In the beginning, there was the .NET Framework. Over time, the .NET Framework struggled to stay competitive, burdened by the weight of backward compatibility. Other languages and frameworks worked on any platform instead of being limited to Windows. To start fresh, the .NET team created a new version called .NET Core that incorporated a lot of new ideas: designing and building in the open, working on any platform, focusing on web performance, and so on.
>
> To make existing libraries port easily between Framework and Core, Microsoft introduced .NET Standard, which defines only the APIs that a .NET implementation needs to fulfill. If you have some projects that are .NET Framework and others that are .NET Core, .NET 5, or later, those projects can use common libraries that target the .NET Standard. So even though no new iterations of .NET Standard will be released, it's still a useful tool for incrementally porting applications to the newest versions of .NET.
>
> Starting with .NET 5, Microsoft tried to simplify by culling Core, Framework, and Standard and having one .NET with some OS-specific targeting capabilities. If you want to develop in .NET, forget about Core and Framework; target the latest long-term support release of .NET. If you need to support older versions of .NET, try targeting .NET Standard, which will give your libraries the broadest reach. Appendix A explores this subject in more detail.

1.1   What is .NET?

.NET is free, cross-platform, and open source; it's a runtime, not a programming language. The .NET runtime understands only one language: Common Intermediate Language (CIL). (This language is commonly referred to as *IL*, but I'll stick with the term *CIL* to differentiate it from other intermediate languages.) CIL is a low-level language similar to Assembly. Don't worry, though; you won't have to learn CIL because .NET comes with compilers that compile high-level languages to CIL.

.NET fully supports three languages: C#, F#, and Visual Basic (VB.NET). C# is the most widely used of those languages by a large margin, and all examples in this book are in C#. F# is a functional language like Clojure and Haskell. C# and F# are active projects, but VB.NET is *done*—Microsoft parlance for continuing support and maintenance but not investing in new features.

Code written in .NET has access to other .NET code, regardless of the language used. If some part of your C# application is better expressed in F#, you don't need to convert everything to F# because all the .NET compilers produce CIL. The C#, F#, and VB.NET compilers are packaged with .NET, but any language that compiles to CIL will work with .NET.

Finally, the .NET community has contributed many other languages. You can even create your own language. Also, the .NET open source community has created compilers for other languages to work in .NET, as shown in the following minitable.

Table 1.1

Project name	Language	Website
PeachPie	PHP	https://www.peachpie.io
IronPython	Python	https://ironpython.net
MoonSharp	Lua	https://www.moonsharp.org
Jint	JavaScript Interpreter	https://github.com/sebastienros/jint

I've mentioned that .NET is a runtime, but what does that term mean? Think of a *runtime* as being an interpreter that can read code in a certain format—such as Intermediate Language (IL); think bytecode if you're familiar with Java—and execute it. The .NET runtime is called the CoreCLR. *CLR* stands for Common Language Runtime, with *Common* referring to the fact that every .NET language uses the same runtime. In the original .NET, the runtime was called simply CLR; the Core part was added with .NET Core to distinguish it from the original CLR (part of the .NET Framework), and the name stuck.

The runtime has important features such as just-in-time (JIT) compilation and memory management, which we'll explore in this book. Figure 1.1 shows how CIL, the compilers, and the CoreCLR fit together.

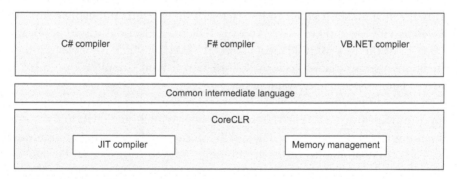

Figure 1.1   .NET compilers, CIL, and CoreCLR

In addition to the runtime and some language compilers, .NET has a class library, which is called the Framework Class Library but referred to as CoreFX. .NET veterans may remember that this library used to be called the Base Class Library (BCL), and Microsoft sometimes called it FX internally. CoreFX provides a set of APIs that handle many base-level functions: collections, algorithms, console output, file I/O, network I/O, and so on.

Besides the .NET class library (CoreFX), some powerful features that come with .NET were built by .NET teams and are supported by Microsoft. This book introduces you to the following key features, as well as to some useful projects created by the open source community:

- Entity Framework Core for access to data stores
- ASP.NET Core for web services and applications
- Testing libraries such as xUnit and FakeItEasy
- Microsoft extensions including logging, localization, dependency injection, and configuration

1.2   *Where is .NET used?*

ASP.NET Core is .NET's web framework and can be hosted in a lightweight, cross-platform server called Kestrel or in the Windows-only Internet Information Services (IIS) host. Kestrel enables ASP.NET Core to run on containers, which makes ASP.NET Core perfect for microservices. Several hosting services available from cloud providers use the container model, IIS, or serverless options.

.NET is also used in desktop (aka thick client) applications, and users have many options. Traditional Windows Forms applications are available; they're helpful in maintaining older applications. Windows Presentation Foundation (WPF) has an XML-based approach and is widely used for desktop applications. An ASP.NET Core feature called Blazor enables building .NET WebAssembly modules, which allows .NET to run in the browser. Blazor also has a hybrid model that can run both on the client and server sides.

You can also write .NET applications for PC, tablet, Xbox, and Hololens with WinUI, which makes it easier to interact with touch, pen, and game controller input as well as a mouse and keyboard. To write iOS, macOS, and Android applications, use Xamarin or the new Multi-Platform App UI (MAUI), which is an evolution of Xamarin. Some open source projects use Blazor to run WinUI applications in the browser, such as Uno Platform and Avalonia UI.

If you're interested in small devices, sensors, and microcontrollers, you have many opportunities to use .NET. .NET runs on boards such as the Raspberry Pi and the Hummingboard, for example. The .NET Internet of Things (IoT) community maintains a set of components for device bindings to work with specific hardware—things such as liquid crystal displays (LCDs), temperature sensors, and analog-to-digital converters. If the hardware is too small to run .NET 6 or later, lighter implementations such as the .NET nanoFramework and Meadow work on embedded devices.

1.2.1   *.NET in gaming and 3D graphics*

.NET Framework developers may be surprised to learn how often .NET appears in game engines. .NET's cross-platform support, along with its deep base class library and its use of the well-liked C# language, has made it an attractive option. Unity has been using C# for scripting game objects since its early releases. Before .NET Core, Unity used Mono, which was an unofficial, cross-platform, open source port of the .NET Framework that had enough capability to handle scripting for many years, but Microsoft didn't support Mono.

Unity migrated to .NET Core after that product came out. Unity uses .NET for scripting game objects but not for writing its engine code, which is written in native C++. The same goes for Godot and CRYENGINE (two other popular game engines).

One objection to using .NET and similar runtimes (such as Java) is that they're managed rather than native. *Native code* is compiled to work on a specific machine and usually manages memory on its own. *Managed code*, by contrast, executes in a runtime by using an interpreter. The runtime often provides memory management via garbage collection, which is undesirable in real-time applications because it can create unpredictable pauses while the garbage collector runs. You'll learn why in chapter 10. But can managed code be used for the entire game engine?

As it happens, two game engines were written with .NET: Evergine (https:// evergine.com) and Stride (https://www.stride3d.net). Evergine is a 3D engine for business and industry that sees use in augmented reality (AR) and virtual reality (VR) projects in areas such as aerospace, architecture, and health care. Stride is a free game engine that handles real-time 3D and VR.

Another project, Ryujinx, provides further evidence that .NET can handle real-time games. Ryujinx is a Nintendo Switch emulator written entirely in C# that emulates the ARM CPU. The Ryujinx team has even driven some performance improvements in .NET. Check out the project at https://ryujinx.org.

1.2.2 *Popular .NET open source projects*

This book introduces many important .NET concepts and reinforces your learning with exercises. Writing code for the exercises helps with the learning process. You may be reading this book because you need to learn or brush up on .NET for a work project, which is great because you get to apply your skills immediately. If you don't have an immediate work project, you can learn from many open source projects.

Reading code from other projects is a great way to see how .NET constructs are used. If you're looking for .NET projects to participate in, the .NET Foundation (https://dotnetfoundation.org) is a good place to start. .NET Foundation projects have common rules about contributor agreements, code of conduct, and licensing. Most but not all projects mentioned in this book are part of the .NET Foundation; all of them are on GitHub.

ASP.NET Core is .NET's web framework and a great starting point for building web applications and services. Naturally, many open source projects are for ASP.NET Core applications. If you want more features than those that are built into ASP.NET Core, you have a few open source and commercial options. DotVVM, for example, has built-in components and reduces the number of round trips to the server by implementing most features in Knockout JS. Another option is ASP.NET Boilerplate, a framework that handles common development tasks by convention and provides a lot of templates. If you're interested in Blazor (the feature that enables .NET in the browser), check out Oqtane or the Ant Design Blazor project.

If you want a full website that handles just about everything and where you can build your application as a custom component, check out some of the .NET content management systems (CMSes), such as Orchard, Umbraco, Piranha, and DNN (aka DotNetNuke).

MAUI is a relatively new product for building applications for any platform. Many other options are also worth investigating. Reactive UI, for example, is a framework for building applications that use functional reactive programming. (If you haven't heard of reactive programming, check out ReactiveX at https://reactivex.io.) Another cross-platform UI framework is Avalonia, which makes the XAML-based UI programming from Windows Presentation Foundation (WPF) work on platforms such as Linux and macOS as well as in the browser (via WebAssembly). Here are a few other interesting projects that you can use or contribute to:

- *Graphics*—ImageSharp, Silk.NET, and SkiaSharp
- *Database*—Dapper, LINQ to DB, and Marten
- *Testing utilities*—xUnit, Verify, BenchmarkDotNet, Moq, FluentAssertions, and FakeItEasy
- *Distributed systems*—Akka.NET and Orleans
- *Workflow*—Elsa Workflows and Durable Task Framework
- *Build tools*—Cake

1.3   *When to use .NET*

At one time, .NET was a Windows-only framework, but that hasn't been the case for years. .NET works in Windows, Linux, and macOS for desktop applications as well as in Android and iOS for phones and tablets. .NET is used in microcontrollers, IoT devices, and games. You can even use .NET in shell scripting via PowerShell. But most jobs in .NET are for web services and applications.

Whether you should use .NET depends on your scenario. Here are a few scenarios in which .NET is an option but not commonly used:

- *Data science*—Although some strides have been made in using .NET for data science and machine learning, starting with Python is a better idea.
- *Hardware drivers*—Managed code in hardware drivers could be useful in that the code is safer and easier to write. But using it requires understanding garbage collection, JIT/ahead of time (AOT) compilation, and trimming. A language such as Rust may be a better starting point.
- *Games*—Game developers using an engine such as Unity or Godot can use C# in their scripts. Books and tutorials that specifically cover C# for these use cases are more targeted than this book. .NET has been used in the past to write entire games, but this book doesn't explore those frameworks.

This isn't to say that you can't use .NET in these scenarios. Choosing what language or framework to use depends on many factors, such as performance, security, the development team's comfort level, what support is available, and how big (and welcoming) the community is. .NET has 20 years of hardening and improvements plus millions of active developers; it's open source, with a large and engaged community. .NET has strong support from Microsoft, even without the support contracts that many companies already have.

Given the fact that you're reading this book, you're at least considering .NET for your application. Try building the examples in the first few chapters to see for yourself how powerful .NET can be, as well as how easy it is to use.

1.4 What will I learn from this book?

This book aims at two types of developers: those who are familiar with other programming languages and are new to .NET and those who have .NET experience but want to catch up on the latest features.

If you're new to programming in general, this book may be difficult to follow. I assume that you have a general idea of the following concepts:

- *Software patterns* (also called *design patterns* and *software design patterns*)—This book uses some basic patterns, such as Singleton, Model-View-Controller (MVC), and method-chaining. Many of these patterns are well known, so the book gives you only a brief introduction to them. Generally, though, knowing what software patterns are is important, as they provide a language for communicating with other software developers.
- *Web services and web applications*—If you know about URLs, HTTP, requests, responses, and web servers, you should be able to follow the examples.
- *Terminal use*—A *terminal* can also be called a *command line, command prompt,* or *shell.* The examples in this book provide instructions that are executed in the terminal. If you're using an IDE such as Visual Studio or Rider, you can use the terminal built into the IDE or translate the commands into UI actions.

Developers who have used .NET in the past may want to consider skimming the first few chapters. If you haven't used .NET for a while, here are some relatively new concepts that are covered in the first three chapters:

- Top-level statements
- Records
- Nullable reference types, null coalescing, and other null operators
- Global and implicit `usings`
- Dotnet watch and hot reload

As you read this book's table of contents, you may wonder how everything fits together. Figure 1.2 shows how the topics align. In this chapter, you're building an understanding of the CoreCLR and the services it offers. On top of that, you'll learn

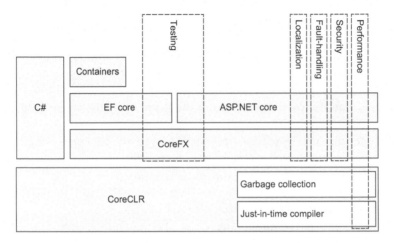

Figure 1.2   High-level diagram of how the topics covered in the book fit together

C# throughout the first few chapters. The class libraries available in CoreFX are essential for understanding what is available in .NET and what has to be pulled in via external packages.

The dashed boxes arranged vertically indicate cross-cutting concerns. Performance, for example, affects everything from understanding how the JIT compiler affects your application to how to use ASP.NET Core more efficiently. Although several areas involve ASP.NET Core, such as security and fault handling, this book focuses on .NET in general; it's not intended to be a comprehensive reference on ASP.NET Core.

By the end of this book, you should be able to write and deploy libraries, console applications, web services, and web applications. Your applications will be able to store and manipulate data in databases and through other services. You'll have intermediate-level understanding of important .NET concepts and features. My goal in this book is to get you quickly to the point where you can develop .NET applications professionally. You can dive deeper into many of the subjects introduced here, and other books from Manning will help you.

1.5   *What is in the .NET runtime?*

I mentioned earlier that .NET is *managed*, which means that it uses a runtime. .NET's runtime, the CoreCLR, has three important concepts that influence how you write code in .NET: intermediate language, JIT compilation, and garbage collection. We'll explore these concepts at a high level first and get into details as they become relevant later in the book.

1.5.1   Intermediate language

The code you write in any language needs to be compiled into some machine-readable form. But what does *machine-readable* mean? For code to execute on a processor, it needs to use the right set of instructions. The two most popular instruction sets for modern computers are x86 and ARM. Many others are available, especially when you include graphical processing units (GPUs), which are used for games (think shaders), crypto-currency mining, and data processing. New generations of processors may add new instructions to an instruction set, so it's important to know the processor's generation. OSes also impose some requirements on application machine code; an Android executable won't run in Windows, for example. Often, you'll need different compilers for different platforms.

Figure 1.3 shows a simplified matrix of producing machine-readable code for one specific OS and CPU. Typically, macOS/iOS applications use the xCode compiler and choose the CPU architecture to build for. OS versions matter. OSX 10, 11, and 12, for example, have compatibility differences. OS flavors matter too (think RedHat versus Ubuntu versus Debian).

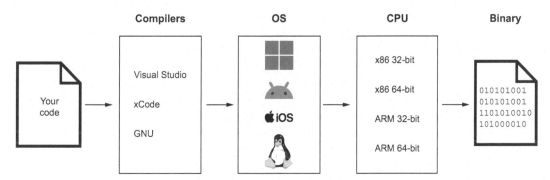

Figure 1.3   Creating an executable application without a runtime (unmanaged)

Intermediate language offers an alternative; it's a language that can be translated quickly into machine code. The compiler is specific to the language, not the OS or processor architecture you're targeting. If you're familiar with Assembly language, CIL is similar but has instructions at a slightly higher level of abstraction. Having your code compiled into CIL means that your application's binaries (the files produced through compilation) can run on any processor or OS with a .NET runtime.

In figure 1.4, the compiler is specific only to the language. The compiler creates CIL code and puts it in a Dynamic Link Library (DLL) file. The DLL file can be transferred to any machine regardless of OS or processor architecture as long as there is a .NET runtime. The .NET runtime converts the CIL to machine-readable code (typically at runtime, using the JIT compiler introduced in section 1.5.2).

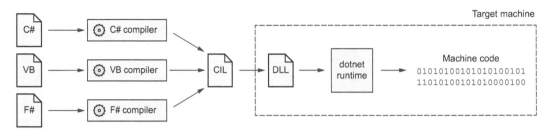

Figure 1.4   .NET languages compile to CIL in a DLL file that can be run on any machine with a .NET runtime.

What is a DLL?

DLL stands for *Dynamically Linked Library*. When you write programs, you almost always make calls into some library to invoke operations. Writing to the console, allocating memory, creating a thread, opening a file, and many other functions are relatively simple operations because of libraries. For some languages, such as C/C++, a link step during the build process links your code to the static libraries it uses. Static linking includes the library in your application, and that library can't be reused by other applications. If the library is updated, the application has to be rebuilt and redistributed.

A more flexible approach to linking uses DLLs, which expose a public surface area and can be reused by any application. The use of DLLs reduces the size of an application while allowing .NET to publish minor new versions with bug fixes without requiring each application to rebuild and redistribute. DLLs are usually installed or registered with the OS, so they can be shared, but if applications use different versions or DLLs reference other DLLs with different versions, you get into what many developers refer to as DLL hell. The concept of a DLL isn't exclusive to .NET.

1.5.2   *JIT compilation*

Figure 1.4 (section 1.5.1) shows that .NET includes compilers for C#, F#, and Visual Basic. Because these languages have already been compiled, why does the CoreCLR (.NET runtime) include another compiler? A *compiler* is a program that translates a program in one language into another language. Typically, a compiler is used for translating a high-level language into a low-level language, and that situation is true of the Visual Basic, C#, and F# compilers.

> **DEFINITION** If a compiler translates one high-level language to another, such as C# to JavaScript, it's typically called a *transpiler*. Some compilers also translate a program in a low-level language to a high-level language and are typically called *decompilers*.

As noted earlier, CIL is at a higher level than machine code. CIL makes no assumptions about the specifics of processor architecture (registers, instruction sets, cache sizes, and so on) so that it can work on as many platforms as possible. Before .NET code can be executed on a processor, the CIL needs to be compiled further down into machine code. The CoreCLR performs this compilation at runtime so that the CIL

DLLs don't need to be compiled into processor-specific DLLs ahead of time. But compilation can be an expensive process, and compiling an entire application every time it runs could affect startup performance. This task is handled by a smart compiler that compiles only the code that is about to be used. In other words, the CIL is compiled just in time, which is where the CoreCLR's JIT compiler gets its name.

> **NOTE** In some cases, you know exactly what processor architecture and OS your application will be running on, such as when you're building a Docker container. You can avoid the effect of JIT compilation in this case by using an ahead of time (AOT) compiler. You can use AOT to trim unused code to reduce the size of the code you distribute. (But test thoroughly, because AOT sometimes removes too much code.) The biggest advantage of AOT is to have an initial compilation of the code so that it runs immediately without waiting for JIT. Later, you use JIT compilation for optimization after gathering data on how the compiled code works. This book doesn't go into the use of AOT, but if you're interested in the subject, take a look at ReadyToRun (http://mng.bz/gv18).

1.5.3 Garbage collection

Earlier in this chapter, I mentioned that the CoreCLR (the .NET runtime) has a memory-management component. The memory manager uses a technique called *garbage collection*. Many functional programming languages (such as Lisp and Haskell) also use garbage collection; so do Java and some JavaScript interpreters. The essence of the technique is to keep track of the references to a chunk of memory; when no references remain, the memory can be safely freed and made available for allocation again.

Garbage collection changes the way you write programs. To see this effect, look at the simple C++ program shown in the following listing.

Listing 1.1 Creating a dynamic array in C++

```
#include <stdio.h>
#include <stdlib.h>

int main() {
   int n = 4, i, *p;
   p = (int*) malloc(n * sizeof(int));      <-------- Allocates an array to hold n ints

   if(p == NULL) {                                    <-------- Checks that memory was allocated
      printf("\nError! memory not allocated.");
      exit(0);
   }
   printf("\nEnter elements of array : ");

   for(i = 0; i < n; i++) {
      scanf("%d", p + i);       <-------- Reads int from input and stores in array
   }
   printf("\nSum : %d", sum(p, n));
   free(p);                          <-------- Frees the array memory
   return 0;
}
```

```
int sum(int *arr, int length) {          ⟵——— Sums array elements
  int i, sum = 0;
  for (i = 0; i < length; i++) {
    sum += *(arr + i);
  }
  return sum;
}
```

In listing 1.1, the array size is hardcoded, but it doesn't have to be. If the number of elements to store in an array isn't known until runtime and could be large, it's better to allocate the array from memory at runtime. But memory allocation can fail, so you have to make sure that it worked and handle it when it doesn't. When you're done with the memory, you have to free it explicitly (free(p)) so that other parts of the program can use it.

The manual method of managing memory is cumbersome and error-prone, but it's preferred in high-performance scenarios such as gaming and real-time devices. By contrast, .NET handles memory management so you don't have to explicitly allocate, free, or handle allocation failures. The .NET garbage collector cleans up unused memory for you. Compare the C++ code in listing 1.1 with the C# equivalent shown in the following listing.

Listing 1.2 Creating a dynamic array in C#

```
public class Program
{
  public static void Main()
  {
    int n = 4, i;
    int[] p = new int[n];                    ⟵——— Allocates an array to hold n ints

    Console.WriteLine("Enter elements of array : ");

    for (i = 0; i < n; i++) {
        p[i] = int.Parse(Console.ReadLine());    ⟵┐ Reads from input, converts
    }                                             │ to int, and stores in array

    Console.WriteLine("Sum : " + Sum(p));    ⟵——— Prints sum
  }

  private static int Sum(int[] arr)
  {
    int i, sum = 0;
    for (i = 0; i < arr.Length; i++)         ⟵——— Array length is part of the array.
    {
      sum += arr[i];
    }

    return sum;
  }
}
```

Notice that the code doesn't check for successful memory allocation and doesn't free any memory explicitly. If memory couldn't be allocated, the garbage collector would run, try to free memory, and then attempt the allocation again. If the collector is unable to free enough memory, an OutOfMemoryException is thrown, giving the host a chance to determine how to handle the problem. .NET also checks array bounds for you, whereas C++ programmers need to implement this task themselves.

What is an OutOfMemoryException?

Some languages, such as Go, communicate errors by function return values. .NET uses exceptions to indicate error conditions. An exception is *thrown* when an exceptional situation occurs. It's the job of the calling code to *catch* the exception and handle it (if it's the right place to handle the exception). An OutOfMemoryException is thrown when .NET is unable to allocate memory. The program is unrecoverable at this point, but you may still want to catch the OutOfMemoryException to return a specific error code and/or give the host or OS a chance to perform a memory dump, which you can analyze to find the source of the memory leak. Make sure that you don't execute any code that would allocate memory when handling this exception; that approach would cause an infinite loop.

.NET memory management isn't free, though. Garbage collection needs to freeze some code execution so that it can reorganize memory safely. The unpredictability of collection events makes the use of managed languages scary in real-time scenarios. (You wouldn't want your pacemaker to pause every now and then to free memory, for example.) For most applications, the benefits of using CoreCLR memory management to simplify an application's code far outweigh the cost. As some developers have found, it's possible to control memory in .NET to minimize the effect of the garbage collector. Chapter 10 explores the garbage collector in greater depth.

Summary

- .NET supports multiple languages, including C#, VB.NET, F#, and community contributions.
- .NET applications compile to an intermediate language (CIL) that isn't specific to any processor architecture.
- .NET runs on a wide variety of platforms and in a broad set of use cases.
- Powerful features such as JIT compilation and garbage collection are built into the .NET platform.

Building
a console application

2

This chapter covers

- Generating projects with templates
- Creating and using namespaces
- Importing NuGet packages

Chapter 1 introduced .NET concepts and the breadth of applications in which it can be used. Now it's time to put this knowledge into practice and start writing apps. If you've programmed with .NET Framework before, you'll want to read this chapter, as there are many differences between .NET and Framework. .NET Core developers will find a lot of similarities but may be surprised by the top-level statements.

To install .NET, follow the instructions for your OS at https://dotnet.microsoft .com/download. All you need are a terminal/command line and a text editor. Most of the code in this book will work with .NET 6 or later, with documented exceptions. Choose the version that works best for you. If you're interested in more information about integrated development environments (IDEs) for .NET, check out appendix B.

As discussed in chapter 1, .NET works in many types of applications. Three types of applications are used in this book: console applications, web applications, and web services. Most of this book's examples use console applications and web services. Many of the samples will work in any of the three types, so you can use whatever you feel most comfortable with. We'll start with console applications.

2.1   Creating new applications from templates

If you're using an IDE, your instructions for creating new projects will vary. The .NET SDK comes with several built-in templates for creating applications.

From a terminal, open a folder in which your .NET projects will go; then execute the command in the following listing, which creates a new console application in the HelloDotnet folder. The code for this application is in the Program.cs file, as shown in listing 2.2.

Listing 2.1 Command to create web API from template

```
dotnet new console --name HelloDotNet
```

> **TIP** Run the commands `dotnet --help` to see a list of commands available in .NET. To get help for a specific command, such as the `new` command you used to create the console application, add the command, as in `dotnet new --help`.

Listing 2.2 Console application Program.cs

```
// See https://aka.ms/new-console-template for more information
Console.WriteLine("Hello, World!");
```

> **NOTE** If you've used .NET Framework, you may be surprised to find no Program file with a `Main` method. .NET uses top-level statements that don't belong to a class. Only one file in a project can have top-level statements, and the file's name doesn't matter. You could think of this file as being code that you'd normally put in the `Program Main` method, but you can also define types.

The other file in the folder, HelloDotnet.csproj, contains important project settings that we'll explore in section 2.2.

2.2   Building and running

From the HelloDotnet folder, execute this command in the terminal: `dotnet build`. When the build is finished, a new bin folder appears below HelloDotnet. The bin folder contains the binaries from the build, organized in subfolders first by configuration, with the default configuration being Debug, and then by run time, with the run time being net*.0. Go to HelloDotnet/bin/Debug/net8.0 (matching whatever .NET SDK version you're using) to find the Dynamic Link Library (DLL) and executable for the console application.

> ### Assemblies
>
> When this book uses the term *assembly*, it's referring to a build artifact that comes from compilation, not the Assembly language. A DLL file contains an assembly, which usually maps one-to-one with a project. The csproj file represents the project and controls how the assembly is built. The HelloDotnet.dll in the net*.0 folder has all the compiled code from the project. I'll use *assembly* and *DLL* interchangeably throughout this book.
>
> Sometimes, a ref subfolder of the net*.0 folder also has a HelloDotnet.dll file in it. This DLL is different: it represents the public surface area of the project but doesn't contain the implementation. This book doesn't use reference assemblies, so you can ignore this folder. For more information about what reference assemblies are and what they're used for, see http://mng.bz/eoPG.

You can run the application by executing `HelloDotnet` from a Windows command prompt, `./HelloDotnet` at a Linux/Mac terminal, or `.\HelloDotnet` if you have a PowerShell console. Note that you execute the command from the build output folder.

The application can execute because you have the .NET SDK installed on your computer. If you copy the same files to another computer with a .NET SDK installed, the executable will still run regardless of any difference in OS or processor architecture. Some OS-specific builds don't require an SDK; we'll explore them in chapter 13.

2.3   Writing code

If you've programmed with .NET Framework or Core, you may be surprised by the simplicity of the Program.cs file. Although it's nice that all the boilerplate code is gone, you have to wonder what happened to all that code, as will become apparent as you progress through this chapter.

Let's try a small example in which we generate some ASCII art based on the parameters passed in from the command line. We'll use an ASCII art-generator NuGet package called `Figgle`. First, we'll add it to the .csproj file, as shown in listing 2.3.

> ### What's a NuGet?
>
> *NuGet* (pronounced *new-get*) is .NET's package manager. Anyone can retrieve from and publish to the public NuGet repository at https://www.nuget.org. Some other places that have public and private repositories use the same protocol, including MyGet and Visual Studio Online. .NET allows the creation and consumption of NuGet packages, which bundle files along with metadata for use in .NET applications.

Listing 2.3   **HelloDotNet.csproj with `Figgle` package reference**

```
<Project Sdk="Microsoft.NET.Sdk">

  <PropertyGroup>
    <OutputType>Exe</OutputType>
```

```
      <TargetFramework>net8.0</TargetFramework>        ◄─┐  Could be net6.0 or net7.0,
      <ImplicitUsings>enable</ImplicitUsings>            │  depending on SDK
      <Nullable>enable</Nullable>
   </PropertyGroup>
                                             │  Add the ItemGroup section.
   <ItemGroup>                            ◄──┘
     <PackageReference Include="Figgle" Version="0.4.0" />
   </ItemGroup>

</Project>
```

In this listing, we add an `ItemGroup` node with a `PackageReference`. I found the value for the package reference by looking up the Figgle package on NuGet.org (https://www.nuget.org/packages/Figgle). A tab on each package called PackageReference shows the exact XML node you can insert into your project file.

NOTE Visual Studio and Rider have package managers on each project that make locating and installing packages much easier.

Replace the code in Program.cs so that you can use the Figgle library to write ASCII art to the console, as shown in the following listing. This code writes a Usage statement if no command-line arguments exist and returns a nonzero exit code; otherwise, it writes the first command-line argument in ASCII art.

Listing 2.4   Code to write ASCII art

```
using Figgle;                     ◄──── Adds the Figgle namespace

if (args.Length == 0)             ◄──── args is an array holding command-line arguments.
{
  Console.WriteLine("Usage: HelloDotnet <text>");
  Environment.Exit(1);    ◄─┐
}                           │  Ends the program with an exit code of 1   │ Converts first
                                                                         │ argument to
Console.WriteLine(FiggleFonts.Standard.Render(args[0]));   ◄──┘ ASCII art
```

Now try running this code from your project folder by executing `dotnet run "Hello, .NET"` from the terminal. The following listing shows what you should see.

Listing 2.5   Output from the ASCII art HelloDotnet

```
> dotnet run "Hello, .NET!"
```

2.4   *Namespaces and conventions*

.NET 6 and later use a minimal style that eliminates a lot of boilerplate code. The Program.cs file has no `Main` method. By convention, the code file is assumed to consist of top-level statements. If you've done shell scripting or JavaScript, this file should look familiar.

> **NOTE**   The top-level statements don't have to be in a file called Program.cs. Try renaming Program.cs, and the application will still work. But if you add another .cs file and put some top-level statements in it, such as `Console.WriteLine`, you'll get a build error. Only one file can contain top-level statements.

Because Program.cs contains top-level code, it isn't part of a namespace. Namespaces are used to organize .NET types. `Figgle`, for example, is a namespace that contains the classes for generating the ASCII art. We include the use of the `Figgle` namespace with the code `using Figgle;`. The package and assembly (DLL) are also named `Figgle`, but the namespace doesn't have to match either of them. Let's move the code that creates the ASCII art to its own class. Create a new file named AsciiArt.cs with the code shown in the following listing.

Listing 2.6   `AsciiArt` class using `Figgle` library to write text and type name

```
using Figgle;                        Puts AsciiArt in the
                                     HelloDotNet namespace
namespace HelloDotnet;       ◁──┘

                                     Marks classes with only
public static class AsciiArt      ◁──┘ static members as static
{
  public static void Write(string text)
  {
    Console.WriteLine(FiggleFonts.Standard.Render(text));
    Console.WriteLine("Brought to you by "         Writes the type name
      + typeof(AsciiArt).FullName);           ◁──── with namespace
  }
}
```

Then modify Program.cs to call the new class, as shown in the following listing.

Listing 2.7   Listing 2.7 Calling `AsciiArt` class from Program

```
using HelloDotnet;          ◁──── Adds the HelloDotNet namespace

if (args.Length == 0)
{
  Console.WriteLine("Usage: HelloDotnet <text>");
  Environment.Exit(1);
}

AsciiArt.Write(args[0]);    ◁──── Calls AsciiArt instead of Figgle
```

Execute the program as before. You should see a line below the ASCII art that says `Brought to you by HelloDotnet.AsciiArt`. The `FullName` property separates the namespace and type name with a dot/period (`.`). Namespace names can also contain dots, which is a way to create a hierarchy of namespaces.

To illustrate how namespace hierarchies work, consider the `Regex` class that's part of CoreFX (the .NET base class library), used for applying regular expressions. Regex is part of the `System.Text.RegularExpressions` namespace. The dots in the namespace indicate the hierarchy. Figure 2.1 shows how this hierarchy works.

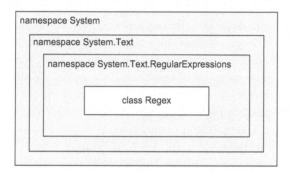

Figure 2.1   Namespace hierarchy of `System.Text.RegularExpressions.Regex`

The `System` namespace is at the top level and has many children, such as `System.IO` and `System.Collections`. `System.Text` focuses on handling text and has some types of its own, such as `StringBuilder`. The `Regex` class is a type that's part of the `System.Text.RegularExpressions` namespace.

What is a type?

Types in .NET are similar to those in other languages, such as Java and Go. A type can be a class, struct, enum, value type (such as int or float), record, and so on. .NET has a Common Type System (CTS) that allows the use of types in any .NET language.

.NET has two kinds of types: reference and value. These categories are determined by how the type's data is stored. A *reference type* stores a reference to its data, and a *value type* contains its data directly. If you're familiar with pointers, references are similar but not the same. (For more information, see section 10.3.4.) In C#, anything can be treated like an object (the base of all reference types) because C# automatically performs *boxing* and *unboxing*, which are the processes of wrapping and unwrapping a value type in an object, respectively. An example is `Console.WriteLine ("Count",` `count)`, where `count` is of type `int`. This statement is valid even though `WriteLine` expects an object as the second parameter. C# boxes the value type `count` automatically. Still, understanding the difference between value and reference types is important because these types behave differently when they're passed as method parameters or copied to other variables.

> *(continued)*
> Keep in mind that C# is a strongly typed language: every expression that evaluates to a value, every variable, and every constant has a specific type. One exception to this rule is the dynamic type, which bypasses static type checking. This book doesn't explore dynamic types but covers some complex types such as generic, implicit, anonymous, and nullable.

A `using` statement indicates that we want to use that namespace in our code. By using a namespace, we get access to the types in that namespace without having to fully qualify them—that is, without having to write the namespace and type name. So we can write `Regex` instead of `System.Text.RegularExpressions.Regex`. Also, we can have multiple types with the same name in different namespaces. If I have my own namespace with a type called `Regex`, and I need to use it in the same code as the CoreFX `Regex` type, the compiler will get confused if I have both namespaces added with `using` statements. In that case, I must fully qualify which `Regex` I want to use.

The types that you write need to be put in a namespace. As of .NET 6, which uses C# 10, namespace declarations can be made at file level. In listing 2.6, you created a class called `AsciiArt` and declared it as part of the HelloDotNet namespace with the statement `namespace HelloDotNet;`. Before C# 10, namespaces declarations could be written only as code blocks with brackets around them and all the types in the file placed inside. C# 10 is backward-compatible, so you still have the option of using this form of namespace declaration. File-level namespaces save one level of indentation—a small but welcome improvement.

The namespace can be declared before or after the `using` statements. Be aware that the placement has meaning. Compare the following two listings.

Listing 2.8 namespace after `using`

```
using System.Text.RegularExpressions;      ⟵──── Full namespace is needed.

namespace System.Text;

public static class Bar
{
   public static readonly Regex Letters = new Regex(@"[a-z]+");
}
```

Listing 2.9 namespace before `using`

```
namespace System.Text;

using RegularExpressions;      ⟵──── Namespace is relative to System.Text.

public static class Bar
{
   public static readonly Regex Letters = new Regex(@"[a-z]+");
}
```

In both listings, we're adding a new static class called `Bar` to the `System.Text` namespace. `Bar` uses the `Regex` class in its code. In listing 2.8, the namespace `Bar` is declared after the `using` statement, so the `using` statement has to be the full namespace of `Regex`. In listing 2.9, the namespace `System.Text` is declared first, which means that the `using`s declared after the namespace can be relative to the namespace that the code is in. If no `RegularExpressions` namespace is at the top level, .NET will look for the `System.Text.RegularExpressions` namespace (figure 2.2).

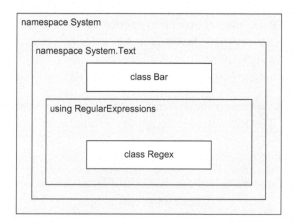

Figure 2.2   Namespace hierarchy of `System.Text.Bar` and `System.Text.RegularExpressions.Regex`

Relative `using`s may make the code cleaner, but many .NET developers avoid them because they can be confusing. If I had a class in the namespace `HelloDotnet.Figgle` and put a `using Figgle;` in my code, it would be unclear which namespace I'm referring to. For clarity, the examples in this book don't use relative namespaces.

2.5 Global using statements

Although we had to declare `using`s explicitly for the namespace of the NuGet package we're using, the same isn't true of the `Console.WriteLine` statements. `WriteLine` is a static method in the `Console` class, which is part of the `System` namespace. We don't need a `using System;` statement in Program.cs because the `System` namespace is included via a global `using` statement. Default global `using`s for the commonly used .NET CoreFX namespaces can be included *implicitly* by means of a flag in the .csproj file, as you saw in listing 2.3, where the property `<ImplicitUsings>` was set to `enable`.

You can add your own global `using`s if your project has namespaces that it uses in many classes. To create a global `using` statement, add a statement such as `global using Figgle;` to one of your classes. The convention is to create a separate file for this purpose in your project, such as GlobalUsings.cs. Another option is to add the global `using` to the .csproj file, as shown in the following listing.

Listing 2.10   Global `using` in Project file

```
<Project Sdk="Microsoft.NET.Sdk">
  <!-- ... -->
  <ItemGroup>
    <Using Include="Figgle" />        ← Add one Using element
  </ItemGroup>                           for each namespace.
</Project>
```

Global `usings` are good ways to reduce the boilerplate code at the top of your code files. The examples in this book use this technique to reduce the size of the listings. Another way to employ the `using` statement in C# is to use a static `using` statement, which reduces the amount of typing required.

2.6   *Static using statements*

A static `using` statement provides access to static members on .NET types without having to write out the type name. The following listing applies a static `using` to the Ascii-Art.cs file.

Listing 2.11   AsciiArt.cs with static `using`

```
using static System.Console;        ←──── Static usings refer to types.
using static Figgle.FiggleFonts;    ←─┐
                                       Full type names are needed
namespace HelloDotnet;                 despite global usings.

public static class AsciiArt
{
  public static void Write(string text)
  {
    WriteLine(Standard.Render(text));        ←─┐ FiggleFonts and
    WriteLine("Brought to you by "              Console aren't needed.
      + typeof(AsciiArt).FullName);
  }
}
```

This code works because `WriteLine` is a static method of `System.Console` and `Standard` is a static property of `Figgle.FiggleFonts`. Static usings can also be paired with global usings. An example is `global using static System.Console;`, which makes `WriteLine` available to all the code in your project without prefacing it with `Console`. Global static usings can also be specified in the .csproj file, as shown in the following listing.

Listing 2.12   Global static `usings` in Project file

```
<Project Sdk="Microsoft.NET.Sdk">
  <!-- ... -->
  <ItemGroup>
    <Using Include="System.Console" Static="True" />        ← Add the Static
    <Using Include="Figgle.FiggleFonts" Static="True" />       attribute.
  </ItemGroup>
</Project>
```

When you use static `usings`, you must balance brevity and readability. This book employs static `usings` only where it's clear that the members come from the static `using` and that the listing is easier to read.

2.7 *Handling more command-line arguments*

In Program.cs, we have an array of command-line arguments stored in the variable `args`. By default, .NET breaks apart the command-line arguments by space. You can use quotes to put terms together. But there are no advanced features such as actions, flags, and options. You'll typically want more control of the arguments, such as converting to types other than string or optional arguments; the `args` array quickly becomes unwieldy. Luckily, NuGet has a few good packages for handling command-line arguments. First, let's establish some rules about the command-line arguments:

- The text to convert to ASCII art should be required. If the text isn't present, or if there are other problems with the arguments, we should show a usage message.
- The usage message should also be available by specifying `--help` as an argument.
- To make things interesting, we'll allow an optional parameter to set the font used for the ASCII art.

> **Command-line parameter conventions**
>
> A generally accepted practice for command-line arguments is that the single dash (`-`) is used for single-letter options and the double dash (`--`) is for long-form word options (called GNU or long-option style). In UNIX-style terminals, you can list all the contents of the current folder by using the command `ls -a`. (The Windows command prompt and PowerShell use different conventions.) The same command can be written as `ls --all` because `--all` and `-a` are both aliases.
>
> The single dash allows you to specify multiple commands quickly. To extract a tar file in Linux\UNIX operating systems, for example, you typically use the command `tar -xvf file.tar`. The letters `x`, `v`, and `f` are single-letter aliases for `--extract`, `--verbose`, and `--file=`, respectively.

A NuGet package called `CommandLineParser` can handle the parameter parsing. NuGet has many command-line parsing libraries, including one published by the .NET team (but still in beta at this writing), so feel free to look into ones other than those I use in this book. Make the changes to the HelloDotnet.csproj file as shown in the following listing.

Listing 2.13 Adding the `CommandLineParser` library to HelloDotnet.csproj

```
<Project Sdk="Microsoft.NET.Sdk">

  <PropertyGroup>
```

```
    <OutputType>Exe</OutputType>
    <TargetFramework>net8.0</TargetFramework>
    <ImplicitUsings>enable</ImplicitUsings>
    <Nullable>enable</Nullable>          ←—— Makes sure that Nullable is enabled
  </PropertyGroup>

  <ItemGroup>
    <PackageReference Include="Figgle" Version="0.5.1" />      ⎤ Add this package
    <PackageReference Include="CommandLineParser"         ←——⎦ reference.
      Version="2.9.1" />
  </ItemGroup>
                                     ⎤ Separates ItemGroup for
  <ItemGroup>                     ←——⎦ organizing (not required)
    <Using Include="Figgle" />                              ⎤ Global static using
    <Using Include="System.Console" Static="True" />   ←——⎦ for WriteLine
  </ItemGroup>

</Project>
```

Next, create a file called Options.cs. This file will hold the parsed command-line parameters. Add the code from the following listing.

Listing 2.14   `Options` record to hold parsed command-line parameters

```
using CommandLine;      ←—— Includes namespace from CommandLineParser package

namespace HelloDotnet;      ←—— Same namespace as AsciiArt class

public record Options      ←—— Uses a record instead of a class; see note
{
    [Value(0, Required = true)]                    ⎤ Custom attribute indicating that
    public string? Text { get; init; }     ←——⎦ first parameter is required

                                            ⎤ Property with init indicates that
    [Option('f', "font")]              ←——⎦ it is set only on construction.
    public string? Font { get; init; }  ←—
}                                          ⎤ Custom attribute indicating
         ⎤ Nullable string property      ⎦ optional font parameter
```

What is a record?

Records are immutable types in C#. The command-line parameters are parsed when the application starts and then put in an `Options` object. After initialization, the contents of the `Options` object shouldn't change. To enforce this practice in the code, use a record type instead of a class type. Besides compile-time checking that the parameters aren't modified, there are advantages to using records for equality checks. C# generates an equality check that compares all the fields of the record.

In listing 2.14, the `Options` record has two properties. The `Text` property holds the text to convert to ASCII art. Because this task is the primary use of the console application, the text doesn't have a parameter name; instead, it's specified by its position in the command-line parameters. Note that the --font parameter can still come before the text because it's a named parameter. The Font property holds the name of the font in which to draw the ASCII art. The font doesn't have to be specified, so this parameter is marked as an Option. The parameter for font can be specified as -f or --font.

2.8 C# properties

The original idea behind properties came from a desire to control access to fields. A *field* in a class is some variable that has scope to the object or static scope to the class. If the field is exposed directly, the class doesn't know when code outside the class is accessing or modifying the field. Some development practices enforced the discipline of creating getters and setters for fields—methods that control access to the field. C# formalizes this discipline into properties. If we remove the shorthand, the Text property from listing 2.14 would look like the code in the following listing.

Listing 2.15 `Options Text` **property without the shorthand**

```
public record Options
{
  private string? _text;          ⏴──── Declares fields to hold text and font values

  [Value(0, Required = true)]
  public string? Text
  {
    get
    {
      return _text;      ⏴──── Returns value of field
    }
    init                 ⏴──── Can also be set; init if set only on initialize
    {
      _text = value;        ⏴──── value is a reserved keyword for setter/init value.
    }
  }
}
```

The record has init statements for the properties but set statements are also valid. Properties can be read-only or can have different visibility for get and set. There are also other shorthand notations for properties such as expression-bodied members. We'll explore more of these permutations of properties throughout the book.

Another question that may come to mind if you're not familiar with C# is the purpose of string?. This property isn't having an identity crisis; it's signifying to the compiler that it can be null. This property may seem weird if you're a .NET Framework programmer because the type string itself is a reference type and therefore can be null.

If you recall, the MSBuild property (no relation to C# property) <Nullable> enable</Nullable> was called out in listing 2.13. Nullable in the project settings tells the compiler that we have to be explicit about when something can be null. Nullable reference types help in compile-time checking of potential problems with null values.

Technically, because `Text` is a required parameter, `CommandLineParser` won't create the `Options` object if the `text` parameter isn't in the command-line parameters, but the compiler doesn't know this and will display a warning that the property needs to be marked as nullable.

> ### The problem with null references
> In 2009, Sir Charles Antony Richard Hoare (aka Tony Hoare) offered an apology for introducing the concept of null references (or pointers). He called it the "billion-dollar mistake" because of its effect on software. C# also struggles with handling nulls correctly and succinctly. The C# language is slowly moving toward a safer design regarding nulls but needs to be backward-compatible, which is why so many operators deal with null as well as nullable types. Using the latest techniques allows for better static analysis when compiling.

Now that we have a record to hold the parsed command-line parameters, let's add the code to perform the parsing. Modify the Program.cs file to match the code in the following listing.

Listing 2.16   Program.cs parsing command-line options with `CommandLineParser`

```
using HelloDotnet;                      Remove Figgle and
using CommandLine;          <───┘       add CommandLine.               Parses args into Options

Parser.Default.ParseArguments<Options>(args)       <───┘              If parse worked, passes
    .WithParsed<Options>(AsciiArt.Write)           <────────────      options to AsciiArt
    .WithNotParsed(_ =>                                        <───
        WriteLine("Usage: HelloDotnet <text> --font Big"));   <───┐   Called if parse failed
                                  Writes usage statement with font parameter
```

The `ParseArguments` method has a modifier before the arguments are passed in. This method uses a generic argument, which is denoted by the angle brackets and placed before the parentheses. To understand how this generic argument works, let's look at the method signature of `ParseArguments` (figure 2.3).

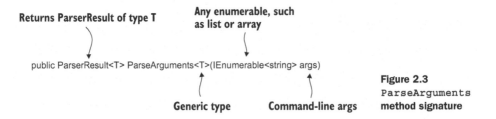

Returns ParserResult of type T

Any enumerable, such as list or array

public ParserResult<T> ParseArguments<T>(IEnumerable<string> args)

Generic type   Command-line args

Figure 2.3
`ParseArguments`
method signature

`T` represents the generic type. `ParseArguments` returns an object of `ParserResult<T>`. The `CommandLineParser` library doesn't know ahead of time what type you use to hold the parsed command-line arguments, which makes it difficult to return the object you

want. The generic allows you to specify the type so that `ParseArguments` can read the
type information and give you the object you want. Similarly, the parameter to `Parse-`
`Arguments`, `IEnumerable<string>`, uses a generic to say that whatever enumerable is provided must be an enumerable of strings. (`IEnumerable` is an interface applied to arrays,
lists, and other collections.)

Interfaces and abstract classes

Like most object-oriented languages, C# has interfaces and abstract classes. An interface defines a contract. A class that implements an interface must provide an implementation of the members defined in the contract. Classes can implement multiple
interfaces. Abstract classes are incomplete implementations for which derived
classes must fill in the missing implementations. A class can derive from only one
base class.

Using interfaces and abstract classes has some important effects, including the
following:

- Abstract classes can't be instantiated into objects directly.
- A class can inherit from only one abstract class but can implement any num-
  ber of interfaces.
- Methods or properties that aren't implemented in an abstract class must be
  marked with the `abstract` keyword.
- Interface properties and methods must be public.

The next method call, `WithParsed<T>`, takes `AsciiArt.Write` as a parameter. We know it's
a method, so how does it work? First, let's look at the method signature (figure 2.4).

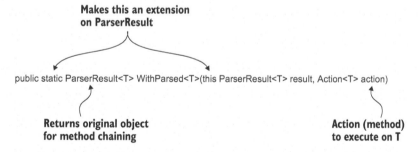

Figure 2.4 `WithParsed` **method signature**

We know from figure 2.3 that `ParseArguments` will return a `ParserResult<T>`. The extension method `WithParsed` can be chained to that `ParserResult` object to check whether
the `ParserResult` was successful and execute some code (`action`) if that's the case.
`Action<T>` specifies that the code we'll execute is a method that takes an object of type
`T` as a parameter—in our case, the `Options` object. We need a method that will take the
`Options` object as a parameter, and luckily, we'll soon have one. The `AsciiArt.Write`

code previously took only a string as a parameter, but we'll soon change it to take the `Options` object so we can use it to determine what font to use for the ASCII art.

Sometimes, you want to add a method to an existing type without modifying or inheriting from that type. Extension methods allow you to do so. Consider a contrived example. The class `string` is part of CoreFX and can't be inherited (sealed), but I'd like to add a method that gives me every other character. I can create my own extension method to accomplish this task, as shown in the following listing.

Listing 2.17   Extension method to get every other character in a string

```
                                                  Extension suffix is a convention
                                                  and not required.
public static class MyStringExtensions  ◁─┘
{                                                      "this string" makes
  public static string EveryOtherCharacter(this string s)  ◁─┘ it an extension
  {                                                           method on string.
    char[] newChars = new char[s.Length / 2 + 1];  ◁─┐ Half the string length rounded
    int sPos, nPos;                            ◁─┐   up should be enough.
    for (sPos = 0, nPos = 0;           Positions in
         sPos < s.Length;              both arrays
         sPos += 2, nPos++)
    {
      newChars[nPos] = s[sPos];      ◁─── A string can be indexed like a char array.
    }

    return new string(newChars, 0, nPos);  ◁─┐ Creates a new string from
  }                                           the char array and returns
}
```

Then this extension method can be used on any string as though it were part of the string type, as in `"abcdefghijklmn".EveryOtherCharacter()`. Likewise, the methods `WithParsed` and `WithNotParsed` aren't part of the `ParserResult` class, but extension methods.

Extension methods don't get access to internal or private members of the class they're extending. In the preceding listing, the code has access to the string and its public members like any other method that operates on a string. `EveryOtherCharacter` isn't part of `string` and available everywhere `string` is. The namespace `MyStringExtensions` must be imported anywhere I want to use the `EveryOtherCharacter` method, but the class name `MyStringExtensions` doesn't need to be mentioned explicitly.

In case the command-line parser is unable to create the `Options` object, we want to write the usage string to the console output. The `WithParsed` extension method uses a design pattern called *method chaining* that allows us to apply another extension method: `WithNotParsed`. `WithParsed` is executed first and checks whether the `ParserResult` indicates that the parsing was successful. If not, `WithParsed` does nothing and returns the `ParserResult` object. The next method in the chain, `WithNotParsed`, checks whether the `ParserResult` object indicated that parsing failed and, if so, executes an action. Figure 2.5 shows the signature of that method.

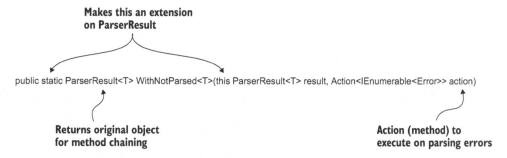

Figure 2.5 `WithNotParsed` **method signature**

This signature is similar to that of `WithParsed` except that the `Action` takes a parameter of `IEnumerable<Error>`. No method like that one is already available, so we could create one in the `AsciiArt` class. But the logic for writing the `Usage` string shouldn't be in `AsciiArt`. We could declare a namespace and type with a method for this purpose, but C# provides a cleaner way: anonymous functions. The following listing shows different ways to write the `Action` used for `WithNotParsed`.

Listing 2.18   Four different ways to write the same `Action`

```
void WriteUsageAndIgnoreErrors1(IEnumerable<Error> errors)      ◁──┐ Most basic form
{                                                                  │ of the method
  WriteLine("Usage: HelloDotnet <text> --font Big");
}

void WriteUsageAndIgnoreErrors2(IEnumerable<Error> _)   ◁──┐ Uses the discard operator
{                                                          │ (_) to ignore the parameter
  WriteLine("Usage: HelloDotnet <text> --font Big");
}

void CallToAction(IEnumerable<Error> errors)
{
  Action<IEnumerable<Error>> action1 = WriteUsageAndIgnoreErrors1;
  action1(errors);
  Action<IEnumerable<Error>> action2 = WriteUsageAndIgnoreErrors2;
  action2(errors);
  Action<IEnumerable<Error>> action3 =
    (IEnumerable<Error> _) =>              ◁────── Creates anonymous function
    {
      WriteLine("Usage: HelloDotnet <text> --font Big");
    }                                                    ┌ Uses expression-bodied
  action3(errors);                                       │ member to simplify
  Action<IEnumerable<Error>> action4 = _ =>      ◁───────┘
    WriteLine("Usage: HelloDotnet <text> --font Big");
  action4(errors);
}
```

An *anonymous function* (sometimes called a *lambda function*, *lambda abstraction*, or *function literal*) is what the name suggests: a function whose name is unimportant. Anonymous functions are among my favorite .NET features because naming is hard, and coming up with a name for a method I use only once is a waste of time. You use a *lambda expression* to create an anonymous function. The term *lambda* originates from lambda calculus, a mathematical system that treats functions anonymously. C# has two types of lambda expressions: expression lambda and statement lambda. An *expression lambda* has a single statement or expression and doesn't need curly braces. A *statement lambda* has multiple statements. The following listing shows some examples.

NOTE   Although there's some distinction between the meanings of *function* and *method*, most .NET developers use these terms interchangeably.

Listing 2.19   Examples of lambda expression types

```
Action<int, int> a1 = (x, y) => WriteLine(x + "," + y);    <──── Expression lambda
Action<string, string> a2 = (left, right) =>    <──┐
{                                                   │  Statement lambda
  if (left == right)
  {
    WriteLine("Matches!");
  }
  else
  {
    WriteLine("Does not match!");
  }
};
                                                        ┌ Expression lambda with return value
Func<int, int, int> multiply = (x, y) => x * y;    <──┘
Func<IEnumerable<int>, int> sum =                  <──── Statement lambda with return value
numbers =>                                     <──┐
{                                                  └ Parentheses aren't needed for a single parameter.
  int running = 0;
  foreach (int num in numbers)
  {
    running += num;
  }

  return running;
};

var parse = (string s) => int.Parse(s);    <──── Compiler infers the type.
```

The first four anonymous functions in this listing are assigned to `Action` or `Func` types. The compiler can infer from the generic arguments applied to `Action` or `Func` what the types are for the input parameters and return types. This feature allows us to write the parameter names, such as `(left, right)`, without needing to add the types, such as `(string left, string right)`. The compiler is also able to infer the other way, as shown in the last anonymous method in the listing. In this case, the type of the `parse` variable is `Func<string, int>`, with `string` being the input parameter type and `int` being the return type. Likewise, in listing 2.16 the compiler can tell from the `WithNotParsed` method signature that the `Action` should take an `IEnumerable<Error>` parameter and use it for the parameter passed to the anonymous function without the code's needing to declare it explicitly.

We're almost done with the modifications to the console application. The next step is updating the `AsciiArt` class to look up the font. Modify AsciiArt.cs to contain the code from the following listing.

Listing 2.20 Looking up the font passed in from the command-line options

```
using System.Reflection;          ◁──── Used for examining the FiggleFonts type

namespace HelloDotNet;

public static class AsciiArt
{
    public static void Write(Options o)      ◁──── Changes parameters to accept Options
    {
        FiggleFont? font = null;             ◁──── font is nullable in this code.
        if (!string.IsNullOrWhiteSpace(o.Font))      ◁──── Looks up font only if the Font
        {                                                   property has something
            font = typeof(FiggleFonts)
                .GetProperty(o.Font,         ◁──── Finds a property with the
                    BindingFlags.Static | BindingFlags.Public)    name specified in Font
                ?.GetValue(null)
                as FiggleFont;               ◁──── "as" is similar to a cast
            if (font == null)                       but protects against
            {                                       type mismatch.
                WriteLine($"Could not find font '{o.Font}'");  ◁──── Writes message if
            }                                                        font is not found
        }       $"" creates an interpolated string.
    }

    font ??= FiggleFonts.Standard;       ◁──── ?? is called the null-coalescing operator.

    if (o?.Text != null)
    {                                            Uses the font to write the ASCII art
        WriteLine(font.Render(o.Text));   ◁──┘
        WriteLine($"Brought to you by {typeof(AsciiArt).FullName}");
    }
    }
}
```

Property must be public and static ("|" is binary operator).

?. is called the null-conditional operator.

2.8.1 Reflection

.NET has an extensive set of reflection libraries in the `System.Reflection` namespace. Many interpreted languages have some form of reflection, which allows you to get information about assemblies and types in .NET code at run time.

In listing 2.20, the `FiggleFonts` type has a static property for each font. The static property we use by default is `FiggleFonts.Standard` and is of type `FiggleFont`. By using reflection, we can attempt to find a property by name and get the `FiggleFont` object that represents it.

Be aware that reflection comes at a cost. Avoid using reflection in code that is called often because of the effect on performance. If you want to use ahead-of-time (AOT) compilation and trim unused code from the output assemblies, AOT may remove code that is accessed only with reflection because it doesn't see a direct reference. Although this book doesn't cover AOT, if you want to use reflection and AOT, you have ways to make them play nicely together; see http://mng.bz/pp9R.

2.8.2   *Interpolated strings*

Normal strings in C# are enclosed in double quotes ("). Interpolated strings allow you to substitute values into strings. If you've used C#, you may be familiar with `string.Format()`, which can substitute values into a string. Interpolated strings are similar to `string.Format()` but not the same. As in listing 2.20, the string value of `o.Font` is inserted into the string by enclosing it in curly brackets ({}). In some cases, the compiler converts an interpolated string into a `string.Format()` in the generated Common Intermediate Language (CIL). But in other cases, other methods of constructing the string are faster, and the compiler will use those instead. Generally, it's better to use interpolated strings. If you're writing code that does a lot of string manipulation and want to understand more about the nuances, check out Stephen Toub's blog post on string interpolation at http://mng.bz/OZQj.

2.8.3   *Null operators*

Listing 2.20 uses two new null operators. The first one is in `GetProperty()?.GetValue()`. If the result of `GetProperty` is `null`, the null-conditional operator will return `null` immediately instead of executing the right side of the expression (`GetValue`). The null-conditional operator is shorthand, especially considering that without it, the alternative is like the code in the following listing.

> **Listing 2.21   Long form of null check on `GetProperty`**

```
PropertyInfo pi = typeof(FiggleFonts).GetProperty(        ⟵  Stores GetProperty
  o.Font, BindingFlags.Static | BindingFlags.Public);          return value
if (pi != null)
{
  font = pi.GetValue(null) as FiggleFont;
}
```

The second null operator, `??`, is called the null-coalescing operator; it evaluates the expression on the left side first. If the left expression is `null`, it evaluates and returns the value of the right expression. This process is similar to how short-circuiting works with the `||` Boolean operator. In listing 2.20, this operator is used in the line `font ??= FiggleFonts.Standard`. As in other languages, this operator is shorthand for `font = font ?? FiggleFonts.Standard`. If `font` is `null`, `FiggleFonts.Standard` is assigned to `font`; otherwise, nothing changes.

2.8.4 *Casting objects to types*

In listing 2.20, the result of the GetProperty().GetValue() is an object that can be null. The value of the expression needs to be casted to type FiggleFont before it can be assigned to the font variable. There's no guarantee, however, that the object returned by the expression will be of that type, so if we use an explicit cast, it may cause an exception at run time. The as operator in C# is a safe way to cast the object; it returns null if the type of object being casted doesn't match the target type.

Exercise 1: Multiple words in ASCII art

The first unnamed parameter passed to HelloDotnet is the text that will be written in ASCII art. A string containing spaces can be used if it's enclosed in quotes. Modify the command-line parameter parsing so that if multiple unnamed parameters are passed, each string will be written to the console separately. For help, see Command-LineParser's wiki at http://mng.bz/Y7wj.

Exercise 2: List all fonts in help text

The help text could be more helpful if it tells the user what fonts are available. You have many ways to accomplish this task. One way is to use reflection to enumerate the public static properties of FiggleFonts and expose them as a static method in AsciiArt. Another way is to grab the list from the Figgle source code and store it as an array or an enum (not covered yet but an option if you know C#).

Summary

- Use dotnet new to create .NET applications from the command line.
- NuGet has an extensive collection of packages with helpful links and instructions.
- Types are organized in namespaces that can be included in a whole project or an individual file.
- C# has many ways to handle null references.
- Anonymous methods and expression-bodied members are common techniques that make C# code more succinct.

Creating web services and applications with ASP.NET Core

The console application from chapter 2 receives command-line parameters and writes the specified string in ASCII art to the console output. The command-line library parses the parameters using common conventions, making the application easy to execute from a terminal. Creating a web service that performs the same function is just as easy.

3.1 Web services

In this section, we'll port the ASCII art program into a web service using ASP.NET Core. In chapter 2, we used the `dotnet new console` command to create a console application from a template. Many other templates are available. You can see a list by running dotnet new list (or, in .NET 7 or earlier, dotnet new --list). We will use the empty web template for the ASCII art service. Use the command shown in the following listing to create a new folder with the new project.

Listing 3.1 Command to create web API from template

```
dotnet new web --name AsciiArtSvc
```

This template will create files similar to the ones shown in figure 3.1.

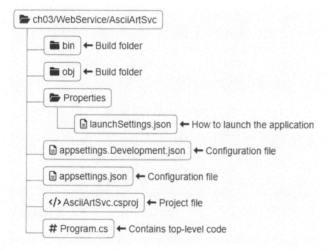

Figure 3.1 Files and folders created by the empty web template

A web API template will look much more like the ASP.NET Core projects you see in the real world. We use the empty template in this example because with the minimal API design of ASP.NET Core, creating a web service is as easy as creating a console application.

From the project's directory, execute the dotnet run command. You should see output similar to the following listing.

Listing 3.2 Output from running the empty web service

```
> dotnet run
Building...
info: Microsoft.Hosting.Lifetime[14]
      Now listening on: https://localhost:7041      ⟵——— HTTPS uses a dev certificate.
info: Microsoft.Hosting.Lifetime[14]
      Now listening on: http://localhost:5292       ⟵——— Port numbers are configurable.
info: Microsoft.Hosting.Lifetime[0]
      Application started. Press Ctrl+C to shut down.
```

Development certificate

.NET includes a certificate for local development to make testing HTTPS endpoints easier. If you installed an IDE such as Visual Studio or JetBrains Rider, the certificate probably was set up for you. Regardless, you can check whether the certificate is trusted with the command `dotnet dev-certs https --check`.

To trust the certificate on your development machine or on a build agent in your continuous integration/continuous development (CI/CD) pipeline, use the command `dotnet dev-certs https --trust`.

Web-service ports for local development

The port numbers used for web services generated from the .NET template are chosen randomly. You may need to change them if they conflict with a port that another application is using. To do so, find the Properties/launchSettings.json file, and look for a section like the one shown in the following code snippet:

```
"profiles": {
  "AsciiArtSvc": {
    "commandName": "Project",          ◁──┐ Used when executing
    "dotnetRunMessages": true,              dotnet run
    "launchBrowser": true,         ◁────── Auto-opens default browser to app URL
    "applicationUrl":
      "https://localhost:7041;http://localhost:5292",   ◁──┐ URLs and port
    "environmentVariables": {                               numbers for
      "ASPNETCORE_ENVIRONMENT": "Development"              https and http
    }
  }
}
```

The default profile generated with the template will launch the default browser and navigate to the configured URL. The browser sends a GET request that the service responds to by returning `"Hello World!"` The browser launch happens with IDEs that use the launch profiles. The `dotnet run` command won't open a browser. The first step in getting the web service to convert strings to ASCII art is to add the `Figgle` package as we did with the console application (shown in the following listing).

Listing 3.3   Adding `Figgle` package to `AsciiArtSvc`

```
<Project Sdk="Microsoft.NET.Sdk.Web">   ◁─── Sdk value includes ".Web".

  <PropertyGroup>
    <TargetFramework>net8.0</TargetFramework>
    <Nullable>enable</Nullable>
    <ImplicitUsings>enable</ImplicitUsings>
  </PropertyGroup>
                                         ┐ Add this ItemGroup.
  <ItemGroup>                        ◁───┘
```

```
  <PackageReference Include="Figgle" Version="0.5.1" />
  </ItemGroup>

</Project>
```

Next, open the Program.cs to see how the current `"Hello World!"` response works. The content should be similar to the following listing.

Listing 3.4 AsciiArtSvc Program.cs

```
var builder = WebApplication.CreateBuilder(args);     ◁—— var declares the variable.
var app = builder.Build();                        ◁—┐
                                                     │ No builder configuration, so defaults are used
app.MapGet("/", () => "Hello World!");            ◁——┐
                                                      │ Maps root level GET to a response
app.Run();
```

In chapter 2, I noted that C# is a strongly typed language. In listing 3.4, however, we use the keyword `var` to declare variables instead of the .NET types. In C#, `var` can be used to declare a variable only if the compiler can determine the variable type. We can make a statement such as `var i = 0;` because the compiler can infer that if `0` is an integer, `i` is an integer. But we couldn't write something like `var myString;` because the compiler can use nothing assigned to `myString` to infer the type. The `var` keyword is a style choice, but it has the benefit of saving characters: you don't need to write the type name, and you don't need to have a `using` statement for that type's namespace (unless you use that type name somewhere else). The drawback is that developers reading the code don't know the type without some investigation.

The empty web template generates little boilerplate code. The bulk of the work is done by the SDK, which assumes a lot of common and helpful defaults. The project includes appsettings.json, for example, and that file is a configuration file. .NET Framework developers are used to the web.config file's having all the configuration. In .NET Core, this file was removed, and configuration loading had to be added explicitly in the code. In .NET 6 and later, JSON configuration is used by default because most developers use this approach anyway.

Order of appsettings configuration

In addition to the appsettings.json, the web empty template includes appsettings .Development.json. The Development portion matches the value of the ASPNETCORE_ ENVIRONMENT environment variable. This variable is set in launchSettings.json. You can modify this value and have matching configuration files.

The appsettings.json file is loaded first. Then the values in appsettings.<ASPNETCORE_ ENVIRONMENT>.json are loaded. The latest configuration values loaded in the chain override the previous values in which the pathname matches. We'll revisit this concept in depth in chapter 13.

The MapGet call does the most interesting work. This method maps requests made to a route (in this case, "/", meaning the root URL) to a function. The function returns a string that's used as the response. The function generated by the template uses a C# anonymous method: () => "Hello World!". We used anonymous methods in the console application, but if you need a refresher, check listing 2.18 in chapter 2.

The ASCII art web API isn't complete until we can pass a string in the request and get the ASCII art back in the response. To do so, we can use the routing mechanism to parameterize the URL. Modify the Program.cs file as shown in the following listing.

Listing 3.5 Program.cs with ASCII art request handling

```
using Figgle;              ⟵——— Add namespace here or globally.

var builder = WebApplication.CreateBuilder(args);
var app = builder.Build();

app.MapGet("/", () => "Hello World!");        ⎤ URL after root is text.
app.MapGet("/{text}",                    ⟵——┘
   (string text) =>                      ⟵——— Parameter name matches route.
   FiggleFonts.Standard.Render(text));   ⟵——┐
                                             ⎦ Render expression returns a string.
app.Run();
```

Run the application and browse to https://localhost:<port>/Testing%20123. You should see the ASCII art in the response. The value of port will differ from project to project. This value is set in the launchSettings.json.

The mapper converts the URL portion to the type of the parameter and matches based on name. The route "/{text}" takes the portion of the URL after the root and converts it to the content of text. The anonymous method for the response takes a parameter of type string with the name text. If the URL portion can't be converted to the type specified or the name doesn't match, the request fails—a useful feature if you want an integer or Globally Unique Identifier (GUID).

In the console application from chapter 2, the font could be specified as an optional command-line parameter. Let's add the font as an optional query-string parameter. First, let's port the AsciiArt class over to this project. Create a new file called AsciiArt.cs and add the code from the following listing.

Listing 3.6 `AsciiArt` class from chapter 2 modified to work with the web service

```
using Figgle;
using System.Reflection;

namespace AsciiArtSvc;

public static class AsciiArt
{
   public static string Write(string text,    ⟵——— Passes in text and font as strings
```

```
      string? fontName = null)
  {
    FiggleFont? font = null;
    if (!string.IsNullOrWhiteSpace(fontName))
    {
      font = typeof(FiggleFonts)                    ←———  Searches for a property with the name
        .GetProperty(fontName,
          BindingFlags.Static | BindingFlags.Public)  ←—  Property must be
        ?.GetValue(null)                     ←————          public and static.
        as FiggleFont;
    }
                                             ←——— Gets the value of the property if found
    font ??= FiggleFonts.Standard;    ←——— Uses standard if no property is found
    return font.Render(text);         ←——
  }                                        Returns as string instead of writing to console
}
```

Now modify Program.cs as shown in the following listing.

Listing 3.7   Rendering with custom font from optional query string

```
using AsciiArtSvc;                ←——— Changes to namespace for AsciiArt class

var builder = WebApplication.CreateBuilder(args);
var app = builder.Build();

app.MapGet("/", () => "Hello World!");      ←  No change in route spec
app.MapGet("/{text}",
  (string text, string? font) =>     ←——— Looks for optional font in query string
  AsciiArt.Write(text, font));    ←——
                                       Calls AsciiArt to render text
app.Run();
```

Notice that font isn't called out explicitly in the route. When you add the font parameter to the anonymous method, MapGet looks for it in the route. Because the name font isn't in the route, MapGet assumes that it will be in the query string. Because font is specified as string? instead of string, the parameter is considered to be optional. Removing the ? and performing a GET request without the query string will result in an error.

Run the application and browse to http://localhost:<port>/Testing%20123?font=DotMatrix. You should see the ASCII art in the response using the DotMatrix font.

3.1.1 Adding a service that responds with a collection of data

Now the web service has a query-string parameter that lets you select the ASCII art font to apply to the text. A developer using this service would want to know the list of possible fonts. Let's modify the root URL endpoint to return a list of all possible fonts instead of "Hello World!". In listing 3.6, we used reflection to match a property by its name. We can also use reflection to get the full list of public static properties on FiggleFonts that are of type FiggleFont, as shown in the following listing.

Listing 3.8 Property getting all fonts with reflection

```
public static class AsciiArt
{
  public static Lazy<IEnumerable<string>> AllFonts =        ◁───  Lazy static property
    new (() =>                                           ◁───  Anonymous method to
      from p in typeof(FiggleFonts)              ◁───          initialize lazy property
      .GetProperties(                       ◁───
        BindingFlags.Public | BindingFlags.Static)           Uses LINQ to query the data
      select p.Name);                    ◁───
  // ...                   Projects the name of the font       All public static properties
}                                                            of FiggleFonts
```

This listing uses a lazy-initialized property. *Lazy* means that the property's value isn't established until its first use. When `AllFonts.Value` is first used, the anonymous method executes. `GetProperties` returns an array of `PropertyInfo` objects, one for each `FiggleFont` property. (There are no other public static properties on `FiggleFonts`.) Lazy-initialized properties are useful when it's expensive to build something and/or the values created take up memory and you want to pay that cost only if those values are used. A list of font names isn't a substantial use of memory, and reflection is relatively fast, so it's not necessary to use `Lazy` in this situation, but it doesn't hurt.

To get only the names of each property, you use a projection (much as you would do in SQL). The keywords `from` and `select` are from a C# language feature called LINQ. *LINQ* (short for *Language-INtegrated Query*) is a means of executing queries on data that uniformly applies to all kinds of data. In this case, the data is an array. In chapter 5, we'll use LINQ to query a database.

LINQ SYNTAX TRANSLATED TO METHODS

Developers who are familiar with SQL are used to the simple query form of `SELECT some-columns FROM sometable WHERE somecondition`. If you've ever used an editor that has SQL autocompletion, you know that the autocomplete can't provide a list of columns after the `SELECT` keyword until it knows the table, which is later in the query. LINQ puts the `from` portion first, which is not only necessary because of how LINQ is parsed, but also nice for autocompletion. Under the covers, the C# compiler is turning the LINQ query shown in listing 3.8 into something similar to the following listing.

Listing 3.9 LINQ query translated to methods

```
public static Lazy<IEnumerable<string>> AllFonts =
  new (() =>
    typeof(FiggleFonts)                        ◁─── No from
    .GetProperties(
      BindingFlags.Public | BindingFlags.Static)           Selects extension method with
    .Select(p => p.Name));                    ◁───          anonymous projection method
```

Arrays, like the one returned from `GetProperties`, implement the `IEnumerable` interface. `IEnumerable` is implemented by all collections in CoreFX (the .NET base class library). The interface has only one method, `GetEnumerator`, which returns an object that implements `IEnumerator`. An enumerator in C# is usually called an iterator in other languages. The iterator pattern is one in which you use a separate object to iterate over a container's elements, usually in a forward-only, one-element-at-a-time way. The same iterator pattern is used in other languages, and the C# documentation sometimes uses *enumerate* and *iterate* interchangeably.

> **WARNING** Enumerators and enumerated types (*enums*) are different things. An enumerated type like `BindingFlags` from listing 3.9 is a type with a set of named constants, each representing some underlying integer. Enumerators are meant to enumerate the items in a container, such as an array or dictionary.

`Select` is an extension method that operates on `IEnumerable` objects and returns an `IEnumerable`. (Extension methods are covered in chapter 2.) Because the output of a select is also an enumerable, the query doesn't need to be executed until some part of the code asks for an enumerator. This deferred execution can be a source of confusion when you're learning to use LINQ, and it's a topic we'll explore more in later chapters.

RETURNING THE LIST OF FONTS IN A RESPONSE

In Program.cs, remove the line to map requests to the root URL (`"/"`) to `"Hello World!"` and replace it with the code in the following listing.

Listing 3.10 Returning all fonts when a request is made to the root URL

```
app.MapGet("/", () => AsciiArt.AllFonts.Value);    ⟵——— Value tells Lazy to evaluate.
```

> **NOTE** The first time the `Value` property of a `Lazy` object is used, the value of the `Lazy` object is constructed and returned. Subsequent calls to `Value` get the already-constructed value.

Run the application, and navigate to the address in a browser. The response should be a JSON array containing all the font names. ASP.NET Core assumes by convention that it should JSON-encode any objects returned in the response unless otherwise specified.

You can choose among more than 250 fonts, which is not a lot, but let's pretend that it is. If we have a client who wants to get only 10, 20, or 50 font names at a time, we should add parameters that allow the caller to specify the page size and offset. First, we'll try limiting the number of font names returned, using a query parameter. No standardized method exists for handling paging for web APIs; some use a cursor-based system because the result data may be unique per query, and others can use the size and offset. We'll use the term *take* as the name of our query parameter. Modify the code as shown in the following listing.

Listing 3.11 Adding `take` parameter to all-fonts query

```
app.MapGet("/",
    (int take) =>                                    ⟵—┤ Must convert to int
    AsciiArt.AllFonts.Value.Take(take));    ⟵——— Take is a LINQ extension method.
```

Now run the application, and open the browser to https://localhost:<port>?take=10. You should see only 10 font names returned.

Now that we can limit the number of results per page, the next step is to specify an offset from the beginning. Some APIs use a page number, but we'll use an offset. The LINQ method for this purpose is called skip, so we'll use the same name for our parameter. Modify the code again to add the skip parameter as shown in the following listing.

Listing 3.12   Adding `skip` parameter to all-fonts query

```
app.MapGet("/",
  (int? skip, int? take) =>          ◁——— Parameter order doesn't matter.
  AsciiArt.AllFonts.Value
    .Skip(skip ?? 0)                 ◁——— Skips before take (doesn't skip if null)
    .Take(take ?? 100));        ◁——┐
                                    └── Takes 100 if not specified
```

Run the application, and open the browser to https://localhost:7250/?skip=100&take=10 to test it. Play around with the numbers a bit to see how ASP.NET Core handles errors. Negative numbers shouldn't break anything and probably will result in an empty array. Specifying values for skip or take that can't be converted to an int will result in a HTTP 500 response code and a page that describes the error.

Use dotnet watch to speed ASP.NET Core development

So far, we've been using dotnet run to run the application. For every code change you made, you had to stop the running application, save the source files, and run dotnet run again. The .NET CLI has a command to watch for file changes in a project and automatically recompile and run. To use this feature, replace dotnet run with dotnet watch run.

FILTERING WITH LINQ

APIs that may return a large number of results often include some kind of filtering—usually a search string if all the results are text. But the filter could also be a manufacturer name for an item in a store, a destination city for a train ticket, or any number of specific attributes. You can use LINQ to apply all kinds of filters to your collections. A FiggleFont object doesn't have much substance, but it has a name and a property to indicate the text direction. We'll add some new parameters to filter fonts by name and/or text direction.

Another common query parameter is sort order. In some advanced queries, you may sort by multiple fields (date in descending order, price from smallest to largest, and so on). The current list of font names returned by our code may look sorted, but it's not. Reflection doesn't guarantee an order for the properties it finds. We'll add default alphabetical sorting by font name and a parameter to switch between ascending and descending.

Because the code needs the whole `FiggleFont` object, not just the name, we'll need to modify the `AsciiArt` class to provide the `FiggleFont` object. The `FiggleFont` class doesn't have a property for the font name, so we'll need something to store both the name of the font and the `FiggleFont` object. One approach is to create a new class or struct with two properties—one for the name and one for the `FiggleFont` object—and then have the LINQ query return objects of that type. C# gives you several ways to do this without explicitly declaring a new type. The technique used in the following listing is called a *named tuple*.

Listing 3.13 Modifying `AllFonts` to return a tuple

```
public static
  Lazy<IEnumerable<(string Name, FiggleFont Font)>>         ◁──┐  Parentheses
  AllFonts = new (() =>                                         │  indicate the
    from p in typeof(FiggleFonts)                               │  tuple.
      .GetProperties(
        BindingFlags.Public | BindingFlags.Static)
    select (                                                 ◁──┘
      Name: p.Name,                                          ◁──┐
      Font: (p.GetValue(null) as FiggleFont)  ◁──┐             Name is the property name.
    ));                                            │
                                                   Font is the property's value.
```

C# tuples

Tuples in C# allow you to group multiple values succinctly. The fields of the tuple don't need to be named, in which case the fields are named Item1, Item2, and so on, depending on order. Tuples can contain any number of terms and aren't limited to two fields. As with LINQ, C# performs some extra work so that you don't have to use the `System.Tuple` or `System.ValueTuple` type explicitly. Parentheses in C# have many meanings, depending on context, but the best way to tell that a tuple is being used is that you find it where you expect a type.

Although the `AsciiArt` class gets the list of all the fonts, it's not doing any of the paging, sorting, or filtering. We'll put that work into Program.cs inside the mapping for this example, but it could be moved wherever it makes the most sense. For the font name and text direction filters, we'll add query parameters called `name` and `dir`, respectively. The order-by parameter will be called `order`, and we'll check only whether its value is `desc` to indicate that the query results should be in descending order. Modify Program.cs to contain the code from the following listing.

Listing 3.14 Adding paging, sorting, and filtering to font list

```
using Figgle;                          ◁────  Add to the top of the file.
const StringComparison SCIC =
  StringComparison.OrdinalIgnoreCase;  ┐  String checks should
                                        │  be case-insensitive.
```

```
app.MapGet("/",
    (
        int? skip,
        int? take,
        FiggleTextDirection? dir,        ◄──        FiggleTextDirection
        string? name,                    ◄───── Font name filter    is an enum.
        string? order                    ◄──
    ) => {                                       Order direction
        var query = from f in AsciiArt.AllFonts.Value    ◄──  Builds the query in steps
            where                        ◄─────  Applies the filter
              (name == null || f.Name.Contains(name, SCIC))
                && (dir == null || f.Font.Direction == dir)  ◄───  Font text direction filter
            select f;
        if (string.Equals("desc", order, SCIC))  ◄────  Looks only for desc
        {
            query = query.OrderByDescending(f => f.Name);  ◄─
        }
        else                                                       Orders by
        {                                                          name
            query = query.OrderBy(f => f.Name);        ◄─
        }

        return query         ◄──  Returns constructed query
            .Skip(skip ?? 0)
            .Take(take ?? 200)
            .Select(f => f.Name);
    });
```

Checks whether text is in the name

Assuming that you're using `dotnet watch run` when you save the code, the code should be ready to test. Check the terminal running the watch in case it's reporting a rude edit. The terminal will have an option to restart. If you pick `always`, .NET will rebuild and restart automatically without prompting. Try a few URLs in your browser, such as https://localhost:<port>/?dir=RightToLeft&order=desc&name=m and https://localhost:<port>/?order=desc&take=10, to see how the parameters work.

3.1.2 Controlling the response

So far, we've used the minimal APIs to return responses as a string or as objects in JSON format. The default response HTTP status code is `200` (`OK`), which makes sense as long as the operation is successful. But what if you'd like to return something other than text? Suppose that you have code that returns text formatted as ASCII art with an optional `font` parameter. If the font was specified in the request but not found, you may prefer to return a `404` (`Not Found`) status code rather than default to the standard font. To control the response code, use an `ActionResult`.

The name `ActionResult` comes from the ASP.NET implementation of the Model-View Controller (MVC) pattern. You'll learn more about the MVC pattern in section 3.2.1. In this pattern, the controller is the entry point for the request and is responsible for selecting the model and view. The controller in ASP.NET was traditionally a class, and each method of that class meant to handle a unique request was an action. The result of an action is the view that is returned to the user—hence, the name

`ActionResult`. Using minimal APIs (such as when we use `app.MapGet` in the Program.cs code) lets us create actions as methods without creating an explicit controller class.

In the code we've written so far, the result of the action is JSON text with a 200 status code. But we could have other types of results, such as HTML or images, and other status codes. ASP.NET Core has a set of built-in `ActionResults`. Let's try modifying the original GET request to return a 404 if the optional `font` parameter isn't a valid font. The `AsciiArt` class needs to be modified to indicate that the font isn't found instead of defaulting to the standard font. In the following listing, the approach is to modify the `Write` method to use an `out` parameter and return a Boolean indicating whether the font was found.

Listing 3.15   Modifying `Write` method to indicate whether font was found

```
public static class AsciiArt
{
  public static bool Write(string text,           ◁———— Returns a Boolean if font found
    out string? asciiText,                   ◁
    string? fontName = null)                 Converted text as an out parameter
  {
    FiggleFont? font = null;
    if (!string.IsNullOrWhiteSpace(fontName))
    {
      font = typeof(FiggleFonts)
        .GetProperty(fontName,
          BindingFlags.Static | BindingFlags.Public)
        ?.GetValue(null)
        as FiggleFont;
    }
    else
    {
      font = FiggleFonts.Standard;        ◁———— Uses default if font not specified
    }

    if (font == null)          ◁———— Doesn't default to Standard font
    {
      asciiText = null;        ◁———— out parameters must be set.
      return false;            ◁
    }                          Indicates font not found

    asciiText = font.Render(text);        ◁———— Success case
    return true;
  }
}
```

Out parameters

Often, we think of parameters as being passed in to a method with only one object or value being returned. This concept is a bit limiting because if we want to return multiple objects or values, we have to wrap them in another type. C# allows us to specify any number of parameters as out parameters.

(continued)
Out parameters must be assigned a value before the method returns. Also, the caller
must provide a place to put the out value. Out parameters allow us to use a pattern
that returns an object when the method is successful and to indicate failure without
throwing an exception.

Now let's return a 404 response if the AsciiArt.Write method returns false. Modify
the Program.cs file as shown in the following listing.

Listing 3.16   Returning 404 if font is invalid

```
app.MapGet("/{text}",
    (string text, string? font) =>
        AsciiArt.Write(text, out var asciiText, font)    ⟵  out object can be created inline.
            ? Results.Content(asciiText!)     ⟵  200 response code with content
            : Results.NotFound());      ⟵  404 response
```

Ternary operators
The anonymous method in the preceding listing is using a ternary operator. Ternary
operators are useful tools for saving space, and many languages have them. Consider
the if/else statement needed to write the method otherwise, as shown in the following code snippet:

```
if (AsciiArt.Write(text, out var asciiTest, font))
{
    return Results.Content(asciiText!);
}

return Results.NotFound();
```

A ternary operator is in the form <boolean expression> ? <true value> : <false value>.
The values returned by Results.Content and Results.NotFound are both the same type:
IResult. Because AsciiArt.Write returns a Boolean value, we can use a ternary oper-
ator in this case.

Exercise: Returning images instead of text
In this chapter, you used a package called Figgle to generate ASCII art. You added
the package to the .csproj file explicitly by adding the PackageReference item group.
When you browse to a package at https://www.nuget.org, the website gives you the
exact PackageReference line you need to add. For this exercise, create a new route in
your web API application that returns text converted to barcode images. The package
you'll use to generate the barcodes is called BarcodeLib. (Note that the code in the
following snippet uses BarcodeLib version 2.4.0; version 3 has breaking API changes.)

Browse to https://www.nuget.org, and find the BarcodeLib package. Then click the PackageReference tab to get the line to add to your .csprojfile.

To return an Image object in a response, you'll use the `File ActionResult`. The code for creating the barcode follows:

```
using BarcodeLib;          <──── Put at top of file
using System.Drawing;             <──── Used for Color
using System.Drawing.Imaging;         <──── Used for ImageFormat


app.MapGet("/barcode/{text}", (string text) => {  <── Different path, text required
  var barcode = new Barcode();                <──── Creates a new Barcode object
  barcode.ImageFormat = ImageFormat.Jpeg;   <──── Sets the image type to jpeg
  _ = barcode.Encode(          <──── Encode returns an Image, which we discard.
    TYPE.CODE128,          <──── Type of bar code to create
    text,            <──── Not all text will work.
    Color.Black,      <──── Foreground color
    Color.White);       <──── Background color
  return Results.File(      <──── File is an ActionResult.
    barcode.Encoded_Image_Bytes,    <──── Gets the bytes of the image
    "image/jpeg");              <──── Content type of the response
});
```

Try this code by browsing to https://localhost:<port>/barcode/hey. You should see the text `hey` converted to a barcode. This library covers many barcode types, each of which has restrictions on input; some types handle only numbers, for example. Try adding parameters to set the barcode type, image format, or colors. Add some error checking for the barcode types that accept only numbers or have other restrictions.

3.2   Web applications

Another powerful capability of ASP.NET is showing a web user interface via Razor. Razor generates HTML from a template that has HTML mixed with .NET code and some Razor-specific directives. We'll create an application that converts text to ASCII art, using a simple Razor page much like the console application and web service covered in the preceding sections.

As before, we'll start by generating a new project from a template, using the command `dotnet new webapp --name AsciiArtWebApp`. The resulting files and folders will look similar to figure 3.2.

NOTE   The files created in the template may vary by SDK version and patch.

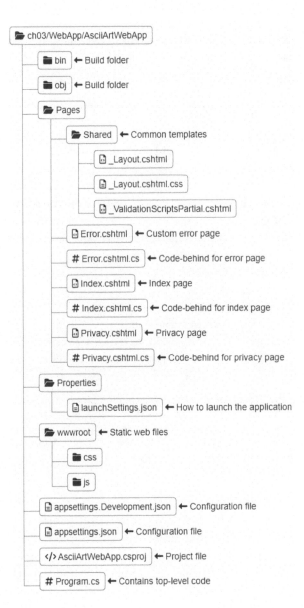

Figure 3.2   Files and folders created by the `webapp` **template**

The csproj file will look like the one generated for the empty web template we used in the preceding example. But the Program.cs file has a few important differences, as shown in the following listing.

Listing 3.17   Program.cs generated for `AsciiArtWebApp`

```
var builder = WebApplication.CreateBuilder(args);    ◁──┐  Same builder as in
                                                           the web service
builder.Services.AddRazorPages();    ◁──┐
                                         Adds Razor support
```

```
var app = builder.Build();

if (!app.Environment.IsDevelopment())          Shows generic error page
{                                               for nondev environment
  app.UseExceptionHandler("/Error");      ◁─┘
  app.UseHsts();                          ◁──── Tells browsers to use only HTTPS
}

app.UseHttpsRedirection();    ◁──── Redirects http to https
app.UseStaticFiles();       ◁─┐
app.UseRouting();             │ Allows static HTML files
app.UseAuthorization();
app.MapRazorPages();        ◁──── Maps the Razor pages in the code to routes
app.Run();
```

The Razor pages are located in the Pages folder inside the project folder. Before digging into the content of the Razor pages, try running the app by executing dotnet watch run in the project folder. Use the link in the command output to open the application in a browser. A home page with a welcome message and a privacy page should be visible.

3.2.1 *Razor pages*

Razor is the name of an ASP.NET Core feature that generates dynamic web pages. It provides a way to embed code in a web page. If you've used Java Server Pages in the past, Razor is similar. This book covers only the basics of Razor syntax so that you can create functional web applications. For this introduction, start with Index.cshtml in the Pages folder. The following listing shows the file's contents.

Listing 3.18 Index.cshtml contents

```
@page                   ◁──── Must be first directive in code
@model IndexModel       ◁─┐
@{                        │ Refers to the Model part of MVC
    ViewData["Title"] = "Home page";   ◁─┐
}                                        │ Properties to share with templates

<div class="text-center">               ◁──── No <html> or <body>
  <h1 class="display-4">Welcome</h1>
  <p>Learn about
  <a href="https://docs.microsoft.com/aspnet/core">building
  Web apps with ASP.NET Core</a>.
  </p>
</div>
```

A directive in Razor is the @ symbol followed by an expression that contains reserved keywords. The @page directive indicates a page. A Razor page handles the request without using a controller (the C part of MVC). The @model directive indicates what class is the model (M), and the page is the view (V).

Model-View-Controller

The MVC concept has been around since the 1970s. It predates named design patterns and is one of the first approaches to divide software constructs in terms of their responsibilities. The model holds the data and logic of the component. The view displays the data to the user and observes the model for updates. The controller handles user input and sends commands to the model or view. The following figure shows the MVC components.

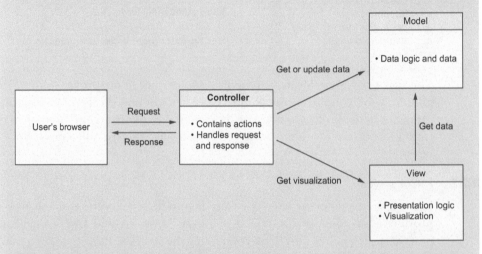

Diagram of the MVC pattern in which the user request goes to the controller, which can update the model and get the latest view to send in the response

Our web application is accessed through the browser, which sends HTTP requests that are typically handled by a controller. User interaction with a web page like the index page in our application is normally a GET request and an HTML response. Because the interaction is so simple, adding a controller in the middle seems to be unnecessary complexity, which is why pages don't have an explicit controller. The figure shows separate controller and view components but consider a Razor page to be a combination of view and controller. The model is still separated because application data and logic don't belong in the view. In section 3.1.2, we saw that web services have a controller that is operated on by actions. There is no view for web services, and the model is not an explicit class.

Note that an MVC template has distinct models, views, and controllers. Our web application isn't a true MVC application in that sense. Understanding MVC is important, though, because its nomenclature is spread throughout ASP.NET Core.

3.2.2   *Code-behind*

The Error.cshtml page generated by the template has some code to show the request ID, as shown in the following listing.

Listing 3.19 Error.cshtml contents

```
@page
@model ErrorModel              ⟵—— Model for this page
@{
    ViewData["Title"] = "Error";
}


<h1 class="text-danger">Error.</h1>
<h2 class="text-danger">
  An error occurred while processing your request.</h2>

@if (Model.ShowRequestId)        ⟵
{                                    "if" is a control structure that
    <p>                              works like a code block.
        <strong>Request ID:</strong>
        <code>@Model.RequestId</code>
    </p>
}
```

The code in the Razor page refers to properties of the ErrorModel. Note that it uses Model instead of referring to the particular ErrorModel type. The ErrorModel type is implemented in the Error.cshtml.cs file, which looks like the following listing. The cshtml.cs file is called a *code-behind file*.

Listing 3.20 Error.cshtml.cs code-behind

```
using System.Diagnostics;
using Microsoft.AspNetCore.Mvc;
using Microsoft.AspNetCore.Mvc.RazorPages;

namespace AsciiArtWebApp.Pages;
                                       The model referred to in
public class ErrorModel : PageModel  ⟵ the Razor page by @model
{
  public string? RequestId { get; set; }

  public bool ShowRequestId =>        ⟵—— Uses expression-bodied member
    !string.IsNullOrEmpty(RequestId);

  private readonly ILogger<ErrorModel> _logger;

  public ErrorModel(ILogger<ErrorModel> logger)
  {
    _logger = logger;
  }

  public void OnGet()
  {                                               Uses null-conditional operator ?.
    RequestId = Activity.Current?.Id  ⟵
      ?? HttpContext.TraceIdentifier; ⟵
  }                                               Uses null-coalescing operator ??
}
```

The `PageModel` processes requests via *handler methods,* which are named based on the HTTP verb used. In listing 3.20, the `OnGet` method handles GET verbs. You could also have an `OnPost` to handle form posts. Handler methods are analogous to actions on a controller. When the `Error` page is requested by the browser with a GET verb, the page sets its model to the `ErrorModel`. ASP.NET Core looks for a handler method to handle the GET request. The `OnGet` doesn't have to exist in the `PageModel`. ASP.NET Core finds the method by convention (`On` followed by a verb) rather than forcing it through an interface or abstract base class.

> **NOTE**   If you need a refresher on null operators, see chapter 2.

> ### Expression-bodied members
> The property `ShowRequestId` is an *expression-bodied member*—a member that consists of only an expression and therefore doesn't need brackets or a return statement. We saw these members in anonymous methods in chapter 2.
>
> The expression in the `ShowRequestId` method is evaluated only when the property is accessed. This detail is important because the `OnGet` method needs to execute before the page uses `ShowRequestId`, which sets the value of the `RequestId` property.

Let's add a page that can show ASCII art based on data posted in an HTML form. The page will look similar to the error page and its model. As before, add the `Figgle` package reference to the csproj file as shown in the following listing.

Listing 3.21   Adding `Figgle` package reference to `AsciiArtWebApp` project

```
<Project Sdk="Microsoft.NET.Sdk.Web">

  <PropertyGroup>
    <TargetFramework>net8.0</TargetFramework>
    <Nullable>enable</Nullable>
    <ImplicitUsings>enable</ImplicitUsings>
  </PropertyGroup>

  <ItemGroup>
    <PackageReference Include="Figgle" Version="0.5.1" />          ⟵──┐ Adds Figgle,
  </ItemGroup>                                                         which should
                                                                       look familiar
</Project>                                                             by now
```

Next, create a new file in the Pages folder called AsciiArt.cshtml. Insert the contents from the following listing.

Listing 3.22   Contents of AsciiArt.cshtml

```
@page
@model AsciiArtModel          ⟵──── We'll create the model in the code-behind next.
```

```
@{
  ViewData["Title"] = "Ascii Art";
}


<form method="post">          <──── Adds a form to the page
  <fieldset>
    <div>
      <label for="Text">Text:</label>
      <input type="text" id="text" name="text" />   <──── Text to convert to ASCII art
    </div>
    <div>
      <label> </label>
      <input type="submit" value="Submit" class="submit" />   <─┐ Button to
    </div>                                                      │ submit form
  </fieldset>
</form>

@if (Model.ShowRenderedText)        <──── Shows section only if some art has been rendered
{
<pre>
@Model.RenderedText        <──── Puts art in a pre section to preserve spacing
</pre>
}
```

In the same Pages folder, create the code-behind file, called AsciiArt.cshtml.cs. Insert the contents of the following listing.

Listing 3.23 Contents of the `AsciiArt` code-behind file, AsciiArt.cshtml.cs

```
using Figgle;
using Microsoft.AspNetCore.Mvc;
using Microsoft.AspNetCore.Mvc.RazorPages;

namespace AsciiArtWebApp.Pages;          │ Indicates that page
                                         │ shouldn't be cached
[ResponseCache(Duration = 0,        <─┘
  Location = ResponseCacheLocation.None, NoStore = true)]
[IgnoreAntiforgeryToken]                  <──── No security on page
public class AsciiArtModel : PageModel
{
    public string? RenderedText { get; set; }   <──── Holds art so it's available to page

    public bool ShowRenderedText =>        <──── Flag indicating that art has been rendered
      !string.IsNullOrEmpty(RenderedText);

    public AsciiArtModel() {}    <──── Empty constructor

    public void OnPost(string text)   <──── Called when form is submitted, an HTTP POST
    {
      RenderedText = FiggleFonts.Standard.Render(
        text ?? "Hello!");                  <──── Uses default if text is null
    }
}
```

The only step remaining is making the page visible in the navbar. Open Pages/ Shared/_Layout.cshtml, and look for the navbar section, which has links for the Home and Privacy pages. Add the new AsciiArt page as shown in the following listing.

Listing 3.24 Adding `AsciiArt` page link to the navbar in _Layout.cshtml

```
<div class="navbar-collapse collapse d-sm-inline-flex
 justify-content-between">
  <ul class="navbar-nav flex-grow-1">
    <li class="nav-item">
      <a class="nav-link text-dark" asp-area="" asp-page="/Index">Home</a>
    </li>                                       | Add this section.
    <li class="nav-item">               ←───────|
      <a class="nav-link text-dark" asp-area="" asp-page="/AsciiArt">
        ASCII Art</a>
    </li>
    <li class="nav-item">
      <a class="nav-link text-dark" asp-area="" asp-page="/Privacy">
        Privacy</a>
    </li>
  </ul>
</div>
```

Assuming that you have the application running with `dotnet watch run`, save all the modified files. The command output in the terminal should have a link to open in your browser. Navigate to the AsciiArt page, and try submitting some text in the form.

Summary

- Minimal APIs and C# shorthand take away a lot of boilerplate and make the code easier to read.
- Web services are as easy to write as console applications.
- Web applications have more boilerplate than services or console applications but are easy to start with.
- LINQ is a C# feature for querying data.

Part 2

Data

Almost all the applications you write will handle external data of some kind. In this part, you'll learn how to store, retrieve, and manipulate data through streams and databases.

In chapter 4, you'll start by building two console applications that read files and folders. Then you'll learn to read and write JSON. Those tasks will give you the skills to make HTTP requests to web services, which you'll practice against a popular website. Working with external data is slow and can often be parallelized, so chapter 4 will give you a first taste of asynchronous programming.

Chapter 5 will get you working with relational databases. You'll use the powerful Entity Framework Core (EF Core) library to retrieve and manipulate data in a real SQL database. Building on this fundamental skill, you'll create a web service with create, retrieve, update, and delete (CRUD) functionality. Then you'll use Swagger to allow others to ingest your service.

File and network I/O

4

This chapter covers

- Reading and writing files
- Working with JSON
- Making HTTP requests
- Unblocking programs with asynchronous programming

Few things are more fundamental to developing applications than file I/O (input/output). A lot of file I/O happens behind the scenes. .NET applications, for example, are typically comprised of multiple DLL files, and the runtime handles when and how to load them. Configuration is often loaded from files. Applications may read text files and parse their contents into objects or transform them into other formats.

4.1 Reading and writing files

In this section, we'll explore how to explicitly locate, read, and write files in code using .NET's built-in libraries. Most of these APIs are available in the `System.IO` namespace, which is automatically included with implicit `using` statements.

4.1.1   *Building a custom template*

In this chapter, you'll create a lot of console applications with some boilerplate code that we used in previous chapters. We'll save a lot of time if we create a custom `dotnet new` template with the code to handle command-line arguments. Let's start by creating a new console application, using the commands from the following listing.

Listing 4.1   Terminal commands to create a new console application

```
dotnet new console --name CmdArgsTemplate
cd CmdArgsTemplate
dotnet add package CommandLineParser        <──── Another way to add package references
```

Note that the `dotnet add package` command will add the latest non-prerelease version of the package reference to the .csproj file. Open the CmdArgsTemplate.csproj file, and add the global static `Using` statement for `System.Console` as shown in the following listing.

Listing 4.2   Adding a global `Using` for System.Console to CmdArgsTemplate.csproj

```
<ItemGroup>
  <Using Include="System.Console" Static="True" />
</ItemGroup>
```

Next, add a file called Options.cs to hold the command-line arguments, as shown in the following listing.

Listing 4.3   Template command-line options file

```
using CommandLine;
                                         Matches to project name
namespace CmdArgsTemplate;       <──┘    so it can be replaced

public record Options
{                                                           Specifies description
  [Value(0, Required = true, HelpText = "Some text")]  <──┘ with HelpText
  public string? Text { get; init; }      <──┐
}                                            └── An example to get the user started
```

In Program.cs, create a template that shows the usage guidance if the options are specified incorrectly, as in the following listing.

Listing 4.4   Template for Program.cs that parses options and shows usage guidance

```
using CmdArgsTemplate;
using CommandLine;
using CommandLine.Text;
                                                          Stores results
var results = Parser.Default.ParseArguments<Options>(args)  <──┘ for help text
```

```
.WithParsed<Options>(options => {
    WriteLine(options.Text);            <---- Placeholder to indicate success
});

results.WithNotParsed(_ =>            <------| If arguments didn't match . . .
    WriteLine(HelpText.RenderUsageText(results)));   <---  . . . write autogenerated
                                                           help text to console.
```

So far, this project is a normal C# project. To make it a template, we need to create a new folder at the same level as the .csproj file called .template.config. Inside this folder, create a file named template.json, and add the JSON from the following listing.

Listing 4.5 template.json defining the `dotnet new` template

```
{
  "$schema": "http://json.schemastore.org/template",
  "author": "Awesome Programmer",
  "classifications": [ "Console" ],
  "name": "Console with arguments",
  "identity": "CmdArgsTemplate",          <---
  "shortName": "consoleargs",             <---
  "tags": {
    "language": "C#",            Uses line      Matches to
    "type": "project"            dotnet new     project name
  },                             consoleargs
  "sourceName": "CmdArgsTemplate",         <---
  "preferNameDirectory": true
}
```

The next steps are building and installing the template. Use the commands from the following listing.

Listing 4.6 Commands to build and install CmdArgsTemplate as a `dotnet new` template

```
dotnet build
dotnet new install .            <---- Refers to current directory
```

> **TIP** If you had any problems installing the package or want to update the template, you can try using the `--force` flag. If that flag doesn't work, try uninstalling the template first, using the command `dotnet new uninstall` from the template's folder.

The `dotnet` console command should indicate success. You can also check that the template was installed correctly by running the `dotnet new list` command. (Templates are alphabetized.) When you're satisfied that the template is installed correctly, try creating a new project in another folder with the template. We'll use this template in the following sections.

4.1.2 Finding files in folders

The first application we'll create lists files in a folder and (optionally) its subfolders. The application will look for filenames that match a filter. We could use it to find .json files, for example. The command-line parameters include the folder to look in, the filter, and a flag to indicate whether to search subfolders recursively. Start by creating a new console application called FindFiles, using the command `dotnet new consoleargs -n FindFiles`. Modify the command-line parameters in the application as shown in the following listing.

Listing 4.7   Command-line options for FindFiles

```
using CommandLine;

namespace FindFiles;

public record Options
{
  [Value(0, Required = true, HelpText = "Root folder")]
  public string RootFolder { get; init; } = ".";

  [Value(1, Required = false, HelpText = "Filename filter")]
  public string Filter { get; init; } = "*";

  [Option('r', "recurse", HelpText = "Search subfolders recursively")]
  public bool Recursive { get; init; } = false;
}
```

0 indicates that this parameter is the first one.

Folder to search

Optional file filter; defaults to wildcard

Searches in subfolders

The important part of the application can be written in a single recursive method. .NET's file APIs are housed under the `System.IO` namespace, which is included by default with `ImplicitUsings` turned on in the project file. The first step is creating a `DirectoryInfo` object, using the folder specified in the options. When we call `EnumerateFiles` on this object, the application can return an `IEnumerable<string>` or throw an exception. Two exceptions are possible with `EnumerateFiles`: a `DirectoryNotFoundException`, which indicates that the directory doesn't exist, and a `SecurityException`, which indicates that the identity under which the application is running doesn't have access to list files in that folder. First, look at the method shown in the following listing.

Listing 4.8   Adding a `find` method to Program.cs that searches subfolders recursively

```
static void RecursiveFind(
  DirectoryInfo folder,           ◁─── Object representation of a folder
  string filter,
  bool recurse)                   ◁─── Expect default to be a wildcard (*).
{
  if (!folder.Exists)             ◁─── Checks whether the folder exists first
  {
    WriteLine($"{folder.FullName} does not exist");
```

```
      return;
   }
   WriteLine(folder.FullName);        ◁──┐  Writes folder name and indicates progress
   try                                ◁────  EnumerateFiles can throw exceptions.
   {
      foreach (var file in folder.EnumerateFiles(filter))  ◁─┐  Finds all the files in the
      {                                                      │  folder matching filter
         WriteLine($"\t{file.Name}");  ◁───┐
      }                                    │  Writes filename and extension indented
   }
   catch (System.Security.SecurityException)  ◁──┐  Thrown if caller doesn't
   {                                             │  have permission
      return;    ◁──── Gives up on this folder
   }

   if (recurse)
   {
      foreach (var subFolder in folder.GetDirectories())
      {                                                    │  Performs same search in
         RecursiveFind(subFolder, filter, recurse);  ◁──┘  all immediate subfolders
      }
   }
}
```

Exceptions

This section is the first place we've seen exceptions in this book. Many languages use exceptions to handle unexpected or exceptional situations. Like most languages, C# has `throw`, `try`, `catch`, and `finally` keywords. The difference in C# is in the details:

- `catch` types are tested in order, so be careful to put subclasses first.
- `catch` doesn't need a named variable if it's not used. Listing 4.8 shows an example.
- When an exception is rethrown from a catch block, the statement `throw;` preserves the original exception's stack trace; `throw exc;` doesn't.
- A `finally` block always executes, whether or not an exception was caught.

`EnumerateFiles` can throw a `DirectoryNotFoundException`, but we don't call that exception out in a `catch` block. The reason is that a folder's nonexistence is something that's easy to check by testing the `DirectoryInfo.Exists` property. Exceptions are generally expensive to throw, as they require collecting a full stack trace, so it's good practice to use them only in *exceptional* situations. If the user doesn't have access to the folder, the code in listing 4.8 relies on the `SecurityException`, mainly because the security check is more difficult to test.

Next, we want to call the `RecursiveFind` method from Program.cs. Replace the `WriteLine (options.Text);` statement in the `WithParsed` clause with `RecursiveFind(new DirectoryInfo (options.RootFolder), options.Filter, options.Recursive);`. Try the application by running a few commands, like those in the following listing.

Listing 4.9   Commands to test FindFiles console application

```
dotnet run . *.cs              ⟵—— Finds C# files in current folder
dotnet run ~/ *.txt --recurse      ⟵
                                    ⌐ Checks user's home folder for txt files recursively
```

> **NOTE** Although a shortened form of the `--recurse` parameter is available, you won't be able to use it directly with `dotnet run` because the `dotnet run` command looks at all the parameters and recognizes the `-r` as its own. If it doesn't recognize a parameter, the command passes it through to your application. That's why `--recurse` works but `-r` doesn't.

Exercise 1: Bare output mode for FindFiles

The FindFiles application writes the folder first and then each file is indented under that folder. This arrangement makes it a bit easier for a human to read but not useful for passing filenames to another application. In section 4.1.3, we'll create an application that can take filenames from the console input. This application will expect the input to be the full path of each file. Add a `bare` command-line option that doesn't write the folder name, doesn't indent filenames, and writes full file paths for each matched file to the console.

4.1.3   Finding text in a file

The next application we'll create searches for text within a file. This application gives the user two ways of specifying which files to search: putting the filename as a command-line parameter or entering the filenames via console input one file per line. The two approaches are mutually exclusive, so we check console input only if no command-line parameter exists. The second method allows us to pipe the files from the FindFiles console output, which is the topic of an exercise at the end of this section.

This application needs one other command-line parameter to specify the text to search for. Start by creating a new console application called FindText, using the command `dotnet new consoleargs -n FindText`. Modify the command-line parameters in the application as shown in the following listing.

Listing 4.10   Command-line options for FindText

```
using CommandLine;

namespace FindText;

public record Options
{
    [Value(0, Required = true, HelpText = "Text to search for")]
    public string? Text { get; init; }              ⟵—— No default text

    [Value(1, Required = false, HelpText = "File to search")]
    public string? Filename { get; init; }        ⟵
                                                   ⌐ Optional single file to search
}
```

NOTE Because no default search string exists, Text is a nullable string type. The compiler is unaware of the Required flag on the attribute, but we know that Text can't be null. Therefore, when we use Text, we'll use the ! suffix to tell the compiler we know it's not null.

To keep things simple, the text search doesn't span lines. We'll add a method to search a file line by line for the Text string. Add the code from the following listing to Program.cs.

Listing 4.11 SearchFile method that looks for text in a file by reading it line by line

```
using System.Security;          ← For exceptions, add to top of file.

static void SearchFile(
  FileInfo file,                ← Object representing a file
  string text)                  ← Text to search for
{
  if (!file.Exists)
  {
    Console.Error.WriteLine(
      $"{file.FullName} does not exist");    ← Reports error to standard error
    return;                     ← Skip if file doesn't exist.
  }

  try
  {
    using var reader = file.OpenText();      ← Creates a StreamReader; using disposes at end of code block
    string? line;
    while ((line = reader.ReadLine()) != null)    ← Reads lines until end of file
    {
      if (line.Contains(text,
        StringComparison.OrdinalIgnoreCase))      ← Case-insensitive, language-invariant search
      {
        WriteLine(line);        ← Writes line if a match is found
      }
    }
  }
  catch (UnauthorizedAccessException)        ← Thrown if we can't open the file
  {
    Console.Error.WriteLine(
      $"Unauthorized: {file.FullName}");
  }
  catch (IOException)           ← Thrown if OS problem occurs when reading
  {
    Console.Error.WriteLine(
      $"IO error: {file.FullName}");
  }
}
```

Reports error to standard error

The standard error output stream

In listing 4.11, the error messages are written to `Console.Error`, which is the standard error output stream. Standard error is separate from standard (console) output, allowing the output and errors to go to different pipes or be ignored independently.

Catch exceptions in order from specific to generic

`catch` blocks run in order, so if you want to handle an `IOException` and a generic `Exception` differently, the `IOException` catch must be above the `Exception` catch. Most IDEs and code analysis tools warn you if your `catch` blocks appear to be out of order.

4.1.4   *Disposing the StreamReader with using*

Chapter 1 introduced garbage collection as an aspect of managed languages. When an object is no longer used, the garbage collector can clean it up to make room in memory for other objects. But we don't know when the collection will happen. Therefore, if any nonmemory resources need to be cleaned up, we have to consider when and how that will happen. A `StreamReader` could be holding on to a file handle. It's a good idea to release that file handle when we're done using it; otherwise, other processes may not be able to access the file until garbage collection or our program ends.

In .NET, cleaning up resources is a common practice, so an accepted pattern exists, called the dispose pattern. To use this pattern, a class needs to implement the `IDisposable` interface, which has a single method called `Dispose`. We won't implement the `IDisposable` interface in this chapter, but because we'll be using many disposable types, learning to use them is important. The explicit call to `Dispose` can be a bit annoying, especially because we have to handle cases in which an exception could occur. The following listing shows how we could handle exceptions.

Listing 4.12   Call `Dispose` even in the case of an exception

```
var reader = file.OpenText();
try
{
  while ((line = reader.ReadLine()) != null);          ←┐ Some code that
}                                                        │ uses reader
finally
{
  reader?.Dispose();
}
```

If anything goes wrong while we're using the reader and an exception is thrown, the `finally` will execute and call `Dispose` on the reader (if it's not null). C# has shorthand for this pattern. Unfortunately, the keyword for the shorthand is `using`. Newcomers to C# may find this keyword confusing because the meaning of `using` changes depending on context. But you'll get used to it soon. The following listing shows a using block that can replace the try/finally approach.

Listing 4.13 Replace try/finally with a using block

```
using (var reader = file.OpenText())          ◁──── reader is the disposable object.
{
  while ((line = reader.ReadLine()) != null);  ◁──── Some code that uses reader
}
```

Note that this using statement is intended for use only on types that implement the IDisposable interface. We can take this example a step farther by getting rid of the using block. The dispose will happen at the end of the enclosing code block. The following listing shows how to replace the using block with a single statement.

Listing 4.14 Replace using block with a single using statement

```
{                                          ◁──── Any enclosing block
  using var reader = file.OpenText();
  while ((line = reader.ReadLine()) != null);
}                                          ◁──── reader disposed at end of block
```

4.1.5 *Parsing command-line arguments*

The next step is parsing the command-line arguments. This process is similar to the one in listing 4.4 except that we also may need to read a list of files from the console input. The following listing shows one way to perform these two operations.

Listing 4.15 Reading files based on command-line arguments and console input

```
var results = Parser.Default.ParseArguments<Options>(args)
  .WithParsed<Options>(options => {             │ If a filename is specified,
    if (options.Filename != null)          ◁────┘ reads only that one
    {
      SearchFile(new FileInfo(options.Filename),  ◁──── Creates object for the file
        options.Text!);                      ◁────
    }                                          │ We know that Text is not null.
    else
    {
      string? filename;                        │ Goes until an empty line
      while (!string.IsNullOrWhiteSpace(  ◁────┘ or end of file (EOF)
        filename = ReadLine()))           ◁────┐
      {                                         │ Short for Console.ReadLine()
        SearchFile(new FileInfo(filename),
          options.Text!);
      }
    }
  });
```

Try the application by running a command such as `dotnet run using Program.cs`. This command shows all the lines that contain `using` in the Program.cs file. If you want to try command-line piping, create a file called Files.txt, and put the text `Program.cs` and `Options.cs` on separate lines. Save the file and then try a piping command like `type Files.txt | dotnet run using` or `cat Files.txt | dotnet run using`. This command shows the lines with the text `using` in both files.

Exercise 2: Search using regular expressions

Add an optional parameter to FindText, `-x` or `--regex`, that allows searching with regular expressions. The regular-expression search will replace `string.Contains` to search for text in a line. .NET's implementation of regular expressions is in the `Regex` class in the `System.Text.RegularExpressions` namespace. You can create the `Regex` object in Program.cs and pass it to the `SearchFile` method or create it inside the `SearchFile` method. Don't forget to pass `RegexOptions.IgnoreCase` in the constructor.

Exercise 3: Use FindFiles and FindText together

The prerequisite for this exercise is completing exercise 1 (creating a `bare` output method for FindFiles). Because the FindFiles `bare` output method writes a full filename per line to standard output and the `FindText` method reads a filename per line of standard input, we can connect the two methods with piping. The resulting command would look something like `findfiles . \*.cs -r -b | findtext using`. First, build both FindFiles and FindText, using `dotnet build`. In the project folder, find the subfolder bin \Debug\net8.0 (if you're using .NET8).

This folder contains the executable and binaries. Put the binaries from both FindFiles and FindText in the same folder, and try the piping command. Note that you can use the parameter short forms (such as `-r` instead of `--recurse`) because you're not calling the `dotnet` executable.

4.2   *Working with JSON*

JSON is likely the most commonly used contemporary text file format for holding structured data. Many .NET libraries read and write JSON, as well as serialize and deserialize it to and from objects. Until .NET Core 3.0 was released, the de facto JSON library was `Newtonsoft.Json`, which was even used directly within ASP.NET. But Microsoft switched to its own implementation, called `System.Text.Json`, shortly after hiring Newtonsoft's developer, James Newton-King. This new library has better performance and integrates well with source generators. If you're working with an older codebase that uses `Newtonsoft.Json`, the APIs are similar enough that you could translate between the two.

In this section, we'll create a new console application, using the same template as before. Use the command `dotnet new consoleargs -n GetJokes` to create the project. This application will read a JSON file with jokes in it, search for jokes in a category, and write the jokes to either console output or to a file. The command-line options will include the input file (required), output file (optional), and an option for setting the category (the default is `"programming"`). The following listing shows how to set the options.

Listing 4.16 Options for the `GetJokes` command-line parameters

```
public record Options
{
  [Value(0, Required = true, HelpText = "Input file")]
  public string? InputFile { get; init; }                    ◁─── Expects a JSON file

  [Value(1, Required = false, HelpText = "Output file")]      ◁─┐
  public string? OutputFile { get; init; }                      │ Writes to console if
                                                                 │ output file isn't set

  [Option('c', "category", HelpText = "Joke category")]
  public string Category { get; init; } = "programming";     ◁─┐
}                                                              │ Category of jokes
                                                               │ to look for
```

4.2.1 Reading JSON documents

First, we need a JSON document to read. You can find a handy list of jokes in JSON format at http://mng.bz/GZOA, courtesy of GitHub user 15DKatz (https://github.com/15Dkatz). Download the file in your browser or use `curl` as shown in the following listing. Put the file in the same folder as the project.

Listing 4.17 `curl` command to download programmer-jokes JSON document

```
curl -o jokes.json https://github.com/dmetzgar/
➥ dotnet-in-action-code/blob/main/ch04/joke_index.json
```

> **Installing curl**
>
> The *Everything curl* book (https://everything.curl.dev) has the most up-to-date explanation of installing `curl`. Depending on your OS, you may already have `curl` installed.

> **curl in PowerShell**
>
> Windows PowerShell has an alias that changes `curl` commands to use `Invoke-WebRequest`, which doesn't support the same options. The command in listing 4.17 works safely with PowerShell. But an example of an option that doesn't work is -o (capital o), which saves the remote file with the same name. `Invoke-WebRequest` doesn't know how to translate the -o parameter.

The JSON file is an array of objects with the format shown in the following listing.

Listing 4.18   Format of the jokes JSON document

```
                        Indicates an array
                               Indicates an object or element
[         ◄─────────┘
  {       ◄──────┘
    "id": 1,                          Integer identifier
    "type": "general",        ◄─────────┘        Category
    "setup": "What did the fish say when it hit the wall?",  ◄───┘
    "punchline": "Dam."
  },
  {
    "id": 2,
    "type": "general",
    "setup": "How do you make a tissue dance?",
    "punchline": "You put a little boogie on it."
  }
  //...
]
```

To open a JSON document and parse it, we need a way to read it from the file. The FindText application from listing 4.11 opened the file by using `FileInfo.OpenText`, which creates a `StreamReader`. A `StreamReader` is a wrapper that lets you read a `Stream` object line by line, which works well for that application. A JSON document isn't parsed one line at a time, so it's better to use the `Stream` itself. Streams are lower-level constructs that can apply to files, HTTP response bodies, memory buffers, console output, and many other areas that involve a stream of bytes.

USING STREAMS

We'll start with an input stream. The code in the following listing should look familiar except for using `OpenRead` instead of `OpenText`. `OpenRead` returns a read-only input `Stream`.

Listing 4.19   Creating an input stream from a file

```
var results = Parser.Default.ParseArguments<Options>(args)         InputFile is required,
  .WithParsed<Options>(options => {                                so not null
    var inFile = new FileInfo(options.InputFile!);          ◄─────┘
    if (!inFile.Exists)                                     ◄──── File must exist.
    {
      Console.Error.WriteLine(
        $"{inFile.FullName} does not exist");
      return;
    }
                                                            Opens a read-only Stream
    using var inStream = inFile.OpenRead();          ◄─────┘
    // Code continued...                         ◄─── Insert output stream
  });                                                 code from listing 4.20.
```

This code gives us a stream of the input JSON file. The next step is getting a stream to write the output to. If the `OutputFile` parameter is specified, we'll create a write-only file stream. But if there is no output file, we can get a stream to write to the console output. The following listing shows the code to get the output stream.

Listing 4.20 Creating an output stream to a file

```
FileInfo? outFile = null;          ⟵——— Create only if OutputFile is specified.
if (options.OutputFile != null)
{
  outFile = new FileInfo(options.OutputFile);      ⎤ If the file exists, a write
  if (outFile.Exists)                            ⟵⎦ stream will overwrite.
  {
    outFile.Delete();              ⟵——— Deletes the existing file
  }
}                                                ⎤ "using" flushes the buffer
                                                 ⎦ and disposes the stream.
using var outStream = outFile != null ?    ⟵
  outFile.OpenWrite() :            ⟵——— Opens write-only stream to file
  Console.OpenStandardOutput();    ⟵⎤
                                    ⎦ Gets stream for console output
```

NOTE Opening a write stream on an existing file allows you to overwrite the file. If the new content is shorter than the existing file's content, however, the old content will still be there. You have options for opening a file and appending new content to the existing contents. You can also seek forward to a certain point in the file to overwrite only a particular section. This book doesn't get into these use cases.

PARSING WITH JSONDOCUMENT

Now that we have streams to read from and write to, we can parse the JSON document. We can parse JSON in many ways. This section uses the Document Object Model (DOM) method, which parses the whole document into an in-memory object representation (analogous to XmlDocument, for .NET Framework veterans). Add the method from the following listing to Program.cs, and add a step in WithParsed to call it after creating the input and output streams (FindWithJsonDom(inStream, outStream, options.Category);).

Listing 4.21 Reading the JSON stream and finding jokes by category

```
using System.Text;          ⟵——— Put at the top of the file.
using System.Text.Json;

static void FinddWithJsonDom(
  Stream inStream,                              ⎤ Creates a Writer, which
  Stream outStream,                             ⎦ lets us write strings
  string category)
{                                               ⎤ Input file is in UTF8; write
  using var writer = new StreamWriter(outStream,  ⟵⎦ it with same encoding.
    Encoding.UTF8,                            ⟵
    leaveOpen: true);      ⟵⎤ "using" disposes Writer, which disposes Stream by default.
```

```
using var jsonDoc =                    ⟵── "using" disposes JsonDocument, which holds memory buffer(s).
  JsonDocument.Parse(inStream);        ⟵─
foreach (var jokeElement in jsonDoc    ⟵──┐ Parse reads whole stream and doesn't dispose.
  .RootElement.EnumerateArray())       ⟵── │ Iterates each element under root
{                                             │ Assumes that root element is an array
  string? type = jokeElement
    .GetProperty("type")               ⟵── Find "type" property; throws exception if not found
    .GetString();                      ⟵──┐
  if (string.Equals(category, type,    ⟵──│ Converts contents of "type" property to string
    StringComparison.OrdinalIgnoreCase)) │ Checks whether "type" matches category
  {
    writer.WriteLine(jokeElement.GetRawText());   ⟵──┐ Writes entire text from
  }                                                   │ joke element to output
}
}
```

Case and language should not matter.

Disposing with using

In listing 4.21, we use the `using` statement to dispose of the `StreamWriter` and `Json-Document` when the method completes. As you learned earlier, this shorthand calls the `Dispose` method and applies only to classes that implement the `IDisposable` interface. `Dispose` methods sometimes call `Dispose` on objects they reference, and sometimes, they don't. When you implement the dispose pattern in chapter 8, you'll see how to protect your own code from multiple calls to `Dispose`.

For code you don't own, it's not clear whether `Dispose` is called. There's no property or method on `Stream` you can check to see whether the stream is disposed, for example. The behavior is often documented, but when it isn't, you may have to read the code. By default, `StreamWriter` disposes the underlying `Stream`. The documentation for `JsonDocument.Parse` doesn't indicate whether it closes the stream, but the code is available on GitHub, and a quick read shows that it doesn't. My approach is to not dispose streams passed into a method because the caller may want to keep working with them.

Try this application by running `dotnet run jokes.json` to write to the console or add a filename parameter to write to a file. Don't forget that the default category is `"programming"`. You can also try `"--category general"` or `"--category knock-knock"`. The output from the application has individual JSON elements but isn't a well-formed JSON document. To write well-formed JSON, we'll need to use a JSON writer.

Exercise 4: Robust JSON parsing

Parsing JSON with code is normally done with the expectation that the JSON will match some schema. If the `type` property doesn't exist in an element, the document root element is not an array, or the JSON is malformed, this code will throw exceptions. Create some JSON documents with these problems to see where and what type of exceptions are thrown; then add `try/catch` blocks to make the code more robust.

4.2.2 Writing JSON documents

The output so far is the raw element text, which isn't valid JSON. To make it valid, we could add commas between elements and enclose the JSON output in an array manually. Or we could replace the `StreamWriter` with the `Utf8JsonWriter`. This writer handles indentation, commas, and other formatting automatically. Also, the `JsonDocument` can use this writer, so we don't have to read and write each property individually. The following listing shows how to rewrite the `FindWithJsonDom` method to use this writer.

Listing 4.22 Using `Utf8JsonWriter` to write well-formed JSON

```
static void FindWithJsonDom(
  Stream inStream,
  Stream outStream,
  string category)
{
  var writerOptions = new JsonWriterOptions
    { Indented = true };
  using var writer = new Utf8JsonWriter(outStream,
    writerOptions);
  writer.WriteStartArray();

  using var jsonDoc =
    JsonDocument.Parse(inStream);
  foreach (var jokeElement in jsonDoc
    .RootElement.EnumerateArray())
  {
    string? type = jokeElement
      .GetProperty("type")
      .GetString();
    if (string.Equals(category, type,
      StringComparison.OrdinalIgnoreCase))
    {
      jokeElement.WriteTo(writer);
    }
  }

  writer.WriteEndArray();
}
```

- **This options pattern is common in .NET.**
- **Turning this off puts all content on one line.**
- **`using` flushes stream but won't dispose it**
- **Root element is an array.**
- **Use JsonDocument as before.**
- **Writes full element to the writer**
- **Indicates array end**

Now the output from the application should have an array of elements and contain commas to separate the elements where necessary. The elements include the `"id"` and `"type"` properties. If we want the output file to exclude these properties and write only the `"setup"` and `"punchline"`, we can write the object and properties directly, as shown in the following listing.

Listing 4.23 Writing only `"setup"` and `"punchline"` properties

```
string? type = jokeElement
  .GetProperty("type")
  .GetString();
```

```
if (string.Equals(category, type,        ◁─── if statement is same as before.
   StringComparison.OrdinalIgnoreCase))
{
   string? setup =                                    ◁─── Gets the setup property
      jokeElement.GetProperty("setup").GetString();
   string? punchline =                                 ◁─── Gets the punchline property
      jokeElement.GetProperty("punchline").GetString();
   writer.WriteStartObject();                          ◁─── Indicates start of object
   writer.WriteString("setup", setup);        ◁─┐
   writer.WriteString("punchline", punchline);  ◁─┤    │ Writes setup property first
   writer.WriteEndObject();            ◁─────────┐│    │ Punchline is next.
}                                               ││
                                                │ Closes the object
```

`JsonDocument` and `Utf8JsonWriter` provide a lot of power in reading and writing JSON documents, but a lot of code is involved for even simple JSON documents. If the schema of the JSON document is known, a simpler way to read and write is via *serialization*, which is the process of converting JSON to objects and vice versa.

4.2.3   JSON serialization

Let's take another look at the structure of the JSON document with jokes, shown in the following listing.

Listing 4.24   Format of the jokes JSON document

```
[          ◁─── Array
   {                 ◁─── Object
     "id": 18,                    ◁─── int property
     "type": "programming",                           ◁─── enum or string property
     "setup": "Why did the programmer quit his job?",
     "punchline": "Because he didn't get arrays."   ◁─── string property
   }
   //...
]
```

The JSON element could be represented with a .NET type. Add a new file called Joke.cs, using the code from the following listing.

Listing 4.25   `Joke` record to hold JSON object

```
namespace GetJokes;

public record Joke(
   int Id,
   string Type,
   string Setup,
   string Punchline
) {}
```

The `Joke` record has the same properties as the element in the JSON file. A serializer called `JsonSerializer` can map the JSON text to this type. Let's add a new method to Program.cs that uses the serializer; the following listing shows the code.

Listing 4.26 Reading and writing JSON with `JsonSerializer`

```
static void FindWithSerialization(        ◁─── Same signature as
  Stream inStream,                              FindWithJsonDom
  Stream outStream,
  string category                                    Different options
)                                                    class from writer
{
                                                     Note that this is a different
  var serialOptions = new JsonSerializerOptions  ◁──┘ name from writer.
    { WriteIndented = true,
      PropertyNameCaseInsensitive = true };  ◁─── JSON file property names, all lowercase
  var jokes = JsonSerializer.Deserialize<Joke[]>(     ◁
    inStream,                                          Deserializes to array
    serialOptions);      ◁───── Input stream           of Joke objects
Writes
objects  ┌─▷ JsonSerializer.Serialize(    └───── Needed for case-insensitive flag
to output│    outStream,
stream   │    jokes?.Where(j => string.Equals(  ◁─── Writes only jokes with given category
         │      category, j.Type,
              StringComparison.OrdinalIgnoreCase))
            .ToArray(),          ◁───── Needs a type (Joke array), not IEnumerable
          serialOptions);   ◁─────┐
}                                 └──── Writes indented
```

Because JSON readers normally expect the JSON to be in a particular schema, many applications prefer to use the serialization method, which can save a lot of code, especially with complex schemas. The output of the serialization method in its current form has two problems, however. One problem is that the property names are capitalized, due to the property names for the `Joke` type; to fix it, use the `[JsonPropertyName]` attribute. We'll use this option in section 4.3. The other problem is that we want only the setup and punchline in the output. Both of these problems can be fixed with a LINQ projection, as shown in the following listing.

Listing 4.27 Writing only the setup and punchline using the serializer and a LINQ project

```
JsonSerializer.Serialize(
  outStream,
  jokes?.Where(j => string.Equals(
    category, j.Type,
    StringComparison.OrdinalIgnoreCase))     │ Select performs the projection.
    .Select(j =>                        ◁────┘
      new {                    ◁───── new creates a new anonymous type.
        setup = j.Setup,
        punchline = j.Punchline})  ┐ Lowercase
    .ToArray(),                    │ property
  serialOptions);
```

4.3   *Making HTTP requests*

Now that we know how to parse and write JSON and how to deal with I/O streams, we can apply this knowledge to making API requests. An interesting free API is the meta-data for each xkcd comic. Visit https://xkcd.com/json.html in your browser to view the instructions. The API provides a comic's metadata only by its number. The following listing shows a sample of the JSON format.

Listing 4.28   Sample of xkcd's metadata JSON

```
{
    "month": "6",          ◁——— int expressed as string
    "num": 2630,           ◁———┐
    "link": "",                │ Comic's number or id
    "year": "2022",
    "news": "",                   ┌ Title with no
    "safe_title": "Shuttle Skeleton",  ◁——┘ special characters
    "transcript": "",
    "alt": "It's believed to be related to the Stellar Sea Cow.",
    "img": "https://imgs.xkcd.com/comics/shuttle_skeleton.png",
    "title": "Shuttle Skeleton",
    "day": "8"             ◁——— int expressed as string
}
```

No search is available for this API, so let's make one. Create a new project called Xkcd-Search, using the same template as before, with the command `dotnet new consoleargs -n XkcdSearch`. This application will try to find only a comic with a given title. Modify the command-line options to have one required parameter: `string? Title`. Then create a new file called Comic.cs and add the code from the following listing.

Listing 4.29   Comic record for deserializing xkcd JSON metadata

```
using System.Text.Json;          ◁——— Used later
using System.Text.Json.Serialization;  ◁——┐
                                          │ For JsonPropertyName
namespace XkcdSearch;                     │ and JsonIgnore

public record Comic
{
    [JsonPropertyName("num")]           ◁——— Maps to num property in JSON
    public int Number { get; init; }
    [JsonPropertyName("safe_title")]    ◁——— safe_title may be easier to match.
    public string? Title { get; init; }
    [JsonPropertyName("month")]
    public string? Month { get; init; }   ◁——┐
    [JsonPropertyName("day")]                 │
    public string? Day { get; init; }    ◁——  Serializer must match
    [JsonPropertyName("year")]                type in JSON.
    public string? Year { get; init; }   ◁——┘
    [JsonIgnore]                         ◁——┐
                                            │ Indicates "Don't serialize this"
```

```
public DateOnly Date =>
  DateOnly.Parse($"{Year}-{Month}-{Day}");      ◁──┐
}                                                    Converts to DateOnly object
```

The name of the property in the `Comic` record is different from the name in the JSON file by more than case, which is why we use the `JsonPropertyName` attribute. The `Date` property parses the date from the metadata into a `DateOnly` object, which is much easier to compare and print in localized form.

The next step is creating a method that will retrieve the JSON via HTTP request and deserialize it into a `Comic` object. Add the method from the following listing to the `Comic` record.

Listing 4.30   Retrieving comic metadata via HTTP request and deserializing

```
                                                        Only one HttpClient is
                                                        needed per application.
private static HttpClient client = new HttpClient()  ◁──
  { BaseAddress = new Uri("https://xkcd.com") };  ◁──
                                                     All calls go to this base address.
public static Comic? GetComic(int number)  ◁──
{                                              static method gets Comic by number.
  try
  {                                          Constructs the path; a 0
    var path = number == 0 ? "info.0.json"  ◁── goes to the latest comic
      : $"{number}/info.0.json";
    var stream = client.GetStreamAsync(path).Result;  ◁── Waits for the response stream
    return JsonSerializer.Deserialize<Comic>(stream);  
  }                                             Aggregates can wrap exceptions
  catch (AggregateException e)                  from async methods.
    when (e.InnerException is HttpRequestException)  ◁──
  {
    return null;                              In case of a 404
  }                                            (it happens)
  catch (HttpRequestException)  ◁──
  {
    return null;
  }
}
```

(left margin annotation: Deserializes response stream into Comic object)

> **NOTE**   The `catch` clause in listing 4.30 uses a `when` keyword, which is a form of pattern matching in C#. Without it, you'd need to check the exception object in the `catch` block. The `is` keyword is checking whether the inner exception is of the type `HttpRequestException`.

The method `GetStreamAsync` sends a GET request to the path. This method is asynchronous, which means that it can be run asynchronously from the calling code. Calling `.Result` on an asynchronous method causes our code to wait until the method is complete, making the call synchronous.

> ### Why does JsonSerializer.Deserialize return a nullable reference?
>
> The return value of `GetComic` in listing 4.30 is `Comic?`, which can be a bit confusing because deserializing an invalid JSON document would throw an exception. In what circumstances would the `Deserialize` method return `null` instead of throwing an exception? This situation isn't mentioned in the API documentation and takes a bit of digging to understand. In some earlier specifications, JSON could be only an object or an array (a bias that I developed unconsciously from experience). But in RFC 7159, JSON text is defined as `JSON-text = ws value ws`, where `ws` means whitespace and `value` is `value = false / null / true / object / array / number / string`. The text `null` is valid JSON, and deserializing it would produce `null`.

The next step is creating a method that searches for a comic with a given title. The procedure is to find the latest comic's number. We know that all the numbers from 1 to the latest are potentially valid addresses. The method performs a simple search, starting from the last value and checking each comic until it reaches the first one. If the title is found, the method returns the `Comic` object. Add the method from the following listing to Program.cs.

Listing 4.31   Method to find a xkcd comic by its title

```
static Comic? GetComicWithTitle(string title)
{
  var lastComic = Comic.GetComic(0);        ◁——— 0 indicates last comic.
  for (int number = lastComic!.Number;      ◁——— Starts a loop at the last comic
      number > 0;
      number--)    ◁—— Decrements number         Checks everything until comic 1
  {                   by 1 each iteration
    var comic = Comic.GetComic(number);     ◁——— Gets Comic object from HTTP request
    if (comic != null &&
      string.Equals(title, comic!.Title,    ◁——— Checks whether the title matches
      StringComparison.OrdinalIgnoreCase))
    {
      return comic;        ◁——— Returns if there's a match
    }
  }

  return null;      ◁——— No match was found.
}
```

The next step is calling the `GetComicWithTitle` method and printing the results. The following listing shows one approach.

Listing 4.32   Calling `GetComicWithTitle` and printing the results

```
var results = Parser.Default.ParseArguments<Options>(args)    Title from
  .WithParsed<Options>(options => {                           command-line
    var comic = GetComicWithTitle(options.Title!);   ◁——      option is required
    if (comic == null)        ◁——
                                      No match was found.
```

```
  {
    WriteLine($"xkcd comic with title " +
      $"\"{options.Title}\" not found");
  }
  else                    ⟵──── A match was found.
  {
    WriteLine($"xkcd \"{options.Title}\" is number " +
      $"{comic.Number} published on {comic.Date}");    ⟵─┐ Writes the number and
  }                                                        the date it published
});
```

Try the application with a command like `dotnet run "Rejected Question Categories"`, or search for one of your favorite xkcd comics. Getting through all the comics can take a while if the title you're searching for isn't found. We'll look at some ways of improving performance in section 4.4.

> **TIP**   If you're looking for the Little Bobby Tables comic, its title is "Exploits of a Mom."

4.4   *Unblocking programs with asynchronous programming*

The code to get the comic via HTTP request was done synchronously: the code waited for the HTTP request to complete before continuing. Because HTTP requests can take a long time and an application can make multiple requests simultaneously, we should be able to speed the search for a comic by title. Before we make the necessary changes, establishing how fast the current application is would be helpful. To do so, we'll use a diagnostic tool called a `Stopwatch`, as shown in the following listing.

Listing 4.33   Measuring `GetComicWithTitle` with a `Stopwatch`

```
using System.Diagnostics;              ⟵──── Place at the top of the file.

var results = Parser.Default.ParseArguments<Options>(args)
  .WithParsed<Options>(options => {
    var stopwatch = new Stopwatch();           ⟵──┐ Creates new Stopwatch object
    stopwatch.Start();                         ⟵──── Starts the timer
    var comic = GetComicWithTitle(options.Title!);  ⟵──┐
    stopwatch.Stop();                          ⟵──┐  Performs the search
    WriteLine("Result returned in " +              │ Stops the timer
      $"{stopwatch.ElapsedMilliseconds} ms");  ⟵──┐
                                                   Reports the elapsed time
    // rest of code continues
});
```

The "Exploits of a Mom" comic is number 327, so searching from the back (more than 2,600 comics) takes quite some time. In my tests, it generally took 35 seconds to find this comic with the synchronous approach. With an asynchronous approach, we can make several HTTP calls at the same time. First, it would help to understand what asynchronous programming is in C#.

WARNING   On some runs of the test, I found that the xkcd server was slow to respond. A search for "Exploits of a Mom" took 160 seconds instead of 35, for example, maybe because the JSON data for the comics isn't commonly requested and isn't optimized. The difference could also be due to throttling. In chapter 11, we'll look at ways to fix cases such as slow response times by making the request again or backing off in case of throttling. For now, kill the running process and try it again if it's too slow.

In C#, we use the Task Parallel Library (TPL) along with the `async` and `await` keywords to write asynchronous code. A `Task` in .NET represents a unit of work. This unit of work can be executed on a separate thread or on the same thread. Typically, `Tasks` are used for long-running work items such as reading from a network or disk. Network and disk access is slow compared with memory, so CPUs are mostly idle during these operations. This situation is similar to a promise in JavaScript or a goroutine in Golang. Let's see how `Tasks` handle long-running work by making a new, asynchronous version of the `GetComic` method, as shown in the following listing.

Listing 4.34   Modifying `GetComic` to be asynchronous

```
public static async Task<Comic?> GetComicAsync(        ← Return type is Task<Comic?> instead of Comic?.
  int number,                                          ← Append Async to name because it uses async/await.
  CancellationToken cancellationToken)                 ←
{
  if (cancellationToken.IsCancellationRequested)       ← Allows us to cancel early if the comic was found
  {                                                       Checks before making the HTTP call
    return null;
  }

  try
  {
    var path = number == 0 ? "info.0.json"             ← Adds await and removes .Result, passes cancel token
      : $"{number}/info.0.json";
    var stream = await client.GetStreamAsync(          ←
      path, cancellationToken);
    return await JsonSerializer.DeserializeAsync<Comic>(   ← This method also takes a cancel token.
      stream, cancellationToken: cancellationToken);
  }
  catch (AggregateException e)
    when (e.InnerException is HttpRequestException)
  {
    return null;
  }
  catch (HttpRequestException)
  {
    return null;
  }
  catch (TaskCanceledException)                        ← May cancel in GetStreamAsync or DeserializeAsync
  {
```

Serializer has Async versions of its methods.

```
        return null;
    }
}
```

> **Cancellation tokens**
>
> If I want to tell an asynchronous block of code to stop, I could send a signal that allows the asynchronous code to detect it and gracefully stop. Cancellation tokens are those signals. It helps me to think of a cancellation token as being one of those pagers that restaurants give you when there's a wait list. The source (`CancellationTokenSource`), or host, gives you the token (`CancellationToken`), which is the pager. When your table is ready, the host triggers the pager.

Async APIs need to add the cancellation token as a parameter explicitly; the process isn't automatic. Your async API isn't required to take a cancellation token, but taking one is a good idea, and you should get into the habit of adding it. In listing 4.34, the cancellation token is tested before the attempt to make the HTTP call. We know that when the first match is found, the application won't be interested in finding any other matches, and we can return `null`. In other cases, you may want to throw an exception. When you're working with applications, ASP.NET Core can trigger a cancellation token for the request if, for example, the client closes the connection.

NOTE The `JsonSerializer.Deserialize` method has an asynchronous version because the stream it reads may not have all the data until it's read. This situation is common for files because the whole file isn't read at once but as it's being parsed. The same thing can happen with HTTP responses when the `Stream` is created on the bytes that have started coming in before the whole response is received.

> **Is there a more succinct way of catching the exceptions?**
>
> Each `catch` block in listing 4.34 targets a different type of exception but performs the same action (returning `null`). We could simplify this process by `catching` only the generic `Exception` type and returning `null`, which would shorten the code, but I try not to get into this habit. Eating all the exceptions means we don't see when something novel is going on or something is wrong with our code. Instead, we can use the `when` clause to filter, as shown in the following code snippet:
>
> ```
> try
> {
>   // ...
> }
> catch (Exception ex) when (
>   (ex is AggregateException
>     && ex.InnerException is HttpRequestException)
>   || ex is HttpRequestException          ◁── Combine into
>   || ex is TaskCanceledException)              when clause.
> {
>   return null;
> }
> ```

> **(continued)**
> We could do the same thing as the when operator with an if statement inside the catch block, being careful to use throw instead of throw ex if the exception doesn't match. The when version is slightly shorter.

The await keyword is a powerful bit of syntactic sugar that tells the C# compiler to split the method. Under the hood, C# sees the await client.GetStreamAsync(); it puts the code up to and including that call in one block and the code after it in another block that is invoked when the await is finished. The async keyword is required to indicate to the compiler (and to developers who are looking at the code) that the method has awaits and is split into parts. (The parts are controlled by a state machine. See appendix D to learn more.) The client.GetStreamAsync method returns a Task object, and awaiting on it means that our code will resume when the HTTP response is received. The thread that executed our code is free to work on something else.

> **For .NET Framework veterans**
> If you used the IAsyncResult and callback pattern in .NET Framework, you probably remember how easy it was to get things wrong. The await keyword and subsequent C# compiler magic in splitting the method is similar to the old callback pattern. The compiler does everything for you, though. It's still possible to use IAsyncResult, but I've yet to meet a programmer who remembers it fondly. Today, you see it mostly when old .NET code is upgraded or being made to work with new .NET code.

NOTE   How the compiler splits an async method isn't important on its own, but knowing that it's happening is helpful because it affects exception stack traces. Suppose that GetComicAsync throws an exception. With synchronous methods, we'd expect the stack to contain something like XkcdSearch.Comic .GetComicAsync line 24. But with async methods, we may get something like XkcdSearch.Comic+<GetComicAsync>d__11.MoveNext line 24. This weird-looking method name is a child class method generated by the compiler to handle the async state machine (appendix D). The line number still points to the right place.

Next, we need to modify the GetComicWithTitle method in Program.cs to be asynchronous. The idea behind this change is to start by retrieving the latest comic to get its number. Then, instead of synchronously checking each number and waiting for the parsed response, we'll create Tasks for each of these calls. If a Task results in a match, we'll use the CancellationToken to cancel all the other Tasks. The following listing shows the code.

Listing 4.35   Asynchronous version of GetComicWithTitle

```
static async Task<Comic?> GetComicWithTitleAsync(     ⟵── Changes to async method
  string title)
```

```
{
    var cancellationToken = new CancellationTokenSource();    ◄——┤ Need this to control
    var lastComic = await Comic.GetComicAsync(0,     ◄——┐         cancellation.
        cancellationToken.Token);                        │  Waits for the last comic
    var tasks = new List<Task>();    ◄——┐                   before proceeding
    Comic? foundComic = null;    ◄——┐   │
    for (int number = lastComic!.Number;    │   Stores all the tasks in a List
            number > 0;                      │
            number--)                    Tasks have access to this in scope.
    {
        var localNumber = number;   ◄——┤ Very important (see note)
        var getComicTask = Comic.GetComicAsync(localNumber,    ◄———— Returns a Task
            cancellationToken.Token);
        var continuationTask = getComicTask.ContinueWith(   ◄——┐
            t => {                    ◄——┐                       Runs another task after
                try                       Previous task is passed in.   GetComic completes
                {
                    var comic = t.Result;
                    if (comic != null &&
                        string.Equals(title, comic!.Title,
                        StringComparison.OrdinalIgnoreCase))
                    {                                   ┌ A match was found; all
                        cancellationToken.Cancel();    ◄┘ other tasks are canceled.
                        foundComic = comic;
                    }
                }                                   ┌ getComicTask may
                catch (TaskCanceledException) {}   ◄┘ have been canceled.
            });
        tasks.Add(continuationTask);    ◄———— Adds the task to the list
    }

    await Task.WhenAll(tasks);    ◄———— Waits for all tasks to complete
    return foundComic;
}
```

Variable scoping with async code

Why does the `number` variable get copied to a `localNumber` variable before calling `Get-ComicAsync`? Why not use `number` directly? This case is where asynchronous code gets tricky, and making mistakes is easy. When the call to `Task.WhenAll` is made with the anonymous method, the `Task` is added to a queue. Then workers get the `Task` and run it. By the time the `Task` is executed, the value of the `number` variable will have changed. C# automatically pulls variables into the `Task`'s context if the code uses them. But the `number` variable in the `Task` context isn't a copy; it's a reference to the original. If you use `number` instead of `localNumber`, you're likely to get a bunch of calls for the number 0. The `localNumber` variable is still pulled in by reference to the anonymous method, but the main difference is that it's scoped to the inside of the `for` loop. Each iteration of the `for` loop creates a new `localNumber` variable to reference, which is a copy of the value in `number`.

The new `GetComicWithTitleAsync` method creates a `Task` for each comic number. Because there are more than 2600 comics, this approach may seem to have too many outgoing HTTP calls. Two things keep this code from exhausting threads or network sockets:

- `Tasks` are queued and workers are assigned to execute the tasks in the queue. The workers use threads from the .NET thread pool.
- The `HttpClient` has a connection pool that manages how many calls are executing simultaneously.

We need to check whether the `GetComicAsync` method has found a matching title. But because this check returns a `Task`, we need to wait for that `Task` to finish to check the results. This situation is where the continuation comes in handy. Putting the continuation task in the `List` means that when we wait for all the `Tasks` to finish with `Task.WhenAll`, we know that every comic has been checked (as when the title isn't found). To call the new `GetComicWithTitleAsync` method, make some adjustments to Program.cs, as shown in the following listing.

Listing 4.36   Updating Program.cs to use `async` method

```
var results = await Parser.Default              ⟵┐
  .ParseArguments<Options>(args)                 │
  .WithParsedAsync<Options>(    ⟵── Uses WithParsedAsync    Add
    async options => {          ⟵                           await
      var stopwatch = new Stopwatch();    Makes anonymous
      stopwatch.Start();                  method async
      var comic = await GetComicWithTitleAsync(   ⟵┘
        options.Title!);
      stopwatch.Stop();
      // Rest of code continues
    });
```

In the synchronous version of this code, the search for the famous "Exploits of a Mom" comic consistently took more than 30 seconds in my tests. The new asynchronous version consistently takes around 1.5 seconds. (YMMV.)

Synchronization is a complex subject that's difficult to get right. Many examples in the rest of this book use async programming and `Tasks`. You'll see more uses of `Tasks` particularly in chapter 8, where we use async enumerables and yields, and chapter 9, where we'll encounter `ValueTask`. I think the most helpful way to learn about asynchronous programming is to get comfortable with the basics and build slowly from there.

Summary

- Create custom `dotnet` project templates to save some copying and pasting of boilerplate code.
- `DirectoryInfo` and `FileInfo` objects help you navigate the filesystem.
- .NET's documentation indicates what exceptions are thrown by each method.
- Exceptions are expensive, so find ways to avoid relying on them.

- Using streams enables your code to work with files or network data, among other things.
- Read or write JSON manually via the DOM or through a serializer.
- Use asynchronous programming to unblock code that waits on long-running operations.

5

Using Entity Framework Core with relational databases

This chapter covers

- Building your first Entity Framework Core application
- Accessing data asynchronously
- Using Entity Framework Core with ASP.NET Core
- Exposing your API via Swagger/OpenAPI

Many applications need to record data to some permanent store so it can be retrieved later, such as when you save a document in Microsoft Word or save to a slot in your favorite game. The state of the document or game can be written to the local filesystem or to cloud-based storage. A file or network stream works well when data can be read sequentially or the data and its relationships are easy to store in memory. When data is too big or complex, such as the catalog of items in a retail store or the list of users and permissions in an identity provider, a more advanced storage system is needed.

5.1 *Storing application data*

CoreFX has a feature called ADO.NET, which is a set of built-in APIs for working with relational databases. ADO.NET allows you to connect to an SQL database and execute SQL queries. The first edition of this book covered ADO.NET and hand-built SQL queries. Writing SQL yourself has some advantages, such as making queries that database administrators can review and getting better performance from the database. But the disadvantages include the extra time and code required when, in most cases, the performance gains are unnoticeable. This edition doesn't cover ADO.NET, however; instead, it focuses on Entity Framework Core (EF Core).

SQL skills still apply

If you're familiar with SQL, those skills are applicable to EF Core. Language Integrated Query (LINQ) has different ordering but uses the same concepts as SQL, such as where, order by, group by, and projection. You don't need to understand advanced concepts such as inner/outer joins, as EF Core handles a lot of that work automatically, but these constructs are available if needed.

Also note that EF Core is a layer of abstraction. Like any layer of abstraction, it has opinions and makes concessions. EF Core is great for many applications, but if SQL performance is important, a tipping point occurs that makes using a lower-level alternative worth the effort.

EF Core is an *object-relational mapper* (ORM), which performs the conversion between objects and relational database entities. Not all data in a database can be represented as an object easily, so using an ORM may impose some constraints on your database schema. An ORM understands certain strategies for mapping database tables to objects and vice versa. Complex ORMs such as EF Core handle advanced concepts such as database functions, stored procedures, and mapping object hierarchies to tables.

EF Core treats objects as *entities*. Although the examples we use in this book map tables one to one with .NET types, EF Core isn't restricted to this behavior. If you have an existing database schema (database-first model), you could combine data from several tables in one entity. EF Core can also start with the entities you've defined in code and generate *migrations* to create a database schema (code-first model). Every database works differently. SQL databases have their own flavor of SQL. To generate migrations for your database, EF Core has a plugin model with existing plugins for SQL Server, Oracle, MySQL, SQLite, and so on.

You can find ORM libraries besides EF Core. The first edition of this book covered a micro-ORM called Dapper, which was used to build the backend services of the popular Stack Overflow website. Micro-ORMs traditionally had a performance advantage over full-featured ORMs such as EF Core because the developer had more control of the SQL queries, caches, type conversions, and the like. As of .NET 6, the gap in performance between Dapper and EF Core has narrowed; see http://mng.bz/Px6n for more information. Learning EF Core provides the most value for the time invested.

In this edition, we'll skip discussing ADO.NET and micro-ORMs to focus on the fundamentals of EF Core. If you're interested in ADO.NET, see chapter 5 of the first edition: https://livebook.manning.com/book/dotnet-core-in-action/chapter-5.

> **Tradeoffs when using ORMs**
>
> Some past ORMs, including Entity Framework (EF Core's predecessor), left a lasting bad impression on some developers. Sometimes, the SQL queries produced were suboptimal, resulting in conflicts with database administrators. In my experience, the queries generated by EF Core may do unexpected things that miss indexes or convert column values for inefficient comparisons. Performance has improved with each new version, but you're not completely absolved of responsibility for query performance. You'll see in chapter 9 how to view the SQL statements that EF Core produces.

5.2   Building your first EF Core application

Consider an example scenario. Manning Publications (the publisher of the book you're reading) wants to expose an API with data about its library. The API should hold metadata about each book and its reviews. Books and reviews can be added, updated, deleted, and retrieved via the API. The library of books needs to be persisted in a data store that won't lose data if the service goes down. The service also needs to be scalable, resilient, and consistent with responses.

Before we can create this API, we need to learn how to use EF Core to communicate with a database. Start by creating a new console application with the commands shown in the following listing.

Listing 5.1   Creating ManningBooks project with in-memory database

```
dotnet new console -n ManningBooks
cd ManningBooks
dotnet add package Microsoft.EntityFrameworkCore.InMemory
```

The package we're adding has an in-memory database provider, which allows us to work with EF Core without creating a separate database. The in-memory database provider should be used only for development. Also, EF Core's documentation recommends against using the in-memory database provider for unit/integration testing (see chapter 8).

The ManningBooks application will represent the books available through Manning Publications. We'll need to store the list of books in the database, so let's make a class that represents the Book object. Create a file called Book.cs, and add the code from the following listing.

Listing 5.2   Book class to represent a book in the Manning catalog

```
namespace ManningBooks;

public class Book
```

```
{
  public int Id { get; set; }         ←——— Primary key by convention
  public string Title { get; set; }
}
```

> ### Primary keys
>
> In a code-first model like the one we're using here, EF Core generates the tables based on the entities. Database tables commonly have keys to identify rows uniquely. If an entity has an `Id` property, EF Core will use it to define a primary key by convention. If you want a property such as `ISBN` to be the key, however, you could add a `[Key]` custom attribute to the property.

`Book` objects can be represented in a database by a table called Books. The convention is that the object is a singular noun and the table uses the plural form. By convention, EF Core recognizes the `Id` field to represent the primary key. When we add this class to our database context, EF Core creates a Books table in the in-memory database that looks like figure 5.1. (We'll ignore the Title for now.)

Figure 5.1 Books table generated by EF Core

NOTE   The key symbol in figure 5.1 shows which column is the primary key.

EF Core knows only that a class represents an entity and relates to a table if it's part of a `DbContext`. The `DbContext` (database context) is EF Core's way of knowing about entities and the relationships among them. You can have multiple `DbContexts` pointing to the same database. Be careful not to have multiple parallel `Tasks` or threads use the same `DbContext`, though; this approach isn't thread-safe.

To add the `Book` class to a `DbContext`, you need to create a new class that inherits from `DbContext`. Create a new file, CatalogContext.cs, and add the code from the following listing.

Listing 5.3   A `DbContext` that holds the `Book` class

```
using Microsoft.EntityFrameworkCore;

namespace ManningBooks;

public class CatalogContext : DbContext        ←——— Inherits from the DbContext class
{
  public DbSet<Book> Books { get; set; }       ←——— Adds Books to the entity model

  protected override void OnConfiguring(DbContextOptionsBuilder options)
    => options.UseInMemoryDatabase("ManningBooks");   ←┐
}                                                       │ Uses the in-memory
                                                        │ database provider
```

If you're using EF Core 6 or earlier, you may see a warning that the `Books` property isn't assigned a value. EF Core is versioned separately but at the same time as .NET, so you usually want to have EF Core's version match your .NET version. (This rule isn't a hard one, though.) Starting in EF Core 7, EF Core suppresses the null value warnings because it assigns values to the DbSet-based properties. If you see the warnings, you can safely get rid of them by assigning a value, as in the following listing.

Listing 5.4   DbSet property set to a default value for EF Core 6 and earlier

```
public class CatalogContext : DbContext
{
  public DbSet<Book> Books => new Set<Book>();
}
```

The DbSet represents a list of entities. EF Core entities are abstract representations not limited to tables; they can represent other objects, such as database views. Also, entities give EF Core its name. For the purposes of this book, we'll consider each entity to represent both a class and a table.

Note that the OnConfiguring method specifies the in-memory database, which doesn't mean that a DbContext is specific to a type of database. You can create database options externally if you create your own DbContextOptionsBuilder. We'll use the external-options method in chapter 8 to switch between a test database for unit testing and a real database for runtime. To test the CatalogContext, modify the Program.cs file with the code from the following listing.

Listing 5.5   Adding Books to CatalogContext and getting ordered list

```
using ManningBooks;                                        Creating the context sets up
                                                           the database connection.
using var dbContext = new CatalogContext();  ⟵──┘
dbContext.Add(new Book { Title = ".NET in Action" });  ⟵──── Creates object shorthand
dbContext.Add(new Book { Title = "API Design Patterns" });  ⟵
dbContext.Add(new Book { Title = "Grokking Simplicity" });    We don't set Id.
dbContext.Add(new Book { Title = "The Programmer's Brain" });
dbContext.SaveChanges();                                    ⟵    Books are added
                                                                 to the database
foreach (var book in dbContext.Books.OrderBy(b => b.Id))  ⟵    only when changes
{                                                                are saved.
  Console.WriteLine($"\"{book.Title}\" has id {book.Id}");  ⟵    Queries books
}                                                                and orders by Id
                                 Interpolated string
```

The call to SaveChanges saves all changes that were made to the context, which means that it creates the books in the in-memory database. Book has an Id property that is assumed to be a primary key by convention. EF Core needs an identifier for each entity that's unique within the database table. Most databases have an identity column that's an autoincrementing integer value assigned to new records. The first Book object added, therefore, has an Id of 1, the second will have an Id of 2, and so on. By querying all the books, you can see this Id populated.

The query uses a LINQ extension (OrderBy) to order the Book objects by Id. If you want to order the Ids in descending order, use OrderByDescending instead. Note also that if you put the SaveChanges after the query, you won't see any books. The Book objects we added to the Books DbSet don't exist in the database until the DbContext is saved. The DbSet is giving you access only to what's in the database—not what you've changed or added only in your code.

LINQ extensions

The books in the database context are an enumerable collection. *Enumerable*, in this context, means something that implements the IEnumerable interface and can provide an enumerator/iterator to step through all the items in the collection. A special type of enumerable is called a *queryable*. IQueryable is a LINQ-specific interface that extends the IEnumerable interface. LINQ extensions cover a wide range of capabilities that are divided into categories:

- *Restriction* (Where)—Filters or restricts an input enumerable to an output enumerable.
- *Projection* (Select)—Creates output elements from input elements.
- *Partition* (Take and Skip)—Partitions or slices the input enumerable into smaller output enumerables.
- *Ordering* (OrderBy and OrderByDescending)—Sorts the input enumerable to an output enumerable.
- *Grouping* (GroupBy)—Groups an enumerable into buckets.
- *Set* (Distinct and Union)—Operations that apply to multiple sets of data, such as intersection, union, and distinct.
- *Conversion* (ToList, ToArray, and ToDictionary)—Converts the enumerable to a different collection. Note that this conversion causes the enumerable to be *materialized*, which means that all the entities are retrieved.
- *Element* (First, FirstOrDefault, and Last)—Retrieves an element based on its position.
- *Quantifying* (Any and All)—Checks that elements match a condition and returns true or false.
- *Aggregation* (Sum, Count, and Min)—Performs calculations on numerical elements.

This list isn't comprehensive but should give you some idea of the power of LINQ extensions. You can also use combinations of functions in single extension methods. A FirstOrDefault, for example, can accept restriction criteria so that you don't have to add the Where. Microsoft has a famous set of documentation on LINQ extensions and examples called the 101 LINQ Samples, which you can check out at https://github.com/dotnet/try-samples#basics.

NOTE We saw interpolated strings in chapter 2. By prefixing the string with $, we can inject values into the string by enclosing the C# expressions in curly brackets {}.

5.2.1   *Object-creation shorthand*

Listing 5.5 shows a method for creating an object of type `Book` with the expression `new Book { Title = ".NET in Action" }`. Until now, we've seen objects created using the constructor. `Book` has no constructor, so C# automatically assumes the default constructor, which is a public constructor with no arguments. In older versions of C# that don't have this shorthand, you might write the code to create the book like the following listing.

Listing 5.6   Creating a new `Book` object without shorthand

```
Book book = new Book();
book.Title = ".NET in Action";
database.Add(book);
```

One obvious way to compress this code is to create a constructor for `Book` that has a parameter for the title. This process can get tedious when you have a large number of properties to set on the object. C# introduced shorthand to set the values of public properties directly during initialization by putting them in a comma-separated list in curly brackets. If you're setting the properties this way, you don't need the parentheses after `Book`. You can use parentheses (`new Book()`), curly brackets (`new Book {}`), or both (`new Book() {}`), but at least one has to be present—that is, you can't write `new Book`).

5.2.2   *Cleaning up the compiler warnings*

When you build or run the ManningBooks console application, you should see several warnings. These warnings appear because C# assumes that you'll explicitly call out when reference types can be null. This behavior is controlled by the `Nullable` property in the ManningBooks.csproj file. Try turning off this property by overriding it with `<Nullable>disable</Nullable>`. The warnings should go away, and the compiler will act more like it did in previous .NET versions. But we want to keep this property enabled because it enforces better discipline for nullable references, so please set it back to `"enable"`.

The first change is to the `Book` class. The `Id` property is an integer, which is a value type that can't be null (unless it's marked as nullable). The `Title` property is a string. C# strings are immutable reference types, so they can be null. The approach you take for fixing the warning requires deciding how that property will be used. One approach is to mark the `Title` as nullable, such as `public string? Title { get; set; }`. The `?` is used after a reference type to indicate that the `Title` is nullable. The problem with this approach is that it allows `Book`s with null `Title`s, which we may not want.

If we decide that the `Title` property shouldn't default to `null`, we have two options. The first option is to set a default value for `Title`. `public string Title { get; set; } = "";` sets the default value to an empty string, for example. The second option is to create a constructor for `Book` that has a `title` parameter, as shown in the following listing.

Listing 5.7   Book constructor

```
public class Book
{
  public int Id { get; set; }          ←─────┐  Non-nullable value type
  public string Title { get; set; }    ←───── No need to mark as nullable

  public Book(string title)            ←───── Adds constructor that requires title
  {
    Title = title;                     ←───── Assigns to Title property
  }
}
```

EF Core can handle the nondefault constructor (a constructor that has parameters), so this approach is a useful way to require `Book` objects to have a title. This style choice may depend on how you populate an entity's properties. Initializing an empty string for the title or requiring the title to be passed into the constructor is your preference. If you decide to use the nondefault constructor, you must change the code in Program.cs to create books from `new Book { Title = "Blah" }` to `new Book("Blah")`. If you try to create a book by using `new Book(null)`, the compiler will generate a warning because `Title` isn't nullable.

> **TIP** If you want the nullable warnings to be considered to be compiler errors, add this property to the .csproj file: `<WarningsAsErrors>Nullable </WarningsAsErrors>`.

5.2.3   Creating a relationship

One powerful aspect of entities (and relational databases) is how they relate to one another. In the requirements stated earlier, the application needs to store ratings for each book. Each rating has a comment and a star rating. Because each rating applies to only one book, we can model the relationship between a `Book` object and a `Rating` object. Listings 5.8 to 5.10 and figures 5.2 to 5.4 show how some sample entities would be modeled as database tables.

Listing 5.8   One-to-one relationship with `Book` as the parent and `Rating` as the child

```
class Book {
  public int Id {get;set;}
  public Rating? Rating {get;}
}
class Rating
{
  public int Id {get;set;}
  public int BookId {get;set;}
  public Book Book {get;set}
}
```

This relationship (figure 5.2) indicates that a `Book` can have one `Rating` optionally. `Book` is considered to be the *parent* or *principal* entity because it can exist with or without a

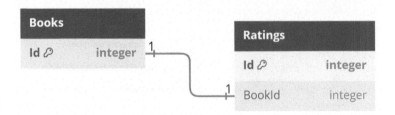

Figure 5.2   One-to-one relationship

`Rating`. `Rating` is called the *child* or *dependent* entity because it can't exist without a `Book`. The `Rating.Book` and `Book.Rating` properties are optional navigation properties, which EF Core can use to perform joins.

The foreign-key relationship between `Rating.BookId` and `Book.Id` is established by convention. EF Core sees the property name `"BookId"` and checks for a `"Book"` entity in the context; then it tries to match to that entity's primary key. If EF Core's conventions don't work in your situation, you can use foreign keys explicitly; see http://mng.bz/ 4JjD. This book uses only the conventions.

Listing 5.9   One-to-many relationship with `Book` as the parent and `Rating` as the child

```
class Book {
  public int Id {get;set;}
  public List<Rating> Ratings
    {get;}
}
class Rating
{
  public int Id {get;set;}
  public int BookId {get;set;}
  public Book Book {get;}
}
```

EF Core recognizes that the `Book.Ratings` property is a collection. By convention, it classifies the relationship of `Book` to `Rating` as one-to-many (figure 5.3).

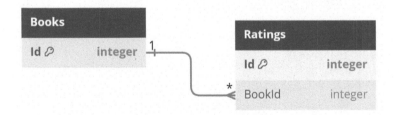

Figure 5.3   One-to-many relationship

When EF Core is generating the tables and foreign keys, no real difference exists between a one-to-one and a one-to-many relationship from the database perspective. The enforcement of the relationship is more on the application side. More complicated techniques can enforce one-to-one relationships at database level—requiring `Book` and `Rating Id` fields to match or add a unique constraint to the `Rating` foreign key, for example—but EF Core won't use them for code-first schemas.

Listing 5.10 Many-to-many relationship between `Book` and `Tag`

```
class Book {
  public int Id {get;set;}
  public List<Tag> Tags {get;}
}
class Tag
{
  public int Id {get;set;}
  public List<Book> Books {get;}
}
```

This code defines a new entity called `Tag`, which would be a metadata tag. A `Tag` could be applied to multiple `Books`, and a `Book` could have multiple `Tags` (figure 5.4). You don't need to add foreign-key `Id` fields to the entities' code.

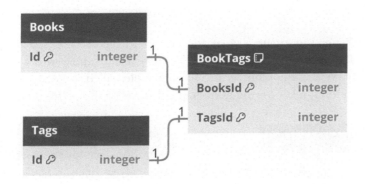

Figure 5.4 Many-to-many relationship

A single foreign key column that relates `Book` to `Tag` or vice versa won't work for many-to-many relationships, so EF Core automatically creates a third table, called a *join table*. The join table has a compound primary key that is both the `Book Id` and `Tag Id`. Then the foreign keys are applied to the join table. First, add a new file called Rating.cs, and enter the code from the following listing.

Listing 5.11 `Rating` class to hold rating data for a book

```
namespace ManningBooks;

public class Rating
{
```

```
public int Id { get; set; }              ◁──── Needs an Id like Book
public int Stars { get; set; } = 5;      ◁──
public string? Comment { get; set; }     ◁──┐        Initializes the rating to 5 stars
}                                            │
                                             └── Comment is not required (but appreciated).
```

The `Stars` property defaults to `0` if we don't provide a value, but I'd much rather make 5 stars the default setting. If the reader didn't provide a comment, we can leave the field as null. The next step is adding a list of ratings to the `Book` class, as shown in the following listing.

Listing 5.12   Adding ratings to the `Book` class

```
public class Book
{
  public int Id { get; set; }
  public string Title { get; set; }
  public List<Rating> Ratings          ◁──┐   Use a List to hold the
    { get; }                              │   Ratings for this book.
    = new();                           ◁──┐
                                          │   No need for init or set
  public Book(string title)               │
  {                                       │   Creates an empty List to initialize
    Title = title;
  }
}
```

Note that we don't need to create a `DbSet` for `Ratings` in the `DbContext`. The `Rating` entity is its own table in the database schema. To associate a `Rating` with a `Book`, EF Core automatically creates a column in the Ratings table called `"BookId"` (or something similar) and a foreign key for the Books table. Figure 5.5 shows this relationship.

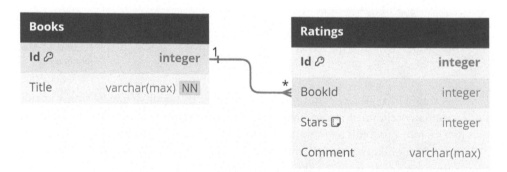

Figure 5.5   Books and Ratings tables generated by EF Core

Note that you have many ways to specify relationships between tables. You could add a `BookId` to the `Rating` class explicitly, for example, and EF Core will assume that it refers to the `Book` class. You could also add a `Book` property to the `Rating` class to get to the

`Book` object from the `Rating` object. For now, test how the relationship works by adding the code from the following listing to Program.cs.

Listing 5.13 Program.cs code to test the relationship between `Book` and `Rating`

```
var dbContext = new CatalogContext();    ⟵── No need to create new context if one exists

var efBook = new Book("EF Core in Action");             ⟵── New book object
efBook.Ratings.Add(new Rating { Comment = "Great!" });  ⟵──
efBook.Ratings.Add(new Rating { Stars = 4 });              Adds a Rating to the List
dbContext.Add(efBook);       ⟵──
dbContext.SaveChanges();         Adds the Book and Ratings to the context

    var efRatings = (from b in dbContext.Books       ⟵── Creates a LINQ query on Books
                     where b.Title == "EF Core in Action"    ⟵── Finds the book we
                     select b.Ratings)   ⟵──                      added by title
                  .FirstOrDefault();        Projects only
                                            the Ratings List
 ⟶ efRatings?.
      ForEach(r => Console.WriteLine(                    ⟵── ForEach extension performs
        $"{r.Stars} stars: {r.Comment ?? "-blank-"}"));  ⟵──    action on each Rating.
```

Gets the first match by title or null (pointing to `.FirstOrDefault()`)

Can be null, so use null-conditional (?.) (pointing to `efRatings?.`)

If comment is null, write blank (null-coalesce).

NOTE The null-conditional (`?.`) operator evaluates only the right side if the left side is not null. In listing 5.13, the whole line is skipped if `efRatings` is null.

If you want double quotes (`"`) in a string, you usually need to escape them: `\"`. The interpolated string in listing 5.13 contains unescaped double quotes, however, because it's part of the expression within the curly brackets. Any valid expression can be included in the interpolated part of the string (the curly brackets in a string that starts with `$"`). It's even possible to nest an interpolated string inside an interpolated string. The following listing, for example, is legal C#.

Listing 5.14 An example of a legal C# statement that uses nested interpolated strings

```
Console.WriteLine($"{ efBook.Title + $", Id={efBook.Id}"}");
```

The query in listing 5.13 specifically targets the ratings of the book. But the query gets only the `Book` objects without the `Ratings`. The `Ratings` are in a separate entity and need to be included in the query explicitly. For this purpose, use the `Include` method as shown in the following listing, which shows how to print all `Books` and their `Ratings`.

Listing 5.15 Printing all `Books` with their `Ratings` to the console

```
using Microsoft.EntityFrameworkCore;    ⟵── Needed for Include extension method

// ...

foreach (var book in dbContext.Books
              .Include(b => b.Ratings))    ⟵── Tells EF Core what relationship to include
```

```
{
  Console.WriteLine($"Book \"{book.Title}\" has id {book.Id}");
  book.Ratings.ForEach(r =>
    Console.WriteLine(
      $"\t{r.Stars} stars: {r.Comment ?? "-blank-"}"));
}
```

Ratings should never be null, no need for ?.

"\t" adds a tab before ratings

Lazy vs. eager loading

If multiple relationships exist in the Book class, each one needs a separate Include if you want the relationships to exist in the returned object. Including the ratings in the Book object is a technique called *eager loading*, which loads Books and Ratings at the same time. By contrast, *lazy loading* retrieves the Book objects but retrieves the Rating objects only when they're used. Eager loading is commonly used for a query that returns more data in one execution. Lazy loading returns less data and retrieves more information only when needed, but it could result in multiple database queries. In some cases, lazy loading is more efficient, depending highly on your application and data.

You have other ways to traverse relationships, such as explicit loading and select loading. This book uses only eager loading, however, because it's the simplest and most common technique. If you're interested in delving deeper into relationship traversal, take a look at http://mng.bz/JlPV.

5.3   *Accessing data asynchronously*

Database access normally involves a network call and some disk access, which makes it slower than searching in memory and a prime candidate for asynchronous programming. The techniques we learned in chapter 4 for using Task, async, and await apply to EF Core as well. The benefits will be more apparent with an SQL database that can record to a local file. Unfortunately, the in-memory database that comes with EF Core doesn't support file storage and also isn't an SQL database. (Entities are stored in memory as is.) An alternative database called SQlite supports SQL and file storage; it's even recommended instead of the EF Core in-memory database in the EF Core documentation. We can use SQlite to see how asynchronous calls would work with a full-featured database such as SQL Server or Postgres. Start by removing the in-memory database and adding SQlite, entering the commands from the following listing in the terminal.

Listing 5.16   Removing InMemory package and installing Sqlite

```
dotnet remove package Microsoft.EntityFrameworkCore.InMemory
dotnet add package Microsoft.EntityFrameworkCore.Sqlite
```

Now modify CatalogContext.cs to use the new database, as shown in the following listing. We'll start with the in-memory mode of SQlite to get the code working and later switch to the file-based mode.

Listing 5.17 Configuring `CatalogContext` to use the Sqlite database

```
using Microsoft.EntityFrameworkCore;

namespace ManningBooks;

public class CatalogContext : DbContext
{
  public const string ConnectionString =
    "DataSource=manningbooks;mode=memory;cache=shared";

  public DbSet<Book> Books { get; set; }

  protected override void OnConfiguring(DbContextOptionsBuilder options)
    => options
      .UseSqlite(ConnectionString);
}
```

Making public so this string can be used in Program.cs ⟵

Creates an in-memory database ⟵

Uses SQLite database ⟵

SQlite's in-memory and file-based modes are controlled by the connection string. Both options still work like SQL databases, unlike the EF Core in-memory database. SQlite's in-memory database has a strange property: when all connections to it are closed, the database is deleted. EF Core doesn't keep an open connection to the database to keep the in-memory database alive, so we have to keep a connection open manually. We'll create this connection in Program.cs by modifying the code as shown in the following listing.

Listing 5.18 Using Sqlite in Program.cs

```
using ManningBooks;
using Microsoft.Data.Sqlite;

using var keepAliveConnection = new SqliteConnection(
  CatalogContext.ConnectionString);
keepAliveConnection.Open();

using var dbContext = new CatalogContext();
dbContext.Database.EnsureCreated();

dbContext.Add(new Book(".NET in Action"));
dbContext.Add(new Book("API Design Patterns"));
dbContext.Add(new Book("Grokking Simplicity"));
dbContext.Add(new Book("The Programmer's Brain"));

dbContext.SaveChanges();

foreach (var book in
  dbContext.Books.OrderByDescending(b => b.Id))
{
  Console.WriteLine($"Book \"{book.Title}\" has id {book.Id}");
}
```

SQlite provider used by EF Core ⟵

Direct connection to SQlite in-memory database ⟵

Uses same connection string as DbContext ⟵

Opens connection and leaves it open ⟵

using disposes dbContext at end. ⟵

Creates database in SQlite

Saves changes to the database ⟵

Gets books in descending order by ID ⟵

NOTE EnsureCreated creates the entity model in the database. If any tables already exist in the database—even ones that aren't part of your context's schema—this method does nothing and returns false. Use a different connection string if you're creating multiple DbContexts.

The DbContext object is a lightweight object that isn't meant to operate as a singleton; it's meant to be created and disposed per request. Let's try it by organizing the code to split the initial database data creation (aka seeding) from a query to show a Book and its Ratings. Start by creating a new static method in the CatalogContext class, as shown in the following listing.

Listing 5.19 Static method to seed books in the database in `CatalogContext`

```
public static void SeedBooks()
{
    using var dbContext = new CatalogContext();          ◁─── Creates DbContext object and
    if (!dbContext.Database.EnsureCreated())             ◁───  disposes at end of method
    {
        return;        ◁─── Skips if database exists          Returns true if new database is created

    }

    dbContext.Add(new Book("Grokking Simplicity"));      ◁─── Initialize however you want.
    dbContext.Add(new Book("API Design Patterns"));
    var efBook = new Book("EF Core in Action");
    efBook.Ratings.Add(new Rating { Comment = "Great!" });
    efBook.Ratings.Add(new Rating { Stars = 4 });
    dbContext.Add(efBook);
    dbContext.SaveChanges();          ◁─── Commits all changes at the end
}
```

This method name uses the term Seed to indicate that if a database is empty, the method will add some initial data or seed values. Next, add another static method to CatalogContext to find a specific book by its title and write its data to the console as shown in the following listing.

Listing 5.20 Finding a book by title and writing to console

```
                                                Returns Task instead of void
public static async Task
    WriteBookToConsoleAsync(string title)       ◁─── Appends Async to method
{                                                    name per convention
    using var dbContext = new CatalogContext();      ◁─── Assumes that database is created
    var book = await dbContext.Books                 ◁───
        .Include(b => b.Ratings)                     ◁───
        .FirstOrDefaultAsync(b => b.Title == title); ◁───  Awaits results of
    if (book == null)                                      FirstOrDefaultAsync
    {
        Console.WriteLine(@$"""{title}"" not found.");    Includes the ratings
    }                                                     async extension method
    else
```

```
  {
    Console.WriteLine(@$"Book ""{book.Title}"" has id {book.Id}");
    book.Ratings.ForEach(r =>
      Console.WriteLine(
      $"\t{r.Stars} stars: {r.Comment ?? "-blank-"}"));
  }
}
```

This code allows us to simplify Program.cs to look like the following listing.

Listing 5.21 **Modifying Program.cs to use the static methods from** `CatalogContext`

```
using ManningBooks;
using Microsoft.Data.Sqlite;

using var keepAliveConnection = new SqliteConnection(
  CatalogContext.ConnectionString);
keepAliveConnection.Open();          ⟵── Needs the keep-alive connection for SQlite

CatalogContext.SeedBooks();          ⟵── Creates the database and adds the books

var userRequests = new[] {           ⟵── C# infers that this is a string array.
 ".NET in Action",
 "Grokking Simplicity",
 "API Design Patterns",
 "EF Core in Action",
};
foreach (var userRequest in userRequests)
{                                                    Each call creates and disposes
  await CatalogContext.WriteBookToConsoleAsync(  ⟵┘  a CatalogContext object.
    userRequest);
}
```

Because the method to write the book to the console is asynchronous, we can start all the tasks at the same time and wait until all of them finish. Instead of using `Task.WhenAll`, which has to be `awaited` (as in chapter 4), the following listing uses an equivalent synchronous method to wait for the tasks to complete.

Listing 5.22 **Running user requests in parallel**

```
var tasks = new List<Task>();          ⟵── A collection to hold the Task objects
foreach (var userRequest in userRequests)
{                                          Adds a Task but doesn't await
  tasks.Add(                          ⟵┘
    CatalogContext.WriteBookToConsoleAsync(userRequest)  ⟵┐
  );                                                       Calls async method
}                                                          that returns a Task

Task.WaitAll(tasks.ToArray());          ⟵── Waits until all Tasks are complete
```

Using Task.Run

Sometimes, you see documentation or examples that use the `Task.Run` method to start a `Task`. `await` and `async` don't move `Task`s to background threads, but `Task.Run` does. In both this chapter and chapter 4, we spend most of our time waiting for web or database query responses. We have no need for multiple threads because as soon as the task is waiting on some I/O operation, another task is free to run. If the task were performing some CPU-intensive work, it would be better to use `Task.Run` to move the task to a separate thread. CPU-intensive work doesn't allow the thread to go idle and look for other tasks to run. But if we move the task to a background thread, the CPU-intensive work can happen on another processor core, allowing the main thread to keep processing other tasks. For in-depth information, check out http://mng.bz/QZWR.

SQlite is a better analog for programming with full-featured databases that you'd use in production (except for the keep-alive connection needed for in-memory). SQlite is also recommended for testing ASP.NET Core applications. The in-memory mode requires the keep-alive connection, which is useful to know if you want to share data between calls. Many applications use file mode because they can embed a database in the application. File mode preserves the data between process executions. By changing the connection string and not using the keep-alive connection, you can try file mode with the ManningBooks code.

Exercise 1: Switch to file-based mode in SQlite

Modify the SQlite connection string to `DataSource=manningbooks.db;cache=shared`. Verify that the database is created on the first start and that `SeedBooks` skips seeding on subsequent starts. Try removing the keep-alive connection when running in file-based mode.

5.4   Using EF Core with ASP.NET Core

So far in this chapter, I've covered EF Core basics such as schemas, relationships, `DbContext`s, and queries. In chapter 3, we created a simple web service that responded to GET requests. We have all the building blocks we need to make a web service with create, request, update, and delete (CRUD) operations.

5.4.1   Request methods

We'll start by building the initial application with a method that returns all the books in response to an HTTP request with a GET verb. Open a terminal, change to a directory where you can create a new project, and then enter the commands from the following listing.

Listing 5.23   Creating ManningBooksApi

```
dotnet new web --name ManningBooksApi    ⟵── Empty web project template
cd ManningBooksApi
dotnet add package Microsoft.EntityFrameworkCore.Sqlite    ⟵── Adds EF Core packages
```

We'll use the same `Book` and `Rating` entities from section 5.2.2. Copy Book.cs and Rating.cs from that section or from the preceding listings. Make sure to change the namespace in these files from ManningBooks to ManningBooksApi. You can also copy the `CatalogContext` code, noting the changes shown in the following listing.

Listing 5.24 `CatalogContext` **adapted to work in the ManningBooksApi project**

```
using Microsoft.EntityFrameworkCore;

namespace ManningBooksApi;                    ⟵──── Change namespace.

public class CatalogContext : DbContext
{
  public const string ConnectionString =
    "DataSource=manningbooks;mode=memory;cache=shared";

  public DbSet<Book> Books { get; set; }

  protected override void OnConfiguring(DbContextOptionsBuilder options)
    => options
      .UseSqlite(ConnectionString);

  public static void SeedBooks()              ⟵──── Keep the seed method.
  {
    using var dbContext = new CatalogContext();
    dbContext.Database.EnsureCreated();
    dbContext.Add(new Book("Grokking Simplicity"));
    dbContext.Add(new Book("API Design Patterns"));
    var efBook = new Book("EF Core in Action");
    efBook.Ratings.Add(new Rating { Comment = "Great!" });
    efBook.Ratings.Add(new Rating { Stars = 4 });
    dbContext.Add(efBook);
    dbContext.SaveChanges();
  }
}
```

The next thing we need to create is the controller. If you remember from chapter 3, the controller is part of the Model-View-Controller (MVC) pattern, shown in figure 5.6. The `CatalogContext` is a model for the purposes of this example. Because this service is a web service, it has no view component unless the JSON response could be considered a view.

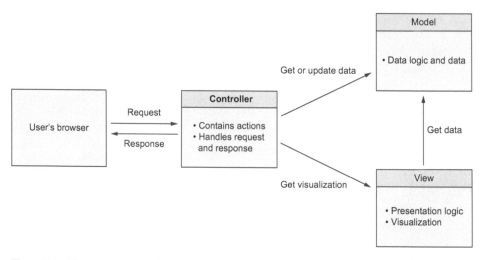

Figure 5.6   Diagram of the MVC pattern in which the user request goes to the controller, which can update the model and get the latest view to send the response

Create a Controllers folder inside the project folder. Then create a new file named CatalogController.cs with the code from the following listing.

Listing 5.25   Adding a new controller that allows requesting a list of books

```
using Microsoft.AspNetCore.Mvc;
using Microsoft.EntityFrameworkCore;

namespace ManningBooksApi.Controllers;          ◁——— Note the namespace.

[ApiController]                     ◁——— Web API controller              URI route is the controller
[Route("[controller]")]                                           ◁——┘  name minus "Controller".
public class CatalogController : ControllerBase
{                                                                  DbContext should be
    private readonly CatalogContext _dbContext;    ◁——┘           created with the request.

    public CatalogController(
        CatalogContext dbContext)           ◁——— Dependency injection will provide this object.
    {
        _dbContext = dbContext;
    }
                                        │ GET requests go to this method.
    [HttpGet]                     ◁——┘
    public IAsyncEnumerable<Book> GetBooks(    ◁——— See description of IAsyncEnumerable.
        string? titleFilter = null)       ◁——┐
    {                                         │ Optional filter by title
        IQueryable<Book> query = _dbContext.Books      ◁——┐
            .Include(b => b.Ratings)                        Can't use "var" because
            .AsNoTracking();           ◁——┐                 query is composed in parts.
        if (titleFilter != null)          │
        {                                 │ Don't track changes.
            query = query.Where(b =>
```

```
        b.Title.ToLower().Contains(titleFilter.ToLower()));
    }

    return query.AsAsyncEnumerable();      ◁─── ASP.NET Core defaults to respond with JSON.
  }
}
```

> ### AsNoTracking
>
> The GetBooks API returns a collection of `Book` objects. No modifications are made to any of these entities. EF Core defaults to recording everything that happens to the entities that it returns from queries or are added to the context. This feature, called *change tracking*, is a major part of what makes EF Core so powerful. If the code modifies the `Title` property of a `Book` object, for example, EF Core records the change, and when `SaveChanges` is called, it converts that change to an UPDATE SQL statement. When you're querying data and don't want to make changes, disable change tracking to prevent accidental changes and also save memory and CPU. On a query level, you can turn off change tracking with the `AsNoTracking` extension method.

> ### What is dependency injection?
>
> *Dependency injection* (aka inversion of control) is used throughout ASP.NET Core applications. A *dependency* is an object on which another object depends. In listing 5.25, the dependency is the `CatalogContext` object. `CatalogController` depends on the `CatalogContext` object to function. Instead of creating the `CatalogContext` on its own, `CatalogController` delegates that control to whatever is calling it. In this case, the ASP.NET Core application has matched the request's route to the `CatalogController` and is responsible for providing the `CatalogContext`. This behavior allows the application to control the lifetime of that object and the specific object that implements it. In unit testing, for example, we may want to provide a fake context—something we couldn't do if `CatalogController` created the object itself.

The `CatalogController` uses a filter like the one used in chapter 4. This filter is specified via a query string. It's optional, so if the value is `null`, we won't add the `Where` clause to the query.

The `GetBooks` method uses something we haven't seen before: `IAsyncEnumerable`. Contrast it with `IEnumerable`, which returns a synchronous enumerator. Synchronous enumerators avoid blocking threads by retrieving all records first and then enumerating. If you want to send records back in the response as they're received from the database without blocking a thread, `IEnumerable` won't work. `IAsyncEnumerable` allows an action to start sending response data as soon as the database query starts getting records from the database. Without `IAsyncEnumerable`, the action must wait to send the response until all the database records are retrieved and the full response content is ready. Although this action doesn't have much advantage for our example service, it's useful for services that deal with a lot of data (or slow queries).

ASP.NET Core returns JSON by default. Because the return value of the `GetBooks` method is an enumerable, ASP.NET Core knows to return a JSON array. No content length is specified in the HTTP response headers. The caller knows that the response is finished when the service closes the connection. Not having to calculate content length before sending a response is another key factor that allows the service to return results as it gets them.

Now that we have a `DbContext` and a controller, we need to let ASP.NET Core know about them. The `DbContext` and controller are registered with the `WebApplication-Builder` (builder variable in the code listing). Modify Program.cs as shown in the following listing.

Listing 5.26   Registering `DbContext` and controller

```
using ManningBooksApi;
using Microsoft.Data.Sqlite;   ⟵── Needed for keep-alive connection

var builder = WebApplication.CreateBuilder(args);
builder.Services.AddDbContext<CatalogContext>();   ⟵
builder.Services.AddControllers();   ⟵

var app = builder.Build();
app.UseHttpsRedirection();
app.MapControllers();   ⟵──── Maps controller URI routes

using var keepAliveConnection = new SqliteConnection(   ⟵
  CatalogContext.ConnectionString);
keepAliveConnection.Open();

CatalogContext.SeedBooks();   ⟵──── Seeds in-memory database

app.Run();   ⟵── App runs until the process is killed.
```

Registers CatalogContext with dependency injection

Looks for ApiControllers

Needs keep-alive connection so database isn't deleted

The `AddControllers` and `MapControllers` methods look for the classes marked with the `ApiController` attribute and map their routes. The `AddDbContext` method registers the `CatalogContext` with the dependency injection module. Dependency injection manages the lifetime of the `DbContext` object so that one is created for a request and is disposed when the response is finished—that is, the `DbContext` is scoped to the request (see chapter 8). Any code running as part of that request gets access to the same `DbContext` object. Because ASP.NET Core is creating the `CatalogController` object to handle the request to that route, it recognizes the `CatalogContext` parameter in the constructor and passes in the object from dependency injection.

The application is ready to run. Execute `dotnet watch run` from the terminal, and open a browser to https://localhost:<port>/catalog to see the full list of books. The catalog path matches the `CatalogController` name with the `Controller` suffix removed by convention.

Try adding the query string ?titleFilter=in to see the catalog filtered by title. If you add a filter that has no matches, the API returns a 404 error, which is expected because the resource wasn't found.

Exercise 2: Add sorting and paging to the CatalogController.GetBooks method

In chapter 3, we used LINQ to sort and page query results. EF Core supports the same LINQ functions. Add optional query parameters for skip, take, and order, and use them to modify the IQueryable.

Because Books have unique identifiers, we can add a method that returns a specific Book object by id. Add the method from the following listing to the CatalogController.

Listing 5.27   HTTP GET method to request a single Book object by id

```
[HttpGet("{id}")]                      ◄——— id is in the URI path.
public Task<Book?> GetBook(int id)     ◄—
{                                         | Returns a Task but is not "async"
    return _dbContext.Books.FirstOrDefaultAsync(   ◄—
        b => b.Id == id);                   | Returns Task directly without await
}
```

Route templates

The string parameter of the HttpGet attribute is called a *route template*. When a request is received, ASP.NET Core uses the URL to determine where to route the request. We've already established that the first segment identifies the controller by name (catalog). When the request is sent to the controller, ASP.NET Core needs to determine which action method to call. It uses the HTTP verb (GET, in this case) and the rest of the URL after the controller segment. The route template "{id}" is indicating a single segment.

Route templates are intuitive for simple cases like those in this book. But if you want to understand the specifics, check out the documentation at http://mng.bz/eonG.

Try opening a browser tab to https://localhost:<port>/catalog/1 to test this method. Because the id parameter is marked as part of the route in the HttpGet attribute, the ASP.NET Core application can distinguish this GET call from the GetBooks method. One technique that we haven't seen before returns the Task directly without using async or await. As noted earlier in this chapter, the await keyword has the effect of splitting the method under the hood (see appendix D); it can also create an extra, unnecessary Task object. Because no async keyword is attached to the method, I set the method name as GetBook instead of GetBookAsync and did the same for GetBooks. The Async method name suffix convention seems to be only for methods marked with the async keyword; the guidance is less clear on methods that return Tasks or IAsyncEnumerables.

5.5   *Exposing your API via Swagger/OpenAPI*

HTTP GET requests are easy to issue with a browser as long as we don't need to put anything in the request body. To add the create, update, and delete methods to our service, we'll need to send requests with different verbs (PUT, POST, and DELETE). Many tools exist for this purpose—including curl, Postman, and Fiddler—and you're encouraged to try those options. But you can do the same thing straight from the browser by using Swagger/OpenAPI. OpenAPI is the name of the specification; Swagger came before the OpenAPI specification and has become part of the OpenAPI initiative. The name *Swagger* is familiar to many developers, is still part of the URL, and is easier to say than OpenAPI, so it's understandable that many developers stick with the old name. Swagger also has a user interface tool called SwaggerUI that's handy for testing the API.

To generate the Swagger documents and expose the SwaggerUI, use a package called Swashbuckle. Add the package to your project, using the terminal command `dotnet add package Swashbuckle.AspNetCore`. Then modify Program.cs as shown in the following listing.

Listing 5.28   Adding Swagger to Program.cs

```
var builder = WebApplication.CreateBuilder(args);

builder.Services.AddDbContext<CatalogContext>();
builder.Services.AddControllers();
builder.Services.AddSwaggerGen();          ◄─┐

var app = builder.Build();                     Add
                                               these
app.UseHttpsRedirection();                     lines.
app.MapControllers();

app.UseSwagger();
app.UseSwaggerUI();

// ...

app.Run();
```

Sometimes, when you save these changes, `dotnet watch` won't pick up the changes correctly, and the Swagger URLs won't work. In this case, stop the process (usually by pressing Ctrl+C) and then restart it. Open a browser tab to https://localhost:<port>/swagger/index.html to view the Swagger UI, which should look similar to figure 5.7.

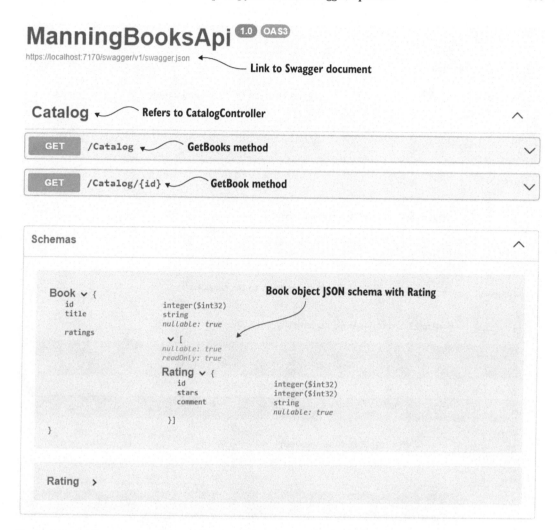

Figure 5.7 Swagger UI index page with the GET APIs on the Catalog controller and the schemas for Book and Rating

In this UI, you can click one of the methods in the API and then click Try It Out to send a request to your service with custom parameters and see the response. Try expanding the GET /Catalog pane and executing a request as shown in figure 5.8. This exercise will be useful for trying the non-GET APIs.

The name *CatalogController* may be a bit misleading. It doesn't mean that the controller should handle CRUD operations on all the entities in CatalogContext. The CatalogController is meant only to provide access to the Books entities.

Catalog   ⌃

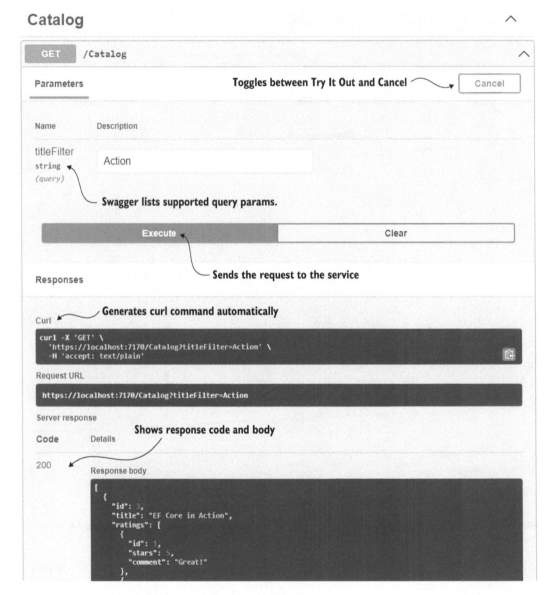

Figure 5.8 Trying the GET /Catalog API via the SwaggerUI

Ratings has a relationship to Books but should have its own controller (and DbSet in CatalogContext). Implementation of a RatingsController is the topic of an exercise at the end of this section. In this section, we'll focus on creating, updating, and deleting Book entities.

A book consists of three components: an ID, a title, and a list of ratings. When a book is created or updated, we don't need to change the ratings. We could make a create statement that has the ID and title in the URI via path or query string. But this approach doesn't leave much room for adding fields such as author, ISBN number, and description. Instead, we can pass all of this information in the body of the request. First, add a description field to Book, as shown in the following listing.

Listing 5.29 Adding description field to `Book` class

```
public class Book
{
  public int Id { get; set; }
  public string Title { get; set; }
  public string? Description { get; set; }        ◁——— Adds the Description as nullable

  public List<Rating> Ratings { get; } = new();
                                                      ┌ Optional to specify
  public Book(string title, string? description = null)  ◁─┤ description in
  {                                                      └ constructor
    Title = title;
    Description = description;
  }
}
```

A book's description can be fairly lengthy—enough to exceed the allowed URL length for most web servers. One option is to have the create method accept a Book object serialized to JSON in the request body. We have only two problems: we want to make sure that the Id isn't set because it's autoassigned by the database, and there are no ratings. Similarly, in the update method we want to allow updates of only the title, the description, or both. To enforce this control, another option is to create a separate class (or record) for creating or updating books, as shown in the following listing.

Listing 5.30 Creating and updating command records

```
public class CatalogController : ControllerBase
{
  // ...
                                                    ┌ Used for CreateBook
  public record BookCreateCommand(        ◁─────────┘
    string Title, string? Description) {}   ◁────── Title is required for creation.
  public record BookUpdateCommand(        ◁────── Used for UpdateBook
    string? Title, string? Description) {}   ◁
}                                                  └ Updates title or description
```

We saw records in chapter 2. Records are immutable types that have lots of built-in features. An immutable type works well in this scenario because we want to preserve what the request provided. In listing 5.30, we used C# shorthand to create the record. The shorthand creates properties for each of the fields specified in the constructor-like syntax, which saves quite a few lines of code.

Now let's add a method to create new books. The HTTP verb typically used for creating new entities is POST. Add the method from the following listing to the Catalog-Controller.

Listing 5.31   POST method to create a new Book

```
[HttpPost]                                          Indicates POST verb          async method that returns
public async Task<Book> CreateBookAsync(                                         new Book object
  BookCreateCommand command,
  CancellationToken cancellationToken)              Default assumes that command is in request body.
{                                                   Gets RequestAborted token
  var book = new Book(
    command.Title,                                  Creates Book with values from command
    command.Description
  );                                                Holds the entity

  var entity = _dbContext.Books.Add(book);          Passes cancellation
  await _dbContext.SaveChangesAsync(cancellationToken);   token
  return entity.Entity;                             Entity holds Book object with Id.
}
```

Cancellation tokens in controller action parameters

The CreateBookAsync method has a parameter for a CancellationToken. ASP.NET Core sees this parameter and automatically adds the HttpContext.RequestAborted token. This token is triggered if the request is aborted for some reason, such as the client's closing the connection. The effect of the cancellation token's being triggered is in doubt because we don't know whether the book was created. You could argue that the create method should make an effort to write to the database even if the connection is closed. But the outcome would still be in doubt, and it would be the client's responsibility to reconnect and check whether the book was created.

When you save the code file, dotnet watch should pick up the change and deploy it. You should see POST /Catalog in the SwaggerUI. The Try It Out function should have an example request body that you can modify and execute. The response should have an id that is greater than 0. Then you can execute the GET /Catalog command to see whether the book you added is part of the catalog.

WARNING   Every time you change the source code and save, dotnet watch reloads. Sometimes, a change is considered to be a rude edit, and the process is restarted, wiping out your in-memory database.

For the UpdateBook method, we want to allow a partial update. If the requester wants only to add a description, they shouldn't have to include the title in the update command. A full update/replacement of an object is usually done with the PUT HTTP verb. The verb for a partial update is PATCH. Take a look at the UpdateBook method in the following listing to see how the process works.

Listing 5.32 `PATCH` method to make a partial update of an existing `Book`

```
[HttpPatch("{id}")]
[ProducesResponseType(StatusCodes.Status404NotFound)]
[ProducesResponseType(StatusCodes.Status204NoContent)]
public async Task<IActionResult> UpdateBookAsync(
  int id, BookUpdateCommand command,
  CancellationToken cancellationToken)
{
  var book = await _dbContext.FindAsync<Book>(
    new object?[] { id },
    cancellationToken);
  if (book == null)
  {
    return NotFound();
  }

  if (command.Title != null)
  {
    book.Title = command.Title;
  }

  if (command.Description != null)
  {
    book.Description = command.Description;
  }

  await _dbContext.SaveChangesAsync(cancellationToken);
  return NoContent();
}
```

Annotations:
- PATCH verb, id in URI path
- Tells Swagger that this can return 404 status code
- Tells Swagger that this can return 204 status code
- Returns IActionResult to control status code
- Assumes id in path and command in body
- Tries to find the Book in the database
- Matches parameter type
- Returns 404 if Book doesn't exist
- Modifies Title only if in the command
- Modifies Description only if in the command
- Indicates success but doesn't return object

NOTE In the call to `FindAsync`, we don't pass the `id` variable and then the `cancellationToken` because the `FindAsync` method has two overloads: one that takes a `params` array and another that takes an object array and a `Cancellation-Token`. A `params` array is a C# technique that allows passing an arbitrary number of parameters to a method without explicitly declaring an array. You can't declare any other parameters after a `params` array because it's supposed to absorb the remaining parameters. `params` arrays usually make code look nicer except in cases like this one.

In the `UpdateBook` method, we make changes to the `Book` object only if those values aren't `null` in the command. The `CreateBook` method returned the `Book` object so that the caller can see the created object with its defaults and the `Id` property filled. We made the assumption that the `UpdateBook` method doesn't need to return the updated `Book` object because the only values changed were in the command, which the caller knows about. If you prefer to return the updated `Book` object, you can replace the line `return NoContent();` with `return Ok(book);` and the attribute indicating the `204` status code with `200`.

The last change to make is the DeleteBook method. This method can work in different ways, depending on your preference. If a Book isn't found with the id specified, for example, you could return a 404. But some clients may interpret this response as an error, and they want a 204 to make sure that the Book no longer exists. The client code could be retrying the command because it didn't get the response previously. In the following listing, we'll use 404 if the Book doesn't exist with the idea that both status codes are acceptable to the client.

Listing 5.33 DELETE method to delete a Book

```
[HttpDelete("{id}")]                                          ←── id in URL path, no body
[ProducesResponseType(StatusCodes.Status404NotFound)]
[ProducesResponseType(StatusCodes.Status204NoContent)]
public async Task<IActionResult> DeleteBookAsync(int id,      ←┐ Returns
    CancellationToken cancellationToken)                        │ IActionResult to
{                                                                │ control status code
    var book = await _dbContext.FindAsync<Book>(id,
        cancellationToken);
    if (book == null)
    {
        return NotFound();          ←── 404 if not found
    }

    _dbContext.Remove(book);                                    ┐ Assumes that delete
    await _dbContext.SaveChangesAsync(cancellationToken);    ←─┘ was successful
    return NoContent();
}
```

Try this method with a few books. The database seeding code you already wrote in the application has one book with ratings. When you try to delete a book that has ratings, you should get an exception. Rating has a relationship to Book, and EF Core assumes by default that if the Book is deleted, any related Ratings should also be deleted, which is called a *cascade delete*. The only problem is that this cascade delete isn't translated into the SQL delete statement. When you try to delete the Book, the database complains that foreign keys from the Ratings table point to that book.

To get EF Core to perform the cascade delete, we need to include the ratings when we get the Book entity. Replace the line var book = await dbContext.FindAsync<Book>(id); with the code from the following listing.

Listing 5.34 Including child entity to perform a cascade delete

```
var book = await _dbContext.Books          ←── Don't forget to add .Books.
    .Include(b => b.Ratings)              ←┐
    .FirstOrDefaultAsync(b => b.Id == id,   │ Add anything to cascade delete.
        cancellationToken);
```

Congratulations—you have a web API that can create, request, update, and delete any book in the catalog. We've only scratched the surface of what's available in EF Core, however. To go deeper, check out Jon P Smith's *Entity Framework Core in Action*, 2nd ed., a comprehensive reference on EF Core, at http://mng.bz/wP4P.

> **Exercise 3: Add a RatingsController that provides CRUD operations on ratings**
>
> Start by adding a `Ratings DbSet` to the `CatalogContext`. Creating a new rating requires the book's ID, which should be in the request body instead of the URL so that it's not confused with the rating ID. Update and delete can use the rating ID. Retrieving ratings makes sense when you do it by book, not by individual rating. Because a book could have a lot of ratings, include optional paging and sorting commands in the retrieval operation.

Summary

- EF Core maps entities to a data source.
- The EF Core in-memory database is useful for prototyping but doesn't use SQL.
- SQLite is a lightweight SQL database that works in memory or with a file.
- Database requests can be slow, and we can avoid blocking threads in our application by using asynchronous techniques.
- We can use controllers in ASP.NET Core to perform CRUD operations on an entity.
- Swagger describes our web API in a standardized document.
- SwaggerUI lets us test controllers from the browser.

Part 3

Testing

Testing your application gives you confidence that your code does what it's supposed to. This part focuses on testing .NET applications.

In chapter 6, you'll learn what unit tests are, what the SOLID principles are and why they matter, and how to build and run unit tests.

Chapter 7 delves into the trickier aspects of testing where external dependencies need to be replaced. You'll see that .NET has some built-in substitutions; for other substitutions, you'll need fakes.

Chapter 8 goes one level higher to integration testing. You'll learn how to write tests for code that interacts with external databases or web services. You'll also get experience with ASP.NET's built-in integration-testing components, which allow you to test a web service from top to bottom. By the end of this part, you'll have the tools to build a full test suite and prove that your code works as intended.

Unit-testing fundamentals

This chapter covers

- Using SOLID design principles
- Understanding the difference between facts and theories
- Executing unit tests with the .NET command-line interface

Like many modern programming frameworks, .NET has built-in support for testing. In this chapter, we'll cover the basics of writing and running unit tests. The `dotnet` command-line interface (CLI) tool has a command to initiate tests but doesn't perform the tests on its own. Instead of forcing one test framework for all of .NET, the `dotnet` CLI tool looks for a test harness. The test harness usually comes from a package. Many test harnesses and frameworks are available, but in this chapter and beyond, we'll use the xUnit framework for testing. Your company may use a different framework, but many of the strategies and concepts should translate.

6.1 Writing code that's easier to test

Testing is an essential part of developing software. In the past, developers and functional testers (engineers testing functionality and correctness) had separate roles. All the members of these groups were programmers, but they were tasked with separate objectives. Developers wrote application code, did some light testing, and then "threw it over the wall" to the testers. Testers went through all the scenarios they could, verified that the application met the requirements, wrote bug reports for all the problems they found, and threw the code back to the developers to fix. This approach may have worked when software was distributed on disks and had long release cycles, but the industry has largely adopted better approaches. Many companies recognized that both roles served the same goal and that the distinction between them was artificial. Developers should be able to test, and testers should be able to develop. This understanding is critical because web applications are often delivered rapidly, sometimes continuously. Developers are responsible for the code they ship, so they're compelled to make their code easier to maintain and test.

> **NOTE** I'm overgeneralizing the testing role and the shift in thinking. During my time at Microsoft, I saw the elimination of the Software Development Engineer in Test (SDET) role. Some companies have made similar transitions, and some haven't, depending on the culture. Testing specializations still exist in areas such as security, performance, compliance, and internationalization. In my opinion, one important takeaway is that a programmer may do more testing than developing, or vice versa, but they're still expected to do both jobs to contribute to the project's and/or company's overall success.

We'll start by testing the smallest units of code: individual methods. Starting from the smallest unit helps build confidence that the code is working as intended. Unit tests should execute quickly and should not rely on external dependencies. Not every method is easy to unit-test, though, such as methods that produce side effects or depend on side effects from other methods. Think of a method that reads a section of an open file and writes some console output.

6.2   SOLID principles

To write code that's conducive to unit testing (with the added benefit of being more maintainable), we'll use the SOLID design principles. Each letter of *SOLID* represents a principle to consider when writing code. The following sections explore these principles and how they look in .NET.

6.2.1   S: Single responsibility principle

Every type should have only one responsibility. In the following listing, we have a class that represents a document in Markdown format.

Listing 6.1   Code that puts two separate responsibilities in the same class

```
public class MarkdownDocument
{
  public void Save() {}
  public void ConvertToHtml(FileStream stream) {}
  public void ConvertToPdf(FileStream stream) {}
}
```

In addition to holding the Markdown data and having the capability to save it, the code has methods to convert it to HTML and PDF. By embedding the conversion methods in the `MarkdownDocument` class, we give that class responsibility for more than just managing the document itself. A correction would be to split the conversion into separate types, as shown in the following listing.

Listing 6.2 Separating conversion methods into their own class

```
public class MarkdownDocument
{
  public void Save() {}
}

public class MarkdownDocumentConverter
{
  public void ConvertToHtml(MarkdownDocument doc,
    FileStream stream) {}
  public void ConvertToPdf(MarkdownDocument doc,
    FileStream stream) {}
}
```

6.2.2 O: Open/closed principle

Types should be open for extension but closed for modification. Let's continue the example in listing 6.2 and focus on the converter class, which is shown in the following listing.

Listing 6.3 Code requiring modification to extend

```
public class MarkdownDocumentConverter
{
  public void ConvertToHtml(MarkdownDocument doc,
    FileStream stream) {}
  public void ConvertToPdf(MarkdownDocument doc,
    FileStream stream) {}
}
```

In this listing, if we want to add another conversion target, such as Microsoft Word, we have to modify the class to add that method. The signature of the method is the same, so we'd have an abstract class or interface that defines a `Convert` method and subclasses/implementations for each target type. We could restructure the code as shown in the following listing. Then adding a conversion to Microsoft Word would require only creating a new class. No modifications to the base class are required.

Listing 6.4 Code open to extension and closed to modification

```
public abstract class MarkdownDocumentConverter
{
  public abstract void Convert(MarkdownDocument doc, FileStream fs);
```

```
}
public class MarkdownToHtmlConverter : MarkdownDocumentConverter {}
public class MarkdownToPdfConverter : MarkdownDocumentConverter {}
```

6.2.3   *L: Liskov substitution principle*

Code can use derived classes without knowing it. In listing 6.4, the conversion methods operate on `FileStream` objects. If we want to add the capability to write to memory or network streams, we have to change the class and methods. Derived classes multiply the work. Consider figure 6.1, in which each class needs to implement file, memory, and network streams individually.

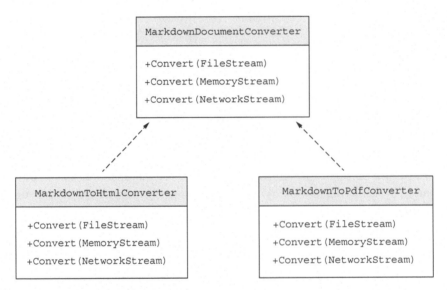

Figure 6.1   A class diagram of `MarkdownDocumentConverter` and derived classes with implementations for writing to file, memory, and network streams

Unless we have some specific need for a `FileStream`, we should use a higher-level abstraction. Writing the converted document to a stream should work the same way regardless of stream type. When we change the code to use a `Stream`, as in the following listing, the code doesn't know or care what type of stream it's writing to.

Listing 6.5   Using Stream as a higher level of abstraction

```
public abstract class MarkdownDocumentConverter
{
    public abstract void Convert(MarkdownDocument doc, Stream stream);
}
```

The Liskov substitution principle makes it easier to replace concrete types with abstract types. This principle also makes it easier to use mocks or fakes, which are types that can be substituted for real implementations and are most often used for testing. (Sometimes, developers use fakes for refactoring old code.) In a unit test, we don't want to get a network stream or file stream every time the test is run. The network or file system isn't what we're trying to test. So we can create a fake stream that checks whether our code is using it as expected. We'll explore fakes in chapter 7.

6.2.4 I: Interface segregation principle

Small, specific interfaces are better than one large, generic interface. One rule that I use when creating interfaces is that if I have classes that implement the interface but leave certain parts blank, the interface is probably too generic. Look at how the interface is used: if most of the code calls only one method on an interface with five methods, consider moving those four methods to another interface. Consider an example in which an object could contain a collection for which we want to generate Markdown text. A collection could be represented in Markdown in a numbered list, bullet points, or table. The following listing shows an interface I'd create for that purpose.

Listing 6.6 Interface for writing a collection to Markdown

```
public interface IMarkdownCollection
{
    string GetNumberedList();
    string GetBulletedList();
    string GetTable();
}
```

Borrowing from the example in chapter 5, if I have a collection of Rating objects for a Book and want to write them to Markdown, a table may be the best choice. I may not want to implement the numbered-list or bulleted-list methods because they don't work for my use case. Using at least two interfaces would be better, as shown in the following listing.

Listing 6.7 Segregating interfaces for specific purposes

```
public interface IMarkdownList
{
    string GetNumberedList();
    string GetBulletedList();
}

public interface IMarkdownTable
{
    string GetTable();
}
```

6.2.5 D: Dependency inversion principle

Depend on abstractions, not implementations. High-level classes shouldn't depend on concrete low-level implementations. Consider a game that uses a deck of cards. We can create a class called `DeckOfCards` that holds all the cards and their order. A `Shuffle` method will order the cards in the deck randomly. Figure 6.2 shows one way to model this class.

Certain sequences of cards may cause different situations in the game. But because `DeckOfCards` uses the `System.Random` class directly, we have no way to control the order of the cards to unit-test these situations. For a single-player game, `System.Random` may be random enough; it uses a seed based on the system clock. For online multiplayer games or competitions (in which people can cheat), we may need a more assured random-number generator. RNGCryptoServiceProvider, for example, is a cryptographic random-number generator and is more secure than `System.Random`. You could even go a step further to get true random numbers from a service like https://www.random.org, which uses atmospheric noise to generate random numbers.

To have better control of the shuffling of cards, we can replace the direct dependency between the `DeckOfCards` class

DeckOfCards
+Shuffle()

System.Random
+Next()

Figure 6.2
A class diagram of
`DeckOfCards` **with**
a dependency on
`System.Random`
to implement the
`Shuffle` **method**

and a random-number generator with an abstraction. The high-level class, `DeckOf-Cards`, works with an interface instead of a low-level implementation. The application can choose the low-level implementation of that interface to fit the situation. Figure 6.3 shows the change in the class diagram.

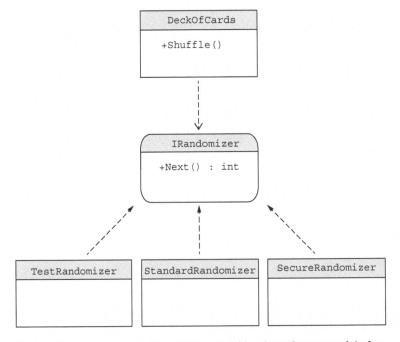

Figure 6.3   A class diagram of `DeckOfCards` **with a dependency on an interface to perform randomization along with implementations of that interface**

.NET extension libraries and ASP.NET Core are full of examples of implementing SOLID principles. We'll explore some of these examples in the next few chapters and implement the principles throughout the rest of the book.

6.3   An example test application: Sodoku

In this chapter, we'll create a *library*, which is a project that can be used in any application (console, web, mobile, and so on). It compiles to a DLL file that isn't executable on its own but that other applications can use. We'll also create a project to hold the unit tests for the library. The library will be used to solve Sudoku puzzles.

Sudoku is a logic puzzle in which you place numbers on a grid based on certain rules. The traditional board is 9x9 cells, and each cell must be filled with a number (1–9) to complete the board. Three rules apply to the numbers in the cells, as shown in figure 6.4:

1. No repeated numbers in a row
2. No repeated numbers in a column
3. No repeated numbers in any of the 3x3 grids that divide the board into 9 separate blocks

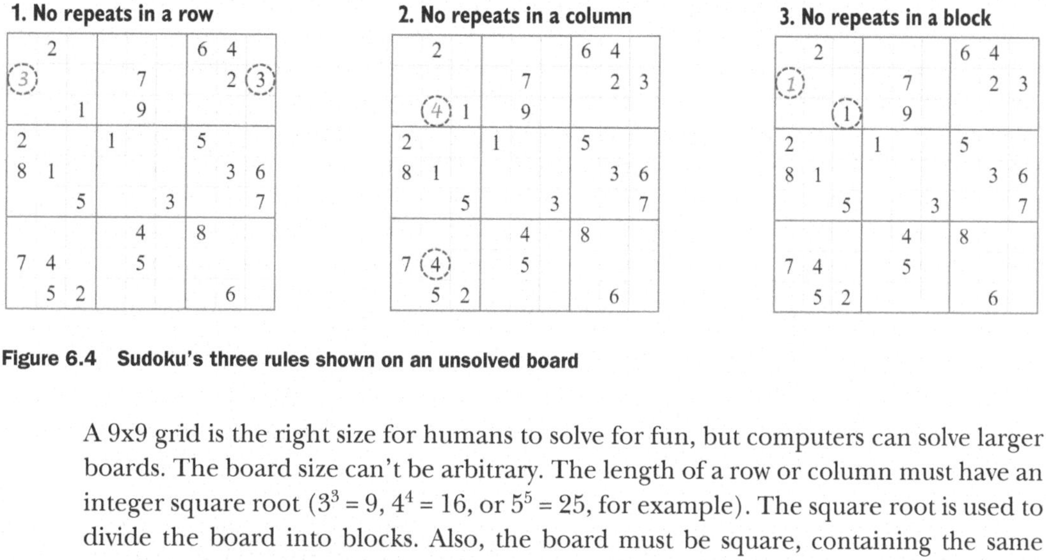

Figure 6.4   Sudoku's three rules shown on an unsolved board

A 9x9 grid is the right size for humans to solve for fun, but computers can solve larger boards. The board size can't be arbitrary. The length of a row or column must have an integer square root ($3^3 = 9$, $4^4 = 16$, or $5^5 = 25$, for example). The square root is used to divide the board into blocks. Also, the board must be square, containing the same number of rows and columns.

We'll create a library that can accept a Sudoku grid of any size with some numbers already filled in. Then the library will either determine that the numbers entered are incorrect or solve the grid. Depending on how many numbers are already filled in, multiple solutions may be possible, but our library needs to produce only one. You could use this library to create a Sudoku game for web, mobile, or desktop applications. You could also use it to cheat on existing Sudoku puzzles to get the fastest time on the leaderboard (theoretically). To make sure that this library is correct, we'll write unit tests to verify each component.

6.4 *Building your first xUnit test project*

.NET has built-in support for unit-testing frameworks. Each framework has a different approach to writing and executing unit tests. My preferred unit-testing framework is xUnit because it uses C# concepts such as constructors, the dispose pattern, and custom attributes in a way that feels natural to me. Other frameworks, such as MSTest and NUnit, have similar capabilities, so don't be concerned that one framework has fewer features than another. Your choice comes down to preference and to what your company or open source project uses.

> **TIP** xUnit.net has a great explanation of the philosophy behind the unit-testing framework in an article titled "Why Did We Build xUnit 1.0?" (https://xunit .net/docs/why-did-we-build-xunit-1.0).

The .NET CLI command to run tests is `dotnet test`, which works similarly to `build` and `run`. The command looks for the project file in the current directory, looks for tests in that project, and then runs those tests. Let's start by creating the SudokuSolver library and the SudokuSolver.UnitTests project, as shown in the following listing.

> **Listing 6.8 Commands to create Sudoku projects**

```
dotnet new classlib --name SudokuSolver
dotnet new xunit --name SudokuSolver.UnitTests          ⟵ Use the built-in xUnit template
cd SudokuSolver.UnitTests
dotnet add reference ../SudokuSolver/SudokuSolver.csproj  ⟵ Unit-test project references the library.
```

> **NOTE** The xUnit template in the .NET CLI adds the xunit.runner.visualstudio package, which is required for both command-line and Visual Studio testing. The template adds a global `using` for the `xUnit` namespace in the Usings.cs file.

In the SudokuSolver library, change the name of the Class1.cs file to Solver.cs. Then add the code from the following listing.

> **Listing 6.9 Initial structure of the `Solver` class**

```
namespace SudokuSolver;

public class Solver
{
  private readonly int[,] _board;          ⟵ A 2D array to hold the board

  public Solver(int[,] board)              ⟵ Passes the board in the constructor
  {
    _board = board;
  }
}
```

```
public bool IsValid()          ◁─── Checks whether the board is valid
{
  return false;                ◁─── Stubs out the method for now
}
}
```

The method `IsValid` checks whether the board is valid by applying the three Sodoku rules. We have it stubbed out for now, meaning that it returns a default value and doesn't yet have an implementation.

---

n-dimensional arrays vs. arrays of arrays (jagged arrays)

A common way of providing a 2D matrix is to use an array of arrays: `int[][] board`, which translates to an array of `int` arrays. This type is different from the 2D array used in listing 6.9: `int[,] board`.

The main difference between a 2D array and an array of arrays is that the latter provides no guarantee that each array is the same length. This type of array is called *jagged*. The code in the following snippet could happen:

```
int[][] jagged = new int[4][];    ◁─── Creates an array of four int arrays
jagged[0] = new int[5];
jagged[1] = new int[10];          ┌ Creates each int array manually. Each
      // ...                      │ int array can be a different size.
```

A 2D array created with a statement like `int[,] board = new int[9, 9];`, however, creates a 9x9 matrix with no extra steps. The same applies to arrays of other dimensions.

In the unit-test project, change the name of the UnitTest1.cs file to SolverTests.cs. In some cases, it helps to write the tests first because we know what to expect from the library, and that knowledge will help us determine when the code is working. We built the scaffold of the `Solver` class, and now we can write the tests to determine whether the code is working properly.

Test-driven development

As far back as the 1960s, NASA used a test-first software development approach. Tests were written to the requirements before the software was developed. This approach was adopted and expanded in the extreme programming (XP) methodology in the early 2000s. Automated tests made for quick feedback on whether the software met the requirements. Test-driven development (TDD) is an evolution of that model that doesn't bring in the other aspects of XP. TDD has both evangelists and critics, as so many other programming philosophies do.

I've used TDD for refactoring legacy codebases and for developing new components when requirements were very clear. When I needed to prototype quickly, I wrote the tests after I settled on a design. The answer to the question "Should I use TDD?" is like the answer to any other question in software: it depends. This book teaches you the skills to test your code but doesn't try to force you toward one philosophy or another.

6.5   Fact tests

The first test we'll write uses the xUnit `Fact` concept. A `Fact` implies that we know something to be true in all cases. We know that an empty Sudoku board is valid, for example; no numbers are entered in the cells, so no repeats are possible.

Before we write the test, I need to clarify two points:

- *The definition of empty*—When the 2D array is created for the board, the default value of each cell is 0. .NET will zero all places in the `int` array when you allocate it. Because the value 0 isn't used in the Sudoku board, we can treat the value as an empty value.
- *The size of the boards to test*—The board size must be a number that has an integer square root. But creating a 9x9 board for every test case is time-consuming (and page-consuming in a book). Instead, we can use 4x4 boards for testing because they'll work just as well.

Let's write one test to verify that a 4x4 empty board is valid, as shown in the following listing. Also, we'll add a test to verify that `IsValid` is false if the board size isn't square. Put this code in the SolverTests.cs file you renamed earlier.

> **Listing 6.10   A `Fact` test that asserts that an empty 4x4 Sudoku board is valid**

```
using SudokuSolver;

namespace SudokuSolver.UnitTests;

public class SolverTests
{
    [Fact]                              ← Applies Fact attribute to test method
    public void Empty4x4Board()         ← Uses descriptive test names
    {
        int[,] empty = new int[4,4];    ← Creates an empty 4x4 board
        var solver = new Solver(empty);   ← Creates a new Solver object
        Assert.True(solver.IsValid());  ← Asserts that the board is valid
    }

    [Fact]
    public void NonSquareBoard()
    {
        int[,] empty = new int[4,9];    ← Creates a non-square board
        var solver = new Solver(empty);
        Assert.False(solver.IsValid());
    }
}
```

An *assertion* is a condition that must be satisfied. Many types of assertions exist, but they ultimately boil down to a Boolean expression that compares an expected value with an experimental value. Try running the test by going to the unit test project's folder on the command line and executing `dotnet test`. The output should look like the following listing.

Listing 6.11 Empty 4x4 board test output

```
Starting test execution, please wait...                    ┐ Searches project code
A total of 1 test files matched the specified pattern.  ◁──┘ for test methods
  SudokuSolver.UnitTests.SolverTests.Empty4x4Board [FAIL]  ◁─┐
    Failed SudokuSolver.UnitTests.SolverTests.Empty4x4Board [6 ms] │ Failed tests
    Error Message:                                              │ are displayed.
      Assert.True() Failure    ◁──── Tells you how the test failed
Expected: True
Actual:   False
    Stack Trace:                                                         ┐ Indicates stack
        at SudokuSolver.UnitTests.SolverTests.Empty4x4Board() in         │ trace of failure
        /ch06/SudokuSolver.UnitTests/SolverTests.cs:line 12  ◁──┘
```

> **TIP** This test method has only one `Assert`, but others can have many. Each `Assert` has an optional string parameter that's displayed in the failure output, such as `Assert.True(solver.IsValid(), "IsValid check");)`. This parameter can make it easier to identify which `Assert` failed.

6.6 Theory tests

Before we implement the `IsValid` method to handle the empty board, we need to learn about another type of test: the `Theory` test. xUnit theory tests are for when there are too many outputs to test, but we know the output for some of the inputs. The Sudoku board is valid if the size has an integer square root, for example. We know that 4, 9, 16, and 25 are acceptable numbers and that the numbers between them aren't. But how many sizes can we test? We don't think it's possible to create a board with a size that exceeds the maximum size of an integer; that approach would take a lot of memory, and testing those bounds makes no sense. So we come up with a reasonable set of values to test. One way to come up with a set of values is to think about upper and lower bounds and edge cases. A size of 4 is the lower bound even though 1 technically has a valid integer square root. No upper bound exists, but we can try numbers close to a known good value. The following listing shows how to write a `Theory` test.

Listing 6.12 A `Theory` test that checks empty boards of different sizes

```
[Theory]                    ◁──── Uses the Theory attribute
[InlineData(0, false)]      ◁─┐
[InlineData(1, false)]        │ InlineData passes
[InlineData(4, true)]         │ parameters to the method.
[InlineData(8, false)]
[InlineData(9, true)]
[InlineData(10, false)]
[InlineData(16, true)]
public void EmptyBoardSizes(int size, bool isValid)    ◁──── Test needs input to run.
{
    int[,] empty = new int[size, size];    ◁──── Creates board based on input size
    var solver = new Solver(empty);
    Assert.Equal(isValid, solver.IsValid());    ◁──── Assert is based on expected value.
}
```

The theory in this listing also covers the Fact case from listing 6.10. Removing the Fact case is reasonable because it provides no new information compared to the theory and the theory tests more conditions. Each piece of inline data is treated as its own test case. When the test fails, it will be written with parameters, such as Solver-Tests.EmptyBoardSizes(size: 9, isValid: True).

We have some tests to start with and can write some code in the Solver class. Modify the IsValid method to check the size of the board as shown in the following listing.

Listing 6.13   Checking whether the board size is correct

```csharp
public bool IsValid()
{
    int rows = _board.GetLength(0);      ⟵  Gets length of first dimension
    int cols = _board.GetLength(1);      ⟵  Gets length of second dimension

    if (rows != cols)        ⟵  Checks if square
        return false;

    if (rows < 4)            ⟵  Checks whether size is at least 4
        return false;

    int sqrt = (int)Math.Sqrt(rows);     ⟵  Gets square root, cast as int
    if ((sqrt * sqrt) != rows)           ⟵  Checks rows for a perfect square
        return false;

    return true;             ⟵  Assumes that board is valid otherwise
}
```

Generic math operations

The code in listing 6.13 uses the System.Math class to get access to math functions. But you may have heard of a .NET 7 feature called *generic math* that puts the math functions on the number types directly, depending on what kinds of numbers they are. int, for example, is represented by the struct Int32. Int32 implements the generic math interfaces IBinaryInteger, IMinMaxValue, and ISignedNumber. (The .NET team knows how to apply the interface segregation principle.) You could replace a statement like Math.Abs(rows) (to get the absolute value of rows) with int.Abs(rows). The Sqrt method applies only to floating-point numbers, so it's not available for integers, and you couldn't do something like int sqrt = (int)double.Sqrt(rows) because rows isn't a double. Generic math has its uses, but not in this case.

Checking whether a number is a perfect square

The Math class, which is built into the core .NET libraries, provides a set of static methods to perform common math operations. The Sqrt method takes and returns a double value. We cast that double value to an int value using (int), which means that we convert the double to an integer. This cast truncates everything after the decimal. We can convert to an integer in other ways by using Math operations like Ceiling, Round, and Floor. In this case, however, we don't want anything after the decimal.

All the tests we've written so far should pass. If you haven't done so already, now is a good time to try running the tests. All the tests deal with empty boards. We know the three rules that must pass for the Sudoku board to be valid, so we can write tests for all three. Creating the boards in the `InlineData` attribute is a bit clunky, but we have another option.

6.6.1 *Applying SOLID principles to SudokuSolver*

SudokuSolver relies on the board's being part of a 2D integer array. An integer array won't enforce the rules that require its size to be a square or both dimensions to be the same size, so the `IsValid` check has to verify those rules as well as the unit tests. The implementation of `IsValid` in listing 6.13 checks only whether the size of the board is correct; it doesn't examine the contents. These responsibilities could be separate, and given the single-responsibility principle, we should divide them into separate classes.

Start by adding a new file to the SudokuSolver project named IBoard.cs. This file will be an interface that defines the properties of the board. Add the code from the following listing to the new file.

Listing 6.14 An interface that defines the properties of a Sudoku board

```
namespace SudokuSolver;

public interface IBoard
{
    int this[int row, int column] { get; set; }    ← Uses an indexer
    int Size { get; }           ←
    int GridSize { get; }       ←      Only one size because board is square
}
                                       Square root of size
```

C# indexers

The notation for accessing the elements of an array is great shorthand. We've seen indexers in action before but haven't called them out explicitly. `Dictionary`, for example, uses an indexer to make access easier. Another example is a specialized collection called `NameValueCollection` in CoreFX (the base class library of .NET) that has both regular `Get` methods and indexers. (Most collections in CoreFX use only the indexer.) The following code snippet shows two ways to get the same values from a `NameValueCollection`:

```
NameValueCollection nvc = new();
// ...
                                           Uses Get method
string? value1 = nvc.Get("key");      ←
string? v.alue2 = nvc["key"];         ←   Uses indexer
```

This code uses an indexer that takes two arguments, allowing the board to be accessed with code that looks the same as that for a 2D array.

Next, let's provide an implementation of the IBoard interface. This interface will still use a 2D array underneath but can provide some guarantee that the size of the board is valid. Create a new file in the SudokuSolver project named ArrayBoard.cs. Add the code from the following listing, which implements the IBoard interface.

Listing 6.15 ArrayBoard class: An implementation of IBoard that uses a 2D array

```
namespace SudokuSolver;

public class ArrayBoard : IBoard
{
  private readonly int[,] _boardArray;
  private readonly int _size;
  private readonly int _gridSize;

  public int this[int row, int column]
  {
    get => _boardArray[row, column];           Returns value from array
    set => _boardArray[row, column] = value;   Sets value in array
  }

  public int Size => _size;        Size can't be changed.

  public int GridSize => _gridSize;

  public ArrayBoard(int size)
  {
    if (!IsValidSize(size, out _gridSize))     Throws exception if size is invalid
    {
      throw new ArgumentException(
        $"Invalid size: {size}", nameof(size));    Interpolated string for message.
    }                                                Nameof gets name of size.

    _boardArray = new int[size, size];     Ensures that board is square
    _size = size;
  }

  private static bool IsValidSize(int size, out int sqrt)
  {
    sqrt = (int)Math.Sqrt(size);           Moves and condenses code from IsValid
    return size >= 4 && (sqrt * sqrt) == size;
  }
}
```

The nameof operator

In listing 6.15, we use the nameof operator instead of writing the string size. This common technique in C# helps in the case of refactoring. Most IDEs have some way to rename a member or type that looks for all instances in which that member or type is used in other code and propagates the name change. This IDE feature can easily tell where the references to the size variable are but may not catch where the string size is used in reference to the member.

Using `nameof` ensures that if the `size` variable is renamed, the IDE will fix the `Argument-Exception` line automatically, or a compiler error will point out that `size` is undefined so you can fix it. Otherwise, the parameter name given to the `ArgumentException` would be incorrect, and you wouldn't notice until runtime or testing.

The `Solver` class needs to be changed to use this new interface. The following listing shows how the `Solver` class has changed to a much simpler form because the `IsValid` method no longer has to verify the size.

Listing 6.16 `Solver` **class using the** `IBoard` **interface**

```
public class Solver
{
  private readonly IBoard _board;

  public Solver(IBoard board)
  {
    _board = board;
  }

  public bool IsValid()
  {
    return true;
  }
}
```

TIP In earlier chapters, we used the `dotnet watch run` command to run our ASP.NET Core applications. This command monitors for changes in the files so that when changes are saved, the hot-reload feature immediately makes those changes available in the running application. The same trick works for testing with the `dotnet watch test` command. When you use this command in the test project, every time you save a change in one of the files, the tests are executed again. This technique is handy for testing a refactoring like the one we're testing now.

The Unified Modeling Language (UML) class diagram for the `SudokuSolver` namespace could be drawn as shown in figure 6.5. UML doesn't have a way to differentiate properties and indexers, so we use `this(int row, int column)` for the indexer. Generally, fields are private (designated by - prefix) and properties are public (designated by + prefix). Indexers operate more like methods than properties because they take arguments.

The SudokuSolver code doesn't have complex relationships or hierarchies to which the other SOLID principles would apply. We'll see examples of other principles—such as dependency inversion, interface segregation, and open/closed—in chapters 7 and 8, which dig further into testing. The Liskov substitution principle made an appearance in chapter 4 where the code was written to use the abstract class `Stream` instead of a

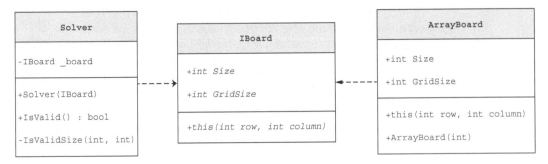

Figure 6.5   A class diagram of the SudokuSolver **namespace with the** Solver **associating with the** IBoard **interface, which is implemented by** ArrayBoard

particular implementation like FileStream. All the SOLID principles are used throughout ASP.NET Core and the Microsoft Extensions libraries that you'll see in later chapters.

6.6.2   Testing for exceptions

The tests we've written so far no longer work because the ArrayBoard will throw an exception if the size is invalid. The unit test needs to verify that the exception is thrown for invalid sizes and not thrown for valid sizes. To make this change, use the Assert.Throws method, as shown in the following listing.

Listing 6.17   Theory test for board sizes

```
[Theory]
[InlineData(8, false)]        ◁——— Subset of cases for brevity
[InlineData(9, true)]
public void EmptyBoardSizes(int size, bool isValid)
{
    if (!isValid)                                Fails test if no ArgumentException
    {                                            is thrown
        Assert.Throws<ArgumentException>(  ◁
            "size",                 ◁——— Verifies parameter name
            () => new ArrayBoard(size));   ◁
    }                                            Anonymous method to run test code
    else
    {                              Using discard operator.
        _ = new ArrayBoard(size);  Exception thrown will fail test.
    }                                      ◁
}
```

Only the constructor of the ArrayBoard class needs to be tested because it verifies the size. The constructor throws an ArgumentException, which the Assert.Throws method catches and checks. If an exception is thrown in a unit test that isn't caught, the test fails.

6.6.3 *Theory testing with MemberData*

MemberData is another attribute that we can use with a Theory test. This attribute tells xUnit to use a member to get the parameters to pass to the test. Listing 6.18 shows the general syntax. The listing adds a new test that checks whether a given board is valid. Creating 4x4 boards to validate the rules is easier in a member than in an attribute. Each new board starts empty (every cell has a 0); then two identical numbers are added in various places.

Listing 6.18 Theory test using `MemberData`

```
[Theory]
[MemberData(nameof(Boards))]     ⟵——|  Member is specified by name; gets the name of Boards.
public void CheckRules(IBoard board, bool isValid)   ⟵—— Passes in the board
{
  var solver = new Solver(board);
  Assert.Equal(isValid, solver.IsValid());
}

public static IEnumerable<object[]> Boards    ⟵——| Required return type.
{                                                 | Member must be static.
  get
  {
    IBoard board = new ArrayBoard(4);    ⟵—— Row repeat check
    board[1, 0] = 1;
    board[3, 0] = 1;
    yield return new object[] { board, false };    ⟵—— Yields return for enumeration
    board = new ArrayBoard(4);    ⟵——|
    board[1, 0] = 1;                 | Column repeat check; must be a new array
    board[1, 2] = 1;
    yield return new object[] { board, false };
    board = new ArrayBoard(4);    ⟵—— Subgrid repeat check
    board[1, 2] = 1;
    board[0, 3] = 1;
    yield return new object[] { board, false };
    board = new ArrayBoard(4);    ⟵—— Valid board with repeat numbers
    board[1, 1] = 1;
    board[2, 3] = 1;
    yield return new object[] { board, true };
  }
}
```

---

yield returns

To return an enumeration of parameters to send to the theory, we could build an array or `List` or use `yield return`. The array/`List` option creates an extra object to hold all the values. When xUnit goes to get the value of `Boards`, it gets the enumerator from the `IEnumerable` and enumerates through to the end. `yield return` means that we don't care what creates the enumeration and want to return the values one at a time.

WARNING   In listing 6.18, each `yield return` uses a new `ArrayBoard` object. If you try to reuse the same board object, xUnit will report this reuse as a duplicate and skip the test. xUnit tries to run tests in random order, so it may be going through the entire enumeration, storing each case, and shuffling before starting to run the theory.

Let's fill in the code to perform each check. The row and column checks are similar. Because I use this example quite often in interviews, I've seen a few implementations. The most common technique that candidates use involves storing each number in the row/column in a `Set` and iterating through with two `for` loops. More efficient ways to do these two checks exist, but the following listing is straightforward.

Listing 6.19   Implementation of first two Sudoku rule checks

```
public bool IsValid()
{
  int size = _board.Size;
  var usedSet = new HashSet<int>();          ←—— HashSet is a Set implementation.
  for (int row = 0; row < size; row++)
  {
    usedSet.Clear();                          ←—— Resets at the start of the inner loop
    for (int col = 0; col < size; col++)
    {
      int num = _board[row, col];
      if (num == 0)                           | Skips 0s
        continue;                             ←—— Goes to next iteration of the loop
      if (usedSet.Contains(num))              ←
        return false;                         | Checks whether the number
      usedSet.Add(num);                       ←  | is already in the set
    }
  }                                           | Puts the number in the set

  for (int col = 0; col < size; col++)        ←
  {                                            | Same but reverses
    usedSet.Clear();                           | inner and outer loop
    for (int row = 0; row < size; row++)
    {
      int num = _board[row, col];
      if (num == 0)
        continue;
      if (usedSet.Contains(num))
        return false;
      usedSet.Add(num);
    }
  }

  return true;
}
```

The third check, determining whether a repeat appears in a subgrid, is less straight-forward. One implementation creates four loops: one for the grid row, one for the grid column, one for the row in the grid, and one for the column in the grid. I prefer to use a different approach that uses modulo and division and needs only two loops, as shown in the following listing.

Listing 6.20   Implementation of third Sudoku rule check

```
int sqrt = _board.GridSize;
for (int grid = 0; grid < size; grid++)        ⟵── Counts through the subgrids
{
  usedSet.Clear();
  int startCol = (grid % sqrt) * sqrt;                  Modulus gives 0,1,0,1.
  int startRow = (grid / sqrt) * sqrt;         ⟵── Division gives 0,0,1,1.
  for (int cell = 0; cell < size; cell++)      ⟵
  {                                                      Counts through cells in subgrid
    int col = startCol + (cell % sqrt);        ⟵
    int row = startRow + (cell / sqrt);                Uses same trick here
    int num = _board[row, col];
    if (num == 0)
      continue;
    if (usedSet.Contains(num))
      return false;
    usedSet.Add(num);
  }
}
```

This code is a bit easier to understand, considering how the grids and cells are arranged. Figure 6.6 shows how the grids are numbered on the left and how the cells are numbered in each grid on the right. The code has to translate the grid and cell numbers into row and column numbers to index into the board.

Numbered grids

Numbered grid cells

0	1	2	0	1	2	0	1	2
3	4	5	3	4	5	3	4	5
6	7	8	6	7	8	6	7	8
0	1	2	0	1	2	0	1	2
3	4	5	3	4	5	3	4	5
6	7	8	6	7	8	6	7	8
0	1	2	0	1	2	0	1	2
3	4	5	3	4	5	3	4	5
6	7	8	6	7	8	6	7	8

Figure 6.6   9x9 Sudoku boards with the grids and cells labeled

Exercise: Solving the Sudoku board

We have yet to implement the solving of the Sudoku board. The IsValid method provides a valuable first step in writing a brute-force implementation that can solve the board. The brute-force method consists of the following steps:

1. If the board isn't valid, return false.
2. Find the next empty space in the board (cell with a 0 value).
3. If no empty space exists, return true.
4. If the space is empty:
   a. Iterate through the possible values for the cell.
   b. Set the value in the board.
   c. Recursively call this method (back to step 1).
   d. If recursive call returns true, return true.
5. If all possibilities have been tried, return false.

Summary

- Use the SOLID design principles to write code that's easier to test and maintain.
- .NET testing frameworks have similar capabilities; using xUnit is a matter of preference.
- Fact tests don't take inputs and usually test one thing.
- Theory tests take inputs, and each input set is considered to be a separate test.
- InlineData is an attribute that can pass constant values to a Theory.
- MemberData points to a static member to get Theory inputs.
- The xUnit Assert class can test equality and look for exceptions.
- An uncaught exception thrown in a unit test fails the test.

Substituting
dependencies in tests

This chapter covers

- Handling time in tests
- Testing with `stream`s
- Adding large multiline strings to code
- Faking dependencies

Depending on the kind of project you're working on, you may feel that you spend more time writing tests than code. As the code you test gets more complex in terms of relationships and dependencies on other code, the tests also become more complex. Code built on a SOLID foundation (pun intended) can take advantage of certain techniques and libraries to help make tests easier to write. This chapter contains a set of commonly used techniques that help make testing easier.

The units in chapter 6 have simple relationships. For more complex code, a unit may depend on several other units, which is true of many ASP.NET Core components. ASP.NET Core has built-in dependency injection and implements the dependency inversion principle. In testing situations, dependencies can be replaced by mocks or fakes that are designed to do nothing except return specific values if needed.

7.1   Testing code that relies on the current time

Consider the implementation of a stopwatch, shown in the following listing.

> **Listing 7.1   An implementation of a stopwatch that uses `DateTime.UtcNow`**

```
public class BasicStopwatch
{
  private DateTime? _startTime;          ◁──── Stores timestamps for start and stop
  private DateTime? _stopTime;

  public void Start()
  {
    _startTime = DateTime.UtcNow;        ◁──── Calling start more than once restarts.
    _stopTime = null;
  }

  public void Stop()
  {
    if (_startTime != null)              ◁──── Timer must be started first.
    {
      _stopTime = DateTime.UtcNow;
    }
  }

  public TimeSpan? ElapsedTimeSpan       ◁──── Difference between start and stop
  {
    get
    {                                                      ┌── Start and Stop
      if (_startTime != null && _stopTime != null)   ◁──── │   need to be called.
      {
        return _stopTime - _startTime;   ◁──── DateTime operator (-) creates TimeSpan.
      }

      return null;
    }
  }
}
```

Operator overloading

In listing 7.1, the elapsed time is calculated by subtracting the start time from the stop time. As in most languages, the subtraction operator (-) in C# is used for subtracting numbers. But here, we're applying subtraction to two structs, which works because `DateTime` has overloaded the meaning of the subtraction operator. The code looks like the following snippet:

```
public static TimeSpan                           ┌── Handles subtraction
  operator - (DateTime d1, DateTime d2)     ◁──── │   between two DateTimes
  => new TimeSpan(d1.Ticks - d2.Ticks);   ◁──── Ticks are long integer (64-bit) values.
```

A tick represents 100 nanoseconds, and `Ticks` is the count of ticks since the beginning of the 21st century (not the same as a UNIX timestamp but similar).

If you were to write unit tests for the `BasicStopwatch` class, you'd be at the mercy of the clock because the class takes a dependency on the `UtcNow` property of `DateTime`. You can put sleeps in your test code, but doing so has a few disadvantages. If the sleep is asynchronous (a delay task), for example, you may have extra time after the delay is finished if no threads are available. This approach also makes the test unnecessarily slow. If you want to test whether restarting the stopwatch worked properly, you might write a test like the one in the following listing.

Listing 7.2   Testing whether restarting the `BasicStopwatch` worked correctly

```
[Fact]
public void RestartStopwatch()
{
  TimeSpan delay = TimeSpan.FromMilliseconds(50);

  var stopwatch = new BasicStopwatch();
  stopwatch.Start();
  Thread.Sleep(delay);
  stopwatch.Stop();                           Waits for 50
                    Start should reset         milliseconds (ms)
  stopwatch.Start();  timestamps.
  Thread.Sleep(delay);
  stopwatch.Stop();

  Assert.NotNull(stopwatch.ElapsedTime);      Elapsed time >50 ms
  Assert.True(stopwatch.ElapsedTime >= delay);   and <100 ms
  Assert.True(stopwatch.ElapsedTime < (delay * 2));
}                                              More operator overloading
```

This test should pass most of the time, but at times, it fails. If many tests are running at the same time, delays could occur, causing the sleep time to be larger than expected. Try setting the delay to 1 ms instead of 50 ms to see whether you can get the test to pass. (I couldn't.) Delays can occur for many reasons:

- The just-in-time (JIT) compiler is compiling the test code.
- Garbage collection paused all threads.
- Other tests are running, and threads or CPU cores aren't available.
- A debugger or profiler is attached.
- Tests are running in a container, and CPU use is limited.

To get the test to pass consistently, you have to set the delay high enough to prevent these problems. If delay is set too low, the test will be flaky (inexplicably works sometimes and doesn't sometimes). But if delay is set too high, it adds unnecessary delay in running tests. If you have a suite of thousands of tests, some of which need delays to work, delays can add up.

I'd love to see a study of the correlation between development/test loop time and developer productivity. Fast unit tests that run instantly on every change are delightful.

The way to fix the timing problem is to apply the dependency inversion principle and abstract the use of `DateTime.UtcNow`. A few Microsoft libraries have an interface called `ISystemClock`. The paraphrased code (paracode?) is shown in listing 7.3; listing 7.4 shows the default implementation.

Listing 7.3   Definition of `ISystemClock`

```
namespace Microsoft.Extensions.Internal;
                                          ◁—— Comments are elided for brevity.
public interface ISystemClock
{
  DateTimeOffset UtcNow { get; }          ◁—— DateTimeOffset is similar to DateTime.
}
```

Listing 7.4   `SystemClock`, the default implementation of `ISystemClock`

```
namespace Microsoft.Extensions.Internal;

public class SystemClock : ISystemClock
{
  public DateTimeOffset UtcNow
  {
    get
    {
      return DateTimeOffset.UtcNow;       ◁—— Yes, that's it.
    }
  }
}
```

NOTE `DateTimeOffset` is a time-zone-aware version of `DateTime`. `DateTime` has a concept of only local versus Coordinated Universal Time (UTC). Handling local time is tricky and can easily create confusion. `DateTimeOffset` identifies a single point in time and should be the default in your .NET code going forward.

For testing, we can create our own `ISystemClock` implementation that provides the exact timestamps we want with no thread sleeps or unpredictability. The first step is modifying the `BasicStopwatch` code to use the `ISystemClock`. *Dependency inversion* (sometimes called *inversion of control*) means that `BasicStopwatch` doesn't control the implementation of the `ISystemClock`. The control goes elsewhere—to the calling code or to a dependency injection component. The reference to the implementation of the `ISystemClock` must be obtainable by calling the dependency injection component or receiving it in the constructor. The constructor method is fairly standard practice in .NET. The following listing shows the new `BasicStopwatch` code.

Listing 7.5   `BasicStopwatch`, `ISystemClock`, and `DateTimeOffset`

```
public class BasicStopwatch
{                                                         Static SystemClock
  private static readonly ISystemClock DefaultClock =  ◁— instance
```

```
      new SystemClock();
  private DateTimeOffset? _startTime;
  private DateTimeOffset? _stopTime;
  private readonly ISystemClock _clock;      ◁——— Not changed after constructor

  public BasicStopwatch(ISystemClock? systemClock = null)
  {
    _clock = systemClock ?? DefaultClock;      ◁——— Uses SystemClock as fallback
  }

  public void Start()
  {
    _startTime = _clock.UtcNow;          ◁——— Gets timestamp from clock
    _stopTime = null;
  }

  public void Stop()
  {
    if (_startTime != null)
    {
      _stopTime = _clock.UtcNow;
    }
  }

  public TimeSpan? ElapsedTime
  {
    get
    {
      if (_startTime != null && _stopTime != null)       Same operator
      {                                                   overloads as
        return _stopTime - _startTime;           ◁——     DateTime.
      }

      return null;
    }
  }
}
```

About default constructors

The BasicStopwatch class in listing 7.5 doesn't have a default constructor. A default constructor takes no parameters. In chapter 3, we used reflection to examine a .NET type to find its properties. Many libraries use reflection to create objects of provided types, including the JsonSerializer we used in chapter 4. Often, these libraries use reflection to look for a default constructor and throw an exception if one doesn't exist. Also, some code that uses C# generics may have constraints that require a default constructor (Method<T>(T t) where T : new()).

If you don't specify a constructor, as in listing 7.1, a default constructor is provided automatically. If you specify a constructor, no default constructor is added. So why can't we use the constructor with the optional parameter in listing 7.5 as a default constructor?

> **(continued)**
>
> If C# implemented optional parameters in such a way that it created overloads for all permutations, it would create two constructors: one with no parameters and one with an `ISystemClock` parameter. That example isn't how optional parameters are implemented, however. The constructor here takes an optional parameter and can't be used by a library or generic constraint that wants a default constructor.
>
> If you're building an ASP.NET Core component, you're likely to create it with dependency injection. For dependency injection, you want only one constructor: the one that takes all the injected objects. (It's acceptable for the parameters to be optional.)

These changes allow the unit test to use its own `ISystemClock` implementation to control the time. The unit test for restarting the stopwatch can be rewritten as shown in the following listing.

Listing 7.6   Using `ISystemClock` instead of `Thread.Sleep`

```
class TestSystemClock : ISystemClock          ⟵── Custom implementation as inner class
{
  public DateTimeOffset UtcNow { get; set; }    ⟵┐ Interface requires get,
}                                                │ but we can add set.

[Fact]
public void RestartStopwatch()
{
  var clock = new TestSystemClock()
  {                                                        ┐ Can be set to any timestamp
    UtcNow = new DateTimeOffset(2023, 1, 1, 0, 0, 0, ⟵──┘
      TimeSpan.Zero)                            ⟵┐ Offset from UTC
  };
  var delay = TimeSpan.FromHours(2);            ⟵┐ Delay time is arbitrary.

  var stopwatch = new BasicStopwatch(clock);
  stopwatch.Start();
  clock.UtcNow += delay;          ⟵── More operator overloading
  stopwatch.Stop();

  // Start should reset
  stopwatch.Start();
  clock.UtcNow += delay;
  stopwatch.Stop();

  Assert.NotNull(stopwatch.ElapsedTime);
  Assert.Equal(delay, stopwatch.ElapsedTime);   ⟵── Exact compare instead of range
}
```

7.2   Testing code that uses Streams

In chapter 4, you used `Stream`s to read and write files. The nice thing about the abstract `Stream` class is that it has many concrete implementations. Writing your methods against `Stream`s makes them flexible enough to work with HTTP request/response bodies, files, network, memory, and custom implementations. Consider the code in the following listing, which reads one line of text from a Stream at a time until it finds some search text.

Listing 7.7   Searching a Stream line by line for matching text

```
public static class Utils
{
  public static string? FindFirstMatchingLine(
    Stream stream, string searchText)
  {
    var reader = new StreamReader(stream);        ◁─── No using; keeps Stream open
    string? line;
    while ((line = reader.ReadLine()) != null)
    {
      if (line.Contains(searchText,                ◁─── Similar to chapter 4
        StringComparison.OrdinalIgnoreCase))
      {
        return line;
      }
    }

    return null;
  }
}
```

7.2.1   Memory stream

To unit-test this method, you need to create a Stream. One way is to build an in-memory stream and write some text to it, as shown in the following listing.

Listing 7.8   A unit test for FindFirstMatchingLine that uses a MemoryStream

```
[Fact]
public void MemoryStream()
{
  using MemoryStream stream = new();        ◁─── Creates an in-memory stream
  StreamWriter writer = new(stream);
  writer.WriteLine("abc");                  ◁─── Writes text to the stream
  writer.WriteLine("def");
  writer.WriteLine("ghi");
  writer.Flush();                           ◁─── StreamWriter may buffer.

  stream.Seek(0, SeekOrigin.Begin);         ◁─── Moves stream position to beginning

  var line = Utils.FindFirstMatchingLine(stream, "f");   ◁─┐ Checks whether the
  Assert.Equal("def", line);                               │ right line was found
}
```

7.2.2   File stream from copied files

If the content you want to use in the test is large, it may be painful to create a memory stream and fill it manually. The content could be saved to a file and loaded by the test at runtime into a `FileStream`. Suppose that you have a file, testdata.txt, that you want to load into a `Stream` for testing. Put this file in the same folder as the unit-test project. Then indicate in the unit test's csproj file that the file should be copied to the output folder, as shown in the following listing.

Listing 7.9   Project file instruction to copy a file to the output folder

```
<ItemGroup>                                      Include
  <None Include="*.txt"          ◄────┘
    CopyToOutputDirectory="PreserveNewest" />   ◄───── Copies only if newer
  <None Update="dontcopy.txt"                   ◄───── Updates metadata
    CopyToOutputDirectory="Never" />     ◄───┐
</ItemGroup>                                   Never copies to output
```

Update or Include?

The first item in the group uses a wildcard to match all .txt files. This wildcard matches each .txt file in the project folder and assigns metadata to those files to indicate that they should be copied to the output folder only if they're newer than files with the same names in the output folder.

The second item in the group uses the `Update` attribute to update the metadata to indicate that a particular .txt file should never be copied to the output folder. .NET Framework programmers may not recognize the `Update` attribute, as traditionally, only `Include` and `Remove` were available. In many situations, `Update` and `Include` are interchangeable.

Tests can load the .txt files copied to the output folder. The following listing shows a test opening a file called testdata.txt and providing the stream to the `FindFirstMatchingLine` method.

Listing 7.10   Test that uses copied text file

```
[Fact]
public void FileStream()
{
  var file = new FileInfo("testdata.txt");
  using var stream = file.OpenRead();      ◄───── Will throw exception if file not found

  var line = Utils.FindFirstMatchingLine(stream, "f");
  Assert.Equal("def", line);
}
```

7.2.3   Manifest resource streams

Another way to get a stream from a file is to embed the file in the project's DLL. Take the dontcopy.txt file that wasn't copied to the output folder in section 7.2.2 and embed it as a resource in the unit-test project DLL. The following listing shows the item group to add to the unit-test project file.

Listing 7.11   Item group that embeds a txt file as a resource in the unit-test project

```
<ItemGroup>
  <EmbeddedResource Include="dontcopy.txt" />        ◄—— Don't use Update here.
</ItemGroup>
```

> **WARNING**   Update won't work for EmbeddedResource unless you've included the item before, likely because files aren't included in the EmbeddedResource group automatically. A file that can't be compiled may be added to the None group by default, so Update and Include work interchangeably there.

Now this file is part of the compiled project assembly. You can access it by using reflection as shown in the following listing.

Listing 7.12   Test that uses manifest resource stream

```
[Fact]
public void EmbeddedResource()
{
  var type = this.GetType();      ◄——┐  The Type of the unit-test class
  var asm = type.Assembly;                 ◄—— Unit-test assembly
  using var stream = asm.GetManifestResourceStream(  ◄—┐
    type.Namespace + ".dontcopy.txt");       ◄—┐      Gets the resource
                                                      from the assembly
  var line = Utils.FindFirstMatchingLine(stream!, "f");
  Assert.Equal("def", line);                   Resource identified by
}                                              namespace and filename
```

> **WARNING**   The name of the resource may depend on the subfolder within the project folder and may not match the namespace name if your assembly name and namespace names are different.

Assembly manifest resources are useful in certain cases. Suppose that you have a JSON file with some information that you don't want a user to change. When you embed the file in the assembly, it's not placed in the output folder with the assemblies. A typical use is for icons or images.

7.3   Finding easier ways to write large strings

If the content of the text you want to use in your tests isn't too large, you could include it in the test file in a string. In listing 7.8, each line is written individually to the StreamWriter to put the text in the MemoryStream. You could write all the lines in one string by using writer.WriteLine("abc\ndef\nghi");. But this approach doesn't scale well, and the escape sequences in the string make it harder for other developers to read. C# has a feature called *verbatim strings* that allows you to write larger sections of text without escape sequences. Verbatim strings start with @" instead of " and have only one escape sequence "" for double quote. The following listing shows two statements that write the same content to the StreamWriter.

Listing 7.13   Normal strings vs. verbatim strings

```
writer.WriteLine("<?xml version=\"1.0\"?>");
writer.WriteLine("<books>");
writer.WriteLine("\t<book title=\".NET in Action\"/>");        ◁——— Tab to indent
writer.WriteLine("</books>");

writer.Write(@"<?xml version=""1.0""?>
<books>
  <book title="".NET in Action""/>
</books>
");
```

In previous chapters, we used interpolated strings to insert values into the string literal. Interpolated strings start with $". You can combine verbatim and interpolated strings by using @$", as shown in the following listing.

Listing 7.14   Verbatim interpolated string

```
writer.WriteLine(@$"<?xml version=""1.0""?>
<books>
  <book title=""{bookTitle}""/>
</books>
");
```

In the case of verbatim interpolated strings, another escape sequence is allowed to write curly brackets ({ }). Instead of writing the opening bracket as {, write {{. Do likewise for the closing bracket. You'll use this technique often if you work with JSON text. The following listing shows an example of JSON in a verbatim interpolated string literal.

Listing 7.15   JSON in a verbatim interpolated string literal

```
writer.WriteLine( /*lang=json,strict*/           ◁——— Used in Visual Studio
@$"{{
  ""RequestParams"": {{
    ""UserId"": ""{userId}"",
    ""ResourceId"": ""{resourceId}""
  }}
}}");
```

The double brackets can make JSON text harder to read in the verbatim interpolated form. For tests, I tend to avoid using interpolated strings for large bits of JSON text. Note that most IDEs escape characters automatically if you paste the text into the string literal. The IDE adjusts the escaping based on the type of string literal you're using.

The inline comment /*lang=json,strict*/ is a poorly documented hint to tell IDEs such as Visual Studio that the string contains JSON. Then the IDE can provide some help in checking whether the JSON is valid. Visual Studio sometimes displays a hint (the light-bulb icon). Figure 7.1 shows the hint.

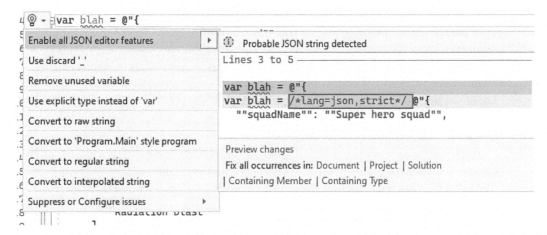

Figure 7.1 A screenshot of the Visual Studio hint that suggests enabling the JSON editor features on a string

So far, the only other text format using these hints that Visual Studio supports is regular expression format. The IDE will provide helpful hints when you're writing the regular expression. Figure 7.2 shows this format in Visual Studio.

```
var emailRegex = /*lang=regex*/ @"(|\^)[\w.\-]{0,25}@(outlook|gmail)\.com(\W|$)";
```

\A	start of string only
\b	word boundary
\B	non-word boundary
\G	contiguous matches
\z	end of string only
\Z	end of string or before ending newline
\k< name-or-number >	named backreference
\1-9	numbered backreference
\a	bell character

The \A anchor specifies that a match must occur at the beginni

Figure 7.2 A regular expression in a verbatim string with a Visual Studio hint that provides help on writing the regular expression

One more type of string literal is useful for large text starting in .NET 7: a raw string, which is similar to a verbatim string but no longer requires the double-quote escaping. Raw strings start and end with three double quotes (`"""`). Also, you can combine a raw string with interpolation by prefixing the opening double quotes with $, as in $`"""`. The following listing shows example JSON in a raw string literal.

Listing 7.16 JSON text written in a raw string literal

```
var jsonString = /*lang=json,strict*/ """
    {
      "RequestParams": {
        "UserId": "myuserId",
        "ResourceId": "myResourceId"
      }
    }
    """;
```

Raw strings allow you to put text in your C# code that looks like the result. One small but useful feature of raw strings is that any whitespace to the left of the closing `"""` is removed from all lines of the raw string. This situation was always an annoyance with verbatim strings; all whitespace was considered to be part of the verbatim string, so you had to remove any indentation if you didn't want it to appear in the string. Raw strings allow the string literal to fit into the code's indentation.

7.4   Replacing dependencies with fakes

Sometimes, a dependency is hard to use during testing. You can put the dependency behind an interface and build a test implementation, called a *fake* or *mock*. Writing fakes can be time-consuming, as many methods and properties aren't used for all tests. The dependency may need to provide different responses depending on the testing situation. The test may want to check whether a method is called in some situations and not in others, for example. To avoid creating different test implementations for each scenario, you can use a fake/mock library.

Fake/mock libraries have been around since the beginning of .NET. The library took advantage of reflection to create an empty implementation of an interface or abstract class. Then it could use a technique such as record/replay to define how a method should respond. Many fake/mock libraries use these kinds of approaches, including NMock, Rhino.Mocks, and TypeMock. The record/replay method is less popular than it used to be. Many new libraries use lambda expressions (and sometimes LINQ expression trees) to allow more expression and control of how a fake or mock behaves.

Let's build an example project to see how to work with fakes. One common dependency to abstract from your code for unit testing is a data store. In chapter 5, you saw two different kinds of in-memory databases that Entity Framework Core supports. Although technically, you could use in-memory databases for unit testing, they're relatively slow and cumbersome to work with. Each test method requires creating a new in-memory database and applying the schema so that tests don't interfere with one another. Also, because multiple test classes can run in parallel, they should have different connection strings so that they're not using the same in-memory database at the same time. A better approach is to abstract the data store completely, and a common method for that purpose is the repository design pattern.

7.4.1   Considering an example repository design pattern

Defined in the book *Domain Driven Design*, by Eric Evans (Addison-Wesley Professional, 2003), the repository pattern separates the domain model from the Data layer. Martin Fowler describes the pattern on his website as such:

> *A Repository mediates between the domain and data mapping layers, acting like an in-memory domain object collection. Client objects construct query specifications declaratively and submit them to Repository for satisfaction. Objects can be added to and removed from the Repository, as they can from a simple collection of objects, and the mapping code encapsulated by the Repository will carry out the appropriate operations behind the scenes.*

Conceptually, a Repository encapsulates the set of objects persisted in a data store and the operations performed over them, providing a more object-oriented view of the persistence layer.

—Edward Hieatt and Robert Mee, *Patterns of Enterprise Application Architecture*

In other words, the objects you use in your business logic and/or user interface may not map directly to your data objects (or entities, in the case of EF Core). Creating a new customer, for example, may take more than one row in one table. Maybe the customer needs to be added to a group or assigned to a role upon creation, or their password is hashed before being written to the data store. Or customer data could be stored in both permanent data storage and a distributed cache. EF Core provides a layer of abstraction from the underlying data source, and in some cases, that abstraction may be enough to make a repository unnecessary. But a big advantage of repositories is that they make your code easier to test.

Let's build a concrete example that uses the repository pattern. The example is a library that can read a stream of customer data and create those customers in a data store. For our purposes, the stream is from a Microsoft Excel worksheet saved in comma-separated values (CSV) format because that format is easiest to parse. The code assumes that the CSV is in the format email,customer name,license. Any line that doesn't have three values is ignored. Customers are uniquely identified by email, so the importer first checks whether a customer with the email exists. If so, it updates that user's name and license. Otherwise, it inserts a new customer with the email, name, and license data from the stream. Figure 7.3 shows the files and folders you'll create for this example.

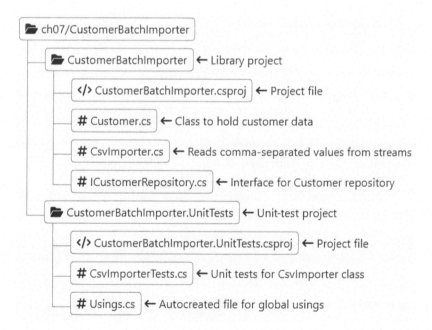

Figure 7.3 Overview of files and folders you'll create for the `CustomerBatchImporter` example

Start by creating a class library called `CustomerBatchImporter` and a unit-test project to go with it, using the commands from the following listing.

Listing 7.17 Commands to create `CustomerBatchImporter` projects

```
dotnet new classlib --name CustomerBatchImporter
dotnet new xunit --name CustomerBatchImporter.UnitTests
cd CustomerBatchImporter.UnitTests
dotnet add reference ../CustomerBatchImporter/CustomerBatchImporter.csproj
dotnet add package FakeItEasy        ◁────┐
                                          │ Adds FakeItEasy package for later
```

NOTE Many faking/mocking libraries have different approaches and merits. FakeItEasy is a popular library that uses easy-to-read semantics. Also check out the NSubstitute and Moq libraries, which perform similar functions.

In the `CustomerBatchImporter` library, create a file called Customer.cs. The `Customer` class would likely be the entity used in EF Core. The information recorded for a customer is the customer's name, email address, and license. For testing purposes, we'll assume that all this information is string data and that there's no need to validate the content of the strings. Add the code from the following listing to the Customer.cs file.

Listing 7.18 `Customer` class

```
public class Customer        ◁──── class not record for entity
{
  public int Id { get; set; }           ◁──── Database unique ID
  public string Email { get; set; }
  public string Name { get; set; }
  public string License { get; set; }
}
```

The repository must be able to look up an existing customer by email address and either update the existing customer or create a new one. The CSV stream doesn't contain the database ID, so let's assume that email uniquely identifies the customer. Updating an existing customer requires the ID and allows updating the name and/or license. Inserting a new customer requires the email address, name, and license. As a result, the repository needs three methods: `GetByEmail`, `Update`, and `Create`. Create a new interface called `ICustomerRepository` with these methods, as shown in the following listing.

Listing 7.19 `ICustomerRepository` interface

```
namespace CustomerBatchImporter;

public interface ICustomerRepository
{
  Task CreateAsync(         ◁──── Defaults to async
```

```
        NewCustomerDto customer);        ◁──── Immutable Data Transfer Object (DTO)

    Task UpdateAsync(
      UpdateCustomerDto customer);

    Task<Customer?> GetByEmailAsync(string email);      ◁──── Gets the Customer entity
}

public record NewCustomerDto(        ◁──── See nearby sidebar on use of DTOs.
    string Email,
    string Name,
    string License
) { }                        ◁──── Can use ; instead of { } for records

public record UpdateCustomerDto(
    int Id,
    string? NewName,
    string? NewLicense
) { }
```

Data Transfer Objects

A Data Transfer Object (DTO) defines how data is sent over a boundary. Although the Customer entity represents how the customer is stored in the database, this approach may not be how you want to communicate about that object externally. In listing 7.19, only two properties can be changed on update. DTOs are often used for web API controllers. By abstracting from the entities used in the data store, they can flatten hierarchies, remove circular references, and hide large or internal properties.

You could decide to use the Customer object directly instead of DTOs. You'd need to make an explicit decision about whether to rely on EF Core change tracking and, if not, document what fields can't be changed or won't be populated from certain operations. Behaviors and side effects are harder for other developers to discover (including yourself a few months later when you have to work on code that you forgot about). I like to use DTOs because developers don't have to find that documentation and keep it updated; the restrictions are part of the types and methods.

The code that reads the CSV stream and creates or updates customers can depend on the repository interface. For testing purposes, you don't need to create a concrete implementation of the repository that writes to a database. Create a CsvImporter class, and add the code from the following listing.

Listing 7.20 Parsing customers from a CSV

```
namespace CustomerBatchImporter;

public class CsvImporter
{
    private readonly ICustomerRepository _customerRepo;

    public CsvImporter(ICustomerRepository customerRepo)      ◁──┐ Gets repository
                                                                 └─ in constructor
```

```
     => _customerRepo = customerRepo;

public async Task ReadAsync(Stream stream)
{
  var reader = new StreamReader(stream);    ⟵──── Creates StreamReader to read lines
  string? line;
  while ((line = await reader.ReadLineAsync()) != null)   ⟵──┐ Reads lines until
  {                                                           │ end of stream
    var customer = ReadCsvLine(line);    ⟵──────┐
    if (customer == null)                        │ null if line is invalid
    {
      continue;      ⟵──── Skips rest of code in loop
    }

    var existing = await                                 ⟵──┐ Sees whether
      _customerRepo.GetByEmailAsync(customer.Email);        │ email exists

    if (existing == null)         ⟵──── Email wasn't found; create customer.
    {
      await _customerRepo.CreateAsync(customer);
    }
    else              ⟵──── Email was found; update customer.
    {
      await _customerRepo.UpdateAsync(
        new UpdateCustomerDto(
          existing.Id,
          customer.Name,
          customer.License
        ));
    }
  }
}
                                                      ⟵──┐ Reads line into
                                                         │ NewCustomerDto
private NewCustomerDto? ReadCsvLine(string line)
{
  var el = line.Split(',');    ⟵──── Splits line into string array by comma
  return el.Length != 3 ? null                   ⟵──┐
    : new NewCustomerDto(el[0], el[1], el[2]);      │ Invalid format returns null.
}
}
```

Exercise 1: CSV parsing

The string.Split(',') method divides a string by a delimiter (the comma, in this case) and creates an array of strings. This method is an overly simplistic way to parse a CSV file. If any of the elements in a CSV contain commas, the method won't work the way we want. Most applications that write CSVs, such as Excel, put double quotes as delimiters around elements that contain commas. If double quotes are also used in the element, they need to be escaped. Try abstracting the CSV parsing behind an interface, and implement it with a capable library from NuGet, such as GenericParser or NReco.Csv.

7.4.2 *Setting up the unit-test class*

Each unit test operates on a `CsvImporter` object. The `ReadAsync` method takes a `Stream` and makes calls to the repository. Because the `Stream` needs to contain only a few lines of text at most, a memory stream will work. The `CsvImporter` constructor takes a repository object, so we'll need one to pass in. The FakeItEasy library can create an empty implementation of an interface. Create the CsvImporterTests.cs file in the unit-test project, and add the code from the following listing.

Listing 7.21 Test class for `CsvImporter`

```
using CustomerBatchImporter;
using FakeItEasy;            ⟵ Can go to Usings.cs instead
using System.Text;           ⟵
using Xunit;                  | For Encoding

namespace CustomerBatchImporter.UnitTests;
                                              Each test can
                                              access fake.
public class CsvImporterTests
{                                             Each test
  private readonly ICustomerRepository _fakeCustomerRepo; ⟵ can access
  private readonly CsvImporter _csvImporter;    ⟵      CsvImporter.

  public CsvImporterTests()  ⟵ Each test is new instance of test class.
  {
    _fakeCustomerRepo = A.Fake<ICustomerRepository>(); ⟵ Creates the fake
    _csvImporter = new(_fakeCustomerRepo);  ⟵
  }                                  | Initializes importer with fake

  private Stream GetStreamFromString(string content) => ⟵ Helper method
    new MemoryStream(Encoding.UTF8.GetBytes(content)); ⟵
}                                          Converts string to bytes
                                           and wraps in Stream
```

xUnit creates a new `CsvImporterTests` object for every test it runs. Therefore, you can place common code that will be used in all tests in the constructor. Because every test performs some operation on `CsvImporter`, the object can be created in the constructor. The fake object for the `ICustomerRepository` is created as a field as well. Tests can modify the fake object as necessary without interfering with other tests.

String content as bytes

The helper method `GetStreamFromString` in listing 7.21 takes a slightly different approach to creating the `Stream` from the one documented in section 7.2.1. That method uses a `StreamWriter` that adds text directly to a `MemoryStream` object. `MemoryStream` can grow its buffer to handle the new text. If you have the exact bytes you want to use, however, the `MemoryStream` wraps that content and can't expand or shrink that byte array. In our case, a single string holds everything the test will use. Strings are essentially arrays of **char**s, and each **char** is a 16-bit value that represents a UTF-16 character.

> *(continued)*
> If you want to construct a MemoryStream by using an existing array, the array must be a **byte** array. A **byte** in C# is 8 bits (as you'd expect). The helper method converts the strings' contents to UTF-8, which uses less memory than UTF-16. Because most text characters fit within the first 128 bytes of ASCII (granted, I'm biased as a native English speaker), most characters can be encoded within the first 8 bits. UTF-8 is a variable length encoding that can handle higher-value Unicode characters. The unit tests don't use UTF-8 to save on memory. StreamReader (and most of CoreFX) defaults to UTF-8.

7.4.3 *Validating faked method calls*

The fake of ICustomerRepository creates an implementation that returns defaults for all method calls. So a call to GetByEmailAsync will return a null, signaling to the CsvImporter that the customer doesn't exist and that a new customer must be created. The call to CreateAsync doesn't return anything, so the test would work if you passed in a Stream with a valid line of input. The test shown in the following listing will pass.

Listing 7.22 Test that imports one customer

```
[Fact]
public async Task OneCustomer()
{
  string email = "some@email.com";
  string name = "A Customer";
  string license = "Basic";
  string csv = string.Join(',', email, name, license);    ← Joins the strings with a delimiter

  var stream = GetStreamFromString(csv);
  await _csvImporter.ReadAsync(stream);
}
```

> **String Join and Split**
> The code in listing 7.20 parses the CSV line by calling Split, using a comma as a delimiter. The inverse operation is Join. As pointed out in the exercise, this example is an overly simple form of CSV that can't handle commas in the string elements.
>
> The Join method uses a C# technique called a params array (see chapter 5). Join can take a delimiter and an array of strings and concatenate them into one string with the delimiter between elements. The signature of Join looks like this: string Join (char separator, params string?[] value). Notice that we don't pass an array into the method; the params keyword tells the compiler that all the arguments after the separator can be combined into a 1D array automatically.

The problem with the OneCustomer unit test is that although the test passes, we don't know whether the test did what it was supposed to. We expect the test to make calls to the ICustomerRepository and create a new customer. With the test as is, the ReadAsync method could be empty and still produce the same result. FakeItEasy provides a way to validate that methods on the fake were called. The code in the following listing checks whether `GetByEmailAsync` and `CreateAsync` were called—and were the only methods called.

Listing 7.23 `OneCustomer` **with validation of repository**

```
[Fact]
public async Task ValidCustomerOneLine()
{
  // Arrange
  string email = "some@email.com";
  string name = "A Customer";
  string license = "Basic";
  string csv = string.Join(',', email, name, license);
  A.CallTo(() => _fakeCustomerRepo.GetByEmailAsync(email))      Setup fake for
    .Returns(default(Customer));                                GetByEmailAsync

                                                     Returns null (see the "default vs.
  // Act                                             null" sidebar in this section)
  var stream = GetStreamFromString(csv);
  await _csvImporter.ReadAsync(stream);      The code should call both methods.

  // Assert
  A.CallTo(() =>
    _fakeCustomerRepo.GetByEmailAsync(email))
    .MustHaveHappened();                             CsvImporter must have called this.
  A.CallTo(() => _fakeCustomerRepo.CreateAsync(
      A<NewCustomerDto>.That.Matches(n =>           FakeItEasy records what was called.
        n.Email == email
        && n.Name == name                           Checks whether new customer is correct
        && n.License == license)))
    .MustHaveHappened();            CsvImporter must have called this.
}
```

FakeItEasy's API makes it read almost like plain English ("A call to this fake object's `GetByEmailAsync` method with this email must have happened"). Before the Act step (see the nearby sidebar), we set up the call to `GetEmailByAsync` to return a null (default for `Customer` reference type). This call should trigger the `CsvImporter` to create a new customer because the null for `GetEmailByAsync` tells the importer that no customer with that email address exists. Notice that before the Act step, we didn't tell FakeItEasy anything about the call to `CreateAsync`. `CreateAsync` doesn't return anything, and FakeItEasy records every call that is made on the fake, which allows us to check what customer was created in the Assert step of the test.

> **The Arrange, Act, Assert (AAA) pattern**
> The Microsoft documentation sums it up best: "The AAA (Arrange, Act, Assert) pattern is a common way of writing unit tests for a method under test."

(continued)

- *The Arrange section of a unit-test method initializes objects and sets the value of the data that is passed to the method under test.*
- *The Act section invokes the method under test with the arranged parameters.*
- *The Assert section verifies that the action of the method under test behaves as expected.*

The FakeItEasy library is designed to work with the AAA pattern. There may be repeated calls to `A.CallTo` on the same method, as in listing 7.23. By design, you can't add a `Returns` and a `MustHaveHappened` on the same `CallTo` line because that approach wouldn't work well with separation between Arrange and Assert.

Also, commenting the section is common practice. Commenting makes it clear to anyone reading the test where each part is.

default vs. null

In listing 7.23, the `GetByEmailAsync` fake returns a value of `default(Customer)`. This C# keyword hasn't been mentioned before. Because `Customer` is a reference type, the value of `default` is `null`. The default of a value type can't be `null`, so for a type like `int`, the default is `0`.

But this requirement isn't the reason why `default(Customer)` is used in this code. `Returns` is a method with two overloads: one that takes a `Customer` object and one that takes a `Task<Customer>`. Usually, the C# compiler can infer the generic type parameter by the parameter you pass in. If the code returned a `Customer` object, as in `Returns(new Customer())`, the compiler will assume that the generic type is `Customer`. But if you try to return `null`, as in `.Returns(null)`, the compiler can't tell the type. The compiler can't tell whether you're saying that the `Task` is null or the return value is null.

You're left with two options. The first option is to create a `Task` with the `null` value, as in `.Returns(Task.FromResult<Customer?>(null))`. The second option is to use `default`, as in `.Returns(default(Customer))`. The `default` gives the right hint to the compiler that it can determine the type. Also, it's easier to read.

We've tested what happens when individual methods are called. But what happens with calls that we weren't expecting? Because FakeItEasy records all the calls made to the fake, it's possible to get a list of those calls. If we don't think that the fake should be called, we can write code to assert this preference. If an invalid CSV line is passed in the stream, for example, it should be skipped. The following listing shows how that test could be written.

Listing 7.24   Test with invalid CSV line

```
[Fact]
public async Task InvalidLine()
{
    var stream = GetStreamFromString("not a valid line");    ⟵—— No commas to split
```

```
await _csvImporter.ReadAsync(stream);

var calls = Fake.GetCalls(_fakeCustomerRepo);    ◁────── Gets all calls to fake
Assert.Empty(calls);                     ◁──────┐
}                                                │  Asserts that there were no calls
```

7.4.4 *Verifying the number and order of calls*

Because one unit test already verifies the contents of the data passed in to the
`CreateAsync` method on the repository, we don't need to verify this information in
every other unit test. When unit tests have a low amount of overlap, test failures can
help you determine problems quickly. We want to verify that a stream with many lines
calls `CreateAsync` only a specific number of times. FakeItEasy has built-in methods to
check the number of calls made to a fake method.

The code in the following listing sends three lines in the stream. Two lines are
valid, but one isn't. The test verifies that the `CreateAsync` method was called exactly
twice.

Listing 7.25   Checking number of calls to `CreateAsync`

```
[Fact]
public async Task ThreeLinesOneInvalid()
{
  // Arrange
  A.CallTo(() => _fakeCustomerRepo.GetByEmailAsync(
      A<string>.Ignored))                     ◁──────┐
    .Returns(default(Customer));                      │  Don't care about email.

  // Act                                              │  Input has three lines.
  var stream = GetStreamFromString(          ◁──────┘
    "a@b.com,customer1,None\ninvalidline\nc@d.com,customer2,None");
  await _csvImporter.ReadAsync(stream);

  // Assert
  A.CallTo(() => _fakeCustomerRepo
    .CreateAsync(A<NewCustomerDto>.Ignored))    ◁────── Don't care about input.
    .MustHaveHappenedTwiceExactly();       ◁──────┐
}                                                 │  Only two valid input lines
```

The call to `GetByEmailAsync` should always return `null`. Here, we see the use of the
`A<>.Ignored` property, which means that we don't care what the input is. The same property is used for the assertion on `CreateAsync`. A variation on the `MustHaveHappened` method
indicates how many times the fake method must have been called. You can find many
other variations on this method through your IDE's autocomplete feature, or go to
FakeItEasy's excellent documentation site at https://fakeiteasy.github.io/docs.

7.4.5 *Throwing exceptions from fakes*

By now, you probably can guess how to make a faked method throw an exception. You
can assume that the repository will throw an exception if the email is null. The unit

test has to verify that the exception is thrown and fail the test if not. The `Assert` class
has a helper method for this purpose, so you don't have to do the `try`/`catch` yourself.
The following listing shows how to throw an exception from a fake and assert that the
test method throws that exception.

Listing 7.26   Detecting expected exception in unit test

```
[Fact]
public async Task GetThrows()
{
  A.CallTo(() => _fakeCustomerRepo.GetByEmailAsync(""))
    .Throws<ArgumentException>();                          ⟵——— Throws instead of returns

  var stream = GetStreamFromString(",name,license");
  await Assert.ThrowsAsync<ArgumentException>(   ⟵——— Catches the ArgumentException
    () => _csvImporter.ReadAsync(stream));       ⟵———┐
}                                                     │ ReadAsync called in a Func
```

`ThrowsAsync` takes a `Func` or `Action` object as a parameter. `Func` represents a method that
has a return value, and `Action` represents a method with no return value. The execution of `ReadAsync` is deferred until `ThrowsAsync` decides to execute it, which means that
it can wrap the call in a `try`/`catch` and assert that the `ArgumentException` is thrown. If
no exception is thrown, the assertion fails. This situation breaks the AAA pattern a little bit because Act and Assert happen together on one line, but there's not much
choice when it comes to throwing exceptions.

Exercise 2: Implementing unit tests for the update method
All tests so far have involved creating new users. If the email address is found, the
`GetByEmailAsync` method returns a `Customer` object. Verify that the code updates the
user with the correct ID and with the parameters from the CSV. One hint to help with
the assertion on the `UpdateAsync` method is to use the `A<>.That.Matches(Func)`
method to check that the DTO matches the expected update values.

Summary

- Adhering to the SOLID principles makes code easier to test.
- Code that relies on timing should abstract the way it gets timestamps.
- Large files can be copied to the unit-test output folder for use in testing.
- Smaller files can be embedded in the code or in the assembly.
- C# has many ways to create large strings.
- Using a fake library saves custom test implementation time and adds powerful
  features.
- The repository pattern is a useful abstraction that makes it easier to test without
  setting up test databases.
- Using a fake or mock library and the AAA pattern makes tests easier to read.

Integration testing

This chapter covers

- Understanding integration tests
- Simulating SQL databases
- Faking HTTP calls
- Using `WebApplicationFactory` for API testing

Unit testing tests individual units in isolation. Dependencies between units are abstracted, usually by interface. The interfaces create a contract to which both the dependent and the dependency adhere, but code rarely has no side effects. Even in previous chapters, we've seen side effects from using streams. A stream's position and whether it's open, closed, or disposed can be changed by any code that touches it. Changes to a database while your code is running may cause an insert to fail or an update to be overwritten. Unit testing isn't enough. We also need to test how units work together—that is, run integration tests.

> **DEFINITION** The clearest definition of integration tests I've found comes from Martin Fowler. (Read the article at http://mng.bz/MZ2D.) The article states, "Integration tests determine if independently developed units of software work correctly when they are connected to each other." Fowler goes on to distinguish between broad and narrow integration tests, the former involving many active modules and the latter using mocks or fakes to test a limited set of interactions.

8.1   Applications with many dependencies

In chapter 4, we built an application that could use some JSON metadata from the XKCD website to find a comic by its title. All the methods were in the top-level Program file. The method call flow looked like figure 8.1.

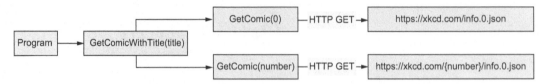

Figure 8.1   Method call flow of the XKCD comic-finding code build from chapter 4

The only way to test code like this is to run it against the actual XKCD website. As noted in chapter 4, this process can take a few seconds to a few minutes to execute. Also, the code didn't attempt to build a cache of the metadata, which is unlikely to change (except for adding new comics).

In this chapter, we'll expand on the earlier searching code. The code will be divided into units using the SOLID principles so that it's easier to test. We'll also add a repository to record the comic metadata to a data store for later retrieval. Figure 8.2 shows the new class diagram.

To unit-test ComicFinder, we normally create fakes for IComicRepository and IXkcd-Client. But for integration testing, we should use the implementations of IComic-Repository and IXkcdClient. The implementation of IComicRepository will use Entity Framework Core (EF Core), which can use an in-memory database that can be created, populated with data, and deleted on each test run. IXkcdClient's implementation will use the HttpClient class as in the original code, but instead of making a call to the XKCD web service, the tests will fake the HTTP responses. Faking the HTTP responses focuses the tests on the integration between IXkcdClient, IComicRepository, and ComicFinder.

Before creating the integration tests for ComicFinder, let's write tests for the implementations of IComicRepository and IXkcdClient. Start by creating a class library called XkcdComicFinder and a test project to go with it, using the commands from the following listing.

Listing 8.1   Commands to create XkcdComicFinder

```
dotnet new classlib --name XkcdComicFinder
cd XkcdComicFinder
dotnet add package Microsoft.EntityFrameworkCore          ◁─── No specific database
cd ..

dotnet new xunit --name XkcdComicFinder.Tests
cd XkcdComicFinder.Tests
dotnet add reference ../XkcdComicFinder/XkcdComicFinder.csproj  ─┐ Test uses Sqlite.
dotnet add package Microsoft.EntityFrameworkCore.Sqlite       ◁─┘
dotnet add package FakeItEasy                            ◁─── Fakes are needed for HTTP calls.
```

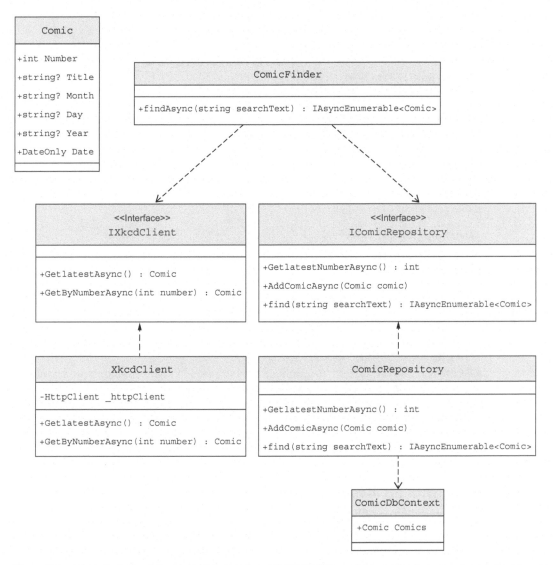

Figure 8.2   Class diagram of the `ComicFinder` (used to find XKCD comics) and its dependencies: a client to make HTTP requests and a repository to store comic metadata

The `Comic` class can be copied from chapter 4 with one modification. Create the Comic.cs file in the `XkcdComicFinder` project, and add the code from the following listing.

Listing 8.2   Comic class that matches the XKCD comic metadata

```
using System.ComponentModel.DataAnnotations;     ◁─── Namespace for Key
using System.Text.Json.Serialization;           ◁─┐
                                                   │ Namespace for Json attributes
namespace XkcdComicFinder;
```

```
public record Comic           ◄─── EF Core can use records.
{
  [Key]                       ◄─── Tells EF Core that this is the ID
  [JsonPropertyName("num")]
  public int Number { get; set; }

  [JsonPropertyName("safe_title")]
  public string? Title { get; set; }

  [JsonPropertyName("month")]
  public string? Month { get; set; }

  [JsonPropertyName("day")]
  public string? Day { get; set; }

  [JsonPropertyName("year")]
  public string? Year { get; set; }

  [JsonIgnore]
  public DateOnly Date =>
    DateOnly.Parse($"{Year}-{Month}-{Day}");
}
```

Using records with EF Core

EF Core can use C# record types without any problems in this scenario, in which making changes to a Comic object isn't necessary. We'll add or retrieve Comic records only because they're not supposed to change. If you're storing something immutable, such as an audit log, using a record type will work. But if the object could be updated, records won't work because a new record has to be created for every change, which will break EF Core's change tracking.

8.2   Testing with an in-memory database

We explored the use of Sqlite in chapter 5 but not in a testing scenario. The DbContext implementation used a specific database implementation in the OnConfiguring method. To make the context easier to use in an integration test, we must leave the database configuration up to the caller (dependency inversion principle). This approach makes for a fairly light ComicDbContext class, shown in the following listing.

> **Listing 8.3   ComicDbContext class with no specified database**

```
using Microsoft.EntityFrameworkCore;

namespace XkcdComicFinder;

public class ComicDbContext : DbContext
{                                                          Gets rid of the warning
  public DbSet<Comic> Comics { get; set; } = null!;   ◄─── (see the nearby sidebar)
```

```
public ComicDbContext(DbContextOptions options) :
    base(options) { }
}
```
← ┐ **Allows constructor only with options**

What does null! mean?

EF Core automatically populates the DbSet properties in DbContext classes, but the compiler doesn't know and will raise a warning that the property could be null. To get the warning to go away, we can set the property to null! This setting doesn't do anything except tell the compiler that the property will be assigned to *something*. What's weird is the syntax. It's not like saying "not null" because the ! as a suffix is the null-forgiving operator, which we use to tell the compiler that we know something won't be null. So it's almost like saying "null for now, but don't worry about it." I like to call it the fuggedaboutit operator or the nothing-to-see-here operator.

With this DbContext, we can create the IComicRepository implementation. Create the IComicRepository.cs file, and add the contents from listing 8.4. Then add the ComicRepository.cs file, and add the implementation shown in listing 8.5.

Listing 8.4 `IComicRepository` interface that matches the earlier class diagram

```
namespace XkcdComicFinder;

public interface IComicRepository
{
    Task<int> GetLatestNumberAsync();

    Task AddComicAsync(Comic comic);

    IAsyncEnumerable<Comic> Find(string searchText);
}
```
← **No Task, so no Async suffix**

Listing 8.5 Storing and retrieving `Comic` objects

```
using Microsoft.EntityFrameworkCore;
```
← **For AsAsyncEnumerable extension**

```
namespace XkcdComicFinder;

public class ComicRepository : IComicRepository
{
    private readonly ComicDbContext _dbContext;

    public ComicRepository(ComicDbContext dbContext)
        => _dbContext = dbContext;

    public Task AddComicAsync(Comic comic)
    {
        _dbContext.Add(comic);
        return _dbContext.SaveChangesAsync();
    }
}
```
← **Specifying Comics DbSet isn't necessary.**

```
public IAsyncEnumerable<Comic> Find(string searchText)        ◁——  Doesn't return Task,
    => _dbContext.Comics.Where(c => c.Title != null &&              so no Async suffix
      c.Title.Contains(searchText))          ◁——
      .AsAsyncEnumerable();                        Case sensitivity depends on database.

  public Task<int> GetLatestNumberAsync() =>         Order by descending to
    _dbContext.Comics                                get the highest number.
      .OrderByDescending(c => c.Number)      ◁——
      .Select(c => c.Number)            ◁——
      .FirstOrDefaultAsync();        ◁——      We don't need the whole
}                                              Comic, just the number.
              Returns 0 if no records are found
```

Indicating that a method is asynchronous (by using the suffix `Async`) and returns a `Task` in an interface feels a bit clunky. The implementation should dictate whether an asynchronous method is necessary. But the caller of the interface needs to know whether the method is async because being asynchronous changes how it's called. Sometimes you see two interfaces: one with synchronous methods and one with asynchronous methods. As general practice, however, it's OK to default to using asynchronous methods where they make sense. The implementations can always return a `Task.FromResult(returnValue)` to avoid creating the whole "async state machine" (see appendix D).

In the case of `IAsyncEnumerable` return values, you don't often see `Task<IAsync-Enumerable<>>` (although you'll see it in this chapter). So what happens if some steps in the implementation method require an `await`? If the implementation does some extra asynchronous processing on each object returned from an asynchronous enumerator, you don't need to return a `Task`. Consider the example in the following listing, which shows a method that operates on each element of an `IAsyncEnumerable` returned from another method.

Listing 8.6   Operating on an `IAsyncEnumerable`

```
private IAsyncEnumerable<Comic> FindComicsByText(
  string searchText) { }                    ◁——
                                                   Implementation
private async Task<Image> GetComicImageAsync(      elided
  string imgUrl) { }                      ◁——

public async IAsyncEnumerable<Comic> Find(     ◁——— async but no Task
  string searchText)
{
  var foundComics = FindComicsByText(searchText);     ◁——| Gets IAsyncEnumerable

  await foreach (var comic in foundComics)      ◁——| awaits foreach needed
  {                                                  for async enumerables
    comic.Image = await GetComicImageAsync(comic.ImgUrl);  ◁——— Gets comic's image
    yield return comic;                ◁——
  }                                         Returns comics as they're processed
}
```

An async is needed on the Find method because it uses awaits. The await foreach/yield return operators allow you to process an IAsyncEnumerable and return an IAsync Enumerable. As we'll see later in this chapter, if we're not using yield return, we need to add Task to the return type. Asynchronous enumerables are part of a .NET feature called *async streams.* To learn about async streams, try the tutorial at http://mng.bz/aED9.

With all the code in place, we can build the integration tests for the repository by using a Sqlite database. We'll create a ComicDbContext with Sqlite in the test class and follow the same approach throughout this chapter. When testing, it's good to start with the smallest units and build up because problems in individual units are harder to diagnose from integration tests alone. In some cases, we can't test the unit directly because the dependency is hard to replace with a fake implementation. In the case of ComicRepository, we want to test whether our EF Core queries are correct and that can be done only against a database, so we need to create narrow integration tests.

Create a ComicRepositoryTests.cs file in the test project. Then add the scaffolding code shown in the following listing.

Listing 8.7 ComicRepository **test scaffolding**

```
using Microsoft.Data.Sqlite;
using Microsoft.EntityFrameworkCore;

namespace XkcdComicFinder.Tests;

public class ComicRepositoryTests : IDisposable     ← xUnit will dispose the test object.
{                                                    ← Used by other test classes
  internal const string ConnStrTemplate =           ← Data source substituted in
    "DataSource={0};mode=memory;cache=shared";
  private readonly ComicDbContext _comicDbContext;   Allows test to add
  private readonly ComicRepository _comicRepo;       or check data
  private readonly SqliteConnection _keepAliveConn;  ← Needs keep-alive connection
                                                        so data isn't erased
  public ComicRepositoryTests()
  {
    (_comicDbContext, _keepAliveConn) =              ← Gets values from tuple
      SetupSqlite("comics");
    _comicRepo = new(_comicDbContext);
  }

  internal static (ComicDbContext, SqliteConnection)  ← Returns tuple
    SetupSqlite(string dbName)                        ← Used by other test classes
  {
    var connStr = string.Format(ConnStrTemplate, dbName);  ← Creates connection
    SqliteConnection keepAlive = new(connStr);                string
    keepAlive.Open();
         Creates and opens keep-alive connection
    var optionsBuilder = new DbContextOptionsBuilder();   ← Options built with
    optionsBuilder.UseSqlite(ConnStr);                       OptionsBuilder
    var options = optionsBuilder.Options;
    ComicDbContext dbContext = new(options);          Sets SQLite as database
                                                   Property get builds options.
```

```
        Assert.True(dbContext.Database.EnsureCreated());        ◁──┐  Makes sure that
                                                                   │  database is new (see
        return (dbContext, keepAlive);  ◁──── Returns tuple        │  the nearby sidebar)
    }

    public void Dispose()       ◁──── Cleans up DbContext and closes connection
    {
      _keepAliveConn.Close();
      _comicDbContext.Dispose();
    }
}
```

We first saw the IDisposable interface in chapter 4 but haven't implemented it. The interface contains only the Dispose method. But a dispose pattern goes well beyond implementing the Dispose method. The dispose pattern protects against multiple calls to dispose, handles the freeing of managed and native resources, and suppresses finalization. The following listing shows a better application of the dispose pattern.

Listing 8.8   Full dispose pattern implementation

```
public class ComicRepositoryTests : IDisposable
{
  private bool _disposed;              ◁──── Already disposed?

  ~ComicRepositoryTests() => Dispose(false);        ◁──── Finalizer

  public void Dispose()
  {
    Dispose(true);
    GC.SuppressFinalize(this);     ◁──── Tells GC not to finalize
  }

  private void Dispose(bool disposing)      ◁──── Indicates dispose or finalize
  {
    if (!_disposed)        ◁──── Checks whether already disposed
    {
      if (disposing)        ◁──── Too expensive for finalize
      {
        _keepAliveConn.Close();
        _comicDbContext.Dispose();
      }
      else               ◁──── Don't make empty finalizers.
      {
        // Some other cleanup
      }

      _disposed = true;
    }
  }
}
```

Finalizers used to be called *destructors*. Finalizers generally clean up native resources, such as unmanaged memory or OS handles. A destructor, which you see in languages such as C++, is antithetical to a constructor in that it's called when an object is being removed from memory. Only the .NET garbage collector can call finalizers, and it does so when cleaning up the object. If a class has a finalizer, the garbage collector has to take extra steps before cleaning up the object, which makes cleanup slower and affects performance. Generally, it's not a good idea to implement a finalizer unless you need one.

For testing purposes, we don't have to worry about multiple calls to `Dispose` on the same object, and we don't need a finalizer for anything in this book. The `GC.Suppress-Finalize` call is needed only if a finalizer is used, so if you don't use a finalizer, you don't need to add this line. For that reason, the tests in this book implement only the `Dispose` method; the rest of the pattern isn't necessary. To learn about the nuances of the dispose pattern, check out http://mng.bz/pp2R.

Assert on EnsureCreated

`EnsureCreated` returns `false` if the database exists and has tables because it doesn't need to apply the schema. We want to make sure that the database is fresh for every test. So if `EnsureCreated` returns `false`, another test is using the same connection string and modifying the same database. Multiple tests working on the same database at the same time often makes tests flaky, sometimes passing and sometimes not. xUnit creates a new `ComicRepositoryTests` object for each test and doesn't run test methods in the same class simultaneously. Because the test class also implements `IDisposable`, xUnit disposes the object after each test. If the `DbContext` isn't disposed or if some code holds a connection to the SQlite database, the database remains in memory for the next test. By asserting that `EnsureCreated` returns `true`, we make sure that no lingering in-memory database is being used, which would fail the test immediately.

Note that this code is called from the constructor. Because xUnit creates a new `Comic-RepositoryTests` object for each test, the constructor is part of the test. When it throws an exception from the `Assert`, that exception is attributed to the test that was was running.

NOTE We still use xUnit for writing integration tests; no xIntegration exists that I'm aware of. There's no real rule that unit-testing frameworks such as NUnit, MSTest, or xUnit must be used only for unit testing.

With the scaffold in place, we can add tests the way we're used to adding them. Listing 8.9 shows the following tests:

- `NoComics_GetLatest`—When the database is empty, `GetLatestNumberAsync` should return `0`.
- `Comics_GetLatest`—If the database contains a list of comics, `GetLatestNumber-Async` should return the highest number.
- `Add`—`AddComicAsync` should add the `Comic` record to the database.
- `Found`—`Find` should match a record in the database based on its title.

TIP   Keep a separate terminal open running dotnet watch test so that you can quickly see whether a test is working by saving files as you go along. To distinguish unit tests from integration tests, you can use traits. See appendix F for information on traits.

Listing 8.9   Narrow integration tests to add to `ComicRepositoryTests` class

```
[Fact]
public async Task NoComics_GetLatest()
{
  var latest = await _comicRepo.GetLatestNumberAsync();
  Assert.Equal(0, latest);
}

[Fact]
public async Task Comics_GetLatest()
{
  _comicDbContext.AddRange(                    ⟵—— Adds several records at the same time
    new Comic() { Number = 1 },
    new Comic() { Number = 12 },
    new Comic() { Number = 4 });
  await _comicDbContext.SaveChangesAsync();

  var latest = await _comicRepo.GetLatestNumberAsync();
  Assert.Equal(12, latest);
}

[Fact]
public async Task Add()
{
  await _comicRepo.AddComicAsync(
    new Comic() { Number = 3 });
                                                     Checks whether the
  var addedComic = _comicDbContext.Find<Comic>(3);  ⟵— record is in the database
  Assert.NotNull(addedComic);
}

[Fact]
public async Task Found()
{
  _comicDbContext.AddRange(
    new Comic() { Number = 1,  Title = "a" },
    new Comic() { Number = 12, Title = "b" },
    new Comic() { Number = 4,  Title = "c" });
  await _comicDbContext.SaveChangesAsync();

  var foundComics = _comicRepo.Find("b")        Converts to regular IEnumerable
    .ToBlockingEnumerable();           ⟵—
                                                     Checks only one element
  Assert.Single(foundComics);            ⟵—
  Assert.Single(foundComics, c => c.Number == 12 );  ⟵—— Single element should be 12.
}
```

While I'm using the term *narrow integration test*, it's debatable whether it should be called a unit test. Each test requires creating a database, applying a schema, potentially inserting test data, running the test, and then cleaning everything up (which makes each test fairly slow). But for a class such as ComicRepository in which we're testing EF Core queries, no smaller unit for testing is available. I'm including this section of the chapter regardless because we'll use the same technique with the Sqlite database for broader integration tests. The same thing applies to section 8.3.

> **Exercise 1: Add alt text to Comic record and allow searching**
> The comic metadata usually contains *alt text* (the text that shows up as a tooltip when you put your mouse cursor over the comic image). Add a property for this text to the Comic record. The repository's Find method should also match the search text in the alt text as well as the title.

NOTE   Chapter 5 discusses the reason for using SQlite instead of the EF Core in-memory provider.

8.3   Testing HTTP calls

The other side of the architecture diagram shown in figure 8.2 is the XkcdClient that makes the HTTP calls to the web service. The interface has two methods: one to get the latest comic and one to get a specific comic by number. Add an IXkcdClient.cs file to the XkcdComicFinder project, and add the contents of the following listing.

Listing 8.10   IXkcdClient interface

```
namespace XkcdComicFinder;

public interface IXkcdClient
{
    Task<Comic> GetLatestAsync();
    Task<Comic?> GetByNumberAsync(int number);    ⟵──── Can return null if no comic is found
}
```

> **Why does GetLatestAsync not return a nullable?**
> When we get a comic by number, that comic may or may not exist. If the comic doesn't exist, we return a null value. When we get the latest comic, we don't expect a 404 not-found response. We should get an exception instead of a null return value in that case.

Next, create an implementation of this interface. Add another file called Xkcd-Client.cs to the project, and insert the code from the following listing.

Listing 8.11 `IXkcdClient` **implementation using** `HttpClient`

```
using System.Text.Json;

namespace XkcdComicFinder;

public class XkcdClient : IXkcdClient
{
  private const string PageUri = "info.0.json";          Every URL ends
  private readonly HttpClient _httpClient;                with "info.0.json".

  public XkcdClient(HttpClient httpClient)          ◁──── Caller passes HttpClient.
    => _httpClient = httpClient;

  public async Task<Comic> GetLatestAsync()
  {
    var stream = await _httpClient.GetStreamAsync(PageUri);
    return JsonSerializer.Deserialize<Comic>(stream)!;
  }

  public async Task<Comic?> GetByNumberAsync(int number)
  {
    try
    {
      var path = $"{number}/{PageUri}";
      var stream = await _httpClient.GetStreamAsync(path);
      return JsonSerializer.Deserialize<Comic>(stream);
    }                                                    Exceptions if no comic
    catch (AggregateException e)                          with that number exist
      when (e.InnerException is HttpRequestException)
    {
      return null;
    }
    catch (HttpRequestException)
    {
      return null;
    }
  }
}
```

> **NOTE** If parts of `XkcdClient` don't make sense, refer to chapter 4, which describes the code in depth.

This implementation should look similar to the one in chapter 4. A specific URL for the latest comic's metadata provides the highest number. Then we can make requests to all the lower numbers to get metadata for specific comics. If a comic with that number doesn't exist (which happens), the response will be status code 404 (not found). Each HTTP response has the metadata in the body; we read it as a stream and deserialize it into a `Comic` object.

To test this class, we need to fake the HTTP requests. The most obvious step is creating the HttpClient directly, but we should avoid this approach. `HttpClient` isn't fake-friendly, and many developers who use `HttpClient` use an extension method. Extension methods can't be faked directly, so you have to fake the methods that the extension calls. The only way to know what the extension calls is to see the code. Fortunately, `Http-Client` eventually calls one method on the `HttpMessageHandler` object it's built on. This method (`SendAsync`) is called regardless of the HTTP verb used in the request, so most developers provide a faked `HttpMessageHandler`.

Create a file in the test project named XkcdClientTests.cs. Add the code from the following listing, which sets up the fields and helper methods that the tests use. The `SetResponse` method shows how to fake the `HttpMessageHandler` to get the `HttpClient` to return the response of our choice.

Listing 8.12 Testing with a mocked `HttpClient`

```
using System.Net;
using FakeItEasy;

namespace XkcdComicFinder.Tests;

public class XkcdClientTests
{
  private readonly XkcdClient xkcdClient;
  private readonly HttpMessageHandler _fakeMsgHandler;    ◀──── Faked message handler

  private const string LatestJson = "...";    ◀──── See figure 8.3 for large string options.

  public XkcdClientTests()
  {
    _fakeMsgHandler = A.Fake<HttpMessageHandler>();         Sets up HttpClient
    var httpClient = SetupHttpClient(_fakeMsgHandler);   ◀──┘ with handler
    xkcdClient = new(httpClient);
  }

  internal static HttpClient SetupHttpClient(
    HttpMessageHandler msgHandler)
  {
    var httpClient = new HttpClient(msgHandler);             All URIs are relative
    httpClient.BaseAddress = new Uri("https://xkcd.com");  ◀──┘ to https://xkcd.com.
    return httpClient;
  }

  private void SetResponse(
    HttpStatusCode statusCode,
    string content = "")                   SendAsync is a
  {                                         protected method.
    A.CallTo(_fakeMsgHandler)          ◀──┘
      .WithReturnType<Task<HttpResponseMessage>>()       Matches call by name
      .Where(c => c.Method.Name == "SendAsync")      ◀── and return type
      .Returns(new HttpResponseMessage()   ◀──┐
      {                                        Responds with status code and content
        StatusCode = statusCode,
        Content = new StringContent(content),
      });
  }
}
```

The JSON string to use for the `LatestJson` constant can be any valid JSON that matches the comic schema. You can get this string by opening one of the comic URLs in your browser. Writing the string as JSON in the test makes it easier for other developers to access. How you write the JSON depends on whether you're using .NET 6 or earlier or .NET 7 or later.

Figure 8.3 shows how to write the text with verbatim strings (.NET 6) or raw strings (.NET 7+). Chapter 7 covers options for long test strings in more depth.

.NET 6 and earlier - verbatim string	.NET 7 and later - raw string
| ```
private const string LatestJson = /*lang=json,strict*/
@"{
  ""month"": ""6"",
  ""num"": 2630,
  ""link"": """",
  ""year"": ""2022"",
  ""news"": """",
  ""safe_title"": ""Shuttle Skeleton"",
  ""transcript"": """",
  ""alt"": ""It's believed to be related to the Stellar Sea Cow."",
  ""img"": ""https://imgs.xkcd.com/comics/shuttle_skeleton.png"",
  ""title"": ""Shuttle Skeleton"",
  ""day"": ""8""
}";
``` | ```
private const string LatestJson = /*lang=json,strict*/ """
{
  "month": "6",
  "num": 2630,
  "link": "",
  "year": "2022",
  "news": "",
  "safe_title": "Shuttle Skeleton",
  "transcript": "",
  "alt": "It's believed to be related to the Stellar Sea Cow.",
  "img": "https://imgs.xkcd.com/comics/shuttle_skeleton.png",
  "title": "Shuttle Skeleton",
  "day": "8"
}
""";
``` |

Figure 8.3 Comparison of writing a comic in JSON format in verbatim strings and raw strings

Now that the scaffolding is in place, it's time to add tests. Listing 8.13 shows the following tests:

- `GetLatest`—Gets the latest comic, which has its own URL
- `NoComicFound`—Tries to get a comic that doesn't exist, resulting in a `404` response code
- `GetByNumber`—Gets a comic that exists

Listing 8.13 Simulating HTTP calls with message-handler fake

```
[Fact]
public async Task GetLatest()
{
  SetResponse(HttpStatusCode.OK, LatestJson);
  var comic = await xkcdClient.GetLatestAsync();
  Assert.Equal(2630, comic.Number);
}

[Fact]
public async Task NoComicFound()
{
  SetResponse(HttpStatusCode.NotFound);
  var comic = await xkcdClient.GetByNumberAsync(1);
  Assert.Null(comic);
}

[Fact]
```

```
public async Task GetByNumber()
{
  SetResponse(HttpStatusCode.OK, LatestJson);
  var comic = await xkcdClient.GetByNumberAsync(2630);
  Assert.NotNull(comic);
  Assert.Equal(2630, comic.Number);
}
```

8.4   Broader integration tests

The narrow integration tests for the repository and HTTP client are in place. We have confidence that the repository and client work correctly on their own. Now it's time to build a broader integration test for `ComicFinder` to verify that the three components work together correctly. The sequence of events in `ComicFinder` follows:

1 Receive as input the text to search for.
2 Check that we have the latest comic by
   a Querying the XKCD client to get the latest number.
   b Querying the repository to get the latest number stored.
3 If we don't yet have the latest comics:
   a Loop starting from the latest we do have, which could be from 0 because the repository could be empty.
   b Request each comic by number until reaching the latest.
   c If the comic exists, add it to the repository.
4 Execute the search on the repository, and return the results.

Create a file called ComicFinder.cs in the `XkcdComicFinder` project. Insert the code from the following listing for the implementation.

Listing 8.14   `ComicFinder` implementation

```
namespace XkcdComicFinder;

public class ComicFinder
{
  private readonly IXkcdClient _xkcdClient;
  private readonly IComicRepository _repo;

  public ComicFinder(
    IXkcdClient xkcdClient,
    IComicRepository repo)
  {
    _xkcdClient = xkcdClient;
    _repo = repo;
  }

  public async Task<IAsyncEnumerable<Comic>> FindAsync(    ⟵ Task of IAsyncEnumerable (see the nearby note)
    string searchText)
  {
    var latestComic = await _xkcdClient.GetLatestAsync();    ⟵ Always checks for the latest
```

```
      int latestInRepo = await _repo.GetLatestNumberAsync();      ◁───┐ Will be 0 if
      if (latestComic.Number > latestInRepo)                           │ repo is empty
      {
        await FetchAsync(latestComic, latestInRepo);
      }

      return _repo.Find(searchText);
    }

  private async Task FetchAsync(
    Comic latestComic, int latestInRepo)
  {
      await _repo.AddComicAsync(latestComic);            ◁──── Add latest to repo.
      int current = latestComic.Number - 1;
      while (current > latestInRepo)
      {
        var comic = await _xkcdClient.GetByNumberAsync(current);
        if (comic != null)                    ◁───┐
        {                                          │ If comic exists, adds it to repo
          await _repo.AddComicAsync(comic);
        }

        current--;
      }
  }
}
```

NOTE   The `FindAsync` method returns a `Task` of `IAsyncEnumerable` instead of only the `IAsyncEnumerable`. First, `FindAsync` performs some async operations and then returns the `IAsyncEnumerable` that it gets from the repository's `Find` method. `FindAsync` doesn't enumerate each value returned from `Find` via an `await foreach/yield return`, so it's not invoking the C# compiler magic on async streams. The `IAsyncEnumerable` is only an object that needs to be returned.

Exercise 2: Modify FetchAsync method to fetch all comics in parallel

The first request to `FindAsync` takes longest to complete because every comic's metadata must be retrieved. In chapter 4, we saw that `Task`s can be run in parallel to greatly reduce the overall time required to populate the repository. Look at how these requests were done in that chapter, and modify the `FetchAsync` method to take a similar approach. Multiple `Task`s shouldn't save changes to the same `ComicDbContext` at the same time. Gather all the `Comic` objects in a collection; then use `AddRange` and save changes, which will require modifying the repository to support adding batches.

The test class uses the helper methods from the repository and client tests to set up the Sqlite database and `HttpClient` message-handler faking. Create a file called Xkcd-ComicFinder.Tests, and add the code from the following listing.

Listing 8.15 `ComicFinder` **test with Sqlite and faked** `HttpClient`

```
using Microsoft.Data.Sqlite;
using Microsoft.EntityFrameworkCore;
using System.Net;
using System.Text.Json;

namespace XkcdComicFinder.Tests;

public class ComicFinderTests : IDisposable
{
    private const string NumberLink = "https://xkcd.com/{0}/info.0.json";
    private const string LatestLink = "https://xkcd.com/info.0.json";
    private readonly ComicDbContext _comicDbContext;
    private readonly SqliteConnection _keepAliveConn;
    private readonly HttpMessageHandler _fakeMsgHandler;
    private readonly ComicFinder _comicFinder;

    public ComicFinderTests()
    {
        (_comicDbContext, _keepAliveConn) =
            ComicRepositoryTests.SetupSqlite("comics_int");
        var comicRepo = new ComicRepository(_comicDbContext);

        _fakeMsgHandler = A.Fake<HttpMessageHandler>();
        var httpClient =
            XkcdClientTests.SetupHttpClient(_fakeMsgHandler);
        var xkcdClient = new XkcdClient(httpClient);

        _comicFinder = new ComicFinder(xkcdClient, comicRepo);
    }

    public void Dispose()
    {
        _keepAliveConn.Close();
        _comicDbContext.Dispose();
    }
}
```

Annotations:
- **Test can alter the database.**
- **Test can alter the HTTP response.**
- **Different database name (see the nearby warning)**
- **httpClient needed to create xkcdClient**

WARNING When you use SQlite for testing, be aware that by default, xUnit runs multiple test classes in parallel. If two test classes are running at the same time and have the same `DataSource` name in their connection strings, they'll be operating on the same in-memory database. Use a different name if you want to allow the tests to run in parallel with their own databases. An alternative is to put the tests in the same collection; see appendix F for details.

`ComicFinder` can make multiple HTTP calls during its search. Each call has a different URL, so we need some way to provide a different response based on the URL. Suppose that we want to set up the fake so that it matches different incoming parameters. Because `SendAsync` is a protected method, the code in listing 8.12 had to match the call based on its name and return type. (We can add a way to check the arguments as well so that we can match a request URI to a specific response content. But we also need a default case of returning `404` for any other URIs. My solution to this problem was to create a dictionary of request URLs to the `Comic` objects for intermediate storage, then loop through each key/value pair and set the call fake. First, I added a catch-all fake that doesn't check the arguments. This fake works because FakeItEasy applies fakes to a stack so that the last added is the first checked. The following listing has the full code for this solution.

Listing 8.16   `SetResponseComics` **helper method**

```
private static Uri GetUri(Comic c) =>
  new(string.Format(NumberLink, c.Number));    ⟵── Creates URL from Comic object

internal static void SetResponseComics(    ⟵── Used in another test class, too
  HttpMessageHandler fakeMsgHandler,
  params Comic[] comics)    ⟵── params arrays are covered in chapter 7.
{
  var responses = comics.ToDictionary(    ⟵┐ Language Integrated Query (LINQ)
    GetUri,    ⟵─────────────────────────────┘ helper to convert to Dictionary
    c => JsonSerializer.Serialize(c));
  responses.Add(new Uri(LatestLink),    ⟵─ GetUri matches signature
    JsonSerializer.Serialize(comics[0]));    (see the nearby note).

  A.CallTo(fakeMsgHandler)                 Latest has an extra URL to match.
    .WithReturnType<Task<HttpResponseMessage>>()
    .Where(c => c.Method.Name == "SendAsync")
    .Returns(new HttpResponseMessage()
    {
      StatusCode = HttpStatusCode.NotFound,    ⟵── Default is 404 not found.
    });

  foreach (var responsePair in responses)
  {
    A.CallTo(fakeMsgHandler)
      .WithReturnType<Task<HttpResponseMessage>>()
      .Where(c => c.Method.Name == "SendAsync")
      .WhenArgumentsMatch(args =>    ⟵── Gets arguments list
        args.First() is HttpRequestMessage req    ⟵── Request is first argument.
        && req.RequestUri == responsePair.Key)    ⟵── Matches request URI
      .Returns(new HttpResponseMessage()
      {
        StatusCode = HttpStatusCode.OK,
        Content = new StringContent(responsePair.Value),    ⟵── Returns the comic
      });
  }
}
```

Value is serialized JSON. (annotation for the Serialize line)

Assumes that first is latest (annotation for the responses.Add line)

NOTE The `ToDictionary` LINQ extension method takes two parameters, which are functions to create the key and value from each object in the enumeration. The signature for the key function is `Func<Comic, Uri>`, a reference to a function that takes a `Comic` object as input and returns a `Uri`. C# developers get used to writing anonymous methods for everything, so we expect to see `c => GetUri(c)`. But if a method already matches the signature, we don't need to wrap it in an anonymous method.

The only thing left to add to the `ComicFinderTest` class is the test itself. The following listing has the code for a test that uses the `SetResponseComics` method and verifies that the find returns the expected values.

Listing 8.17   Testing whether `Comics` are created correctly

```
[Fact]
public async Task StartWithEmptyRepo()
{
  SetResponseComics(_fakeMsgHandler,                    ← Takes a params array      First in array is
    new Comic() { Number = 12, Title = "b" },                                      the latest comic.
    new Comic() { Number = 1,  Title = "a" },           ←
    new Comic() { Number = 4,  Title = "c" });

  var foundComics = (await _comicFinder.FindAsync("b"))    ← Returns IAsyncEnumerable
    .ToBlockingEnumerable();                               ← Converts to regular IEnumerable

  Assert.Single(foundComics);                             ← Only one comic is expected.
  Assert.Single(foundComics, c => c.Number == 12);        ←
}
                                                          Only comic 12 is expected.
```

If you've been following along with `dotnet watch test` running on the test project, you should see all these tests light up. This chapter has a lot of code to follow, so be sure to check out the supplemental code repo (at https://github.com/dmetzgar/dotnet-in-action-code) if you get stuck.

8.5   *Integration-testing ASP.NET Core APIs*

`XkcdComicFinder` is a library that any application can use. The next step is using this library from an ASP.NET Core web API and building broader integration tests for the web API all the way down to the repository and XKCD client. First, we'll add a project called `ComicFinderService`. We'll also include some new packages in the test project to help with the integration tests. The following listing shows the terminal commands for these steps.

Listing 8.18   Adding packages to `Tests` project and creating `ComicFinderService`

```
cd XkcdComicFinder.Tests
dotnet add package Microsoft.AspNetCore.Mvc.Testing      ← For WebApplicationFactory
dotnet add package Microsoft.Extensions.Http             ←   (shown in listing 8.22 later
cd ..                                                        in the chapter)

                                                        For HttpClient service replacement
dotnet new web --name ComicFinderService
cd ComicFinderService
dotnet add reference ../XkcdComicFinder/XkcdComicFinder.csproj   ← Could be any
dotnet add package Microsoft.EntityFrameworkCore.Sqlite         ←   database
mkdir Controllers
```

The web template creates an empty web application using the ASP.NET Core minimal APIs. We'll replace this code to use the Controller style. By convention, all the controllers go inside a Controllers folder in the project, which we created in listing 8.18. In the Controllers folder, create a new file called SearchController.cs, and add the code from the following listing.

Listing 8.19 `SearchController.FindAsync` method

```
using Microsoft.AspNetCore.Mvc;
using XkcdComicFinder;

namespace ComicFinderService.Controllers;

[ApiController]
[Route("[controller]")]
public class SearchController : ControllerBase
{
  private readonly ComicFinder _comicFinder;

  public SearchController(ComicFinder comicFinder)        ◁──┐ Passed in by
    => _comicFinder = comicFinder;                            dependency injection

  [HttpGet]
  public Task<IAsyncEnumerable<Comic>> FindAsync(          ┐ Expects a searchText
    string searchText) =>                            ◁──── │ query parameter
    _comicFinder.FindAsync(searchText);
}
```

Next, we'll replace the contents of Program.cs. In .NET 6 and later, the templates use the minimal APIs and top-level statements. Later in the test code, we'll want to reference the `Program` class, so we'll make it a traditional start point with a `Main` method. The following listing has the new code for Program.cs.

Listing 8.20 Setting up dependency injection in `Program.Main`

```
using XkcdComicFinder;
using Microsoft.Data.Sqlite;
using Microsoft.EntityFrameworkCore;

namespace ComicFinderService;

public class Program
{
  public static void Main(string[] args)                      ┐ Config comes from
  {                                                             appsettings.json by default.
    var builder = WebApplication.CreateBuilder(args);
    var services = builder.Services;                          ┐ Connection strings have
    var cfg = builder.Configuration;                  ◁────── │ their own section.
    var connStr = cfg.GetConnectionString("Sqlite");  ◁─┘
    var baseAddr = cfg.GetValue<string>("BaseAddr");  ◁──┐ Makes the base
                                                          address configurable

    services.AddScoped<IComicRepository,      ◁───── Scoped to request
      ComicRepository>();                     ◁───┐
                                                  Register interface's implementation
```

```
services.AddScoped<IXkcdClient, XkcdClient>();            ◁──        Order matters!
services.AddScoped<ComicFinder>();    │ Finds SearchController       (See the sidebar
services.AddControllers();            ◁─┘                            "Order matters
services.AddDbContext<ComicDbContext>(option =>     ◁──              with dependency
  option.UseSqlite(connStr));         Uses OptionsBuilder │          injection.")
services.AddHttpClient<IXkcdClient, XkcdClient>(         ◁──
  client => client.BaseAddress =
  new Uri(baseAddr!));

var app = builder.Build();
app.MapControllers();         ◁──── Maps routes

using var keepAliveConn =           ◁──── Needed if in-memory database is used
  new SqliteConnection(connStr);
keepAliveConn.Open();

using (var scope = app.Services.CreateScope())     ◁──── DbContext is scoped.
{
  var dbCtxt = scope.ServiceProvider          │ Required means throw
    .GetRequiredService<ComicDbContext>();    ◁─┘ exception if not found.
  dbCtxt.Database.EnsureCreated();       ◁──
}                                         │ Creates database and applies schema

app.Run();         ◁──── Runs forever until killed
  }
}
```

I mentioned dependency injection a couple of times in earlier chapters, including the use of `AddDbContext`, but listing 8.20 introduces some new concepts. ASP.NET Core's dependency injection allows control of object lifetimes and initializations. `AddScoped`, for example, indicates that the object is scoped to the request: the object will be created once per request and cleaned up when the request is complete. Other lifetimes include transient (create on each injection) and singleton (one object for the whole process). `DbContext`s use connection pooling, so creating one per request won't have a significant performance effect. `AddHttpClient` registers the `HttpClient` as a singleton (per the .NET guidelines at http://mng.bz/OZGj) and also uses connection pooling. If you want your type to be registered as a singleton, you have to make sure that it's thread-safe (won't fail when used by simultaneous threads).

> **TIP**   `DbContext`s use connection pooling, but the `DbContext` objects still need to be constructed. EF Core has a setting that allows pooling of `DbContext` objects, which cuts down on memory allocation and garbage collection. Some caveats exist, so check out http://mng.bz/Y7gj for more information about this setting.

Order matters with dependency injection

If you put the `AddHttpClient` call before `services.AddScoped<IXkcdClient, Xkcd­Client>()`, the service will throw an exception about an invalid URI. Problems like this one can be particularly difficult to diagnose in larger projects. You may notice that `AddDbContext` is after the `ComicRepository` is registered, for example, yet no problem exists.

> **(continued)**
> The difference is due largely to the way these extension methods are implemented. If an extension method uses `CreateScope` to resolve one of the services as in listing 8.20, for example, the service types must be registered already. I recommend adopting this practice: if type A depends on type B, register type B first.

The program uses configuration to get the connection string and base address for the XKCD service. .NET Framework programmers are used to having configuration in the app.config file. .NET Core had no default configuration mechanism, probably in part because app.config was XML. Developers quickly converged on a new file called appsettings.json, and libraries were added to read that configuration. In .NET 6, appsettings.json became the default, and explicit code is no longer required to read it.

NOTE Chapter 13 provides more details on .NET configuration.

Modify the appsettings.json file already included in your project to match the following listing.

Listing 8.21   appsettings.json that includes the connection string and base address

```
{
  "ConnectionStrings": {
    "Sqlite": "DataSource=svc;mode=memory;cache=shared"   ⟵ Different database name
  },
  "Logging": {                    ⟵ Included by default
    "LogLevel": {
      "Default": "Information",
      "Microsoft.AspNetCore": "Warning"
    }
  },
  "AllowedHosts": "*",
  "BaseAddr": "https://xkcd.com"        ⟵ XkcdClient base address
}
```

This web service is working now. You can test it by using `dotnet run` in the ComicFinderService folder and opening a browser to http://localhost:<port>/search?searchText=something. Note that the output of the `dotnet run` command gives you the port number. `search-text` can be whatever you want to search for. I find that the term over produces a lot of results. Note that the first query takes a long time because the service is calling the XKCD server to get all the comic metadata. Parallelizing the comic metadata retrieval process will make the first query faster. Also note that the database goes away as soon as the process stops. You can change that behavior by modifying the Sqlite connection string to use a file instead of memory (as in `DataSource=xkcd.db;cache=shared`).

ASP.NET Core has a feature that allows you to test a web service as though you were making an HTTP call to it. This feature enables a broader integration test in which you can verify that the whole system works top to bottom, including configuration and dependency injection. Some people would call this test an *end-to-end* (E2E) test. The definition of an E2E test varies on environment. If many microservices are involved in a call chain, for example, an E2E test would include more than one service. Because the HttpClient is faked instead of calling the XKCD website, everything involved in the test is in one process, which is why I consider this test to be integration rather than E2E.

To see how WebApplicationFactory works, add a new test class to the test project. Create a file called SearchControllerTests.cs, and add the code from the following listing.

Listing 8.22   Using `WebApplicationFactory`

```
using System.Text.Json;
using ComicFinderService;                          │ Namespace for
using Microsoft.AspNetCore.Mvc.Testing;      ◄──── │ WebApplicationFactory
using Microsoft.Extensions.DependencyInjection;   ◄──── For ServiceDescriptor

namespace XkcdComicFinder.Tests;

public class SearchControllerTests
{
  private const string BaseAddress = "https://xkcd.com";
  private readonly WebApplicationFactory<Program>      ◄──
    _factory;
  private readonly HttpMessageHandler _fakeMsgHandler;   ◄──

                                Still fake HTTP message handler  │  Why we didn't use
  public SearchControllerTests()                                 │  top-level statements
  {
    _fakeMsgHandler = A.Fake<HttpMessageHandler>();

    _factory = new WebApplicationFactory<Program>()     ◄──
      .WithWebHostBuilder(builder =>
      {
        builder.ConfigureServices(services =>          │ Finds HttpClient added
        {                                              │ by Program.cs
          ServiceDescriptor sd = services.First(
            s => s.ServiceType == typeof(HttpClient)); ◄──┘  │ Removed from
          services.Remove(sd);                     ◄──       │ dependency injection
          services.AddHttpClient<IXkcdClient, XkcdClient>(  ◄──
            h => h.BaseAddress = new Uri(BaseAddress))        │ Replaced by
            .ConfigurePrimaryHttpMessageHandler(    ◄──       │ test version
              () => _fakeMsgHandler);
        });                                          │ Uses fake message handler
      });
  }
}
```

WebApplicationFactory creates an in-memory host that we can use for testing. First, the Program.Main method reads the configuration and sets up the dependency injection. The builder.ConfigureServices function enables us to make modifications. In this

case, we want to use our fake `HttpMessageHandler`. The message handler can't be
replaced in an existing `HttpClient`, so the only approach is to replace it with our own
`HttpClient`. The `services` variable is an `IServiceCollection` object on which we can use
LINQ extension methods as we would like on other collections. Only one `HttpClient`
was registered, so we find the first one and remove it. Notice that when we add the test
`HttpClient`, the message handler has to be set with the `ConfigurePrimaryHttpMessage-`
`Handler` extension method because we don't have direct access to the message handler
in `AddHttpClient`.

The `WebApplicationFactory` provides a client that we can call as though we're trying
to make an HTTP call to our service. Note that the service isn't set up and started until
this client is created. To see how the client works, add the test from the following listing.

Listing 8.23 Testing the `WebApplicationFactory` client

```
[Fact]
public async Task FoundB()
{
  ComicFinderTests.SetResponseComics(
    _fakeMsgHandler,
    new Comic() { Number = 12, Title = "b" },      <--- First is latest.
    new Comic() { Number = 1,  Title = "a" },
    new Comic() { Number = 4,  Title = "c" });
                                                     No relation to XkcdClient's
                                                     HttpClient
  HttpClient client = _factory.CreateClient();     <---
  var response = await client.GetAsync(            <--- Allows us to call our service
    "/search?searchText=b");                       <---
                                                     Can use relative URLs
  Assert.Equal(HttpStatusCode.OK, response.StatusCode);
  string content = await response.Content
    .ReadAsStringAsync();
  var comics = JsonSerializer.Deserialize<Comic[]>(    <---
    content);                                          IAsyncEnumerable is
  Assert.NotNull(comics);                              turned into a JSON
  Assert.Single(comics);                               array.
  Assert.Single(comics, c => c.Number == 12);
}
```

NOTE The `HttpClient` created here sends requests to the `ComicFinderService`
and has nothing to do with the `HttpClient` used by the `XkcdClient`.

Setting up `WebApplicationFactory` can be a bit slow compared with setup of a unit test.
Reviewing what's created as part of your service's startup is a good idea. Expensive
items that have nothing to do with the test could be removed. A common approach is
to use configuration to control what gets created. The test class can manipulate the
configuration through code.

Using different configuration files for testing

You may have noticed an appsettings.Development.json file in the `ComicFinder-Service`. By convention, ASP.NET Core loads the appsettings.<environment>.json file after the appsettings.json and uses it to override any duplicate configuration. The environment can be set by environment variable, as we'll see in chapter 13, but it can also be set explicitly by the test. You can add the line shown in the following code snippet to the `WithWebHostBuilder` function and add an appsettings.Integration.json file to the `ComicFinderService` with different configuration that is used only for the test.

```
_factory = new WebApplicationFactory<Program>()
  .WithWebHostBuilder(builder =>
  {
    builder.UseEnvironment("Integration");      <──── Line to add
    builder.ConfigureServices(services =>
    { /* ... */ });
  });
```

Summary

- Integration testing determines how units work together.
- EF Core enables the use of lightweight in-memory databases such as SQlite, which are helpful for testing.
- Fake HTTP calls in tests by faking the `HttpMessageHandler`.
- `WebApplicationFactory` enables you to fake a web API end to end.
- Order matters when you register services with dependency injection.
- `WebApplicationFactory` can set the environment, modify configuration, and manipulate dependency injection.

Part 4

Getting ready for release

The previous parts of this book helped you build functional applications with enough tests to give you confidence that your code is correct. This part works on all the other important aspects of developing software with .NET that go beyond functionality.

In chapter 9, you'll evaluate a web service that you already built for security issues. You'll learn about threat modeling and common vulnerabilities. Then you'll authorize functionality in your application so that only authenticated users have access.

Chapter 10 talks about performance, which means measuring, profiling, and investigating performance problems. You'll use performance tools such as BenchmarkDotNet, PerfView, and NBomber. You'll learn why benchmarks are important and how you can analyze profiles to understand performance problems. You'll also get some insight into how garbage collection works.

Chapter 11 discusses common techniques for handling failures. Dependencies can fail for many reasons, so knowing how to apply failure strategies and policies will make your applications more resilient.

If any of your clients uses a different language, date format, or number format or anything else that's culture-dependent, you'll get a lot of useful information from chapter 12. That chapter shows you how to build world-ready applications.

Chapter 13 teaches you how to package your .NET applications in Docker containers. The chapter also covers configuration and secrets, which help you prepare your applications to run outside your development environment.

When you finish this part, you'll understand the breadth of .NET development and know where to go when you need more depth. You'll be ready to build real-world .NET applications!

Security

Most of the software you'll write will be connected to the internet in some way. We've all seen the high-profile data breaches in the news. Even password managers (which you could reasonably expect to be secure) have been compromised. A breach could cost your company not only in reputation and lost customers, but also in ransom money. Although it's impossible to make an application 100 percent secure, you can take a few straightforward approaches to make it harder for attackers to compromise.

> *Security in IT is like locking your house or car. It doesn't stop the bad guys, but if it's good enough, they may move on to an easier target.*
>
> —Paul Herbka, cybersecurity expert

189

9.1   *Securing applications*

A framework or library isn't going to make your application secure. The topic of security is too vast for this book, but I'll cover some of the basics. It's helpful to start with an existing application, explore some of its vulnerabilities, and apply the tools and techniques available in .NET.

In chapter 5, you created a web service for the Manning book catalog. This application is an ASP.NET Core web API using Entity Framework Core (EF Core) to store and retrieve data from a database. The service is insecure, so let's fix that problem. Copy the code to a new folder if you've already built the application; otherwise, grab the code from the supplementary GitHub repo at https://github.com/dmetzgar/dotnet-in-action-code.

Next, we need to make some tweaks so that this project is easier to test. First, rewrite the `CatalogContext` code as shown in the following listing.

Listing 9.1   `CatalogContext` class with options passed in

```
using Microsoft.EntityFrameworkCore;

namespace ManningBooksApi;

public class CatalogContext : DbContext
{
  public DbSet<Book> Books { get; set; } = null!;

  public CatalogContext(DbContextOptions options) :    ⟵── Passes in options
    base(options) { }
}
```

This version of the `DbContext` doesn't control what database is used, and it doesn't have a method to seed the database. To use it correctly, modify the Program.cs file as shown in the following listing.

Listing 9.2   Using Sqlite file database for `CatalogContext`

```
using ManningBooksApi;
using Microsoft.EntityFrameworkCore;

var builder = WebApplication.CreateBuilder(args);

builder.Services.AddDbContext<CatalogContext>(options =>    ⟵── DbContextOptionsBuilder
  options.UseSqlite(
    "DataSource=manningbooks.db;cache=shared"));            ⟵── Uses file-based database

builder.Services.AddControllers();
builder.Services.AddSwaggerGen();                Services are available
                                                 only after building.
var app = builder.Build();    ⟵──┘

                                                          Scope is needed to
using (var scope = app.Services.CreateScope())     ⟵── resolve services.
{
  using (var dbContext = scope.ServiceProvider
    .GetRequiredService<CatalogContext>())         ⟵── Gets the DbContext
  {
```

```
        dbContext.Database.EnsureCreated();     ◁    Ensures that the database
    }                                                schema is applied
}
app.UseHttpsRedirection();
app.MapControllers();
app.UseSwagger();
app.UseSwaggerUI();

app.Run();
```

NOTE A keep-alive connection is required only for the Sqlite in-memory database.

9.2 *Threat modeling*

Threat modeling is a process that reveals some of the vulnerabilities in your architecture. You start by drawing the components, such as services and data sources, and the connections among them. Then you establish your trust boundaries. If you have a service that accesses a database that's not exposed to the outside internet, for example, those two components are within the same trust boundary. If a client calls in to the service from outside your network, that call crosses the trust boundary. Many Microsoft developers (both current and former) use the Microsoft Threat Modeling Tool to analyze the vulnerabilities when crossing trust boundaries.

TIP The Microsoft Threat Modeling Tool is available at http://mng.bz/z8Q6 (Windows only).

The tool not only helps you create the threat model diagram, but also identifies vulnerabilities at each point. With a threat model, you can see how a data source could be accessed; it reminds you of important checks at each point. Consider a typical ASP.NET Core web application that connects to a database. The threat model would look something like figure 9.1.

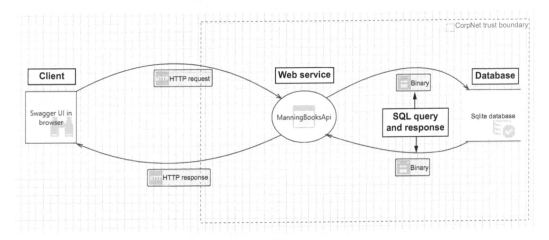

Figure 9.1 A threat model for a web application hosted within a company's network that accesses a database

The figure shows three components: the database (SQlite database), the web service (ManningBooksApi), and the client accessing the service (Swagger UI in browser). A dashed box labeled "CorpNet trust boundary" indicates what components are inside the company's network. The HTTP request sent from the web browser crosses that trust boundary.

The Microsoft tool points out many potential threats even in this simple model. We'll look at ways to implement fixes for the threats that affect our .NET code, including the following:

- JavaScript Object Notation (JSON) processing
- Data flowing across HTTP request/response, which an attacker might sniff or tamper with
- Potential SQL injection vulnerability for SQL database
- Weak database access control
- Elevation using impersonation
- Weak authentication scheme
- Weak web-service access control

The JSON libraries in .NET handle the JSON processing weaknesses. Both `System.Text.Json` and `Newtonsoft.Json` are kept up to date on the latest security problems. But any dependencies you take on your code, such as a NuGet package or the .NET SDK, can contain vulnerabilities. Many sites and services can notify you when new security problems are discovered. The standard term for a security problem is *Common Vulnerabilities and Exposures* (CVEs). CVEs should help you assess whether your code is affected and the level of risk. Following are some sites that can help you keep on top of the latest CVEs:

- *Microsoft Security Update Guide* (https://msrc.microsoft.com/update-guide)— The latest information on vulnerabilities in Microsoft products. .NET and ASP.NET Core and each of their versions are listed as separate products.
- *OpenCVE* (https://www.opencve.io)—A tool for downloading a local copy of the National Vulnerability Database that periodically checks for updates and provides search capabilities.
- *GitHub Dependabot alerts* (http://mng.bz/0GwE)—A bot that scans your GitHub repository for vulnerable dependencies. This tool can be useful for finding out whether a NuGet package you use has a known problem. The bot can also suggest what version to upgrade to.

To patch a vulnerable application, you need to deploy updates safely, which means updating without causing downtime for your users. The requirement seems to be simple. But consider the fact that no downtime during an update means deploying a new version while running the old version. Are database schema changes compatible with both old and new code? Will any behavior changes break user flows? Can you roll back to the old version if a problem occurs? Figuring out how to deploy well is fundamental to fixing security problems quickly.

9.3 **Setting up HTTPS**

The next threat to address is that an attacker might sniff or interfere with data flowing across the HTTP request/response, as shown in figure 9.2. HTTP is unencrypted, and anyone who intercepts the request or response can read it or tamper with it. We can prevent this problem by using HTTPS. (If you wonder why HTTPS isn't the default in ASP.NET Core, you'll learn more in chapter 13.) The secure part—the *S* in *HTTPS*—requires a certificate. For a service or application that's exposed publicly, you'll need a certificate from a trusted authority. This requirement is a bit inconvenient for development, so the .NET command-line interface (CLI) includes a command that installs a development certificate: `dotnet dev-certs https --trust`. (Chapter 3 mentioned development certificates.)

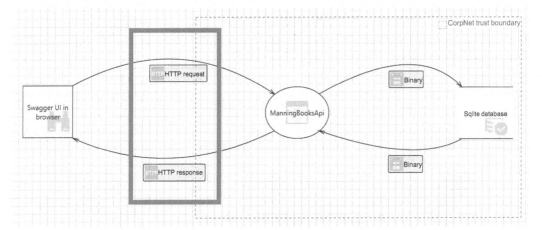

Figure 9.2 The threat model with the HTTP request and response highlighted

The code in the ManningBooksApi application already enables HTTPS. You can see the line `app.UseHttpsRedirection();` in the Program.cs file. This line responds to any HTTP requests with a redirect status code to the same URL in HTTPS. You can test this response by opening your browser's development tools to the Network tab and navigating to http://localhost:<port>/swagger/index.html. The initial response should be a status code `307` with a Location response header that has the HTTPS address.

Status code `307` means "temporary redirect," which seems a bit strange if our application is always going to run as HTTPS. ASP.NET Core intentionally chose temporary redirect over permanent redirect because browsers tend to cache permanent redirects, which can cause problems during development. The application should operate differently in production, though. You have a few options:

- Don't open an HTTP port to your service.
- Put the service behind a proxy such as Istio (https://istio.io), which handles HTTPS and the certificate and then communicates with your service via HTTP.
- Permanently redirect HTTP requests to HTTPS (in production only).

If you choose the redirection route, whether temporary or permanent, ASP.NET Core recommends using the HTTP Strict Transport Security (HSTS) protocol. That way, browsers visiting the site will record that the whole site should be HTTPS instead of testing and caching individual URLs. Put simply, HSTS is a means to tell clients (browsers) that the site they're visiting is accessible only via HTTPS, which it does by including a response header called Strict-Transport-Security.

Browsers caching the fact that the site is HTTPS-only is good for two reasons: less overhead from repeated wasted calls via HTTP and less opportunity for a monster-in-the-middle attack. HTTP requests that are unencrypted are vulnerable to any threat actor that can intercept (and possibly modify) the request before the client receives the redirect signal. HSTS should be enabled only in production and is relatively simple to add, as shown in the following listing.

> **Listing 9.3   Enabling HSTS in production**

```
var app = builder.Build();

if (app.Environment.IsProduction())       ⟵——— Determined by config or env var
{
    app.UseHsts();                  ⟵——— Adds HSTS with default options
}
```

> **WARNING**   The code in listing 9.3 checks specifically for the production environment. Other examples may check whether the environment is *not* development. Many companies have several environments, such as alpha, beta, and preproduction. Because these environments have frequent changes and HSTS has a long-term effect, I prefer not to use HSTS until production. Your service may have multiple production regions, however, in which case you'll want to check for your own production-environment values.

The default settings for HSTS in ASP.NET Core don't use the preload feature. *Preload* is a registry of sites maintained by Google but used by all major web browsers. If you attempt to visit a site with an HTTP address and the browser finds that site on the registry, preload changes the URL to HTTPS without sending the HTTP request and getting the redirect with the HSTS header. You can use a public site to check the preload settings of any domain: https://hstspreload.org. To use preload, configure HSTS in the services collection as shown in the following listing.

> **Listing 9.4   Configuring HSTS**

```
                                            Put before builder.Build().
builder.Services.AddHsts(options =>    ⟵——┘
{                                           Turns on preload
  options.Preload = true;          ⟵——┘
  options.IncludeSubDomains = true;        ⟵——— Includes subdomains of this domain
  options.MaxAge =                            ⟵—┐
    DateTime.UtcNow.AddYears(1) - DateTime.UtcNow;   ⟵—┐   Must be >= 1 year
                                                     │   for preload
                    No TimeSpan.FromYears        ┘
```

```
    options.ExcludedHosts.Add("test.manningcatalog.net");
});
```
Subdomains with
no HSTS header

```
var app = builder.Build();
```

NOTE Listing 9.4 sets the MaxAge to 1 year by adding 1 year to the current time-stamp and subtracting the current timestamp. If you remember from the beginning of chapter 7, the subtraction operator is overloaded for DateTime and produces a TimeSpan object. TimeSpan has methods such as FromSeconds and FromDays but doesn't have a FromYears method. Although we could use TimeSpan.FromDays(365), it would be less than a year every leap year. Technically, we could use the preload's documented minimum of 31,536,000 seconds. Also note that this age doesn't have to match the certificate's expiration.

HSTS preload has many rules because it's a common registry. Also, the registry contents are hardcoded into the Google Chrome browser's source code, which explains the age requirements. Preload is only one feature of HTTPS; we haven't even looked at certificates yet!

TIP To learn more about HSTS, check out the RFC at https://tools.ietf.org/html/rfc6797.

9.4 Checking for SQL injection vulnerability

The next threat on the list is a potential SQL injection vulnerability for the SQL database. This threat involves the database and how the service communicates with it (highlighted in figure 9.3). For a long time, SQL injection was the top vulnerability on the Open Worldwide Application Security Project (OWASP) Top 10 list (https://owasp.org/www-project-top-ten). OWASP is a not-for-profit foundation devoted to software security; it publishes an annual list of the 10 most critical security concerns for web applications. In 2021, SQL injection finally slid from first to third place in the list. Obviously, this problem is still huge, and EF Core does a great job of addressing it. But simply using EF Core won't guarantee that you're immune to injection attacks.

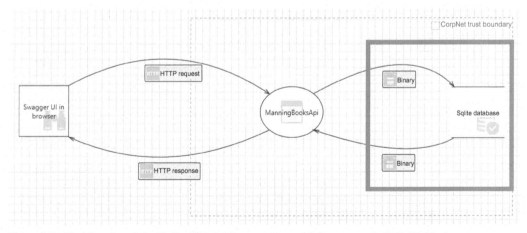

Figure 9.3 The threat model with the SQL database and requests/responses to it highlighted

9.4.1   *Adding an interceptor*

EF Core's DbContext has methods such as FromSqlRaw, FromSqlInterpolated, and Database
.ExecuteSqlCommand that run hand-coded SQL statements. A quick search in the codebase for these methods would be a helpful step in an audit of injection vulnerabilities.
Queries that you write with Language Integrated Query (LINQ) don't use string manipulation, and the EF Core documentation indicates that they're immune to injection
attacks. In my experience, this explanation rarely satisfies database administrators and
security auditors. What we can do is produce a full list of the SQL statements that the
code will execute by using an interceptor. An *interceptor* does what its name implies:
intercepts the SQL generated by EF Core before it's sent to the data store.

   We'll add the interceptor to the DbContext in a test project. The ManningBooksApi
project from chapter 5 didn't have a test project, so we'll have to add one. Use the
commands in the following listing to create the test project.

> **Listing 9.5   Command to create a test project for ManningBooksApi with references**

```
dotnet new xunit --name ManningBooksApi.Tests
cd ManningBooksApi.Tests
dotnet add package Microsoft.EntityFrameworkCore.Relational   ◁──┐  Adds support for
dotnet add reference ../ManningBooksApi/ManningBooksApi.csproj      interceptors
dotnet restore
```

Next, create a file called LogSqlInterceptor.cs, and add the code from the following
listing.

> **Listing 9.6   LogSqlInterceptor logging SQL generated by EF Core**

```
                                         For DbCommand and DbDataReader
using System.Data.Common;                ◁────┐
using Microsoft.EntityFrameworkCore.Diagnostics;   ◁──── For DbCommandInterceptor
using Xunit.Abstractions;                ◁─┐
                                           └─  For ITestOutputHelper
namespace ManningBooksApi.Tests;

public class LogSqlInterceptor : DbCommandInterceptor
{                                              ┌  Keeps output
  private readonly ITestOutputHelper _testOutput;  ◁──┘  with test results

  public LogSqlInterceptor(ITestOutputHelper testOutput)
    => _testOutput = testOutput;
                                               ┌  See the nearby
  public override                              │  sidebar on ValueTask.
    ValueTask<InterceptionResult<DbDataReader>>   ◁──┘
    ReaderExecutingAsync(                      ◁─┐
      DbCommand command,                         └  Called when EF Core uses DbDataReader
      CommandEventData eventData,
      InterceptionResult<DbDataReader> result,
      CancellationToken cancelToken)
  {
```

```
    _testOutput.WriteLine(command.CommandText.Trim());
    return base.ReaderExecutingAsync(
      command, eventData, result, cancelToken);
  }
}
```

◁————— **Writes SQL to test output**

Executes command on reader

Using ITestOutputHelper to write test logs instead of Console

In listing 9.6, the interceptor writes the SQL text to an `ITestOutputHelper` because using `Console.WriteLine` to get test output is problematic. xUnit typically runs tests in parallel, so console output will overlap between tests. Also, if you're using some build automation system to run tests, `ITestOutputHelper` will associate the output with its respective test.

ValueTask vs. Task

The `DbCommandInterceptor.ReaderExecutingAsync` method returns a `ValueTask` instead of a `Task`. `ValueTask` is used for async methods that are expected to perform synchronous work, which makes sense in the interceptor case because the usual purpose is to manipulate the SQL. Stephen Toub wrote an excellent article on `ValueTask` (http://mng.bz/KZBg), in which he lists some use cases for it:

- You expect consumers of your API to `await` the method directly (as opposed to passing back the `Task`, as we've done in this book).
- Allocation-related overhead is important to avoid for your API.
- You expect synchronous completion to be a common case, or you can pool objects effectively for use with asynchronous completion.

In most cases, the performance benefit of using `ValueTask` instead of `Task` isn't enough when weighed against the additional complexity of using it properly. For that reason, I avoid using `ValueTask` in this book except when a dependency requires it.

The next step is writing some tests. The ManningBooksApi doesn't divide its code neatly into easily testable units, and it would take too long (and too many pages) to refactor it. Luckily, ASP.NET Core relies on dependency injection, which means that we can create a `DbContext` in the test class and pass it to the `CatalogController`. Give the UnitTest1.cs file created by the template a new name, CatalogControllerTests.cs, and add the code from the following listing.

Listing 9.7   Writing test logs with `ITestOutputHelper`

```
using ManningBooksApi.Controllers;
using Microsoft.Data.Sqlite;
using Microsoft.EntityFrameworkCore;
using Xunit.Abstractions;

namespace ManningBooksApi.Tests;
```

```
public class CatalogControllerTests : IDisposable
{
  private const string ConnStr =
    "DataSource=test;mode=memory;cache=shared";
  private readonly CatalogContext _catalogContext;
  private readonly SqliteConnection _keepAliveConn;
  private readonly CatalogController _controller;

  public CatalogControllerTests(ITestOutputHelper testOutput)
  {
    _keepAliveConn = new(ConnStr);
    _keepAliveConn.Open();

    var optionsBuilder = new DbContextOptionsBuilder();
    optionsBuilder
      .AddInterceptors(new LogSqlInterceptor(testOutput))
      .UseSqlite(ConnStr);
    _catalogContext = new(optionsBuilder.Options);
    Assert.True(_catalogContext.Database.EnsureCreated());
    _controller = new(_catalogContext);
  }

  [Fact]
  public async Task GetBook()
  {
    SeedBooks();
    var book = await _controller.GetBook(1);
    Assert.NotNull(book);
  }

  public void Dispose()
  {
    _keepAliveConn.Close();
    _catalogContext.Dispose();
  }

  private void SeedBooks()
  {
    _catalogContext.Add(new Book("Grokking Simplicity"));
    _catalogContext.Add(new Book("API Design Patterns"));
    var efBook = new Book("EF Core in Action");
    efBook.Ratings.Add(new Rating { Comment = "Great!" });
    efBook.Ratings.Add(new Rating { Stars = 4 });
    _catalogContext.Add(efBook);
    _catalogContext.SaveChanges();
  }
}
```

Annotations:
- Test still uses an in-memory database.
- Needs a keep-alive connection for the in-memory database
- Interceptor added via builder
- Creates controller
- Adds some books to the database
- Gets the first book (1-based index)
- Makes sure that the book exists
- Stolen from old CatalogContext code

When you run the tests with dotnet test, by default, you won't see the test output on the command line. To see the test output, add the command-line parameter --logger "console;verbosity=detailed". Now you should see EF Core's SQL statements in the output, as shown in the following listing.

Listing 9.8 SQL statement generated by EF Core to get a `Book` by its `ID`

```
SELECT "b"."Id", "b"."Description", "b"."Title"
FROM "Books" AS "b"
WHERE "b"."Id" = @__id_0          ◄────  Id as parameter
LIMIT 1
```

In this SQL statement, we see that EF Core uses parameters, which prevents a user from passing in values that try to hijack the SQL statement. If EF Core constructed the SQL statement by concatenating strings and using the raw parameter values, the service would be open to SQL injection attacks. Suppose that we have an API that searches for a book by title but doesn't check the contents of the title argument and doesn't use SQL parameters. Someone could pass in a string like `atitle'); DELETE FROM Books; --` that would result in an SQL query, as shown in the following listing.

Listing 9.9 Example SQL injection attack on a query that searches for a book by title

```
SELECT "b"."Id", "b"."Description", "b"."Title"                    ┐ Unchecked
FROM "Books" AS "b"                                                │ title string
WHERE "b"."Title" LIKE '%atitle'); DELETE FROM Books; --%'  ◄──────┘
LIMIT 1
```

Attackers don't need to know your table schema ahead of time. They could try different combinations of inputs until they see strange behavior such as an exception or error. Then they can try querying the table schema and eventually get to the point where they can extract sensitive data from your database and hold it for ransom. Even if the database contains no sensitive data, attackers can delete data, add garbage, drop tables, and generally cause harm.

Least privilege for connection strings
Full-featured databases have configurable authorization. One user might have full access to create schemas, and another might have read-only access on one schema in one database. Your application needs to authenticate with the database in some way, usually with a user ID or machine key. That user should be authorized to do only what they need to do—no more. This authorization could help stop an attacker from dropping tables or getting a list of users.

In some cases, EF Core doesn't use parameters. Consider the example code in the following listing.

Listing 9.10 EF Core query that produces SQL without parameters

```
List<string> titles = new List<string>() {      ◄──── List of titles to search for
   "Robert'); DROP TABLE Students;--",          ◄──┐
   "Book", "Grokking Simplicity" };                 │ XKCD's "Bobby Tables"
return _dbContext.Books.FirstOrDefaultAsync(
   b => titles.Contains(b.Title));              ◄──── Checks whether the title is in the list
```

EF Core produces the SQL shown in the following listing.

Listing 9.11   SQL produced by EF Core when using the code from listing 9.10

```
SELECT "b"."Id", "b"."Description", "b"."Title"
FROM "Books" AS "b"
WHERE "b"."Title" IN
  ('Robert''); DROP TABLE Students;--',     ⟵———— Escaped string
  'Book', 'Grokking Simplicity')
LIMIT 1
```

Before EF Core 8, developers had no good way to pass in an array via parameters. They had options such as creating a temp table, but this approach is fragile and has overhead. (If you need to use it, however, you can find a NuGet package called `EFCore.BulkExtensions`.) Although I'm certain that the EF team has spent a lot of time figuring out how to escape a string correctly, I'm not as certain that every community-contributed EF Core database provider has been as rigorous—a good reason to watch for CVEs. Also, keep in mind that because the query is different based on the contents of the list, the query plan is less likely to be cached in the database, which produces a slight performance penalty.

In EF Core 8, however, databases such as SQL Server can pass a list in a parameter. The trick is that EF Core 8 uses a JSON data type; it can pass in the list in JSON format, and the SQL query will parse the JSON to create a list. The following listing shows an example of this type of query.

Listing 9.12   EF Core 8 SQL query using JSON for list parameter

```
SELECT "b"."Id", "b"."Description", "b"."Title"
FROM "Books" AS "b"
WHERE EXISTS (
    SELECT 1
    FROM OPENJSON(@__titles_0) AS [t]     ⟵———— Converts JSON to table
    WHERE [t].[value] = [b].[Title])
LIMIT 1
```

The `LogSqlInterceptor` overrides the `ReaderExecutingAsync` method and won't get called if the LINQ query is synchronous. To get all the SQL queries produced by EF Core, override the other methods, including the following:

- `ReaderExecuting`
- `NonQueryExecuting`
- `NonQueryExecutingAsync`
- `ScalarExecuting`
- `ScalarExecutingAsync`

With this interceptor, you can get a sample of the SQL queries produced by your application. This sample is helpful for security audits for injection vulnerabilities and for performance optimization by looking for inefficient queries or places to add indexes. The tests here use SQlite, so everything can be in memory, which is a good analogue for other SQL databases, but the SQL generated for the production database may be different. The interceptor could be turned on via a feature flag, used to detect unrecognized SQL queries, or enabled only for end-to-end (E2E) testing with a real database.

TIP Don't try optimizing queries by starting with the SQL. Instead, build performance tests that stress the application (see chapter 10). Then use tools like SQL profilers to identify ill-performing queries. Cloud databases usually have dashboards that surface performance problems. When you find a query to investigate, you can match it to the interceptor output to find it in the code.

Exercise 1: Implementing remaining interceptor methods

The SQL statements generated by EF Core reveal nuances of the database and can show inefficient LINQ queries. Implement the remaining interceptor methods to record the SQL to the test output. Create some tests that create, update, and delete books and ratings in the catalog.

Exercise 2: Use Verify test library to check for SQL changes

You may have some SQL queries that have an outsized effect on your application's performance. You've spent time making sure that the database indexes are correct and the query plans are optimized. But another developer might unwittingly change the LINQ query, producing a different SQL query that misses an index, or they might change a schema and drop a table column or return a value in a response that could pose a security vulnerability. This vulnerability might not be discovered until the code is deployed to a full-scale environment like production. (All these scenarios have happened to me.)

A tool can make this sort of vulnerability a little easier to catch in code review. The Verify test library (https://github.com/VerifyTests/Verify) compares the output of a test from one run to another and fails the test if a change occurs. If you take the SQL queries captured by an interceptor and write them to a stream, Verify can compare that stream with the accepted version and flag any changes, forcing the change author and code reviewers to acknowledge the SQL change. This tool isn't a foolproof way to prevent SQL problems, but it can help.

Take a look at the documentation for the `Verify.EntityFramework` extension at http://mng.bz/9dKq. A feature called Recording records all SQL queries made (probably using an interceptor as we did). Add the `Verify.EntityFramework` extension to the tests in `CatalogControllerTests`; then adjust the LINQ queries to see how this change affects the SQL.

9.4.2   *Configuring the connection string safely*

The next threat we'll address is weak database-access control. The threat model describes this threat as follows: "Improper data protection of SQlite database can allow an attacker to read information not intended for disclosure. Review authorization settings." So far, we've hardcoded the database connection string. This practice isn't acceptable in production, however, as each environment has its own database with its own connection string. But we need a way to provide the connection string without exposing it to attackers.

The most common way to get the connection string in the code is via configuration, but if the string contains a password, we can't put it in the appsettings.json file. At every company where I've worked, accidentally checking in a password usually results in a lot of annoying work to change the password on the target resource, as well as all the places where that password is stored or used, in addition to cleaning up the Git history. Remember that access to the Git repository (Git has replaced every other source control by now, right?) is a threat vector, whether the threat comes from outside hackers or unscrupulous employees.

In production environments, the continuous deployment (CD) pipeline usually grabs the secrets from a secure store and puts them in a place that the application can access. Kubernetes, for example, has secrets that pods can access. We'll explore how secrets are exposed to applications in a container environment in chapter 13. One method of providing secrets to applications involves environment variables. Azure App Services, for example, allows secrets to be accessed through environment variables. Environment variables are also an option in Kubernetes but no longer recommended because they're less secure than secrets.

The production environment's method of handling secrets is a bit cumbersome for local development, which is why the .NET CLI has commands for managing secrets that keeps them out of your code. The Secret Manager tool has to be initialized in your project. From the ManningBooksApi project directory, run the command `dotnet user-secrets init`. (Visual Studio users can right-click the project and choose Manage User Secrets from the shortcut menu.) This command adds a `UserSecretsId` property to the csproj file. The value of this field is an uninteresting Globally Unique Identifier (GUID) that can be checked in to your code repository safely and used by other developers. The GUID refers to a secret file stored on your machine.

> **WARNING** Connecting to a database with a secret (such as username and password) adds extra risk. It's best to avoid handling secrets where possible because there are safer ways to connect to a database. The most prevalent method in the past was to use integrated security, which connected to the database with the identity that the application's process was running in. .NET Framework developers usually hosted their applications in Internet Information Services (IIS). IIS could run the application in its web server under an Active Directory (AD) domain account. In newer versions of .NET, the application is more often hosted in a container running on a Linux host (which

can still use AD through Kerberos, but it's more difficult to set up). Options for managing identities vary depending on the hosting environment and the database. If you're ready to move on from username/password, the best way to start is to look at the database client documentation.

Let's add our connection string to the secrets file, using the statement from the ManningBooksApi project directory in the following listing.

> **Listing 9.13 Adds the connection string to Secret Manager for ManningBooksApi project**

```
dotnet user-secrets set "ConnectionStrings:Catalog"
  "DataSource=manningbooks.db;cache=shared"
```

Now modify the AddDbContext statement in Program.cs to get the connection string from the secret, as shown in the following listing.

```
var builder = WebApplication.CreateBuilder(args);      Gets Configuration
var config = builder.Configuration;            ◁───── object, also used later

builder.Services.AddDbContext<CatalogContext>(options =>
{                                              Gets Catalog from
  var connStr = config.GetConnectionString("Catalog");  ◁── ConnectionStrings section
  options.UseSqlite(connStr);
});
```

Access to the configuration depends on where the code is. In this case, the application has not been built, so we use the builder object. An IConfiguration object can also be passed in via dependency injection. The defaults for ASP.NET Core configuration include appsettings.json, environment variables, and user secrets. In chapter 13, we'll explore how to use secrets in container environments.

9.5 ASP.NET Core Identity

We've ensured that we're not allowing SQL injection and that our connection string is secure. But anybody can call the APIs and do anything they want. This scenario is one in which two more threats—elevation using impersonation and weak authentication scheme—take effect (figure 9.4). The Manning catalog should allow only authenticated users to access its API. ASP.NET Core comes with a prebuilt authentication and authorization system called ASP.NET Core Identity. Identity is another vast subject, even in ASP.NET Core alone, but we can simplify it by not handling user accounts ourselves.

I think that in many authentication guides, tutorials, and blogs, the approach is to create a website with a login/sign-up section. Then we're walked through the various steps of using ASP.NET Core Identity to create a new user with a hashed and salted password. My concern about introducing authentication this way is that we're encouraged to have our users create yet another username-and-password combination, which itself is a threat vector. Even though ASP.NET Core Identity handles the hard work of hashing

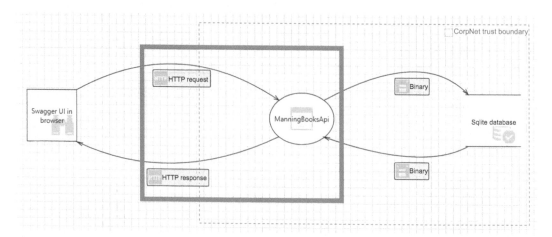

Figure 9.4   The threat model with the HTTP request/response and the web service highlighted

and salting the password so that our users will never have their passwords compromised, it still stores all the user data: name, email address, and potentially other forms of personally identifiable information (PII) such as phone numbers for multifactor authentication. So if a hacker gets access to our database, our users are exposed.

I'd rather show how to use OpenID Connect because it applies broadly across many identity providers: Microsoft, Facebook, X, Auth0, Okta, and so on. OpenID Connect has a complex and storied history that's impossible to do justice to here. The important point for our purposes is that this specification allows a client of any type to get authentication information about users. This arrangement allows us to offload the burden of managing user accounts to an external identity provider; then we can focus on verifying that the token presented to us in the request is correct, which ASP.NET Core Identity will help us do. Our web API has to worry only about the authentication tokens, which usually come in JSON Web Token (JWT) format.

> **TIP**   To dive further into OpenID Connect, read the Manning book on the subject: *OpenID Connect in Action*, by Prabath Siriwardena (https://www.manning.com/books/openid-connect-in-action).

The first step is adding the NuGet package that allows us to authenticate JWTs. Run the command `dotnet add package Microsoft.AspNetCore.Authentication.JwtBearer`. Then modify the ManningBooksApi application to require the request to come from an authenticated user. Add the lines from the following listing to Program.cs to turn on authentication and authorization, both of which are needed for authentication.

Listing 9.15   Adding authentication and authorization

```
using Microsoft.AspNetCore.Authentication.JwtBearer;     ◁──── Needed for JWT types

builder.Services
```

```
.AddAuthentication(
    JwtBearerDefaults.AuthenticationScheme)    ⟵—— Sets Bearer scheme as the default
.AddJwtBearer();                               ⟵
                                                    ⌐ JWT auth scheme (defaults to bearer)

var app = builder.Build();         ⟵
                                       ⌐ Provided to show relative position

app.UseAuthentication();    ⟵
app.UseAuthorization();  ⟵             ⌐ Enables authentication

                               ⌐ Enables authorization
```

> ## Schemes
>
> The term *scheme* as used by ASP.NET Core Identity is a bit confusing. The HTTP protocol has its own list of authentication schemes: basic, bearer, digest, NTLM, and so on. Schemes in ASP.NET Core Identity don't match the HTTP schemes. I could have several JWT bearer schemes configured that allow different bearer tokens, such as Microsoft or Google. All those schemes need different names so that they can be listed in the authorization policies (see section 9.6). The fact that `JwtBearerDefaults` `.AuthenticationScheme` has the value `Bearer` is unintentionally confusing. You can name the scheme whatever you want, but be sure to set the name in the `AddJwtBearer` method.

Next, add the `Authorize` custom attribute to the `CatalogController`, as shown in the following listing.

> **Listing 9.16   Turning on authorization for the `CatalogController`**

```
[ApiController]
[Route("[controller]")]
[Authorize]                           ⟵——— Add this line.
public class CatalogController : ControllerBase
{ /*...*/ }
```

Try running the application and navigating to the Swagger UI at https://localhost :<port>/swagger/index.html. Choose the `Get` method with no parameters to get the full list of books. Click Try It Out and Execute. The response should be a `401` status code (meaning unauthorized) with the response header `www-authenticate: Bearer`. This header indicates that the method is looking for an `Authenticate` header in the request, using the `Bearer` type.

> ## Authentication vs. authorization
>
> In simple terms, *authentication* is who you are, and *authorization* is what you're allowed to do. Authorization doesn't always require authentication. I could have a policy that anonymous users are allowed to access certain parts of my application. But if I restrict a portion of an application to registered users, I need the user to prove that they have registered (via authentication). OpenID Connect is mainly about authentication (with the exception that scopes in the token can be considered to be a form of authorization).

> **(continued)**
> In ASP.NET Core, the lines between authentication and authorization can be blurry. To prevent anonymous users from using the `CatalogController`, for example, we have to tell ASP.NET Core Identity to authorize the controller's access. The default authorization is to check that the user is authenticated.

TIP Getting ASP.NET Core Identity to do what you want may take a lot of research, not to mention trial and error. If you want to get deeper into the subject, check out Manning's *ASP.NET Core Security*, by Christian Wenz (https://www.manning.com/books/asp-net-core-security).

9.5.1 *Setting up Microsoft authentication*

This section shows how to set up an application registration in an Azure Active Directory (AD) tenant for OpenID Connect and the Swagger UI. The section is optional because it requires signing up with Microsoft Azure. Instead, you can use your company's OpenID Connect provider (if it has one) or sign up for a free Auth0 or Okta account. Another option is to set up your own identity provider by using Duende Software's Identity Server (https://github.com/DuendeSoftware/IdentityServer) or OpenIddict (https://documentation.openiddict.com).

> **TIP**   If you need more context on setting up an Azure account, Azure AD tenant, or the application in Azure AD, Microsoft has a comprehensive guide at http://mng.bz/jXy8.

For this example, I'll assume that you have an Azure account and an Azure AD tenant. Both are available for free for limited development use, which is fine for our purposes. Follow these steps to register the application:

1 Navigate to the Azure portal in your browser (https://portal.azure.com).
2 On the search bar, type **app registrations**, and click the App Registrations link that appears.
3 Click *New Registration*.
4 Enter a name for the registration, which can be anything.
5 Set the supported account type to Accounts in This Organizational Directory Only.
6 **Do not** enter a redirect URI yet; you'll do that later.
7 Click *Register*.
8 On the application's registration Overview page, copy the client and tenant IDs to the appsettings.json file, as shown in listing 9.17.

Figure 9.5 shows images for steps 2–8.

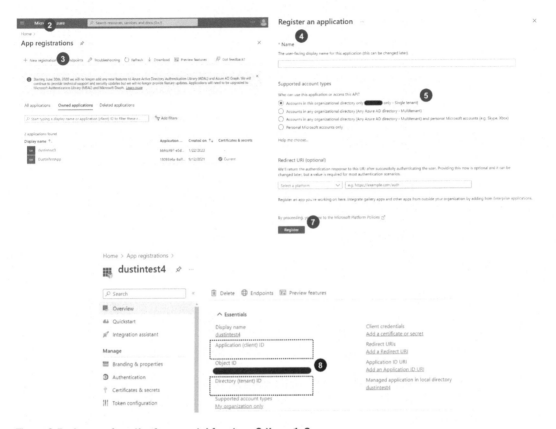

Figure 9.5   Images from the Azure portal for steps 2 through 8

Listing 9.17   Adding Authentication section to appsettings.json

```
{
  "Authentication": {
    "Microsoft": {
      "ClientId": "<clientid>",
      "TenantId": "<tenantid>"
    }
  }
}
```

9   Go to the *Expose an API* section.

10   Click *Add a Scope*.

11   The portal first tells you that you need to set an Application ID URI, which is usually api://<client id>.

12   Click *Save and Continue*.

13   Enter a scope name, which can be anything.

14   Set *Who Can Consent?* to *Admins and Users*.

15 In the *Admin Consent Display Name* and *Admin Consent Description section,* type whatever you want.

16 Click *Add Scope.*

Figure 9.6 shows images for steps 9–16.

Figure 9.6   Images from the Azure portal for steps 9 through 16

17 Go to the *Manifest* section.

18 Find the accessTokenAcceptedVersion setting and change its value to 2.

19 Click *Save.*

20 Go to the *Authentication* section.

21 Click *Add a Platform.*

22 Choose *Single-Page Application.*

(The Swagger UI could be considered to be an SPA.)

23 Set the *Redirect URI* to https://localhost:<port>/swagger/oauth2-redirect.html.

24 Check the boxes for both *Access Tokens* and *ID Tokens.*

25 Click the *Configure* button.

Figure 9.7 shows images for steps 17–25.

You're all done! You completed a lot of steps, so be sure to check your work against the figures. The name of the scope you created doesn't matter, but a custom scope must exist for Azure AD to issue a valid JWT (a quirk of Azure AD). On step 18, you set the accessTokenAcceptedVersion to 2. This setting seems weird, but its purpose is that older versions of Azure AD tokens were signed by a different issuer (another quirk of Azure AD). The issuer for the access token is supposed to match the authority in the OpenID configuration document; otherwise, the token will be considered to be invalid.

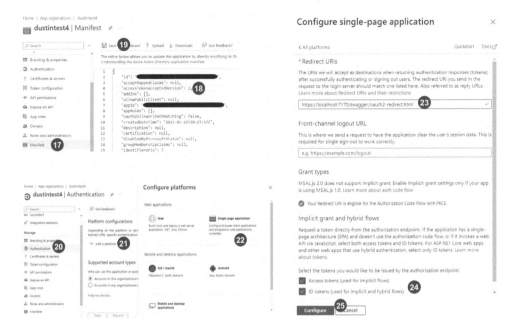

Figure 9.7   Images from the Azure portal for steps 17 through 25

The OpenID Connect specification allows some leeway in how access tokens are implemented, and some vendors take advantage of that fact. Google, for example, doesn't use JWT format for its access tokens. Microsoft does use JWT, but it also places a *nonce* (number used only once) in the header that makes the JWT invalid to everyone but Microsoft. Google and Microsoft do these things because the tokens are meant for accessing their own properties; using their tokens for your application requires some custom settings. ASP.NET Core Identity has authentication mechanisms for Microsoft, Google, and other identity providers that hide some of the complexity. We'll focus on generic JWT bearer authentication, which applies more broadly.

9.5.2   *Authenticating with Swagger UI*

Now that we've turned on authentication for the Catalog API, the Swagger UI needs to authenticate. Swagger UI is capable of authenticating as long as you provide enough information. A bit of complex coding is involved, so let's isolate that part into its own helper class. Create a new file called MsAuthHelper.cs in the ManningBooksApi project, and add the code from the following listing.

Listing 9.18   Setting up Swagger UI to communicate with Azure AD

```
using Microsoft.AspNetCore.Authentication.JwtBearer;
using Microsoft.OpenApi.Models;

namespace ManningBooksApi;
```

```
public static class MsAuthHelper
{
  private const string UrlPrefix =                        ⟵  AAD login base URL
    "https://login.microsoftonline.com/";
  private const string TenantIdConfig =                   ⟵  Location of tenant ID in appsettings
    "Authentication:Microsoft:TenantId";
  private const string ClientIdConfig =                   ⟵  Location of client ID in appsettings
    "Authentication:Microsoft:ClientId";
                                                          ⟵  Defines a flow for Swagger UI
  public static OpenApiOAuthFlow GetImplicitFlow(
    IConfiguration config,                                ⟵  Needs the configuration
    params string[] extraScopes)
    {                                                     ⟵  List of custom scopes
      var tenantId = GetTenantId(config);
      var scopes = new Dictionary<string, string>() {     ⟵  Dictionary of scope
        { "openid", "" },                                     name to description
        { "profile", "" },                               ⟵  Standard scopes
        { "email", "" }
      };
      foreach (var extraScope in extraScopes)
      {
        scopes.Add(extraScope, "");
      }

      return new OpenApiOAuthFlow {
        AuthorizationUrl = new Uri(                       ⟵  Get from discovery
          $"{UrlPrefix}{tenantId}/oauth2/v2.0/authorize"),    document
        TokenUrl = new Uri(                              ⟵
          $"{UrlPrefix}{tenantId}/oauth2/v2.0/token"),
        Scopes = scopes,
      };
    }

  public static string GetTenantId(IConfiguration config)
    => config.GetValue<string>(TenantIdConfig);

  public static string GetClientId(IConfiguration config)
    => config.GetValue<string>(ClientIdConfig);

  public static string AddScopePrefix(
    this string scopeName, IConfiguration config)         ⟵  Helper for custom
    => $"api://{GetClientId(config)}/{scopeName}";            scope name

  public static JwtBearerOptions ValidateMs(              ⟵  Helper for JwtBearerOptions
    this JwtBearerOptions options,
    IConfiguration config)
  {
    options.Authority =                                  ⟵  Must match token
      $"{UrlPrefix}{GetTenantId(config)}/v2.0";              issuer (iss claim)
    options.Audience = GetClientId(config);              ⟵
    return options;                                         Must match token
  }                                                         audience (aud claim)
}
```

> **What is a discovery document?**
>
> The OpenID Connect specification indicates that an identity provider must provide a publicly accessible document that indicates all the important configuration. This document contains a list of important URLs, scopes available, and so on. Microsoft's document for social accounts, for example, is available at https://login.microsoftonline.com/consumers/v2.0/.well-known/openid-configuration. The Swagger UI configuration can take a discovery document instead of specifying URLs explicitly like the `authorize` and `token` URLs configured in listing 9.18. When you take this approach, the flows aren't configurable, so this book doesn't use it.

With the helper method defined, the next step is configuring the authentication and the Swagger UI. Add the lines from the following listing to Program.cs.

Listing 9.19   Lines to add to Program.cs to configure authentication and the Swagger UI

```
using Microsoft.OpenApi.Models;

builder.Services.AddControllers();              ← Provided to show relative position
builder.Services.AddSwaggerGen(options => {     ← Configures the Swagger UI
  var scheme = new OpenApiSecurityScheme() {
    Name = "Authorization",                      ← OpenID Connect is built on OAuth 2.0.
    Type = SecuritySchemeType.OAuth2,           ←
    Scheme = JwtBearerDefaults.AuthenticationScheme,   ← HTTP bearer auth scheme
    BearerFormat = "JWT",                        ←
    In = ParameterLocation.Header,              Bearer token format
    Flows = new OpenApiOAuthFlows {
      Implicit = MsAuthHelper.GetImplicitFlow(  ← Enables only implicit flow
        config,
        "somescope".AddScopePrefix(config))     ← Name of your custom scope
    }
  };
  options.AddSecurityDefinition("token", scheme);   ← Definition name must match.
  options.AddSecurityRequirement(
    new OpenApiSecurityRequirement { {          ← Dictionary
      new OpenApiSecurityScheme {
        Reference = new OpenApiReference {
          Type = ReferenceType.SecurityScheme,
          Id = "token",                          ←
        }                                        Definition name must match.
      },
      Array.Empty<string>()
    }
  });
});

builder.Services
  .AddAuthentication(
    JwtBearerDefaults.AuthenticationScheme)      Uses custom
  .AddJwtBearer(options => options.ValidateMs(config));   ← JWT config

var app = builder.Build();                       ← Provided to show relative position
```

Where to put bearer token — `In = ParameterLocation.Header,`

When the code is in place, try running the application. In this example, dotnet watch run may not pick up the code changes, so it's better to stop the application and use dotnet run. Navigate to the Swagger UI (https://localhost:<port>/swagger/index .html). You'll notice a new Authorize button. Click that button to bring up the authorization dialog box, and configure it as shown in figure 9.8. The client_id field should match the client ID you copied to the appsettings.json file. Select all the scopes, which should include the custom scope you added to the registration. Then click Authorize. A new browser tab should open to allow you to log in to your Microsoft account. You also need to approve the application to get access to your account. When you finish those tasks, you should return to the Swagger UI, and the authorization dialog box will close. Try Get API again, and instead of a 401, you should see a 200 status code and a response, which means that you've authenticated successfully!

Figure 9.8   Swagger UI authorization dialog

Be mindful of using Swagger UI in production

Swagger UI has been known to have vulnerabilities. This fact doesn't mean that there are vulnerabilities in Swagger or OpenAPI, which is a standardized way of communicating your API schema. If you don't need to expose Swagger UI to your customers, it's better to turn it off in production. (Run app.UseSwaggerUI() if the environment is set to Development.) Otherwise, keep on top of CVEs for Swagger UI in case exploits are discovered so that you can patch quickly.

> ### Exercise 3: Store client and tenant ID in Secret Manager tool
>
> Although the client and tenant ID of your Azure AD application may not be secrets, they could be different for each environment, including for each developer working on the application. Add the client and tenant ID to user secrets instead of configuring them in the appsettings.json file.

9.6 Authorization

The last threat vector we'll look at in this chapter is weak web-service access control, which affects the highlighted section in figure 9.9. This threat involves a user's permissions to read or modify the application data. In section 9.5, we enforced a rule that only authenticated users can access the Controller API. But anyone on our Azure AD instance can read, add, update, or delete any of the books in the catalog. If we want to limit the ability to modify the catalog to a certain group of people, we need to introduce authorization.

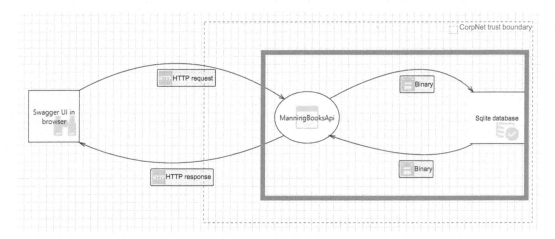

Figure 9.9 The threat model with the web service and database highlighted

For this experiment, suppose that any authenticated user can get books, but only you (the developer) can create, update, or delete. We'll need to remove the `Authorize` custom attribute from the `CatalogController` class and mark each method individually. To distinguish between the two cases (authenticated versus you), we'll need to specify different authorization policies. Authorization policies are indicated by name. To see how this technique works, modify the `Authorize` custom attributes as shown in the following listing.

Listing 9.20 Controller action-level authorization

```
[ApiController]
[Route("[controller]")]
```

```
public class CatalogController : ControllerBase          ◄─┐  Removes Authorize
{                                                          │  attribute here
  [HttpGet]
  [Authorize("AuthenticatedUsers")]                      ◄─┐
  public IAsyncEnumerable<Book> GetBooks(                  │  Read-only
      string? titleFilter = null)                          │  policy
  { /*...*/ }                                              │
                                                           │
  [HttpGet("{id}")]                                        │
  [Authorize("AuthenticatedUsers")]                      ◄─┘
  public Task<Book?> GetBook(int id)
  { /*...*/ }

  [HttpPost]
  [Authorize("OnlyMe")]                                  ◄─┐
  public async Task<Book> CreateBook(                      │
    BookCreateCommand command)                             │
  { /*...*/ }                                              │
                                                           │
  [HttpPatch("{id}")]                                      │
  [ProducesResponseType(StatusCodes.Status404NotFound)]    │
  [ProducesResponseType(StatusCodes.Status204NoContent)]   │
  [Authorize("OnlyMe")]                                  ◄─┤  Read-write
  public async Task<IActionResult> UpdateBook(             │  policy
    int id, BookUpdateCommand command)                     │
  { /*...*/ }                                              │
                                                           │
  [HttpDelete("{id}")]                                     │
  [ProducesResponseType(StatusCodes.Status404NotFound)]    │
  [ProducesResponseType(StatusCodes.Status204NoContent)]   │
  [Authorize("OnlyMe")]                                  ◄─┘
  public async Task<IActionResult> DeleteBook(int id)
  { /*...*/ }
}
```

The next step is figuring out how to determine whether the authenticated user is you. We can look at the contents of the bearer token to see what information is available. If you run the application before making the changes in listing 9.20, browse to the Swagger UI, authenticate, open the browser's developer tools to the Network tab, and call a Get method. You should see a request to the CatalogController. In that request is an authorize header containing the word Bearer followed by a long string of base 64-encoded data. Copy the base 64 data, and open a JWT decoder tool like JWT.io (https://jwt.io) to view the contents.

WARNING Many good JWT decoder tools are available, such as DevToys (https://devtoys.app); JWT.io; jwt.ms (https://jwt.ms); and my favorite, JWT Decoder, Verifier, Generator, Decryptor (https://dinochiesa.github.io/jwt). All the browser tools indicate clearly that any data you paste into the site doesn't get transmitted to a backend service. But you have no guarantee that these sites won't be compromised in the future. A safer bet is DevToys, which is an open source desktop application. The JWT may contain PII; worse, it's valid until the expiration date, and an attacker can use it to impersonate you.

The JWT is like a JSON object divided into the three parts: header, payload, and signature. The header indicates the type of token and what algorithm was used to sign it. The signature is compared to the signing key (made available from a link in the discovery document) and can be used to ensure that the token's contents weren't tampered with. The payload is like an object in which every property is called a *claim*. Following are a few interesting claims:

- `aud` (Audience)—The client for which the token was intended. It allows the recipient of the token to detect whether the token was meant for it or may have been stolen from another client.
- `iss` (Issuer)—The authority that created the token.
- `nbf` (Not before)—Timestamp noting that the token can't be used until at least this timestamp.
- `iat` (Issued at)—Timestamp showing when the token was created.
- `exp` (Expiration)—Timestamp showing when the token expires.
- `sub` (Subject)—Often, the ID of the user whom the token represents.
- `preferred_username`—A custom Azure AD claim that contains the username (usually, the email address).

You can get the `preferred_username` claim from the token and use it to determine whether it matches your Microsoft account's email address. But first, you need access to the token. Also, this check must be done for the `OnlyMe` authorization policy. Let's establish our two policies by adding the lines from the following listing to Program.cs.

Listing 9.21 Creating authorization policies

```
using Microsoft.AspNetCore.Authorization;

builder.Services.AddAuthorization(options =>        ◁──── AuthorizationOptions
{
    options.AddPolicy("AuthenticatedUsers",          ◁──── Read-only policy
      policyBuilder => {                             ◁──── AuthorizationPolicyBuilder
        policyBuilder
          .RequireAuthenticatedUser()               ◁──── User must be authenticated.
          .AddAuthenticationSchemes(                 ◁──┐
            JwtBearerDefaults.AuthenticationScheme);    │ Auth scheme to use for this policy
      });
    options.AddPolicy("OnlyMe",          ◁──── Read-write policy
      policyBuilder => {
        policyBuilder
          .RequireAuthenticatedUser()
          .AddAuthenticationSchemes(
            JwtBearerDefaults.AuthenticationScheme)
          .AddRequirements(new OnlyMeRequirement());   ◁──── Adds a requirement
      });
});
builder.Services.AddSingleton<IAuthorizationHandler,   ◁──┐ Registers requirement
  OnlyMeRequirementHandler>();                            │ handler(s)
                                          ◁──── Handles OnlyMeRequirement
var app = builder.Build();    ◁──── Provided to show relative position
```

Multiple policies can use the same scheme. *(annotation pointing to `.AddAuthenticationSchemes(` in the first policy)*

The default policy when `AuthorizationOptions` isn't specified is `RequireAuthenticate-dUser` with the default authentication scheme. We established in section 9.5 that the default authentication scheme is `JwtBearerDefaults.AuthenticationScheme`. Now that we need named authorization policies, we have to add those policies as shown in listing 9.21. The `OnlyMe` policy has an extra requirement that we need to create. Create a new file called OnlyMeRequirement.cs, and add the code from the following listing.

Listing 9.22   Custom authorization requirement and handler

```
using Microsoft.AspNetCore.Authorization;

namespace ManningBooksApi;
                                                    Requirement class needs to exist.
public class OnlyMeRequirement :        ←
  IAuthorizationRequirement { }           ←——— Empty interface

public class OnlyMeRequirementHandler :
  AuthorizationHandler<OnlyMeRequirement>     ←——— Handles the OnlyMeRequirement
{
  protected override Task HandleRequirementAsync(   ←——— Only one method to override
    AuthorizationHandlerContext context,         ←
    OnlyMeRequirement requirement)                 Has some request context
  {
    if (context.User != null)        ←——— If user is authenticated . . .
    {
      var emailClaim = context.User
        .FindFirst("preferred_username");    ←——— . . .get the username claim.
      if (emailClaim != null
        && emailClaim.Value == "your@email.com")    ←——— If it matches your email . . .
      {
        context.Succeed(requirement);    ←——— . . . mark the requirement as successful.
      }
    }

    return Task.CompletedTask;    ←——— No async methods are called.
  }
}
```

A policy can have multiple requirements, and a requirement can have multiple handlers. Notice that when the email matches, the handler marks the requirement as successful, but it doesn't mark the requirement as failed in any other case. Because many handlers can handle the same requirement, another handler may find a reason to succeed the requirement. If one handler marks failure but another marks success, the requirement is in doubt and therefore failed. We mark failure only if we explicitly want the requirement to fail.

Try the web application to see the different responses. If you don't authenticate, you should get a `401` response code. If you authenticate and call a `Get` method, you should get a `200` response code. If you change the email check in `OnlyMeRequirement-Handler` to not match your email and try to create a book, you should get a `403` response code (unauthorized).

WARNING The `OnlyMe` requirement that checks for a hardcoded email address isn't how you'd ship a production application. This example is meant to show how handlers and requirements work. If you're checking by email, make sure that the email list comes from a safe place (not hardcoded) and that the email is verified (usually by a claim in the token, depending on the identity provider).

Exercise 4: Add a requirement to the OnlyMe policy
ASP.NET Core Identity checks whether all the requirements in a policy are satisfied. To verify, create a new requirement called `MatchEmailDomainRequirement` that takes a domain name as a string in the constructor. Then build a handler for the requirement that gets the domain from the user's email address and compares it to the requirement's domain name.

Exercise 5: Add another handler to the OnlyMeRequirement
Multiple handlers can handle the same requirement. Create a new handler for the `OnlyMeRequirement` that checks the claim name against your name. Try authenticating with an account with a different email address but with your name to see whether it works.

TIP A couple of books mentioned earlier in this chapter dive deeper into the topic of security: *ASP.NET Core Security*, by Christian Wenz, and *OpenID Connect in Action*, by Prabath Siriwardena.

Summary

- Threat modeling tools help you identify vulnerabilities and threat vectors in your application.
- Use HTTPS by default, and think carefully about how it will work in development versus production.
- EF Core guards against SQL injection attacks, but take a "trust but verify" approach with the SQL queries it generates.
- Swagger UI can authenticate with an identity provider and send bearer tokens to APIs.
- Authentication policies are referred to by their scheme name.
- Authorization policies are referred to by their policy name.
- Policies can have multiple requirements, and requirements can have multiple handlers.

10

Performance and profiling

This chapter covers

- Seeing why performance testing is important
- Benchmarking code with `BenchmarkDotNet`
- Collecting profiles with `BenchmarkDotNet`
- Analyzing profiles with tools
- Understanding the garbage collector
- Writing web API tests with `NBomber`

We tend to notice when applications are slow but take for granted ones that aren't. Sometimes, performance is about perception, as when you click a button and nothing happens, so you don't know whether you clicked it. A way to handle this situation is to make the button inactive or change its color immediately so you'll get the impression that it's working fast even if the underlying action takes the same amount of time.

This chapter doesn't go into these kinds of techniques; instead, it focuses on how to make your .NET applications faster. You'll learn about some tools and techniques that measure, profile, and analyze performance. Like security, performance is a vast topic that can't be covered in a chapter, but we'll explore some of the basics.

10.1 Why test performance?

Premature optimization is the root of all evil.

— Sir C. Antony R. Hoare

This quote by Sir Tony Hoare (A.M. Turing Award winner and creator of the quicksort algorithm), popularized by Donald Knuth (another Turing Award winner and creator of the TeX typesetting system), is perhaps the most misunderstood guidance for writing applications that perform well. *Optimization*, in this context, refers to CPU cycle counting and tuning low-level operations. Programmers love to do these things, but they often get lost in the minutiae and miss the big picture. Sir Tony wasn't trying to tell us to forgo considering performance when designing our applications; he was warning us against getting mired down by optimizing the wrong things.

Performance considerations need to start at the design phase—that is, at the macro level. We need to understand the components involved and how they perform under load. For some components—Kafka, RabbitMQ, Cosmos DB, and so on—it's easy to find benchmarks and blog posts about optimizations, so you can get a general sense of how well the component will perform. The performance of other components, such as relational databases, depends greatly on how they're used (in terms of complexity of schema and queries).

Becoming proficient at architecting software while considering performance, security, maintenance, and the like comes with training and experience that applies almost universally to the discipline of software engineering. Much like security, performance needs to be considered in many stages of application development. This book can cover only unique aspects of .NET performance.

When each new version of .NET is close to release, Stephen Toub writes a detailed, lengthy blog post about its performance improvements. One example is Toub's "Performance Improvements in .NET 8" post at http://mng.bz/VxlN. You may find it helpful to skim the categories in these posts to see whether your code uses any features that have been improved. Often, simply updating to the newest version of .NET provides some performance boost. But the fact that .NET may be faster doesn't mean it's going to be faster in your application. As a Microsoft architect who specializes in performance (Vance Morrison) said: "Good perf does not just happen. You have to plan, and to plan you have to measure."

Just as we have unit and integration tests, and ideally security tests, we want to create performance tests. We have many ways to improve the performance of our applications, such as caching, using compiled queries in Entity Framework Core (EF Core), and avoiding reflection. Blindly making changes to improve performance works sometimes, but at other times, it has the opposite effect. This chapter focuses on how to measure performance because when you have measurements, you know what parts of your application to focus on.

10.2   *Introduction to BenchmarkDotNet*

Testing libraries have become progressively simpler to use over time. Throughout this book, we've used xUnit because it's terse and easy to understand. BenchmarkDotNet (https://benchmarkdotnet.org) takes a similar approach, looking almost like a unit test. It has become the de facto standard for .NET performance benchmarking.

Let's build a simple benchmark to see how BenchmarkDotNet works. Use the commands in the following listing to create a console application called FirstBenchmark and add the BenchmarkDotNet library to it.

Listing 10.1   Commands to create `FirstBenchmark` application

```
dotnet new console --name FirstBenchmark
cd FirstBenchmark
dotnet add package BenchmarkDotNet
dotnet add package Newtonsoft.Json          The libraries we'll
dotnet add package System.Text.Json         be comparing
```

Next, we'll write a test class. BenchmarkDotNet is a great tool for exploring areas that you might be curious about. The numbers produced from a test may help you understand the general range of performance of some bits of code, but the real power is in comparing different approaches. The real "wall clock" time of code may differ depending on what environment an application runs in. When we run a comparison benchmark, the absolute numbers aren't as important as how the numbers relate to one another.

For the test class, we'll perform an experiment to find out what's faster for JSON deserialization: Newtonsoft.Json or System.Text.Json. We'll use the jokes.json file from chapter 4 as a decently large file to deserialize. The file is also available in the supplemental repository at https://github.com/dmetzgar/dotnet-in-action-code. Make sure to copy the file to the build output folder by adding the contents of the following listing to the project file.

Listing 10.2   Copying the jokes.json file to the build output as part of the build

```
<ItemGroup>
  <None Update="jokes.json">
    <CopyToOutputDirectory>PreserveNewest</CopyToOutputDirectory>
  </None>
</ItemGroup>
```

Also copy the Joke.cs file from the older project, and change the namespace. You can use the code from the following listing.

Listing 10.3   `Joke` record

```
namespace FirstBenchmark;

public record Joke(
```

```
    int Id,
    string Type,
    string Setup,
    string Punchline
) {}
```

Now we can write the test. Create a file called JsonDeserializationTest.cs in the project, and add the code from the following listing.

Listing 10.4   Benchmark comparing JSON deserialization

```
using BenchmarkDotNet.Attributes;        ◄─── For the Benchmark attribute
using Newtonsoft.Json;
using STJ = System.Text.Json;            ◄─── JSON libraries have similar class names.

namespace FirstBenchmark;

public class JsonDeserializationTest
{
  private readonly string _jsonString;

  public JsonDeserializationTest()
  {                                                      Reading the file isn't
    var reader = new StreamReader("jokes.json");  ◄──── part of the test.
    _jsonString = reader.ReadToEnd();
  }

  [Benchmark]
  public Joke[]? Newtonsoft() =>                                   Deserializes with
    JsonConvert.DeserializeObject<Joke[]>(_jsonString);  ◄──────── Newtonsoft

  [Benchmark]
  public Joke[]? SystemText() =>                                   Deserializes with
    STJ.JsonSerializer.Deserialize<Joke[]>(_jsonString);  ◄─────── System.Text
}
```

Why do the benchmark methods return values?

The .NET compiler is clever. It can look at code like the following code snippet and determine that it doesn't do anything.

```
[Benchmark]
public void Power()
{
  Math.Pow(Math.E, Math.PI);
}
```

The compiler may notice that nothing is done with the value that's returned and decide to remove that code from the Release-mode compilation. The JSON deserialization may not be removed because the compiler may not be able to determine whether there are side effects, but that action will depend on how clever the compiler is. Even though the compiler may not catch a do-nothing method in the current version of .NET, it may become smarter in the future.

> **(continued)**
> Returning the calculated result from the benchmark causes the compiler not to opti-
> mize away the method contents. The compiler assumes that some code might need
> the returned value from the method. Returning the result is a best practice for `Bench-
> markDotNet` tests.

Add the code from the following listing to the Program.cs file to invoke the JSON
deserialization benchmark when this application executes.

Listing 10.5 Bare-minimum Program.cs code to run the benchmarks

```
using BenchmarkDotNet.Running;

BenchmarkRunner.Run<JsonDeserializationTest>();
```

Running the application with the command `dotnet run` won't work. Instead, you need
to use `dotnet run -c Release` to use the Release-mode configuration. `BenchmarkDotNet`
wants to run only in Release mode. By default, .NET uses Debug mode, which turns
off performance optimizations and adds information to the resulting binaries to make
the code easier to debug. These debug changes skew the results and provide misleading information. When you're ready to deploy or ship, using Release mode is normal
practice, so the performance tests should use the same configuration.

A trick that I use with my `BenchmarkDotNet` projects is using Debug mode to verify
that the tests are correct. To do so, I take advantage of something that C# borrows
from its C/C++ lineage: preprocessor directives. A *preprocessor directive* is a statement
that the compiler executes before compiling the C# code. If you're familiar with C or
C++, you may be familiar with creating macros by using preprocessor directives. C#
doesn't support macros, but it does allow for conditional compilation. In the following listing, the application verifies the tests when it's compiled in Debug mode or runs
the benchmark in Release mode.

Listing 10.6 Using preprocessor directives

```
using BenchmarkDotNet.Running;
using FirstBenchmark;

#if DEBUG                          <---- Preprocessor directive

var test = new JsonDeserializationTest();
CheckJokes(test.Newtonsoft);                    <---- Passes in test method
CheckJokes(test.SystemText);

static void CheckJokes(Func<Joke[]?> func)       <---- Takes a method parameter
{
  try
  {
    var jokes = func();                 <---- Executes the method
```

```
    if (jokes == null || !jokes.Any())        ◁──── Checks whether jokes were deserialized
    {
      throw new Exception();
    }

    Console.WriteLine("Succeeded");
  }
  catch
  {
    Console.WriteLine("Failed");
  }
}

#else            ◁──── For configs other than Debug

BenchmarkRunner.Run<JsonDeserializationTest>();

#endif           ◁──── if must have an endif.
```

> ### Debug and Release aren't the only options
> The default build configurations are Debug and Release. But Debug and Release are only names that have properties associated with them. You could decide to have multiple build configurations. You could use a build configuration to match the environment (ReleaseDocker, ReleaseOnPrem, and so on), for example. Configuration is a well-known build property that we can check in project files (such as csproj) and preprocessor directives. Visual Studio also has specific tools for build configurations; see http://mng.bz/x2v7.

When you're running the benchmark (using Release-mode configuration), BenchmarkDotNet sends a lot of output to the console to show how the test is going. BenchmarkDotNet runs the test methods through the pilot and warmup phases to understand how fast the methods are. It also tries to give the just-in-time (JIT) compiler enough time to complete. The .NET JIT normally operates in a tiered manner, doing a quick compilation to native code at first and then doing a second compilation based on how that code is being used under load (although the default behavior can change in newer .NET versions). When the tests are complete, BenchmarkDotNet generates a summary including information on the environment in which the tests were run and a table comparing the results, such as table 10.1. (Note that us=microseconds.)

Table 10.1 Result table from the benchmark tests

Method	Mean	Error	StdDev
Newtonsoft	657.7 us	12.72 us	28.19 us
SystemText	285.2 us	5.61 us	10.39 us

Newtonsoft.Json is the original standard JSON library for .NET. In this context, *standard* means that even Microsoft relied on it for JSON serialization in ASP.NET Core. Microsoft built System.Text.Json later for a few reasons, including reducing the dependencies ASP.NET Core takes on libraries outside Microsoft's control and pursuing better performance. (The ASP.NET Core team was pushing for better results on the TechEmpower Benchmark, a third-party benchmark that compares many web frameworks; see https://www.techempower.com/benchmarks.)

10.3 Profiles

A *profile* records what your application does when it's running. You could get a memory profile to see how memory is being allocated and freed, or you could get a disk profile to see disk reads and writes. Network profiles record network traffic and activity. CPU profiles tell you how your application uses the processor. Profiling tools are powerful because they can connect these resources (memory, CPU, and so on) to specific lines of code in your application by getting the contents of the currently executing thread's stack. When the profile is collected, the frames found in the stack can be matched to symbols that provide the namespace, class, and method names.

What's a stack?

We hear about stack traces in exceptions or stack overflows that can happen when we make too many recursive calls. But what is a stack? Consider the program in listing 10.6, which contains a top-level statement that calls the CheckJokes method. CheckJokes calls the Newtonsoft test method, which calls the DeserializeObject method. The stack in this scenario is CheckJokes > Newtonsoft > DeserializeObject, with DeserializeObject at the top and CheckJokes at the bottom of the stack, as shown in the following figure.

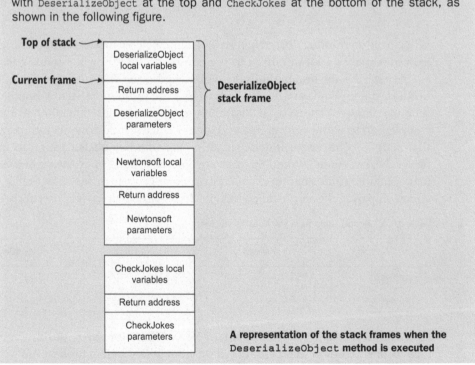

A representation of the stack frames when the DeserializeObject method is executed

Method calls have been around for ages, and they have an accepted pattern. The calling code is working on values in the CPU registers. Before calling a function/subroutine/ method, it wants to save its state, which it does by pushing the contents of the registers to the stack; then it pushes the arguments for the function/subroutine/method to the stack and makes the call. When the call is finished, the items can be removed from the stack to get the return value from the function/subroutine/method and restore the state of the calling code. The figure shows a simplified view of the stack frames when `DeserializeObject` executes.

Each level of the stack (called a *frame*) needs some uniquely identifying information. Programs are divided into assemblies, assemblies into classes (and other types), and classes into methods. Most profilers write each level of the stack with assembly, class name, and method name. Line-number information usually isn't available in CPU profiles because the binaries are compiled in Release mode. But most of the time, the stack information can provide enough clues to determine what the code is doing.

10.3.1 Capturing profiles with BenchmarkDotNet

`BenchmarkDotNet` has an advantage in capturing profiles: it can isolate the profile to specific test methods. `BenchmarkDotNet` can collect two kinds of profiles, the first of which is available only in Windows. Windows has powerful support for recording profiles via a feature called Event Tracing for Windows (ETW). If you're using Windows, this method is preferred because it can include lots of other information, such as custom .NET events and disk access. The second option, `Event Pipe`, works cross-platform. To test `Event Pipe` profiling, add the attribute to the benchmark test class as shown in the following listing.

Listing 10.7   Adding `EventPipeProfiler` to a benchmark class

```
[EventPipeProfiler(EventPipeProfile.CpuSampling)]    ⟵── Other profile types are available.
public class JsonDeserializationTest { }
```

Run the benchmark again, and look for a folder in the FirstBenchmark project titled BenchmarkDotNet.Artifacts. In that folder, you should find a .nettrace file and a .speedscope.json file for each benchmark method.

10.3.2 Analyzing profiles

You can view `Event Pipe` profiles in three ways: speedscope, Visual Studio, and Perf-View. First, you can view .speedscope.json files in speedscope, which is available at https://www.speedscope.app. speedscope shows a flame graph of the call stacks (see figure 10.1). The problem with this graph is that as `BenchmarkDotNet` moves between steps (pilot, warmup, and actual), each step is a separate method call. speedscope doesn't have the flexibility to combine these steps so that we can focus on the JSON deserialization.

**Different stages
of WorkloadPilot**

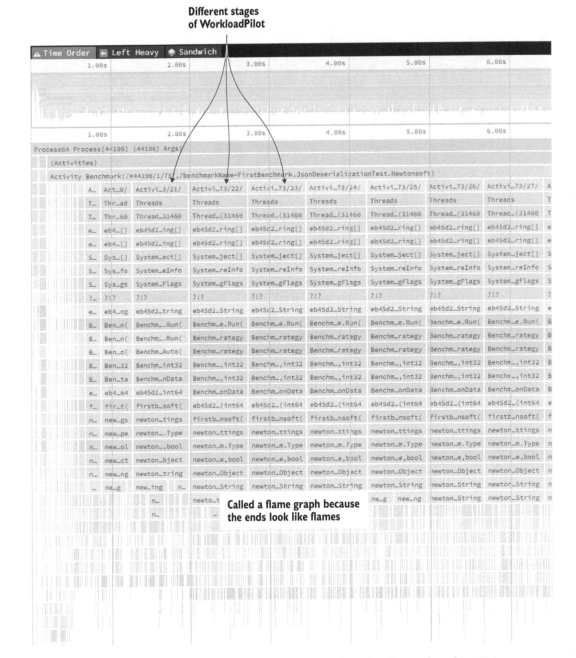

Figure 10.1   The speedscope flame graph of the `Event Pipe` **profiler taken by** `BenchmarkDotNet`

If you have a Windows machine, you can open the .nettrace in two ways, the first of which is through Visual Studio. Visual Studio 2022 includes performance-profiling tools in all editions, including Community. If you're using Visual Studio normally, the profiling tool has many options and capabilities that are worth digging into. To view the .nettrace profile in Visual Studio, simply drag the file to Visual Studio. Figure 10.2 shows how the profile looks in Visual Studio 2022 (with Just My Code turned off).

TIP BenchmarkDotNet can limit to a particular benchmark and generate profiles as part of a continuous integration build. If the build agent is Windows, consider using the ETW-based profiles because you can use those profiles to include more information. Generating profiles from a continuous integration can be useful if you have a performance-sensitive application and need to track regressions. Although speedscope and Visual Studio can't compare profiles, PerfView (covered in section 10.2.3) has powerful diffing capabilities for this purpose.

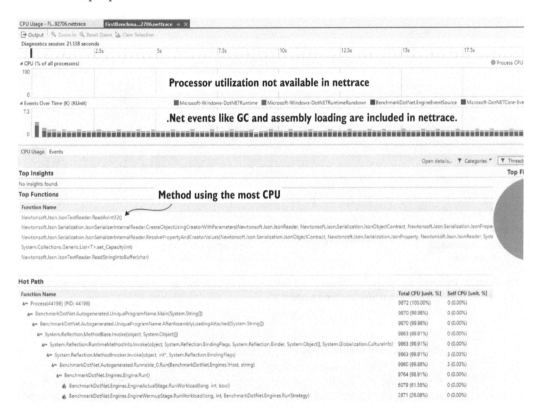

Figure 10.2 Visual Studio can show the methods that use the most CPU over the length of the profile.

10.3.3 Using PerfView

Also available in Windows is my favorite tool: PerfView (https://github.com/Microsoft/perfview). PerfView takes some time to learn. Its power is in its ability to group, fold, and filter data. Using a group pattern to combine frames that include the string "BenchmarkDotNet" and a fold pattern to fold frames that start with "Activity Workload", PerfView can show a less noisy version of the call tree (figure 10.3).

Group pattern   **Folds anything 5% or less into parent frame**   **Fold pattern**

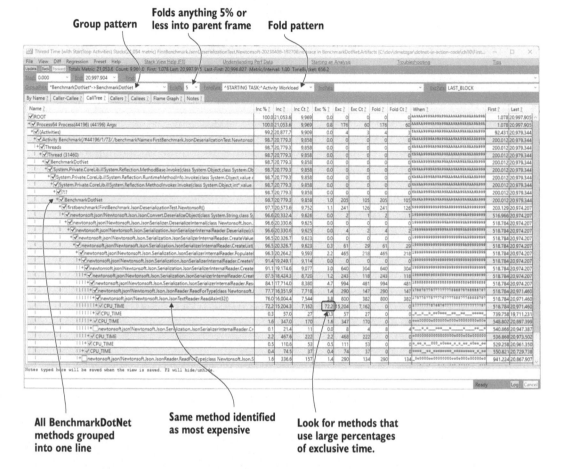

All BenchmarkDotNet methods grouped into one line   **Same method identified as most expensive**   **Look for methods that use large percentages of exclusive time.**

Figure 10.3   PerfView has powerful grouping and folding capabilities that can reduce noise in profiles by grouping or folding frames that you don't care about.

Inclusive vs. exclusive costs

Every method contains some instructions that run on the CPU. The amount of time spent executing the instructions within a particular method is considered to be the *exclusive cost* of that method. Because that method is likely called multiple times, profiles sum the total time and show that time as the exclusive cost of the method. Costs are usually presented as percentages of the total CPU cost for the whole profile.

The inclusive cost of a method is its exclusive cost plus the cost of any methods it calls. Suppose that you have a method A, which calls methods B and C. The exclusive costs of A, B, and C are 1%, 5%, and 6%, respectively. Assume that B and C don't call anything else, so their inclusive costs are equivalent to their exclusive costs, which makes method A's inclusive cost 12%: 1% exclusive for itself, plus 5% and 6% for the inclusive costs of B and C.

Group vs. fold vs. filter

These three operations perform similar operations but with important differences. Using combinations of these functions gives you the powerful ability to focus on the parts of the stack that are important to you:

- *Filter*—Removes the stack frame and anything below it. If you have a method that performs work in which you're not interested, remove it and anything it calls with a filter.
- *Fold*—Folds the matched frame into the one above it. In figure 10.3, the frame that starts with `Activity Workload` has a unique string for each workload. This folding divides the stack trace into individual activities that by themselves aren't interesting. Folding skips the `Activity Workload` frame, and any frames below it are still included in the stack trace.
- `Group`—Combines several linked stack frames into one group. We don't care about what `BenchmarkDotNet` is doing, for example, but it's good to know when it's called and how much it contributes to the overall profile. Typically, this grouping is used for .NET CoreFX libraries so that you can focus on your own code; PerfView has built-in groups for this purpose. If a stack frame contains the string `"BenchmarkDotNet"` as in figure 10.3 and any frames below it have the same string, all these frames will be combined into one group. Groups don't include any frames that don't have the `"BenchmarkDotNet"` string.

PerfView can also display interesting information about the performance of the garbage collector during the profile. Below the `"Memory Group"` item in the tree view is a `GCStats` item. Opening this item brings up a window containing details about the garbage collector. Figure 10.4 shows this window.

Chapter 1 looked briefly at garbage collection, but didn't get into details. To interpret what the profile tells you about the garbage collector, you'll have to know some key concepts, such as collection, compaction, and generation.

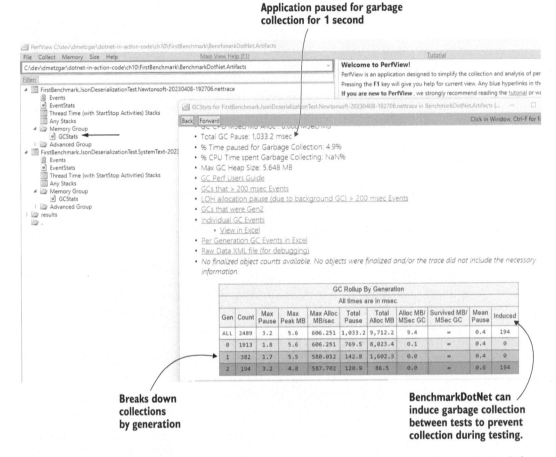

Application paused for garbage collection for 1 second

Breaks down collections by generation

BenchmarkDotNet can induce garbage collection between tests to prevent collection during testing.

Figure 10.4   PerfView's `GCStats` window provides details on the performance of the garbage collector during the profile.

10.3.4 *Understanding garbage collection*

The .NET garbage collector manages your application's memory use. To understand how it works, it helps to think about how C/C++ memory management works. Memory is divided into a few parts, but we're interested only in the stack and the heap. The *stack* contains variables declared inside a function, function arguments, and return addresses. The *heap* contains chunks of contiguous memory allocated dynamically by the program.

The currently executing function in a program has variables declared and stored on the stack. When function A calls function B, function B has its own variables that need to go on the stack. Function B isn't allowed to manipulate function A's stack variables. When function B completes, it needs to return to the correct point in function A. All this data is kept in the stack frame. By contrast, any function can manipulate any part of the heap when it's given pointers to the right heap memory addresses.

Stack overflows

For recursive calls, each new invocation of a function has to have a new stack frame. If your program has too many recursive calls, the stack frames can exceed the stack's maximum size. Typically, this situation happens with infinite loops when a function calls itself. This is the infamous stack-overflow error comes from.

You may not know the amount of memory that an application needs when you're writing the program. A program might load a file from disk that can range from a few kilobytes to a few hundred megabytes, and the data loaded from the file needs to be stored in memory dynamically allocated from the heap. Consider the C++ code in the following listing.

Listing 10.8 C++ code to read numbers into a dynamic array

```
int* readNInts(int count) {
  int* ptr;                      ←── Pointer to memory address in heap
  ptr = new int[count];          ←──┐
  for (int i = 0; i < count; i++) {  │ Dynamically allocates memory from heap
    ptr[i] = readInt();          ←──┐
  }                                  │ Stores values in an array
  return ptr;        ←──┐
}                        │ Returns a pointer
```

Contrast the statement in listing 10.8, `ptr = new int[count]`, with an array declaration statement like `int arr[100]`. The statement `ptr = new int[count]` allocates memory from the heap, whereas `int arr[100]` creates an array on the stack. When you're creating arrays on the stack, the number of elements needs to be a constant or literal value because the compiler has to know how much stack space to allocate. If the size of the array isn't known until runtime, you can create the array by using the heap method. Also, the heap generally has more memory available than the stack.

The nice part of the stack method is that the array is cleaned up when the program closes the stack frame (when the method returns and the local variables in that method go out of scope). Heap memory isn't cleaned up automatically, though. The function in listing 10.8 allocates the array and stores a pointer to the memory address where that array is located. That pointer can be passed around to other functions while the array is needed. Passing the array's size along with the pointer is a good idea because no bounds checking occurs while heap memory is accessed. `ptr[count + 10]` is a legal C++ statement, for example, but it accesses memory outside the bounds of the array that could belong to something else in the application.

When the array is no longer needed, its memory should be returned to the heap. The program would accomplish that task with the `delete[] ptr` statement. If the heap memory isn't returned (or freed, in the C vernacular), other parts of the program can't use it. This situation is referred to as a *memory leak*; the pointer is lost and the program could continue to allocate new arrays from the heap until it runs out of memory.

Managing memory explicitly has advantages, the most notable of which is performance, which is why videogame programmers prefer writing their core engines in languages such as C++. Also, the programmers are in complete control of how the application works, which is important for things such as embedded devices; where memory is tight, and the application needs to respond in real time without delay.

A lot of applications don't have tight memory budgets and can tolerate a few milliseconds of delay. The discipline of freeing memory explicitly adds time to development, code review, testing, and bug fixing because it can be difficult to detect and fix memory leaks. In object-oriented programming, the number of pointers to manage can become untenable. In .NET, the garbage collector handles memory management. Although the garbage collector is a huge boon to productivity, it involves a tradeoff. Sometimes, it helps to know how this machine works so you can use it efficiently.

WHAT DOES A GARBAGE COLLECTOR DO?

The stack, frame, and heap concepts work similarly in .NET. The difference is how memory is dynamically allocated and freed. The following listing shows the C# equivalent of the code from listing 10.8.

Listing 10.9   C# code to read numbers into a dynamic array

```
int[] ReadNInts(int count)
{
  int[] arr = new int[count];        ⟵——— arr is a reference, not a pointer.
  for (int i = 0; i < count; i++)
  {
    arr[i] = readInt();       ⟵——— for loop works the same way.
  }
  return arr;          ⟵——— Returns reference
}
```

The code in listing 10.9 creates an array of integers in the heap. Arrays in C# are *reference types*. References *refer* to objects in memory. This reference isn't the same as a pointer in C++. In the C++ example, `ptr` is an address to a physical memory location. The array created there stays until it is freed. In C#, the runtime handles the physical memory location, allowing the array to be moved to a different memory location. To illustrate the differences between references and pointers, look at the sample code in the following listing, which creates a copy of an array by using pointers in C#.

Listing 10.10   C# copy array using pointers instead of references

```
int[] CopyArray(int[] source)
{
  int length = source.Length;                   ⎤ Creates a target array of the same size
  int[] target = new int[length];     ⟵————⎦
  unsafe                              ⟵——— Pointers in C# need to be in unsafe blocks.
  {
    fixed (int* pSource = source,      ⟵——— fixed tells the runtime not to move the arrays.
```

```
            int* pTarget = target)
  {
    for (int i = 0; i < length; i++)
    {
      pTarget[i] = pSource[i];
    }
  }
}
  return target;
}
```

fixed pointers can't be moved but can be dereferenced.

Returns target array reference

The unsafe keyword tells the compiler that the code within isn't verifiably safe. *Verifiably safe* code is code that .NET can verify won't attempt to access memory it's not allowed to access (access violation), exceed array boundaries, and so on. unsafe isn't implying that the code is inherently dangerous. Within an unsafe code block, C# code can use pointers, allocate and free memory, and call methods by using function pointers.

Before we can copy the contents of the source array to the target array, we need to make sure that the arrays don't move, which is the purpose of the fixed keyword. fixed tells the .NET garbage collector that the arrays must stay in the same physical memory location until the fixed code block is finished. This situation begs a question: why would the .NET garbage collector move the arrays?

HEAP FRAGMENTATION AND COMPACTION

Suppose that when your .NET application starts, a heap is created with 1 MB of memory. We'll represent the heap as a contiguous section of memory, as in figure 10.5.

Figure 10.5   1 MB of heap memory

When you allocate memory for an array, the runtime needs to provide a contiguous chunk that matches the array size. Then the runtime has to keep a record of where that chunk is so that when it allocates memory for something else, the chunks don't overlap. When your program is starting, each new memory chunk is allocated in the memory location after the previous one, as shown in figure 10.6.

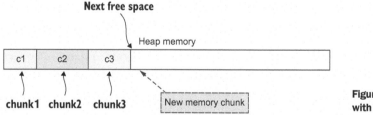

Figure 10.6   Heap memory with chunks allocated

When you get close to the end of the 1 MB heap, the next chunk may not fit in the remaining memory. In figure 10.7, we need to allocate a new chunk, but the heap doesn't have enough remaining space to hold it.

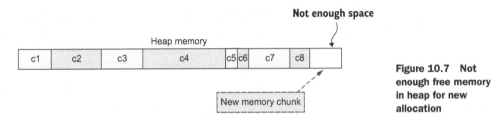

Figure 10.7   Not enough free memory in heap for new allocation

The garbage collector looks at all the chunks of memory that were allocated previously and determines which ones are unused and can be freed. This process is called *collection*. In figure 10.8, some of the chunks have been removed, but still, no space is big enough to allocate the new chunk.

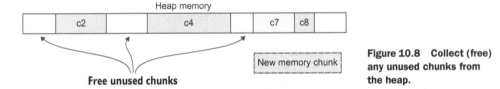

Figure 10.8   Collect (free) any unused chunks from the heap.

Although the total unused heap may have more than enough space for the new chunk, not all that space is contiguous. Suppose that we can't increase the total heap size. The best way to get a contiguous space large enough to allocate the new chunk is to compact all the allocated chunks together. Because C# arrays are reference types instead of pointers, we can move the memory without affecting the code using the array. Figure 10.9 shows that after compaction, we have enough space to allocate the new chunk.

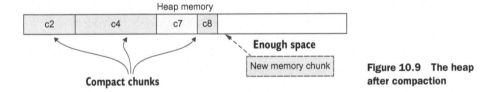

Figure 10.9   The heap after compaction

Compaction can take time. While the garbage collector is moving chunks of memory, the parts of the code that use those memory chunks have to wait. We can see from the GCStats information in the profile that more than 1 second is spent in collection. For BenchmarkDotNet profiles, don't put too much weight into garbage collector use, because BenchmarkDotNet can induce a collection manually between tests to get more reliable results. Normal applications don't control when collection and compaction occurs, and they may become unresponsive during these processes. For this reason, developers who work in real-time scenarios in which unpredictable latency can be problematic, if not devastating (such as embedded devices or graphically intense videogames), may have reservations about using garbage-collected languages.

WARNING Don't induce garbage collections in your application. Inducing garbage collections makes sense for collecting benchmarks; in almost all other scenarios, this action won't improve performance.

Garbage collectors can employ many techniques to reduce the effect, frequency, and duration of compaction. The .NET runtime team has invested heavily in the garbage collector over the 20 years .NET has been around. Given the breadth of applications in which .NET is used, I'd say that this investment has paid off.

GENERATIONS

The GCStats information shows how many collections were performed by generation. Table 10.2 shows a snippet of the table. The first generation, Gen0, is the fastest. Gen0 collections try to avoid long pauses or compaction. If a chunk of memory is still being referenced, the collector can't free the memory. The chunk of memory survives to the next generation, Gen1. Gen1 happens less frequently than Gen0.

Table 10.2 GCStats **table from PerfView from the** Newtonsoft **benchmark method profile**

Gen	Count	Total pause	Total alloc
ALL	2489	1,033.2 ms	9,712.2 MB
0	1913	769.5 ms	8,023.4 MB
1	382	142.8 ms	1602.3 MB
2	194	120.9 ms	86.5 MB

Chunks that survive Gen1 move to Gen2. Gen2 items are generally considered to be long-term. Keeping references longer than they're needed could result in that memory's getting into Gen2. Gen2 collections don't happen often. (Table 10.2 shows 194 Gen2 collections, all of which were artificially induced by BenchmarkDotNet). The garbage collector would rather expand the heap than perform a compaction, and if you have lots of Gen2 objects lying around, your program will allocate more heap space. If your application spends a lot of time in garbage collection or takes up more memory than you think it should, these GCStats can be helpful. Also, some memory profiles can show which objects are being allocated and freed.

10.4 Web performance testing

BenchmarkDotNet works best for measuring code that runs in milliseconds or less and produces stable results. Code that relies on external systems, such as network calls or database queries, generally isn't reliable enough for low-level benchmarking. In functional testing, we write unit tests to look at individual units and integration tests to see how components work together at a higher level. You can think of BenchmarkDotNet as being equivalent to unit testing. Other tools are better suited to higher-level testing, such as via web API calls.

The most popular tool for high-level performance benchmarking is JMeter, an Apache open source project with an active community. JMeter can interface with applications via HTTP requests and perform scripted operations that mimic user interactions. These features make it a great tool no matter what language the application is written in.

JMeter is written in Java, however, and this book is a .NET book. Also, good .NET alternatives to JMeter exist. The tool we'll use is NBomber (https://nbomber.com). NBomber isn't the only .NET load testing tool, but it's free for certain uses and easy to use for writing tests.

The example application we'll use is the `ComicFinderService` from chapter 8. Copy the XkcdComicFinder root folder to a new directory or make changes in place. Make sure to update the appsettings.json for the `ComicFinderService` to use a local file SQlite database (`"Sqlite": "DataSource=xkcd.db;cache=shared"`), and set the `BaseAddr` setting to `https://xkcd.com`. Run the service in one terminal, and try a search to prepopulate the database (such as http://localhost:5123/search?searchText=Shuttle). It may take a while for the service to retrieve all the comics and record them to the database file.

Next, create a new console application for load-testing the `ComicFinderService`. Use the commands in the following listing.

Listing 10.11   Command to create `ComicFinderLoadTest`

```
dotnet new console -n ComicFinderLoadTest
cd ComicFinderLoadTest
dotnet add package NBomber
dotnet add package NBomber.Http
```

Next, add the contents of the following listing to the Program.cs file.

Listing 10.12   NBomber load test

```
using NBomber.CSharp;
using NBomber.Http.CSharp;

using var httpClient = new HttpClient();

var scenario = Scenario.Create("search_mom",      ⟵── Creates one scenario
  async context =>
  {
    var request =                          ⎤ Makes a GET HTTP request
      Http.CreateRequest("GET",      ⟵──┘
        "http://localhost:5123/search?searchText=Mom");  ⟵── Uses search text "Mom"

    var response = await Http.Send(httpClient, request);  ⟵── Sends the request
    return response;                 ⟵┐
  })                                   │ Lets NBomber check status code, latency, and so on
.WithoutWarmUp()                 ⟵┐
.WithLoadSimulations(          │ Warmup is unnecessary if the database is primed.
  Simulation.Inject(
    rate: 100,                        ⟵── Requests per interval
    interval: TimeSpan.FromSeconds(1),   ⟵┐
    during: TimeSpan.FromSeconds(30))    ⟵┤ Interval time
);
                                          │ Duration of scenario test
```

```
NBomberRunner
  .RegisterScenarios(scenario)      ⟵——— Multiple scenarios are allowed.
  .Run();
```

Run the application and watch the console output. While the test is running, NBomber shows real-time statistics, which is helpful in case something isn't working correctly. At the end of the 30-second test, NBomber creates a reports folder inside the project folder. One report folder is created per run, and the reports are saved in multiple formats. Figure 10.10 shows one of these reports.

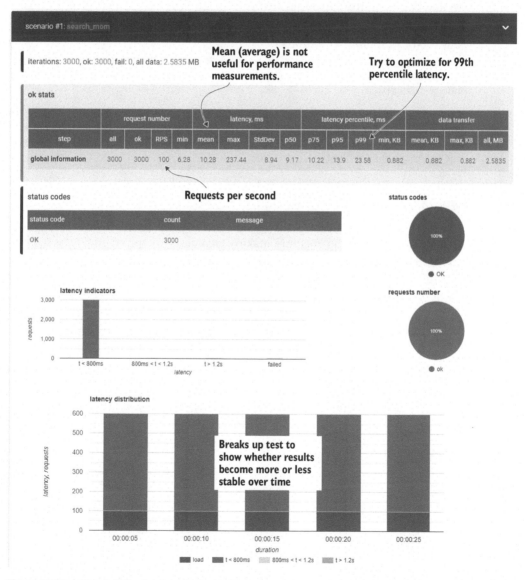

Figure 10.10 Sample NBomber load test report

This figure shows the latency of the requests in milliseconds broken into different categories. I avoid mean or average wherever possible because this number can be skewed by small or large numbers in the data set. For the most part, P99 is the most important; it's the latency for 99% of the requests. If you have 10K visitors to your site per day, 1%, or 100 users, will be getting latencies at or worse than this value. As the numbers of users and requests grow, the number of users affected gets larger, so you'd go farther than P99 into P99_5 (99.5%) or P99_9 (99.9%). Maximum latency is difficult to investigate sometimes because spikes usually don't happen in reproducible ways and can result from external factors.

Exercise: Add more scenarios

Create several scenarios that search for different texts. Try including texts that don't match anything. Also try adding invalid requests. Increase the overall requests per second to the service.

Performance tests enable you to see how an application will break under load. You may not be able to break the application with only one client machine, but trying to do so is fun. Mostly, you'll be stretching the limits of the SQlite database, which isn't meant for production load.

Summary

- Incorporate performance into design decisions early.
- Measure performance before making changes.
- Benchmarking tools work best for comparing measurements in relation to other measurements rather than as absolute measurements.
- Use benchmarks to answer questions with data.
- Collect profiles to understand where time is spent.
- Understanding collection, compaction, and generation will help you make sense of memory problems.
- Higher-level testing tools such as NBomber provide a picture of overall application performance.
- For tracking request latency, P99 is the preferred measurement.

Handling failures

Code can fail for many reasons. Maybe a dependency isn't responding, or something else has a lock on a resource you want. Your customers may have found an unexpected way to use your application or hit corner cases you didn't anticipate. If we adopt a mindset that our code will fail, we can move to adopt strategies that handle failures well. In this chapter, we'll look at common .NET tools and techniques that isolate problems, retry, and compensate.

11.1 Operating in the real world

Sometimes, it seems that the things we build today don't last long. Even though it's only 20 years old, my driveway is slowly crumbling, and the concrete needs to be removed and replaced. Yet the Roman Pantheon, built almost two millennia ago, is still standing strong. Researchers recently discovered that the reason why this concrete lasts so long is that it has properties that allow it to heal. Whether by accident or intention, Roman concrete was designed to handle failure. My driveway, by contrast, was designed to be inexpensive.

Like physical items, software fails all the time. Phone applications, websites, and operating systems all fail for a variety of reasons. It can be unsettling to think that software powers all kinds of critical infrastructure, such as airplanes, train schedules, telecommunications, and bank transactions. Luckily, the engineers behind these systems developed ways to handle failure. The Erlang programming language, for example, was invented to handle telephone exchanges; its design traits include fault tolerance and containment. Controllers on commercial airplanes sometimes provide conflicting data—a situation sometimes called the Byzantine Generals Problem. Many distributed consensus algorithms and implementations are available to address this problem. These software systems are designed to handle failure.

How much effort you put into handling failure depends on the nature of your application. In my experience, temporary measures (the ones marked with a TODO comment about fixing later) rarely get fixed, so I find it best to put more effort into testing and fault handling than seems necessary. Some failures come from bugs in the implementation, which we try to handle by rigorous testing and code reviews. Other failures can come from environment problems, hardware problems, and dependency outages. In this chapter, we'll look at common failures and the facilities in .NET to handle them.

11.2 EF Core

One of the most common failure points in an application is interaction with the database. Some databases have thousands of error codes, each labeling a different type of failure. Errors can also occur while an application is in the middle of making changes, either at the database or application level. Using some well-known techniques, we can make our applications resilient to database failures.

11.2.1 Database transactions

Suppose that you're building a payment service for an online game. Players can send and receive in-game money from other players in exchange for items. A transfer of money involves debiting from one account and crediting another. With EF Core, we could have an Account entity (table), and the transfer would be to select the rows for the accounts affected and update them. Sometimes, EF Core doesn't go directly to the database if it already has a copy of the Account entity cached in its change tracker, so the transaction process looks like figure 11.1.

A database is an external dependency; it's not running in the same process as our .NET code. Our .NET application doesn't have control or knowledge of what's going on with the database. The connection to the database uses another external dependency: the network, which can have its own problems. The .NET application runs on a machine that could lose power at any time. Our code runs in a process on the OS that could be killed at any point. We have to treat the database, our connection to it, the

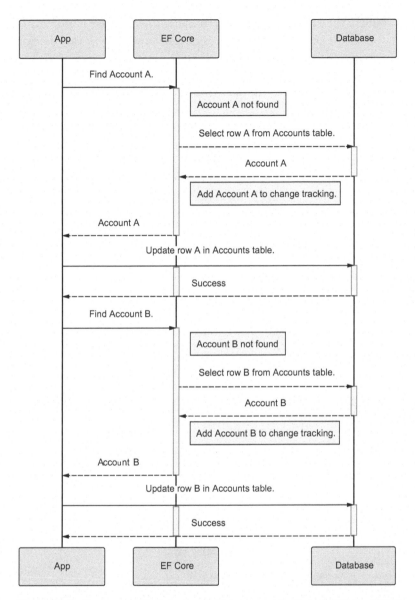

Figure 11.1 A sequence diagram showing how our application checks the change tracker for the `Account` entity, queries the database, and then performs the updates

process that our app runs in, and the host machine/container in which our app runs as being capable of going down at any time.

If each account's balance is stored in a database table row, two rows need to be updated at the same time. Databases have a standard means of performing this task: a transaction. The idea is simply that all the changes within the transaction succeed (*commit*) or fail (*rollback*). The transaction protects against partial completion, in which only some of the changes succeeded. Because the database handles the transaction, it can rollback if our app loses connection or crashes. We can use a database transaction to protect our money transfer.

To see how this process works, we'll build an application that credits and debits two accounts. We'll simulate a failure in one of the steps to show how a transaction protects in that case. SQlite supports transactions, but not nested transactions, so it has problems with EF Core. For this example, I picked SQL Express as the database, but any relational database that supports transactions will work. SQL Express is free to download and comes with Visual Studio. You can also use any other SQL Server database, which are available for Linux or for macOS via a Docker container. Start by creating a class library project for the bank code and a test project, using the lines from the following listing.

Listing 11.1   Commands to create `MoneyTransfer` projects

```
dotnet new classlib --name MoneyTransfer
cd MoneyTransfer
dotnet add package Microsoft.EntityFrameworkCore
cd ..
dotnet new xunit --name MoneyTransfer.Tests
cd MoneyTransfer.Tests
dotnet add reference ../MoneyTransfer/MoneyTransfer.csproj
dotnet add package Microsoft.EntityFrameworkCore.SqlServer
```

In the `MoneyTransfer` class library, create a file called Account.cs, and add the code from the following listing.

Listing 11.2   `Account` class in the `MoneyTransfer` project

```
using System.ComponentModel.DataAnnotations;

namespace MoneyTransfer;

public class Account
{
  [Key]                                          ⟵——— Defines primary key
  public string AccountNumber { get; set; }
  public decimal Balance { get; set; }           ⟵——— Uses decimal for currency

  public Account(string accountNumber, decimal balance)
  {
    AccountNumber = accountNumber;
    Balance = balance;
  }
}
```

Next, create a file called BankContext.cs for the `DbContext` implementation that holds the `Account` entity, as shown in the following listing.

Listing 11.3   BankContext class

```
using Microsoft.EntityFrameworkCore;

namespace MoneyTransfer;

public class BankContext : DbContext
{
  public DbSet<Account> Accounts { get; set; } = null!;

  public BankContext(DbContextOptions options) :          No default constructor
    base(options) { }                                     is needed.
}
```

Next, we'll build a repository for controlling credits and debits to accounts. Create a file called BankRepository.cs, and add the code from the following listing.

Listing 11.4   BankRepository class

```
namespace MoneyTransfer;

public class BankRepository
{
  private readonly BankContext _ctxt;

  public BankRepository(BankContext dbContext)
    => _ctxt = dbContext;

  private async Task<Account> GetAccountAsync(string acc)    ◁──── Helper method
  {
    var account = await _ctxt.Accounts.FindAsync(acc);    ◁──── FindAsync searches by key
    return account ??
      throw new ArgumentException(          ◁──── Throws exception if account isn't found
        "No account found: " + acc,
        nameof(acc));
  }
}
```

Find and transactions

We've used Find/FindAsync before, but it's worth pointing out that this method has some nuance. Using a query like Single, First, or Select on a DbSet always results in a query to the database. But Find is one of the ways in which EF Core checks its local cache first and queries the database only if the entity isn't there. As you use the DbContext in your code, EF Core keeps track of the entities you retrieve and modify through *change tracking*. Find grabs the local version and prevents a database round trip, which is faster but comes with a caveat. When a transaction rolls back, locally cached entities sometimes don't get the memo and have the wrong values. We'll see how to combat this problem by clearing the change tracker later in this section.

To credit an account, we need only add the credit amount to the account balance. We'll assume that there's no upper limit to the account balance or amount. The following listing shows the `CreditAsync` method that increases the balance and saves the result to the database. The listing also includes a method to retrieve the `Account` entity from the database.

Listing 11.5   `GetAccountAsync` and `CreditAsync` methods

```
public async Task CreditAsync(string acc, decimal amt)
{
  var account = await GetAccountAsync(acc);
  account.Balance += amt;              <--- Modifies account entity
  await _ctxt.SaveChangesAsync();      <---
}                                          Immediately saves changes to database

private async Task<Account> GetAccountAsync(string acc)
{                                                        Finds account by
  var account = await _ctxt.Accounts.FindAsync(acc);  <-- account number
  return account ??
    throw new ArgumentException(      <--- Throws exception if account isn't found
      "No account found: " + acc,
      nameof(acc));
}
```

The `CreditAsync` method should also check whether the amount is a positive number and not a tiny fraction (unless tiny fractions are allowed). I omitted those checks because they don't serve the example.

Debiting an account is similar but has the necessary check of not reducing the account below a zero balance. It's normal to check whether the account has enough balance before initiating the transaction, but it's still necessary to check again because the balance may have changed between the time of the check and the actual debit. Listing 11.6 shows the `DebitAsync` method.

NOTE   A real payment system would take the debit command as a message that's added to a queue; then the items in the queue are processed one at a time and in order to prevent the balance from being incorrect due to simultaneous transactions. If you're interested in this approach, check out Martin Fowler's excellent description of the Command-Query Responsibility Segregation (CQRS) pattern at https://www.martinfowler.com/bliki/CQRS.html.

Listing 11.6   `DebitAsync` method

```
public async Task DebitAsync(string acc, decimal amt)
{
  var account = await GetAccountAsync(acc);

  if ((account.Balance - amt) < 0)
  {
    throw new InsufficientFundsException(      <--- Custom exception
```

```
        $"Account {acc} funds insufficient");
    }

    account.Balance -= amt;
    await _ctxt.SaveChangesAsync();        ◁────── Immediately saves changes to the database
}
```

DebitAsync throws an exception if the balance is too low. Instead of using one of the built-in exceptions, we can create our own exception so that the error is clear to the caller. For this example, create an exception class in a file called InsufficientFunds-Exception.cs, and add the code from the following listing.

Listing 11.7 Custom insufficient-funds exception

```
namespace MoneyTransfer;                                    ┐ Inherits from
                                                            │ System.Exception
public class InsufficientFundsException : Exception    ◁────┘
{
    public InsufficientFundsException(string message) :    ◁────── Requires a message
        base(message) { }
}
```

Custom exceptions

.NET veterans may be accustomed to implementing custom exceptions by using a template such as the one in the following code snippet:

```
[Serializable]                                    ┐ Indicates that the
public class MyException : Exception    ◁─────────┘ object is serializable
{
    public MyException() { }

    public MyException(string message)
        : base(message) { }
                                                  ┐ Wraps another exception
    public MyException(string message,            │ with this one
        Exception innerException)        ◁────────┘
        : base(message, innerException) { }
                                                       ┐ Serialization-only
    protected MyException(SerializationInfo info,  ◁───┘ constructor
        StreamingContext context)
        : base(info, context) { }
}
```

Although nothing is wrong with implementing all the constructors for Exception this way, the serialization stuff isn't necessary. If you're not familiar with the term, *serialization* is the process of taking an object's representation in memory and translating it into something that can be transmitted or written to a file. (We've serialized objects to JSON before.) Originally, the *Serializable* attribute was meant for binary and XML serialization; it indicated to the serializer that the public and private fields of an object should be serialized by default. When the object is deserialized, taking the transmitted form and converting it to an in-memory object, the special constructor bypasses any logic that would execute if we created the object anew.

(continued)

`Newtonsoft` doesn't use the special serialization constructor. The binary serializer is available only for .NET Framework and doesn't appear in modern .NET due to safety concerns. The XML serializer's main usage was for Simple Object Access Protocol (SOAP) messages created by Windows Communication Foundation (WFC). WCF, SOAP, and to some extent XML has fallen out of favor and aren't used often now.

Unless you're writing code for .NET Standard to be portable with older .NET Framework applications, the serialization constructor isn't necessary. The default constructor is helpful if you deserialize an exception, but if you don't transmit `Exception` objects directly and don't create exceptions without a message, the default constructor isn't necessary. The inner exception is needed only if another exception could trigger your custom exception, which isn't the case in listing 11.6. The custom-exception template has become a habit for .NET developers, though. Sometimes, we stick with the ceremony to satisfy our code reviewers.

Now that we have both credit and debit methods defined in the `BankRepository` class, let's add a method to transfer a sum from one account to another. The following listing shows the `TransferAsync` method, which credits one account and debits another.

Listing 11.8   `TransferAsync` method

```
public async Task TransferAsync(
  string from, string to, decimal amt)
{
  await CreditAsync(to, amt);
  await DebitAsync(from, amt);
}
```

In the test project, create a file called BankRepositoryTests.cs, and add the code from the following listing to verify that the `TransferAsync` method works as intended.

Listing 11.9   Unit test of `TransferAsync` method

```
using Microsoft.EntityFrameworkCore;

namespace MoneyTransfer.Tests;

public class BankRepositoryTests : IDisposable
{
  private readonly BankContext _bankContext;
  private readonly BankRepository _bankRepo;

  public BankRepositoryTests()
  {
    var optionsBuilder = new DbContextOptionsBuilder();      ⟵ Uses Microsoft
    optionsBuilder.UseSqlServer(                                  SQL Server client
```

```
        "Server=.\\SQLExpress;Database=bank;" +        ◁——— Local SQL Express database
        "TrustServerCertificate=true;" +               ◁——— Needed for newer
        "Trusted_Connection=Yes;");                     ◁——— EF Core versions
      var options = optionsBuilder.Options;            ◁——— Needed for SQL Express connection
      _bankContext = new(options);
      _bankContext.Database.EnsureCreated();           ◁——— Creates database and schema
      _bankRepo = new(_bankContext);
    }

    [Fact]
    public async Task TransferSucceeds()
    {
      _bankContext.Accounts.Add(new("A", 100));        ◁——— Creates test bank accounts
      _bankContext.Accounts.Add(new("B", 100));
      await _bankContext.SaveChangesAsync();           ◁——— Saves accounts to the database

      await _bankRepo.TransferAsync("A", "B", 30);     ◁——— Transfers 30 units from A to B

      var fromAccount = _bankContext.Accounts.Find("A");    ◁—┐
      Assert.NotNull(fromAccount);                             │ Verifies that
      Assert.Equal(70, fromAccount.Balance);                  │ transfer was
                                                              │ successful
      var toAccount = _bankContext.Accounts.Find("B");     ◁—┘
      Assert.NotNull(toAccount);
      Assert.Equal(130, toAccount.Balance);
    }

    public void Dispose()
    {
      _bankContext.Database.ExecuteSqlRaw(             ◁——— Runs unadulterated SQL
        "TRUNCATE TABLE [Accounts]");               ◁——┐
      _bankContext.Dispose();                            │ Removes all rows from Accounts
    }
  }
}
```

If you're not using SQL Express, you need to modify the optionsBuilder statements and possibly the truncate SQL command to match your (transaction-capable) database of choice. Run dotnet test to verify that all the code works correctly and you're able to connect to the database.

Next, let's see what happens when something goes wrong during the transfer. In our case, we can trigger the InsufficientFundsException by transferring an amount that exceeds the account's balance. Keep in mind that any number of exceptions can happen during the transfer, such as network or database outages, update conflicts, or crashes (service or host). These exceptions trigger similar outcomes. Figure 11.2 shows the sequence of events.

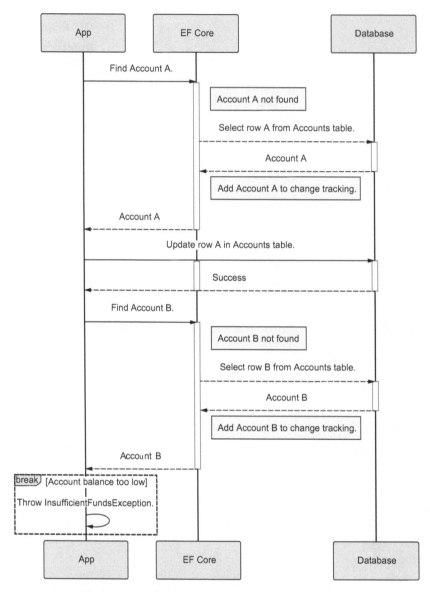

Figure 11.2 A sequence diagram showing that the exception occurs after account A is credited but before account B is debited

Add the test method from the following listing to show that in the case of an exception, the current transfer method will leave account B with money it shouldn't have.

Listing 11.10 `TransferAsync` **leaving accounts in invalid states**

```
[Fact]
public async Task TransferFails()
{
  _bankContext.Accounts.Add(new("A", 100));
  _bankContext.Accounts.Add(new("B", 100));
  await _bankContext.SaveChangesAsync();

  await Assert.ThrowsAsync<InsufficientFundsException>(      ⟵── Expects the exception
    () => _bankRepo.TransferAsync("A", "B", 120));

  var fromAccount = _bankContext.Accounts.Find("A");
  Assert.NotNull(fromAccount);
  Assert.Equal(100, fromAccount.Balance);      ⟵── Not able to debit this much from A

  var toAccount = _bankContext.Accounts.Find("B");
  Assert.NotNull(toAccount);
  Assert.Equal(100, toAccount.Balance);      ⟵── B was not supposed to be credited.
}
```

Running this test should produce a failure, as B's balance is 220 when it should be 100. The simple solution to this contrived example is to reorder the debit and credit, but either operation could fail for circumstances beyond the control of the .NET code. To handle this case, we can tell the database to perform these two operations as part of a single transaction. Then, if the transaction isn't committed, no change is made to the accounts. Rewrite the `TransferAsync` method as shown in the following listing.

Listing 11.11   A transactional version of the `BankRepository.TransferAsync`

```
public async Task TransferAsync(
  string from, string to, decimal amt)
{
  using var tx = await
    _ctxt.Database.BeginTransactionAsync();      ⟵── Creates a database transaction

  try
  {
    await CreditAsync(to, amt);      ⟵── Performs credit/debit as normal
    await DebitAsync(from, amt);
    await tx.CommitAsync();      ⟵── Commits if no exception is thrown
  }
  catch      ⟵── Catches any exception
  {
    await tx.RollbackAsync();      ⟵── Explicitly undoes changes
    _ctxt.ChangeTracker.Clear();   ⟵─┐
    throw;                       ⟵──┤ Clears EF Core's cache
  }                                  │
}                                    └ Propagates exception to caller
```

What happens if I don't explicitly commit or roll back?

It's entirely possible that you won't capture all the failure conditions in the transaction and call `Rollback`. The transaction object is disposable, which is why we use `using`. When the transaction object is disposed, and if an explicit rollback or commit wasn't called, the transaction will roll back by default. If you don't use `using`, the garbage collector will dispose the object eventually, but you don't control when.

Many ways to create transactions may depend on the database provider. This method should work for most databases (but not for SQlite). Running the unit tests again will show that both A and B remain at their original balances even though the `CreditAsync` clearly changed the balance and called `SaveChangesAsync` on the `DbContext`. If you set a debug breakpoint after that `SaveChangesAsync`, you won't find the updated account balance in the Accounts table because the transaction holds the changes in a separate construct until the transaction is committed. If the service crashed before committing the transaction, the database would eventually abort or rollback the transaction due to timeout or lost connection. Figure 11.3 shows the sequence of events in the transaction and rollback.

Earlier, I mentioned that the `FindAsync` method searches EF Core's local cache before querying the database for a record. While you're inside the transaction and using `FindAsync`, you want EF Core's cached copy because that copy will have the updates. When the transaction is rolled back, however, the cached records are invalid. EF Core isn't aware that the rollback occurred because of the particular way that this transaction was created and rolled back, so it doesn't have a trigger to clear the rolled-back records from its cache. That is why it's necessary to clear the change tracker cache as part of the rollback. Otherwise, the unit test, which performs a `FindAsync` to get the Account records using the same `DbContext` object, will get account B with a balance of 220 even when the database shows that the balance is 100. This subtle problem can go undetected if the tests use a different `DbContext` from the repository.

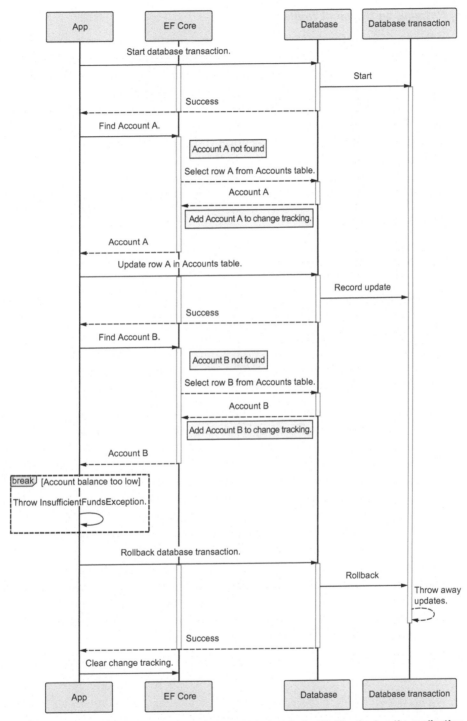

Figure 11.3 A sequence diagram showing the transaction start and rollback when the application finds that the account balance is insufficient

11.2.2 *Retrying on transient faults*

If the database or the database client returns an error, usually an associated code indicates the error type. EF Core's SQL Server client has a list of error codes that it considers to be *transient*, which means that the operation can be retried. Luckily, you don't need to sprinkle retry logic throughout your code on every SaveChanges call. EF Core has a concept called execution strategies that allows for automatic retry of transient problems. The execution strategy should be specific to the type of database. For SQL Server, EF Core has a built-in execution strategy that you can enable via the options builder, as shown in the following listing.

Listing 11.12 Enabling EF Core retry on failure

```
public BankRepositoryTests()
{
  var optionsBuilder = new DbContextOptionsBuilder();
  optionsBuilder.UseSqlServer(
    "Server=.\\SQLExpress;Database=bank;" +
    "TrustServerCertificate=true;" +
    "Trusted_Connection=Yes;",
    sqlOptions => sqlOptions.EnableRetryOnFailure());     <--- Options specific to SQL Server
  var options = optionsBuilder.Options;
  _bankContext = new(options);
  _bankContext.Database.EnsureCreated();
  _bankRepo = new(_bankContext);
}
```

You may notice that after you add this option, the tests stop working. The reason is that the default execution strategy isn't designed to handle transactions. The EF Core team likely made the code fail on purpose to get you to consider how transactions work in terms of retry. During the call to commit the transaction, the connection to the database could be lost. When this situation happens, the application doesn't know whether the transaction succeeded. Ideally, your code can verify whether the transaction succeeded by executing a query on the database. Verification also influences the design of the application. Figure 11.4 shows the sequence of events that occur when a transaction's outcome is in doubt.

You rarely lose a connection specifically during transaction commit. If it's difficult to verify that the transaction succeeded, you can choose to ignore this situation and retry on all exceptions, including connection loss during commit. If it's possible to verify that the transaction succeeded, however, you can include that verification in the execution strategy. Listing 11.13 shows two extension methods for DbContext in a new class called Extensions in the MoneyTransfer project.

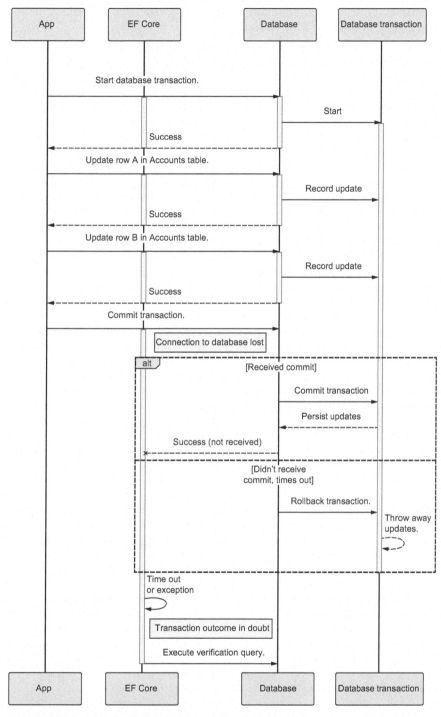

Figure 11.4 A sequence diagram showing a transaction's outcome in doubt as a result of connection loss during transaction commit

One method retries the transaction if any exception occurs; the other verifies whether the transaction worked before retrying.

Listing 11.13   Transaction execution strategies

```
using Microsoft.EntityFrameworkCore;
using Microsoft.EntityFrameworkCore.Storage;

namespace MoneyTransfer;

public static class Extensions
{                                                          Retries on any
  public static Task ExecuteRetryableTransactionAsync(     exception
    this DbContext ctxt,
    Func<Task> action)                                     Extension on DbContext
  {
                                                           Function to execute in transaction
    IExecutionStrategy strategy =
      ctxt.Database.CreateExecutionStrategy();             Strategy includes retry.
    return strategy.ExecuteAsync(async () =>
    {
      using IDbContextTransaction tx =
        await ctxt.Database.BeginTransactionAsync();
      try
      {
        await action();            Runs function
        await tx.CommitAsync();
      }
      catch
      {
        await tx.RollbackAsync();
        ctxt.ChangeTracker.Clear();    Remember to clear cache on rollback.
        throw;
      }                              Rethrows to trigger retry
    });
  }

  public static Task ExecuteVerifyingTransactionAsync(     Verifies before retry
    this DbContext ctxt,
    Func<Task> action,
    Func<Task<bool>> didItWork)      Function checks for success.
  {
    IExecutionStrategy strategy =
      ctxt.Database.CreateExecutionStrategy();
    return strategy.ExecuteInTransactionAsync(    EF Core should clear change tracker.
      action, didItWork);
  }
}
```

Using the `Retryable` extension, you can simplify the `TransferAsync` method to the code shown in the following listing.

Listing 11.14 Using retryable transaction in `TransferAsync`

```
public Task TransferAsync(
  string from, string to, decimal amt)
  => _ctxt.ExecuteRetryableTransactionAsync(async() => {
    await CreditAsync(to, amt);
    await DebitAsync(from, amt);
  });
```

We don't want to repeat this transaction if we don't have to. With the verifying extension, when the database connection is lost during transaction commit, EF Core will establish a new connection and check whether the transaction succeeded. Unfortunately, we have no reliable way to determine whether the transaction succeeded by looking at the balances of the two accounts. The problem is that other transactions may have occurred between retries and changed the account balances. Even if we get the balances from both accounts before the transaction and then use the didItWork function to check whether the balances have changed by the transfer amount, those balances may have been changed by other bank transactions.

The only reliable way to check whether the transaction succeeded is to redesign how the bank transfers are processed (perhaps by using the CQRS pattern mentioned in section 11.2.1). This case is one in which how well your application handles failures depends on your requirements and budget. Being able to retry a transaction is a net gain over not retrying at all, and the case for connection loss specifically during commit is rare, so most developers go with the simpler execution strategy.

11.3 Polly

EF Core's built-in retries are nice, but what about other areas of the application that don't use EF Core but need to retry? Before writing your custom retry loop, consider one of the libraries on NuGet that offer sophisticated error handling. The de facto standard for error handling in .NET is Polly. The Microsoft extension library for the HttpClientFactory (Microsoft.Extensions.Http.Polly) even uses Polly to apply policies to HTTP requests. If you want to learn more about Polly or its policies, check out the excellent documentation at https://github.com/App-vNext/Polly/wiki.

To try Polly, create some policies for HTTP requests to the XKCD API. You can follow along with this code by copying the code from chapter 8. This code includes a test project that mocks the HttpMessageHandler, which we can use to simulate an invalid response code, such as 500. The XkcdClient class takes an HttpClient parameter in its constructor, which is normally populated by dependency injection. The GetLatestAsync method calls GetStreamAsync on the HttpClient but doesn't use a try/catch to handle any exceptions. Thanks to the Microsoft extension library for Polly, we can apply a retry policy to the HttpClient.

Let's start by looking at the HttpClient registered in dependency injection for the XkcdClient in the ComicFinderService. Start by adding the Microsoft extensions NuGet package with the command dotnet add package Microsoft.Extensions.Http.Polly.

Then add a line to the `HttpClient` registration to add a Polly policy, as shown in the following listing.

```
services.AddHttpClient<IXkcdClient, XkcdClient>(
  client => client.BaseAddress =          Sets the address
  new Uri(baseAddr!))
  .AddPolicyHandler(GetRetryPolicy());     Extension method
```

Add the method `GetRetryPolicy` to create the Polly policy, as shown in the following listing.

```
using Polly;              Add usings.
using Polly.Extensions.Http;
                                                    HttpResponseMessage
static IAsyncPolicy<HttpResponseMessage> GetRetryPolicy()   is the request return
  => HttpPolicyExtensions                                    type.
    .HandleTransientHttpError()                      Polly helper class
    .WaitAndRetryAsync(6, retryCount =>        Retries on transient errors
      TimeSpan.FromMilliseconds(            Retries up to six times
        100 * Math.Pow(2, retryCount)));

    100 ms times a power of 2      Delays before each retry
```

The Microsoft extension library allows you to set a Polly policy on the `HttpClient`—nothing else. Polly has a core set of functionality for retry logic as well as other useful error-handling concepts. Because HTTP retries are common, Polly has an out-of-the-box handler for HTTP. Network failures, timeouts, and 500-level status codes are included in the `HandleTransientHttpError` handler.

The `HandleTransientHttpError` method isn't required, but it does a lot of heavy lifting. You could write your own policy that specifically retries on the transient error codes identified by Polly but excludes network timeouts and includes the 429 status code, which means that the server is receiving too many requests. Such a policy would be written as shown in the following listing.

```
static IAsyncPolicy<HttpResponseMessage> GetRetryPolicy()   Indicates the
  => Policy<HttpResponseMessage>                             result type
    .HandleResult(r => r.StatusCode ==
      System.Net.HttpStatusCode.TooManyRequests)      429 status code
    .OrTransientHttpStatusCode()
    .WaitAndRetryAsync(6, retryCount =>        Polly helper method
      TimeSpan.FromMilliseconds(
        100 * Math.Pow(2, retryCount)));     Same backoff-retry as before
```

11.3.1 Simulating HTTP errors

Although it's great to add error-handling policies to our code, how do we know that our policies work? When a policy is applied to custom code that throws exceptions, throwing exceptions is straightforward enough to write tests for. But simulating HTTP error responses is a little more involved. The Microsoft extension library has a class called PolicyHttpMessageHandler that allows it to apply policies. We can make a subclass of this class for testing purposes and use it in the HttpClient. Assuming that you copied the code from chapter 8, find the XkcdComicFinder.Tests project and add a file called Test-PolicyHttpMessageHandler.cs. Then add the code from the following listing.

Listing 11.18 Extending the PolicyHttpMessageHandler

```
using Microsoft.Extensions.Http;
using Polly;

namespace XkcdComicFinder.Tests;

internal class TestPolicyHttpMessageHandler
  : PolicyHttpMessageHandler              ◁──── Base class
{
  public Func<HttpRequestMessage, Context,
    CancellationToken, Task<HttpResponseMessage>>
    OnSendAsync { get; set; } = null!;      ◁──── Test provides this Func.

  public TestPolicyHttpMessageHandler(
    IAsyncPolicy<HttpResponseMessage> policy)   ◁──── Polly policy
    : base(policy) { }

  public TestPolicyHttpMessageHandler(        ◁──── Another constructor
    Func<HttpRequestMessage,
    IAsyncPolicy<HttpResponseMessage>> policySelector)
    : base(policySelector) { }

  protected override Task<HttpResponseMessage>
    SendCoreAsync(
    HttpRequestMessage request,
    Context context,
    CancellationToken cancellationToken)
    => OnSendAsync(request, context, cancellationToken);   ◁──── Calls Func
}
```

Next, create a new file called XkcdClientRetryTests.cs, and add the code from the following listing.

Listing 11.19 Simulating calls that fail and then succeed

```
using Polly;
using static System.Net.HttpStatusCode;

namespace XkcdComicFinder.Tests;
```

```
public class XkcdClientRetryTests
{
  private const string LatestJson =         ←———| Copies from other tests
    /*lang=json,strict*/ """           ←——— If .NET 7 or later
    {
      "month": "6",
      "num": 2630,
      "link": "",
      "year": "2022",
      "safe_title": "Shuttle Skeleton",
      "title": "Shuttle Skeleton",
      "day": "8"
    }
    """;

  [Fact]
  public async Task FailsTwiceThenSucceeds()
  {
    var policy = Policy<HttpResponseMessage>     ———| Doesn't check status code
      .Handle<HttpRequestException>()       ←——
      .RetryAsync(retryCount: 3);         ←——— Retries three times

    var handler =new TestPolicyHttpMessageHandler(policy);  ←——|
    var httpClient = new HttpClient(handler);                  | Uses test message
    httpClient.BaseAddress = new Uri("https://xkcd.com");      | handler

    var callCount = 0;
    handler.OnSendAsync = (req, c, ct) =>        ←——— Sets handler's Func
    {
      if (callCount < 2)
      {
        callCount++;
        throw new HttpRequestException();   ←——— First two calls throw exceptions.
      }
      else
      {
        return Task.FromResult(
          new HttpResponseMessage()
          {
            StatusCode = OK,          ←——| Third call returns a valid response.
            Content = new StringContent(LatestJson)
          });
      }
    };
    var xkcdClient = new XkcdClient(httpClient);

    var comic = await xkcdClient.GetLatestAsync();
    Assert.Equal(2, callCount);          ←——
    Assert.Equal(2630, comic.Number);       | Checks whether exceptions happened
  }
}
```

If you have a particular set of requirements for how error handling should work with your code, the custom PolicyHttpMessageHandler gives you a way to verify that the policy is in place and correct. Otherwise, adding tests to make sure that the policy is working as configured isn't useful.

11.3.2 Other Polly capabilities

I've only scratched the surface of what Polly can do. In addition to executing back-off retries with customizable time values, you can execute methods on each retry. This approach can be helpful if you're using an expired authorization token that needs to be refreshed or are verifying that an update hasn't already happened. Beyond retries, you can use all kinds of error-handling strategies:

- *Timeouts*—Don't implement your own timeout logic. Polly has you covered.
- *Fallbacks*—When an operation fails to the point where recovery in a reasonable period is impossible, we can fall back to another value instead of returning a failure response.
- *Circuit breakers*—If a resource isn't available, each request making separate calls and getting errors back wastes time and effort. During a database failover, for example, there's a small window of time in which connections could time out if used. Each incoming request that uses the database makes a query and timeout on its own, tying up the available database connections in the pool. It would be great to detect this error condition and hold any queries until we establish that the database is reachable again. This procedure is what a circuit breaker does. If the number of exceptions on a particular policy exceeds a threshold, the circuit breaker opens, and all calls are paused, preventing excessive retries that could keep the resource down longer. The circuit breaker periodically attempts to test whether the resource is available again; if the test is successful, it closes the circuit.
- *Bulkhead*—This strategy is good when a resource can handle only a certain number of parallel requests. You might depend on a web API that limits throughput or has a steep increase in pricing tiers when a certain parallel request threshold is crossed. Bulkheads can limit the number of requests going through at the same time and queue up subsequent requests, with a configurable limit on queue length. Although this error-handling policy may not sound like much, it's a proactive means of preventing errors.
- *Rate limiting*—Like the bulkhead strategy, rate limiting governs how many operations are being made, but it applies to the number of requests during a time window; it doesn't limit parallel requests. If you know that your resource can handle only five requests per second, you can create a rate-limit policy for five requests per second.
- *Caching*—This strategy is in the same vein as bulkhead and rate limiting, in that it's a means of prevention instead of an error-handling policy. Polly can cache responses, which is useful if the same inputs produce the same output. The actual cache implementation is outside Polly and uses standard .NET/Microsoft cache providers.

Summary

- Use database transactions to ensure that all updates in a set of updates either happen or don't happen.
- EF Core has built-in retry logic through default execution strategies.
- Default execution strategies usually don't cover transactions.
- Rarely, transactions can fail in a way that leaves the result in doubt. EF Core provides a mechanism to check the outcome.
- Transactions can fail at the commit phase, leaving the outcome uncertain.
- Use Polly in places that require retries outside or in addition to EF Core.
- Testing Polly policies can give you confidence that they work as expected.

12

Building
world-ready applications

This chapter covers

- Making your application world-ready
- Performing a localizability review
- Localizing your application

When I say *world-ready*, I don't mean it in the sense of `"Hello, World!"`, and I don't mean that your application is ready to be released to production. Before making an application available to the world, consider that most of the world doesn't speak your language. Even if your application is a web API used as a backend service or a library in a NuGet package for use in other applications, anything that can be exposed to an end user should be in a form that the user can understand. Dates, time zones, languages, measurements, and even sorting order depend on region and culture.

.NET includes powerful capabilities for internationalizing applications. In this chapter, you'll learn about the recommended process for internationalization. We'll disambiguate the terms *localization*, *globalization*, and *internationalization*. (World-ready is a Microsoft term to describe the whole process.) We'll also explore the techniques and APIs for localization in .NET, beginning with an example application.

12.1   *Creating the sample application*

One company that I had the privilege of consulting for built a unique type of commercial air conditioner. The idea was simple: run the air conditioner at night to create a block of ice and then use the block of ice to create cool air during the day. Even though creating the ice takes energy, some areas have lower electricity rates during off-peak hours. For power companies, this ice is a form of stored energy (like a battery) that evens out power use during the day. The software that comes with these air conditioners enables power companies to monitor and control the air conditioners. We'll model this air conditioner software as an ASP.NET Core web API.

Suppose that you're a developer for this company, based somewhere in California. The sales team has landed its first international deal, which is great news for expanding the company. But the API was developed with the assumption that all your customers would be English-speaking and located in California. You need to go through the process of internationalization.

You can think of an air conditioner as being an Internet of Things (IoT) device. In this example, the device has an HTTP endpoint that can be reached by a central controller at the power station and by the owners of the site where the units are installed. The endpoint is an API that returns a set of measurements from each unit's sensors. The unit periodically records the measurements on a hard drive. Although the API would likely provide access to download all the measurements and allow long-polling or HTTP/2 to get live updates, we don't need those capabilities for this example. In this case, the API will return the last set of measurements it collected. The response would look like the following listing.

Listing 12.1   Example response from the air conditioner's API

```
{
  "UnitId": 1,           ◁──── Identifies unit at site
  "Site": "TIJ1",
  "Timestamp": "2022-10-10T00:05:00.000Z",     ◁──── UTC instead of localized time
  "Measurements": {
    [
      "SensorName": "ExhaustAirTemp",      ◁──── Sensor name
      "Value": 15.2,
      "Description": "Exhaust Air Temperature"       ◁──── Localized description
    ],
    [
      "SensorName": "CoolantTemp",
      "Value": 3.4,                  ◁──── Temperature in Celsius
      "Description": "Coolant Temperature"
    ],
    [
      "SensorName": "OutsideAirTemp",
      "Value": 24.1,
      "Description": "Outside Air Temperature"
    ]
  }
}
```

The z in the timestamp string means *zero offset*, which is a way to represent Coordinated Universal Time (UTC). Most developers stick with UTC times in all their code except when it's presented to a user. Local time depends on where the unit is and what laws are in effect at the time. UTC is easier to handle than local times and prevents some ambiguity.

> **NOTE** The acronym for *Coordinated Universal Time* seems as though it should be CUT, not UTC. The agencies in charge wanted an abbreviation that was the same in all languages. English speakers proposed CUT, and French speakers proposed TUC, so the agencies compromised by using neither of those proposals.

UNIX epoch time

.NET's DateTime class has methods to convert to UNIX epoch time (also called UNIX time but not epoch time, which is ambiguous). Some developers prefer to use UNIX time because it's a signed integer that expresses the seconds (or higher granularity) since 00:00:00 UTC on January 1, 1970. The signed integer takes up less space than a full timestamp string like the one in listing 12.1. But UNIX time doesn't account for leap seconds. UTC does include leap seconds, which can cause UNIX timestamps and UTC timestamps to be out of sync. Also, UNIX time has in the past been stored in 32-bit signed integers, which will overflow soon. This situation is called the Year 2038 problem or the Epochalypse (see https://www.epochalypse.today). Recording a timestamp in the string UTC format prevents these complications.

> **TIP** If you're curious about the minutiae of dates and times and why localization is difficult, check out Noda Time (https://nodatime.org), a .NET library for handling dates and times more accurately. The user guide indicates the rationale for the library and shows where CoreFX falls short.

Create a new web API project from the built-in template called AcController, using the command dotnet new webapi --name AcController --use-controllers --use-program-main. The default template includes one controller, the WeatherForecastController, that returns a random set of WeatherForecast objects. You can rename these files MeasureController and Temperatures, respectively, or create new files. The following listing shows the contents of the Temperatures file.

Listing 12.2 Contents of Temperatures.cs

```
namespace AcController;

public record Temperatures (
    int UnitId,
    string Site,
    DateTimeOffset Timestamp,              ←── DateTimeOffset contains time zone offset.
    IEnumerable<Measurement> Measurements  ←── Any readable collection of measurements
) { }
```

```
public class Measurement          ⟵——— Not using record to allow updates
{
  public string SensorName { get; set; }
  public decimal Value { get; set; }     ⟵——— Uses decimal for accuracy
  public string Description { get; set; }

  public Measurement(string sensorName, decimal value,
      string description)
  {
    SensorName = sensorName;
    Value = value;
    Description = description;
  }
}
```

Decimal vs. double or float

A *floating-point number* is a means of representing a real number (real as opposed to integer) by using a fraction. Because the parts of the fraction are represented in base 2 rather than base 10, some loss of precision can occur. Many implementations of floating point, including the one used in .NET, can't represent the value `0.1` accurately, for example. The C# documentation states that types such as `float` and `double` are normally used to improve performance or reduce the number of bytes needed to store the number, and it recommends using `decimal` in all other cases. Decimal numbers in .NET are more accurate than double or float.

Next, set the contents of the MeasureController file to match the following listing.

Listing 12.3 `MeasureController` class with `GET` action handler

```
using Microsoft.AspNetCore.Mvc;

namespace AcController.Controllers;

[ApiController]
[Route("[controller]")]
public class MeasureController : ControllerBase
{                                                          ⟵  Updated by
  private static readonly Measurement ExhaustAirTemp =        background
    new (nameof(ExhaustAirTemp), 0, "Exhaust Air Temperature");  process (not
  private static readonly Measurement CoolantTemp =            coded)
    new (nameof(CoolantTemp), 0, "Coolant Temperature");
  private static readonly Measurement OutsideAirTemp =
    new (nameof(OutsideAirTemp), 0, "Outside Air Temperature");

  private static readonly Measurement[] _measurements =    ⟵  Measurements
    new[] {                                                   to return
      ExhaustAirTemp, CoolantTemp, OutsideAirTemp
    };

  [HttpGet("{site}/{unitId}")]          ⟵——— Site and unit id in URI
  public Temperatures Get(
```

```
    [FromRoute] string site, [FromRoute] int unitId)
{
  return new Temperatures(unitId, site,
    DateTimeOffset.UtcNow, _measurements);
}
}
```

The Program file will have to change so that it doesn't use top-level statements. If you're modifying an existing application or forgot to use the `--use-program-main` option when creating the project, it's straightforward to move the top-level statements to a Main method. The reason for changing this behavior is to give the `WebApplication-Factory` a target class to point to (chapter 8). The existing Program code can be wrapped in the `Main` method, as shown in the following listing.

Listing 12.4   Wrapping Program.cs code in `Main` method

```
namespace AcController;

public class Program
{
  public static void Main(string[] args)
  {
    // Existing Program code goes here
  }
}
```

The default webapi template should enable the Swagger UI, which gives a good indication that the controller is configured correctly. Verify that the API is working by running the application and visiting Swagger in your browser via http://localhost:<port>/swagger. Next, create a test project, using the steps from the following listing.

Listing 12.5   Commands to create AcController.Tests project

```
dotnet new xunit --name AcController.Tests
cd AcController.Tests
dotnet add package Microsoft.AspNetCore.Mvc.Testing   ⟵—— For WebApplicationFactory
dotnet add reference ../AcController/AcController.csproj
```

In the Usings.cs or GlobalUsings.cs file (depending on which version of .NET you're using), add a global `using` for the `AcController` namespace. Rename the default Unit-Test1.cs file to MeasureTests, and add the code from the following listing.

Listing 12.6   Tests for `MeasureController`

```
using Microsoft.AspNetCore.Mvc.Testing;   ⟵—— For WebApplicationFactory
using static System.Net.HttpStatusCode;   ⟵
                                              Prevents writing
namespace AcController.Tests;                 HttpStatusCode in every test
```

```
public class MeasureTests
{
  private readonly WebApplicationFactory<Program>        ◁──── Targets Program class
    _factory;

  private readonly HttpClient _client;     ◁──── Most tests will use client.

  public MeasureTests()
  {
    _factory = new WebApplicationFactory<Program>();
    _client = _factory.CreateClient();
  }

  [Fact]
  public async void RespondsOK()
  {
    var response = await _client.GetAsync(
      "/measure/TIJ1/1");             ◁──── Verifies that the service is working
    Assert.Equal(OK, response.StatusCode);
  }
}
```

Check whether the test is working by running `dotnet test`. Now we have the scaffolding in place and can begin the process of internationalization.

12.2 *Getting resource strings*

The `MeasureController` code in listing 12.3 contains a hardcoded description of the sensor written in English. If this service is consumed by a client that uses a different language, we want the description to be translated into the client's language. To do so, we need three things: the client's preferred language, a translation of the description in that language, and a way to get the translated description at runtime. We'll start with the last one.

In .NET, the localized description text is considered to be a resource. Resources don't have to be strings. You might have a client application that shows a flag representing the user's region, for example, and the flag image could be a resource. To get access to resources, we use a class called `ResourceManager`, which is available in the `System.Resources` namespace and doesn't require adding a separate NuGet package.

Modify the `Measurement` class as shown in the following listing to use the `ResourceManager` to get the description resource. You can use the sensor name as the key for the resource as long as it remains the same for all languages.

> **Listing 12.7   Using `ResourceManager` to get localized sensor description**

```
using System.Resources;       ◁──── Put at the top.

public class Measurement
{                                                              ┐ Creates only one
  private static readonly ResourceManager s_resMan =      ◁────┘
    new ("AcController.SensorNames",          ◁──── Resource file(s) to use
```

```
    typeof(Measurement).Assembly);        ◁──── Assembly containing the resources

  public string SensorName { get; set; }
  public decimal Value { get; set; }
  public string Description {
    get => s_resMan.GetString(SensorName)!;   ◁──── Gets localized description
  }

  public Measurement(string sensorName, decimal value)   ◁─┐ Removes description
  {                                                          │ parameter
    SensorName = sensorName;
    Value = value;
  }
}
```

Because this code modifies the constructor, you need to remove the description parameters from the `MeasureController`. Before this code can be tested, `Resource-Manager` needs a resource file to get strings from. The root name of the resource in listing 12.7 is `"AcController.SensorNames"`. The `AcController` portion matches the assembly name, and the `SensorNames` portion points to a resource in that assembly.

If you've worked with .NET, you're probably familiar with .resx files. A *ResX* is a file that contains resources and is in XML format. Most of the time, we don't see the actual XML in the resource file because IDEs like Visual Studio have designers built specifically for this format. In this book, I try to stay away from using IDEs unless they're necessary. Unfortunately, ResX files are too big to put in a book because they include their schema at the top instead of referencing it by URI.

Luckily, we can use another format for resource files: ResText, a resource file in text format. ResText is meant only for strings, so it isn't as powerful as ResX, but it has a succinct, lightweight format that's easy to use. Create a file in the AcController project called SensorNames.restext, and add the contents from the following listing.

Listing 12.8   Contents of SensorNames.restext

```
# Sensors        ◁──── Allows comments

ExhaustAirTemp=Exhaust Air Temperature       ◁──── key=value
CoolantTemp=Coolant Temperature
OutsideAirTemp=Outside Air Temperature
```

The .restext file isn't a code file, so .NET needs to build it differently. To do so, you'll need to add the section from the following listing to the AcController.csproj file.

Listing 12.9   Embedding .restext files as resources

```
<ItemGroup>
  <EmbeddedResource Include="*.restext" />       ◁──── Adds any .restext file
</ItemGroup>
```

An embedded resource is part of the assembly. We used embedded resources in chapter 7 to store test assets. The asset stored in the assembly isn't the .restext file itself but the .resources file generated from it. SensorNames.restext is considered to be a default resource that's embedded in the assembly; it's used as a fallback in case a resource matching the client's language isn't found.

Now that everything is in place, modify the test to check for the appropriate descriptions, as shown in the following listing.

Listing 12.10   Testing for sensor descriptions

```
public class MeasureTests                               Add to the
{                                                       beginning.
  private static JsonSerializerOptions s_jsonOptions =
    new() { PropertyNameCaseInsensitive = true };       ASP.NET Core
                                                        lowercases first letters.
  // Keep existing fields and constructor

  [Fact]
  public async void RespondsOK()        ⟵── Changes this test case
  {
    var response = await _client.GetAsync(
      "/measure/TIJ1/1");
    Assert.Equal(OK, response.StatusCode);
    var responseBody = await response.Content
      .ReadAsStringAsync();                      Reads response content
    var temps = JsonSerializer.Deserialize<TempsDto>(   ⟵── Deserializes with options
      responseBody, s_jsonOptions);
    Assert.NotNull(temps);
    Assert.Collection(temps.Measurements,    ⟵   Checks count where actions succeed
      m => Assert.Equal("Exhaust Air Temperature", m.Description),
      m => Assert.Equal("Coolant Temperature", m.Description),
      m => Assert.Equal("Outside Air Temperature", m.Description)
    );
  }

  // Add to bottom
  internal record TempsDto(           ⟵── For deserializing only
    int UnitId,
    string Site,
    DateTimeOffset Timestamp,
    IEnumerable<MeasurementDto> Measurements
  ) { }

  public record MeasurementDto(
    string SensorName,
    decimal Value,
    string Description
  ) { }
}
```

> ### Why use DTOs?
>
> Chapter 7 defined Data Transfer Objects (DTOs) for transferring data in and out of a controller. These DTOs were defined as records because records are immutable, which works well for objects passed in and out of controllers. In this chapter's example, the `Measurement` type represents a model that presumably is updated regularly to show the latest sensor readings. Allocating a new object for each of these readings isn't necessary because each request doesn't necessarily receive a unique response. But on the test side, where we need to deserialize the JSON into objects, the get-only localized `Description` property causes problems. Creating the DTO types in the test allows deserialization without putting constraints on the original model types.

> ### Assert.Collection in xUnit
>
> The `Collection` assertion in listing 12.10 expects a set of `Action` methods to check for elements in the collection. The number and order of the `Action` methods must match the contents of the collection precisely. If your collection isn't in exactly the same order each time or if the number of items could vary, use the `All` or `Contains` assertion instead.

12.3 Adding resource languages

How does `ResourceManager` make the application world-ready? To answer that question, you'll make a Spanish-language version of the SensorNames.restext file.

A power company in Mexico has purchased some of your company's air conditioners. The culture code for the Spanish language in Mexico is `es-MX`. You need to create a resource file for this culture code. Add a new file named SensorNames.es-MX .restext to the AcController project with the contents of the following listing.

Listing 12.11 String resources for the sample application for the Spanish-Mexico culture

```
ExhaustAirTemp=Temperatura del aire de escape
CoolantTemp=Temperatura del refrigerante
OutsideAirTemp=Temperatura del aire exterior
```

NOTE Apologies if these terms aren't translated well; I used a translating tool.

WARNING As mentioned in chapter 7, .NET's build system often doesn't detect changes to `EmbeddedResource`. Therefore, incremental builds won't rebuild the assembly when only an embedded resource was changed. You'll need a full build (use `dotnet build --no-incremental`) if you're changing only the .restext file.

SensorNames.es-MX.restext should be included in the assembly automatically because we used a wildcard for .restext files. Build the project, and look into the output folder (bin/Debug/net8.0/ or whatever .NET version you're using). This folder contains the AcController files. In addition, you'll find a subfolder named es-MX that contains a file named AcController.resources.dll. This file is called a *satellite assembly* and is meant specifically to hold culture-specific resources. Figure 12.1 shows where the files are in the AcController folder.

Figure 12.1   Files and folders for the AcController project, including the resource files and satellite assemblies

The purpose of separating nondefault culture code resources into their own assemblies is to allow them to be built as part of a separate pipeline if necessary. Localization is a separate step from development in most organizations. The localization team needs to be in charge of what languages to support and when those translations will happen. Translating strings too early in the development cycle can result in a lot of repeated work as developers will change the content of the strings. Requiring the application to be rebuilt to update localized resources is unnecessary and slows the localization team's development cycle.

Setting a culture as default (neutral)

SensorNames.restext is the default resources file because it has no culture code. It's considered to be the neutral culture. Notice that no AcController.resources.dll satellite assembly is in the same folder as the AcController.dll. The reason is that the neutral resources are embedded in the AcController.dll.

You don't need to embed a neutral resource, though. As an alternative, you can set a particular culture code as the neutral culture with a custom attribute, as shown in the following code snippet:

```
using System.Resources;          ←┘ Namespace for the attribute

[assembly:                       ←  This custom attribute applies on the assembly level.
    NeutralResourcesLanguageAttribute("en-US",   ←  Sets neutral/default culture code
    UltimateResourceFallbackLocation.Satellite)] ←┐
        Falls back to satellite assemblies
        instead of main assembly
```

This assembly-level custom attribute can go in any file, preferably a dedicated file. This attribute tells the `ResourceManager` to look for an `"en-US"` satellite assembly whenever it can't find a satellite assembly that matches the requested culture. Note that if it the `ResourceManager` can't find the designated neutral satellite assembly, it throws an exception. To test this behavior, you could rename SensorNames.restext to Sensor-Names.en-US.restext.

12.4 ASP.NET Core's built-in culture support

To get the Spanish version of the descriptions, the client needs to communicate to the service what language it wants. One way to communicate this information explicitly is to set the culture code in the request URL. Microsoft's documentation site uses the URL method, for example. (Try replacing the `en-us` in a `learn.microsoft.com/en-us/` URL with `es-mx` to see this behavior in action.) ASP.NET Core also has built-in middleware to handle culture specification through a query string, a cookie, or the `Accept-Language` header. The good news is that you don't have to choose; all three of these options are available by default, applied in priority order: first query string, then cookie, and then header. You can add a custom culture provider, but the built-in providers should cover most cases.

To add culture-provider support, add the code from the following listing to Program.cs. Note that the placement of this code matters because the middleware that checks the culture code must come after the middleware that determines the code. That's not the case for our web API, but we'll put the code before `app.MapControllers();` as a habit.

Listing 12.12 Enabling ASP.NET Core culture provider

```
var cultures = new[] { "en-US", "es-MX" };   ←  Support culture codes
var localizationOptions = new RequestLocalizationOptions()
    .SetDefaultCulture(cultures[0])          ←┐
    .AddSupportedCultures(cultures)          ←  Tells what code the default is
    .AddSupportedUICultures(cultures);       ←  See the nearby tip.
app.UseRequestLocalization(localizationOptions);
```

What's the difference between Culture and UI Culture?

Generally, you want the Culture and UI Culture to be the same. *Culture* is used for formatting, such as for dates, times, and sort order. `ResourceManager` uses *UI Culture* to determine which resources to search for, such as strings or images.

Now that we have an accepted way of passing the culture, we can add a test to check whether we get localized descriptions in the response. The only differences between this test and the `RespondsOK` test that's already in the test class are the URL and the actions to check the collection. Instead of writing another fact test, we can replace both tests with a single theory, using a Language Integrated Query (LINQ) projection to create the actions. The following listing shows how to write this theory test.

Listing 12.13   Testing that descriptions match culture

```
[Theory]
[InlineData("/measure/TIJ1/1",          <---- URL
  "Exhaust Air Temperature",          <--
  "Coolant Temperature",                |  Descriptions in order
  "Outside Air Temperature")]
[InlineData("/measure/TIJ1/1?culture=es-MX",       <---- Sets culture to es-MX
  "Temperatura del aire de escape",
  "Temperatura del refrigerante",
  "Temperatura del aire exterior")]
public async void CultureDescriptions(
  string url, params string[] descriptions)   <---- Parameters after url become an array.
{
  var response = await _client.GetAsync(url);
  Assert.Equal(OK, response.StatusCode);
  var responseBody = await response.Content
    .ReadAsStringAsync();
  var temps = JsonSerializer.Deserialize<TempsDto>(
    responseBody, s_jsonOptions);
  Assert.NotNull(temps);
                                                    Select is the
                                                    projection.
  Assert.Collection(temps.Measurements,
    descriptions.Select(d => new Action<MeasurementDto>(    <--   Actions are a
      m => Assert.Equal(d, m.Description))).ToArray());     <--   params collection.
}
```

Setting culture via query string

ASP.NET Core's localization library checks for two query strings: `culture` and `ui-culture`. If you set only one of these parameters on the query string, the library will copy the same value to the other parameter.

The last line of the test converts the array of description strings to an array of `Action` objects that perform the assertions. `Assert`'s `Collection` method takes two parameters:

the collection and a params array of `Action` objects on the collection's type. The `params` keyword in C# is flexible in that it still works if you pass it an array of the expected type.

This test should pass, but it raises a question: how does the `ResourceManager` know what the culture is? Notice that we don't explicitly get the culture from the query string and pass it through to the controller or the `Measurement` objects. At some point, this process may start to seem like magic. What's actually happening is that the culture provider reads the culture code from the query string and sets the culture on the current thread (using `System.Globalization.CultureInfo.CurrentCulture` and `Current-UICulture`). The culture is maintained for the request even if it's going to different threads while executing async `Tasks`. `ResourceManager` uses the `CurrentUICulture` value to get the culture code.

12.5 *Internationalization*

Often abbreviated as *i18n* (*i* + 18 letters + *n*), *internationalization* means different things to different companies. In Microsoft and .NET terms, internationalization refers to a process consisting of three steps.

- Globalization (g11n)
- Localizability review (l12y)
- Localization (l10n)

The definitions of these terms in Microsoft's documentation are vague and circular. A more helpful way to understand what they mean is to go through each step of the process.

12.5.1 *Globalization*

Globalization, aka world-readiness, involves designing and developing an application that can adapt to the region and culture of the user. Any data that can be exposed to the user—such as strings, dates, and numbers—needs to be adaptable to the region's and culture's language, sort order, and formats.

Note that although globalization means that the software must be adaptable to the user's region and culture, it doesn't mean that each culture is supported. You shouldn't need to alter the code when you want to support an additional language or region, and you don't need to have that language built into your code when you ship. Although adding new cultures sounds easy to achieve, making incorrect assumptions is fairly common. To see why, create a new console application (the example repo uses the name AcController.Client), and add the code from the following listing to the Program file.

Listing 12.14 Code for AcController.Client

```
using System.Globalization;
using System.Net.Http.Headers;
using System.Text.Json;
```

```
var culture = CultureInfo
    .CreateSpecificCulture("es-MX");    ◁──┘    Or some other culture code
Thread.CurrentThread.CurrentCulture = culture;    ◁────  Sets culture on the application
Thread.CurrentThread.CurrentUICulture = culture;

                                                  Fills in port number
var client = new HttpClient() {
  BaseAddress = new Uri("http://localhost:<port>")  ◁──┘
};                                                        Uses Accept-Language
client.DefaultRequestHeaders.AcceptLanguage.Add(   ◁──     header
  new StringWithQualityHeaderValue(culture.Name));  ◁──┘
                                                        Sets culture code
var responseBody = await client.GetStringAsync(   ◁──
  "/measure/TIJ1/1");                               Gets only response body
var temps = JsonSerializer.Deserialize<TempsDto>(  ◁──
  responseBody, new JsonSerializerOptions() {       Uses DTOs to deserialize
    PropertyNameCaseInsensitive = true
  }
);

Console.WriteLine("Timestamp: " +
  temps!.Timestamp.LocalDateTime);         ◁────  Writes local time
Console.WriteLine("Site     : " + temps.Site);
Console.WriteLine("Unit ID  : " + temps.UnitId);
foreach (var measure in temps.Measurements)
{
  Console.WriteLine(
    measure.Description.PadLeft(36)    ◁────  Right-aligns description to 36 chars
    + ": " + measure.Value + " C");   ◁──
}                                             Temperature is in Celsius.

internal record TempsDto(    ◁────  Copies DTO code from tests
  int UnitId,
  string Site,
  DateTimeOffset Timestamp,
  IEnumerable<MeasurementDto> Measurements
) { }

public record MeasurementDto(
  string SensorName,
  decimal Value,
  string Description
) { }
```

The purpose of this code is to call the AcController web API and write the sensor data to the console. Make sure that AcController is running before you execute this application. One important note: having a culture set on the current thread doesn't mean that the HttpClient will automatically add it to requests.

The code in listing 12.14 writes the current sensor readings to the console, but this code isn't world-ready. The problem is in the string concatenation, which makes an assumption about the order of elements in a sentence that may not make sense in all languages. In languages that read right to left, for example, the C should appear on the left.

One way to fix this problem is to alter the strings in the SensorNames.restext file. Instead of returning the description by itself, you could treat the description like a label. Then the label could allow substituting the temperature value wherever necessary. The following listing shows what these labels could look like. The placeholders for string substitution are part of the resource file.

Listing 12.15 Using placeholders in resources

```
ExhaustAirTemp=Exhaust Air Temperature: {0} C
CoolantTemp=Coolant Temperature: {0} C
OutsideAirTemp=Outside Air Temperature: {0} C
```

Exercise: Display temperatures in Fahrenheit

.NET doesn't provide facilities for converting temperatures based on region. Use of Fahrenheit is by region, not by language. You can determine the region by the country code and match to the table of International Organization for Standardization (ISO) country codes at https://www.iso.org/obp/ui/#search. To get the country code, create a `RegionInfo` object as shown in the following code snippet:

```
var culture = CultureInfo
  .CreateSpecificCulture("en-US");
var region = new RegionInfo(culture.LCID);     ◁—— Can also use "en-US"
Console.WriteLine("Country code = " +
  culture.TwoLetterISORegionName);
```

Only a few countries use Fahrenheit: the United States and island nations such as the Bahamas and the Cayman Islands. To calculate Fahrenheit, multiply by 9, divide by 5, and add 32. You also need to make the Celsius designation in the resource strings a substitutable parameter (such as `Coolant Temperature: {0} {1}`).

Then the client can use `string.Format(description,  value)` to write the label. Resource files in other languages can position the placeholders wherever appropriate.

Although this solution is one way to deal with the problem, it forces the service to conform to how the client will use it. Instead, the client could have its own resource strings to write the labels. This approach normally isn't the best one. We can take a shortcut because we can assume that the order is different only for right-to-left languages. The following listing shows how to detect this situation and adjust the output.

Listing 12.16 Reversing label for right-to-left languages

```
var reading = culture.TextInfo.IsRightToLeft
  ? $"C {measure.Value} :{measure.Description}"
  : $"{measure.Description}: {measure.Value} C";
Console.WriteLine(reading);
```

Note that this listing doesn't include the padding, which makes the code easy to read. Also, the `WriteLine` statements for the timestamp, site, and unit ID should be reversed.

Suppose that all these items are taken care of and the code is world-ready. The next step is going through a localizability review.

12.5.2 Localizability review

A localizability review is a chance to review your application and test whether it's globalized (world-ready) and ready for localization (translation to different languages). Think of localizability as being similar to a code review but with a focus on globalization. Your team needs to check all the input and output to determine whether it's user-facing, including persisted data that could be affected by the culture in which the data is used.

No complete list of cultures exists because that list would change all the time. Because nothing checks whether your culture code is a real one, you can create a dummy culture for testing. Dummy cultures can be useful for finding areas of your code that break during build or testing. With a dummy culture, you can play with string contents, image sizes, sort orders, date formats, and the like. Sometimes, developers make assumptions about the length of strings, for example. In some languages, translations may be much longer strings that could cause problems. This situation is easy enough to check with a dummy culture. Because translation of all the string resources (localization) usually happens late in the product-development life cycle, building a few dummy cultures early can help you avoid last-minute fixes.

There's no prescribed way of doing a localizability review. Doing a code review and using dummy cultures are two helpful approaches. You can also enlist the help of a team or organization that specializes in internationalization.

12.5.3 Testing right-to-left languages

Suppose that your company has signed a deal with a power company in Saudi Arabia. Arabic is written right-to-left. To allow your logs to be translated into Arabic, you'll need to create an Arabic resource file. Create a new file in AcController named SensorNames.ar-SA.restext. This file will have contents like those in the following listing. You can get this file from the companion code on GitHub or get the Arabic strings by using a translation app.

Listing 12.17 Sensor descriptions in Arabic

```
ExhaustAirTemp=درجة حرارة الهواء العادم
CoolantTemp=درجة حرارة المبرد
OutsideAirTemp=درجة حرارة الهواء الخارجي
```

Next, add the `"ar-SA"` culture to the list of supported cultures in the Program file, as shown in the following listing.

Listing 12.18 Adds "ar-SA" as a supported culture to AcController Program.cs

```
var cultures = new[] { "en-US", "es-MX", "ar-SA" };
```

Next, in the client console application, change the culture to `"ar-SA"`. The output of the application should look something like the following listing.

Listing 12.19 Output when using `"ar-SA"` culture code

```
Timestamp: 24/  8/  1444 ص12:38:03 بعد الهجرة
Site     : SA1
Unit ID  : 1
درجة حرارة الهواء العادم: 0 C
درجة حرارة المبرد: 0 C
درجة حرارة الهواء الخارجي: 0 C
```

Arabic characters not supported in Windows console

If you're using the Windows command prompt, the Arabic strings may show up as "?????" in the console output. The fix for console output is complex. You'd need to install a font that supports Arabic and then change the code page in the console to see the results. Even then, the console doesn't support right-to-left languages. To check whether your code works, redirect your output to a file by using this command: `dotnet run >> output.txt`. The strings should look correct in most text editors. PowerShell doesn't have this problem.

What's up with that date in the output?

We set `Thread.CurrentThread.CurrentCulture` to the `"ar-SA"` culture. As mentioned earlier, culture controls how dates and times are written. The date shown for Saudi Arabia uses a lunar calendar. Whether or not this format is acceptable depends on the customer, as not all Saudi Arabian customers want to use the lunar calendar.

Another consideration is that Saudi Arabia may change its official calendar to use the Gregorian calendar in the future. Most of Saudi Arabia already uses the Gregorian calendar, but the `"ar-SA"` culture code still officially uses the lunar calendar. The important takeaway is that seemingly simple outputs can be complex. Look for these kinds of assumptions during localizability review.

12.5.4 Other considerations for globalization

The key to making world-ready applications is not making assumptions about any communications with the user. When you're writing software, keep the following points in mind:

- Sort order and string equality depend on culture.
- Numbers should be stored in the invariant culture because number formats depend on culture.
- Although currency values don't depend on culture, they can depend on the denomination you're using. Store this data alongside the currency value.

Invariant culture

A world-ready application shouldn't need to ship patches to keep up with politics (well, at least not politics outside the company). Data communicated by backend services needs to use a culture that doesn't change and doesn't require separate installation. In .NET, this culture is called the *invariant culture*.

Some things aren't built into the .NET Framework but are culture-sensitive:

- Addresses
- Telephone numbers
- Paper sizes
- Units of measure (length, weight, area, volume, and so on)
- Temperature

TIP The `RegionInfo.IsMetric` property on the current culture tells you whether the region uses the metric system.

LOCALIZATION

In this chapter, you've already done some localization. You produced the Spanish and Arabic translations of the sensor description resources used in the `AcController` web API. Localization is the process of creating versions of your resources that apply to specific cultures. Although Bing Translate may work for a sample application, the translations could be nonsensical, misleading, or perhaps offensive to a native speaker. Most companies hire the services of a firm that specializes in translation.

An example of incorrect Bing/Google translation

A colleague showed me the difficulty of translating with online tools. If you use Bing/Google Translate to convert the English word *turkey* (the animal) to Arabic, you'd get an appropriate translation referring to the animal. But if you want the word *Turkey* (the country), you'll have a harder time getting the translation to work. The capitalized first letter doesn't affect the translation, and *Turkey country* just gives you a country of turkeys. Luckily, the country has changed its name with the United Nations to Türkiye, which prevents this particular gaffe for English-speakers.

You don't need all the localized resources while you're writing your code. The resource files are independent enough that you can avoid giving an external translation company access to your source code by giving them only the resource files.

Context is also important in translation. The resources file on its own doesn't give the translator much context. You can help by adding comments to the .restext file (using # or ; at the beginning of a line). Developers need to remember to write these comments, but they may forget or might not have enough information. You could decide to let the translator see the running application, but if the application is specialized, such as an MRI machine, this help might not be enough. You may need a translator who understands your business, or you'll have to give them enough context to figure out the appropriate translations. Bottom line: don't take localization lightly.

Summary

- Internationalization is a process involving globalization, localizability review, and localization steps.
- Localization files are embedded resources that turn into satellite assemblies.
- Challenge your assumptions about any of your code that interacts with users.
- ASP.NET Core has built-in culture providers to get the culture code from query strings, cookies, or request headers.
- The current culture is set on the current thread and follows async `Tasks`.

Working with containers 13

Containers have become increasingly prevalent in software development. The core concept boils down to providing an isolated and portable environment to run software. One of the difficulties of developing software is the fact that things run differently depending on the machine. The OS provides access to all kinds of resources: network ports, filesystem, environment variables, other processes, kernel APIs, and so on. These resources may change from one machine to another (which is where the infamous line "It works on my machine" comes from).

13.1 Why use containers?

Machine-specific settings lead to diagnosing problems such as not having a certain dependency installed, having network ports already in use, or needing environment variables for a process that hamper other processes. These problems can take a lot of time to figure out—time that developers would rather spend writing software. By

280

writing software that runs in a container, a developer guarantees that resources and dependencies are specified clearly so that the host OS can provide them. Containers can also be built on top of other container images.

> **An example of a breaking change in .NET Framework**
>
> You use .NET Framework 4.5 to build an application that reads a list of files from a folder and puts the filenames in a database table. The maximum length of a file path in this version of .NET Framework is 260 characters, so the column's data type is set to `varchar(260)`. The application catches exceptions of type `System.IO.PathTooLong-Exception` when the path exceeds 260 characters, reports to the console, and skips saving the row to the table. But on some customer machines, this process doesn't work, and the application breaks. The customer has .NET Framework 4.6.2, which supports long paths, and the `PathTooLongException` is thrown only if the path exceeds maximum `int` (32,767) characters. Your application is broken by a dependency that you can't control.

Contrast the .NET Framework example in the preceding sidebar with the container model. The container you build will be based on the official Microsoft image for a specific .NET version. Even if new .NET versions are released with breaking changes, the container has its version of .NET within. This container can be run on any machine (with matching OS) regardless of whether .NET is installed on the machine or what other containers are running. Containers give you greater control of distribution.

13.2 Container landscape

For many developers, the word *container* is almost always preceded by *Docker*. But the idea of process isolation goes way back. Early UNIX added a way to set the root directory of a process to a different location in the filesystem (chroot), allowing segregation of file access per process. In 2004, Solaris introduced Solaris Zones and Solaris Containers, which allowed isolated OS-level virtualization. Some people described Solaris Containers as "chroot on steroids". In 2006, Google launched a means of isolating resource use in Linux that would later be merged into the kernel. Early Docker built on a system called LXC (LinuX Containers) before replacing it with its own library, called `libcontainer`.

There is no single way to build and run containers. Docker wasn't the first in the space, but it provided the most complete ecosystem for container management. I haven't found an equivalent alternative to Docker, but plenty of tools to make containers are available. For local development, especially in macOS and Windows, Docker is the best.

Before .NET 7, the easiest way to build containers was to use Docker's tools. .NET 7 and later have built-in support for creating containers. But knowledge of Docker is still helpful, especially because Docker is the easiest way to host a container locally. We'll use Docker to host .NET containers for development.

NOTE   To get started, download Docker Desktop at https://www.docker.com/ products/docker-desktop and follow the instructions provided. Linux users can use either Docker Desktop or Docker Engine.

When it comes to hosting containers in production, you have a bit more choice. Docker has a product called Docker Swarm, Azure has Azure Container Instances, and Amazon has Elastic Container Service. The most common choice for hosting containers in production environments is Kubernetes, often abbreviated as K8s (*K*, 8 letters, *s*). Setting up Kubernetes by yourself can be daunting, though. Some cloud providers have managed Kubernetes offerings such as Google Kubernetes Engine, Amazon Elastic Kubernetes Service, and Microsoft Azure Kubernetes Service. Any of these options should be able to host your containers in production; their use falls outside the scope of this .NET book.

13.3 *Building a container image*

The method you use to build containers depends on your .NET version. .NET 7 and later have built-in container publishing. For .NET 6 and earlier, you have to create your own Dockerfile. Even in .NET 7, the published container provides only the most basic form of container image (equivalent to a boilerplate Dockerfile); you still need to install Docker Desktop. Any customizations require creating a Dockerfile.

Before trying the different methods, you need an application to containerize. In the supplemental code, I copied the AsciiArtSvc from chapter 3. It's better to pick an application like a service for this example because we want the application to stay running. A console application that does some work and completes is short-lived and harder to observe. Also, if the console application requires input, you have to figure out how to get console input to the container.

The AsciiArtSvc has only the default launch profiles in the launchSettings.json file. The default launch profiles won't work because they indicate that the web server should listen on http://localhost:<port>/. The identifier localhost is called a *loopback*. Loopbacks work well on regular machines, but they don't work the same way in containers. To get the web application to work properly, add the code from the following listing to the profiles section of launchSettings.json (in the Properties folder).

Listing 13.1 **Docker launch profile without** `localhost` **loopback**

```
"docker": {
  "commandName": "Project",
  "dotnetRunMessages": true,
  "launchBrowser": false,                    ⟵——| No browser in container
  "applicationUrl": "http://*:5101",         ⟵—— Listens for anything on this port
  "environmentVariables": {
    "ASPNETCORE_ENVIRONMENT": "Development"        ⟵—— For debugging
  }
},                              ⟵—— Be careful of trailing commas.
```

TIP   C# supports trailing commas, but most JSON parsers don't. Trailing commas are helpful when you write a list of comma-separated items with one item per line. If the last line doesn't have a trailing comma and you add another line, you have to put a comma at the end of the preceding line. When you look at this list in code review, you see two lines changing instead of one. This process is also helpful if you're generating text or code and don't know how many items to write ahead of time. Sometimes, JSON parsers support trailing commas, but not using them in JSON is generally safer.

Note that the `applicationUrl` in listing 13.1 is `http`, not `https`. The use of `https` means that a certificate is needed. Container images are immutable, so adding a certificate to them doesn't work and also creates a security concern. Through tools such as Docker Swarm and Kubernetes, you can expose secrets to containers. The secrets are managed separately so that you can rotate the certificate without creating a new image. Most production environments, however, route traffic to the container through a proxy such as Envoy (https://www.envoyproxy.io) or Istio (https://istio.io), which handles the SSL certificate. This practice eliminates the complication of requiring every container to handle certificates.

13.3.1   Using .NET 6 and earlier or custom Dockerfile

Docker provides a command-line utility to build containers. This utility looks for a file named Dockerfile to specify details about the container. The Dockerfile format has only two types of elements: comments and instructions. Assuming that you've grabbed the AsciiArtSvc code, add a new Dockerfile to the project directory, and insert the code from the following listing.

Listing 13.2   Dockerfile for AsciiArtSvc

```
# Use the official .NET 6 container
FROM mcr.microsoft.com/dotnet/sdk:6.0

# Copy files from the current folder on your machine to
# the /src folder in the container
COPY . /src

# Set working directory in the container
WORKDIR /src

# Expose HTTP port from "docker" launch profile
EXPOSE 5101

# Run the application when the container is started
ENTRYPOINT ["dotnet", "run", "--launch-profile", "docker"]
```

The Dockerfile format generally doesn't have leading whitespace, although it's allowed (and ignored). Comments are sometimes used for parsing directives, but we won't use them here.

The interesting part of the Dockerfile is the instruction. An instruction is always given in the form INSTRUCTION arguments. A Dockerfile *must* begin with a FROM instruction. A Dockerfile can have multiple FROM instructions; we'll get into that topic later in this chapter. The FROM indicates the *base image*—some existing image that we'll modify. Images are immutable, so to change them, we have to start from a base, make modifications, and save to a new image. The changes we make copy the source of AsciiArtSvc to a folder and set an entry point that runs the application. Everything from the current folder gets copied over unless we specify otherwise. The bin and obj folders that are part of our local build shouldn't go into the image, so we should tell Docker to ignore them. We do so by using a .dockerignore file. Create this file, and add the lines from the following listing.

Listing 13.3 Contents of .dockerignore

```
/bin/
/obj/


# Ignore any Visual Studio Code-specific artifacts        ⟵── If you're using VS Code
/.vscode/
```

.NET and any IDE produce many more artifacts than you need to be in the container image. You can get a more comprehensive .dockerignore file at https://www.gitignore .io/api/csharp. (gitignore.io is owned by and redirects to toptal.com.)

   With the two Docker files created, we're ready to build the image. Make sure that Docker Desktop is installed and that the docker command works on the command line. From the AsciiArtSvc project folder, run the command from the following listing to build the container image and register it with Docker under the tag asciiartsvc (must be lowercase).

Listing 13.4 Building AsciiArtSvc image and applying tag

```
docker build --tag asciiartsvc .
```

The first run takes longer because Docker needs to retrieve the base image(s). Subsequent builds can use cached images because they're immutable. When the image is created, you should see it in Docker Desktop, as shown in figure 13.1.

TAGGING AND VERSIONING

Notice in figure 13.1 that the new image is tagged latest. By default, if you don't specify a version in the tag, the version is considered to be the latest. Try making some changes to the Dockerfile or to the AsciiArtSvc code and then run the docker build command again. You'll see the new image in Docker Desktop, but the old image will be marked dangling, as shown in figure 13.2.

   The image needs to have a tag and a version. The first image we built, however, had only a tag (latest). When we built again, the new image had the same tag. The

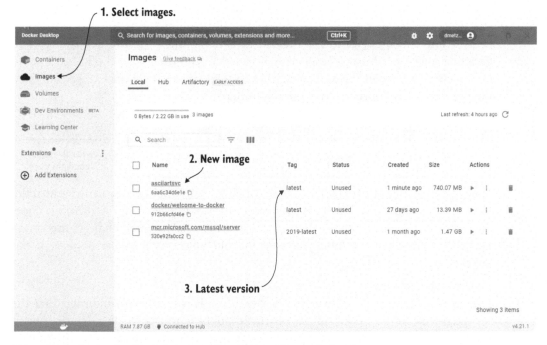

Figure 13.1   Docker Desktop's Images section showing the asciiartsvc image

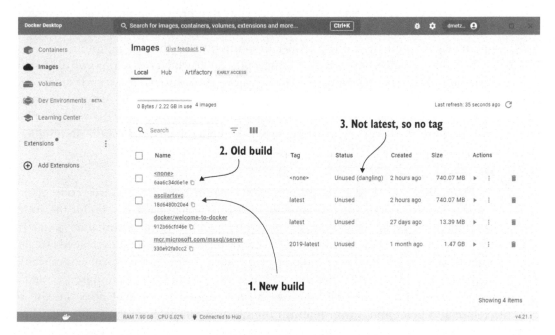

Figure 13.2   Docker Desktop's Images section showing an image tagged asciiartsvc/latest and another marked unused/dangling

old image still has an ID (the 6aa6c34d6e1e shown below the name), so any currently executing containers that use that image are still functional. But any new containers created with the latest version of the asciiartsvc tag will go to the new image. The dangling image is a bit ugly, especially because we can't tell what the image's name used to be. To prevent this situation, you can set a version tag and a latest tag each time you build, as shown in the following listing.

Listing 13.5   Building and tagging AsciiArtSvc image with `latest`

```
docker build -t asciiartsvc:latest -t asciiartsvc:0.1 .
```
◁── -t and --tag are equivalent.

Now when you view the images in Docker Desktop, you should see two entries with the same ID: 0.1 and latest. When you change the Dockerfile or the AsciiArtSvc code, build with an updated version (such as 0.2) and latest. This build changes the latest tag to the new image without marking the old image as dangling because it has another tag.

RUNNING THE CONTAINER

Listing 13.2 contains the instruction EXPOSE 5101. This instruction indicates that the service listens on port 5101. All this instruction does is inform Docker that the port is used. The instruction doesn't publish the port, which means that if you start the container, the port won't be available from outside the container. The host must assign a port to map to the exposed port when running the container.

To see how this process works, click the Play/Run button on the asciiartsvc image. This button should bring up a dialog box with a button you can click to specify optional arguments (figure 13.3). Click this button to see the port assignment.

In figure 13.3, the host machine assigns port 5000, which maps to port 5101 in the container. If you run the container, Docker shows the console output, and you can see the service listening on port 5101. Visiting http://localhost:5101 in your browser should yield an error message that the site is unreachable. Change the port to 5000, and you'll see the list of ASCII art fonts. Now you have a web application running in a container.

MULTISTAGE BUILDS

The container you created in the preceding section has all the source code of the AsciiArtSvc project. The dotnet command gets the NuGet packages, builds the code, and then runs the application, which would happen every time a container is started with this image. Ideally, we want the container to have only the files it needs to run without any NuGet restore or build steps on startup. You can perform several build steps with a build or continuous integration system or use Docker's multistage build.

You might break the build into two stages: a publish step that does the NuGet restore and build and a run step with the entry point. Each time a FROM instruction appears in a Dockerfile, it signifies a new build step.

**2. Exposed port
from Dockerfile**

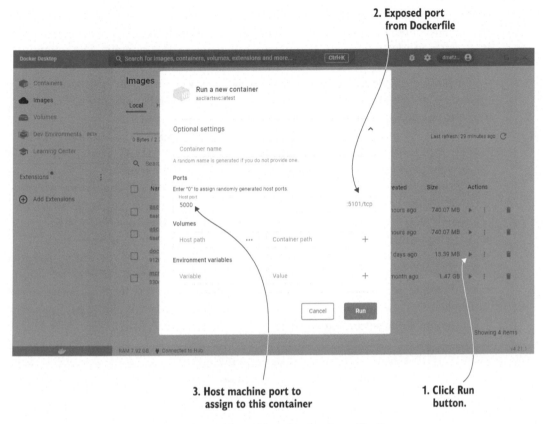

**3. Host machine port to
assign to this container**

**1. Click Run
button.**

Figure 13.3 Docker Desktop starting a container with optional port specification

The following listing shows this two-stage build.

Listing 13.6 Dockerfile with two build stages

```
FROM mcr.microsoft.com/dotnet/sdk:6.0        ⟵——— SDK base image
COPY . /src
WORKDIR /src
RUN dotnet publish -o /publish    ⟵——— Publishes binaries

                                                    ⟵─┐ New base image
FROM mcr.microsoft.com/dotnet/aspnet:6.0     ⟵─┘
COPY --from=0 /publish /publish    ⟵——— Copies from first image
WORKDIR /publish
EXPOSE 80                                     ⟵——— Default HTTP port
ENTRYPOINT ["dotnet", "AsciiArtSvc.dll"]      ⟵─┐
                                               └─ No launch profile
```

TIP You can replace the contents of the existing Dockerfile or create a separate file (such as Dockerfile-multistage) and use the -f option on the docker
build command to specify the Dockerfile to use.

In the first stage, we use the .NET SDK image. The SDK has the tools to do the NuGet restore and build and to publish the binaries. The second stage is on the second FROM instruction; it uses a different base image called aspnet that contains just enough to run ASP.NET Core applications and is much smaller than the SDK base image.

Each build stage gets assigned a number, which is why we see the instruction COPY --from=0. The 0 refers to the first image where we published the binaries. Stages can also have names to make them easier to identify, as we'll see next.

The EXPOSE instruction now exposes port 80. Published binaries don't use the launch profiles from launchSettings.json. By default, the HTTP port is 80, so we expose that port (which is only for inside the container). We removed the launch profile argument from the entry point, but it still has the dotnet command, which is included in the base image.

When you run a container with this new image, you should see the startup time improve significantly. The time savings comes from the shift of the dotnet publish command to execute when building the image. When you change the source and run docker build, Docker notices that the files have changed and won't use the previously cached data for that step. This cached data is called a *layer*. If you examine the image in Docker, you see a Layers section that contains each layer (figure 13.4). Typically, you have one layer per instruction.

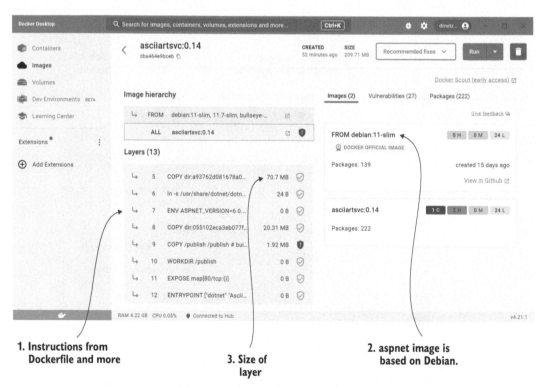

1. Instructions from Dockerfile and more

3. Size of layer

2. aspnet image is based on Debian.

Figure 13.4   Docker Desktop with the asciiartsvc image open to the Layers section

Because each layer is separate, we can make smaller steps within each stage. This approach creates a greater opportunity for the layer to be cached, which will make the overall build faster. A common optimization for .NET is to perform the dotnet restore on a separate layer. Only the project file is needed to restore the NuGet packages, so we can copy only the project file, run restore, and then copy the source code. As long as the project file hasn't changed, we can use the cached layer with the restored packages. The following listing shows how the Dockerfile would be modified for this purpose.

Listing 13.7   Dockerfile with named stages

```
FROM mcr.microsoft.com/dotnet/sdk:6.0 AS build-stage   ⟵──┐   Name the image build-stage.
WORKDIR /src                                        ⟵──┐  The working directory can be set first.
COPY AsciiArtSvc.csproj .                   ⟵──┐  Copies only the project file
RUN dotnet restore                       ⟵──┐  Gets NuGet packages
COPY . .                               ⟵──┐  Copies source code
RUN dotnet publish -o /publish

FROM mcr.microsoft.com/dotnet/aspnet:6.0
WORKDIR /publish
COPY --from=build-stage /publish .         ⟵── Uses label instead of number
EXPOSE 80
ENTRYPOINT ["dotnet", "AsciiArtSvc.dll"]
```

> **NOTE** For production images, you should add the -c Release option to the dotnet publish command. Release versions have optimizations that make the binaries smaller and faster. These versions also leave out debugging information, which is useful during testing but not desirable in a final version.

In section 13.3.2, we'll look at .NET 7's built-in support for creating container images. Even after upgrading to the latest .NET, your team may choose to stick with custom Dockerfiles; some customizations in the Dockerfile may need to be preserved.

13.3.2 Using .NET 7 and later

With .NET 7 and later, you can build containers with the dotnet command-line interface (CLI). Docker still needs to be installed but you don't have to create a Dockerfile. Start by copying the AsciiArtSvc to a new folder. Remove the bin and obj folders, as well as any Docker files such as .dockerignore and Dockerfile. Next, modify the csproj file as shown in the following listing.

Listing 13.8   Supporting container image building in .NET 7 and later

```
<Project Sdk="Microsoft.NET.Sdk.Web">

  <PropertyGroup>
    <TargetFramework>net7.0</TargetFramework>       ⟵── Target framework 7+
    <Nullable>enable</Nullable>
```

```
    <ImplicitUsings>enable</ImplicitUsings>
    <ContainerImageName>asciiart-net7</ContainerImageName>    ⟵— Adds image name
  </PropertyGroup>

  <ItemGroup>                                                      ⎤ Exposes port
    <ContainerPort Include="80" Type="tcp" />    ⟵——┘
  </ItemGroup>                                          ⟵—— ContainerPort isn't a property.

  <ItemGroup>
    <PackageReference Include="Figgle" Version="0.4.0" />
    <PackageReference Include="BarcodeLib" Version="2.4.0" />
    <PackageReference
      Include="Microsoft.NET.Build.Containers"    ⟵—— Use dotnet add package.
      Version="7.0.306" />
  </ItemGroup>

</Project>
```

> **WARNING** Microsoft's documentation says that the functionality from the
> `Microsoft.NET.Build.Containers` package should be part of new web projects
> created with .NET SDK 7.0.300 or later, so you don't need to add it. When
> you upgrade older projects (such as AsciiArtSvc) or create new nonweb proj-
> ects, you'll likely need to add the package. (A work item is open at this writing
> to address the problem of needing to add the package; this problem will most
> likely be fixed in future .NET releases.) If the `container publish` command
> fails with the message `The target "PublishContainer" does not exist in the`
> `project`, you'll need this package. The best indication that the package is no
> longer needed is if you see a compiler warning that suggests removing the
> explicit reference, which started with the latest SDKs.

Save the csproj file, and run the `publish` command with an extra option to build the
container image, as shown in the following listing.

Listing 13.9   CLI command to publish a .NET application as a container image

```
dotnet publish /t:PublishContainer --os linux --arch x64
```

> **NOTE** Production images should be built with the additional `"-c Release"`
> option to use the release configuration. The default configuration is `Debug`,
> which includes details that are helpful for debugging, such as line numbers.
> These details can be helpful for diagnosing problems but shouldn't be part of
> a production version.

You should see the asciiart-net7 image in Docker Desktop as before. Run with the
optional setting to map a port to the exposed port 80. Also notice from the layers of
the container image that .NET isn't doing a multistage build. The `dotnet publish`
command restores, builds, and publishes the application for a specific run time
(Linux, x64) and then copies it to the container, using the aspnet base image.

TIP   The version number for the application is used for the container image tag. This tag is a default setting that you can change by adding the `Container-ImageTags` property to the csproj file. If you don't change the version of the project or set an explicit version for the container, the same `1.0.0` tag will be used. If an image with that tagged version already exists, it will be replaced by the new image.

13.4 Configuration

We've learned that containers isolate applications, which makes them behave predictably in any environment. We've also learned that container images are immutable. But some parts of an application change depending on the environment. An application that accesses a database, for example, would have a different connection string in one region versus another; a staging environment might have different logging levels from a production environment; or a web API that we depend on may have a different address depending on the region. Producing a separate container image for each environment, region, or configuration change would be nonsensical.

First, distinguishing configuration from secrets is important. Configuration could be different based on environment, but there's little or zero risk if these values are exposed. Secrets are things like cryptographic keys, connection strings, and API keys that could pose a risk if they were exposed. The application needs access to the secrets, but developers don't. We'll concentrate on configuration values first.

Start by creating a new web API application called EnvTest (using `dotnet new webapi -n EnvTest`). Notice that this project contains two configuration files: appsettings.json and appsettings.Development.json. The Development part of the filename is meant to match an environment. Change the contents of appsettings.Development.json to match the following listing.

Listing 13.10   Environment-specific configuration values in appsettings

```
{
  "EnvironmentName": "Development",
  "RegionName": "My Desk"
}
```

Next, add a new controller called ConfigController.cs to the Controllers folder, and add the contents of the following listing.

Listing 13.11   `ConfigController` returning configuration values

```
using Microsoft.AspNetCore.Mvc;

namespace EnvTest.Controllers;

[ApiController]
[Route("[controller]")]
public class ConfigController : ControllerBase
```

```
{
  private readonly IConfiguration _config;          ⊲——— Allows access to config values

  public ConfigController(IConfiguration config)    ⊲——┐
  {                                                      │ Populated by
    _config = config;                                    │ dependency injection
  }

  [HttpGet]
  public string Get() => $$"""                        ⊲——— Use verbatim instead for .NET 6.
  {
    "EnvironmentName" : "{{_config["EnvironmentName"]}}",   ⊲——— Gets config value
    "RegionName" : "{{_config["RegionName"]}}"
  }
  """;
}
```

Run the application and open a browser to http://localhost:<port>/config to see the response. (I recommend installing a browser extension that formats JSON.) You should see the configuration values in the response.

13.4.1 *Controlling the .NET environment*

For a different environment or region, we may want some configuration values to be different. We'll need to tell ASP.NET Core what environment we're in, which we can do by setting an environment variable. Unfortunately, *environment* is an overloaded term, and getting confused is easy. ASP.NET Core has an environment concept that's completely separate from environment variables. An *environment variable* is a feature of the OS that the process can use to get some configuration. The "PATH" environment variable in Windows, for example, has the directories that the command prompt or shell can search to find an executable. A container host can use environment variables that are specific to the container. We can control the ASP.NET Core environment by using an environment variable on the container. To test this feature, try running (in the same terminal where you run dotnet run) the command from either of the following two listings, depending on your OS.

> **Listing 13.12   Windows PowerShell command to set environment variable**

```
$env:DOTNET_ENVIRONMENT="Prod1"
```

> **Listing 13.13   Linux/macOS shell command to set environment variable**

```
export DOTNET_ENVIRONMENT=Prod1
```

This command sets the ASP.NET Core environment to "Prod1". Next, create a new file called appsettings.Prod1.json, which has configuration settings specific to one region in production, and add the text from the following listing to the new file.

Listing 13.14   Contents of appsettings.Prod1.json

```
{
  "EnvironmentName": "Production",
  "Region": "Antarctica"
}
```

Run the application and open a browser to the same config endpoint as before. The values in the response should reflect the contents of the new configuration file.

13.4.2 Configuration order

If appsettings.Prod1.json is applied when the environment is set to `"Prod1"`, what is the point of the appsettings.json? Configuration in ASP.NET Core comes from multiple sources and is applied in a specific order. The sum of the configuration sources is flattened and made available via the `IConfiguration` interface (and other ASP.NET Core configuration primitives). When a configuration key is used in more than one source, the source that is applied later in the order overrides what came before. Configuration values are applied in the following order:

1 appsettings.json
2 appsettings.Environment.json
3 User secrets (covered in section 13.5)
4 Environment variables
5 Command-line arguments

Exercise 1: Confirm configuration order

Try out the configuration-override order by adding a key called `TestOverwrite` to appsettings.json and adding the key to the output of the config controller. One at a time, try each of these in order:

1. Set `TestOverwrite` to `one` in *appsettings.json*, and check whether it shows in the /config GET response.
2. Set `TestOverwrite` to `two` in *appsettings.Development.json*, set DOTNET_ ENVIRONMENT back to `Development`, and check whether /config GET replaced the previous value.
3. Create an environment variable in your terminal called `TestOverwrite`, set its value to `three`, run the application from the same terminal, and confirm the override.
4. Run the application with `dotnet run TestOverwrite="four"`, and confirm that it overrides everything else.

13.4.3 *Hierarchical configuration*

The configuration is expressed in appsettings.json, and JSON allows organizing content in a hierarchical form. We can take advantage of this feature to organize configuration into logical groups. Suppose that appsettings.json has the contents of the following listing.

Listing 13.15   An example of hierarchical configuration in appsettings.json

```
{
  "Level1": {
    "Level2": "test",
    "Level2Array": [                    ⟵——— Array of JSON objects
      { "Level3" : "first" },
      { "Level3" : "second" }
    ]
  }
}
```

When we're trying to get a value from IConfiguration, the key is using a composite of the hierarchy separated by colons (:). We get a value from Level2, for example, by using "Level1:Level2". This process gets a bit trickier when it comes to arrays. If you want to get the value of Level3 in the first array element below Level2Array, use "Level1:Level2Array:0:Level3". Also, the delimiter is put between array indices. Use this same delimiter when specifying configuration values as command-line parameters.

> **WARNING**   The overriding logic isn't applying intelligence when it comes to arrays; it only matches objects in the array by index.

When you're setting or overriding a configuration value from an environment variable, the delimiter isn't a colon. Instead, the delimiter is __ (two underscores). This setting means that to override the first array element below Level2Array, the environment variable name would be Level1__Level2Array__0__Level3.

13.4.4 *Applying configuration in Docker Desktop*

When running a new container from an image, you have the option of setting environment variables for that container. You can use the optional settings in Docker Desktop to set the DOTNET_ENVIRONMENT environment variable, which chooses the appsettings file to use, and to set specific configuration values (such as Level1__Level2). These settings are available in the same options section that you used to map the exported port (figure 13.5).

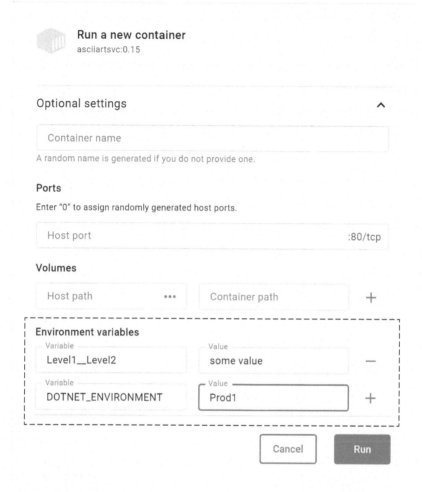

Figure 13.1 Docker Desktop starting a container with optional environment-variable settings, including DOTNET_ENVIRONMENT set to Prod1

13.4.5 *Mapping configuration to objects*

The hierarchical grouping of configuration values does more than organize the appsettings file. The IConfiguration interface also allows you to get only the parts you're interested in. An application might need to connect to Azure Cosmos DB, for example. The Cosmos DB settings would go in their own configuration section, as shown in the following listing.

Listing 13.16 An example appsettings JSON file with a section for Cosmos DB settings

```
{
  "CosmosDbSettings": {
    "DatabaseName": "somedb",
```

```
    "Endpoint": "https://somedb.documents.azure.com/"
  }
}
```

Then you could create a `CosmosDbRepository` class that's interested only in this configuration section, as shown in the following listing.

Listing 13.17   Gets Cosmos DB configuration in repository

```
public class CosmosDbRepository
{
  private readonly IConfiguration _config;          ◁──── Section is still IConfiguration.

  public CosmosDbRepository(IConfiguration config)
  {
    _config = config.GetSection("CosmosDbSettings");      ◁──── Path to section
  }

  private void Connect()
  {
    var dbName = _config["DatabaseName"];        ◁──── Gets values from section
    var endpoint = _config["Endpoint"];
  }
}
```

Although grouping configuration values is nice, a better approach would be to deserialize those groups into objects. ASP.NET Core has a built-in feature for this purpose. Let's start by creating a record that will hold the Cosmos DB settings, which should be similar to the following listing.

Listing 13.18   A C# record to hold the Cosmos DB configuration

```
public record CosmosDbSettings          ◁──── Uses this form; needs default constructor
{
  public string DatabaseName { get; init; } = null!;
  public string Endpoint { get; init; } = null!;
  public string AuthKey { get; init; } = null!;      ◁──── Secret we'll use later
}
```

Then modify the Program.cs file to tell the dependency-injection service container to bind the record to the configuration section, as shown in the following listing.

Listing 13.19   Binding `CosmosDbSettings` to configuration section

```
builder.Services.Configure<CosmosDbSettings>(          ◁──── Type to bind
  builder.Configuration.GetSection("CosmosDbSettings"));     ◁────┐
                                                                 │ Config section
var app = builder.Build();     ◁──── Included to show position   │ to bind
```

NOTE The section is an IConfiguration itself, so you can create one type for the whole appsettings file and bind to it. (I'm not saying that you should do this—only that you could.)

Now you can change the repository class to use the options pattern to get the bound configuration record. The options pattern in .NET has many useful capabilities and nuances, but the most common use is the one shown in the following listing.

Listing 13.20 Using the options pattern to get `CosmosDbSettings`

```
using Microsoft.Extensions.Options;          ◁──── Namespace for IOptions

public class CosmosDbRepository
{
  private readonly CosmosDbSettings _settings;     ◁──── Keeps the record object

  public CosmosDbRepository(
    IOptions<CosmosDbSettings> options)            ◁──── Specifies options type
  {
    _settings = _options.Value;      ◁──── Gets the bound object
  }

  private void Connect()
  {
    var dbName = _settings.DatabaseName;      ◁──── Config values in object
    var endpoint = _settings.Endpoint;
  }
}
```

NOTE Binding in this case happens only on startup. If the configuration values are changed (by changing appsettings or through a custom configuration source), those changes aren't reflected in the bound object(s). Any changes made to the bound objects won't be reflected back to the configuration file or made available to any other classes that use the options pattern.

Using a .NET type to bind to configuration allows stronger typing. (Think of using ints and bools.) Also, unit-testing is easier because mocking an IConfiguration takes more work than creating an IOptions instance. The following listing shows an example test class for CosmosDbRepository that uses the options pattern.

Listing 13.21 Creating test configuration with options pattern

```
public class CosmosDbRepositoryTests
{
  private readonly CosmosDbRepository _repo;

  public CosmosDbRepositoryTests()
  {
    var config = new CosmosDbSettings(      ◁──── Creates settings object
      "somedb",
```

```
        "https://somedb.documents.azure.com/");
    _repo = new(Options.Create(config));          ◁──── Returns IOptions object
  }
}
```

13.5   Secrets

If your team is working on an application that uses a database, each developer may want to use a different database. One developer has a local SQL Express, another uses a full SQL Server, and a third experiments with SQlite. Committing the connection string to your Git repo not only forces other developers to use your database, but also reveals any secrets such as usernames and passwords for the database. You also want to use different connection strings for each environment to which the application is deployed. Although you can give connection strings to the application through configuration, this process isn't something that you want to check in.

Specifying secrets such as connection strings through environment variables has been common practice. But this practice is one to avoid because any maintainer in your cluster (think about a container management tool like ArgoCD) can view environment variables.

.NET has a feature called *user secrets* that works with the configuration system and allows developers to keep secrets locally. (We saw user secrets in chapter 9.) In section 13.4.5, we defined a record for holding Cosmos DB connection information. This record included an `AuthKey` field that we haven't yet populated. We don't want to put this key in the appsettings.json file because it will expose the secret to anyone who manages to get access to the source code (which isn't good for open source). Each developer who has access to this database can add a user secret on their development machine with the `AuthKey` value. First, enable user secrets with the `dotnet` CLI command shown in the following listing. Be sure to run this command in the project directory.

> **Listing 13.22   `dotnet` CLI command to initialize user secrets for a project**

```
dotnet user-secrets init
```

This command adds a property to the csproj file called `UserSecretsId` with a Globally Unique Identifier (GUID) value. A file corresponding to this GUID will be created in a user's local folder. In Windows, this folder is %APPDATA%\Microsoft\UserSecrets\ <user_secrets_id>\secrets.json; in Linux or macOS, it's ~/.microsoft/usersecrets/ <user_secrets_id>/secrets.json. Because the file was initialized at only this point, it's empty. Let's add the `AuthKey` secret, using the command from the following listing.

> **Listing 13.23   `dotnet` CLI command to add or update a secret value for a project**

```
dotnet user-secrets set "CosmosDbSettings:AuthKey" "12345"
```

If you look in your user-secrets file now, you should see a JSON document containing the newly added secret. After all the configuration sources are combined, the

`CosmosDbSettings` section will include the values from both appsettings and user secrets. Remember that user secrets are applied after appsettings, so you could put an empty or dummy value for `AuthKey` in the appsettings file if you want to.

Exercise 2: Modify ConfigController to show contents of CosmosDbSettings
We've looked at how configuration data is composed and used the `ConfigController` to show the order in which configuration is combined. Extend the `ConfigController` to show the `CosmosDbSettings` along with the `AuthKey` data. Try adding empty values to the configuration, updating or removing the user secret, and overriding with environment variables or command-line parameters.

The .NET CLI user-secrets function is meant only for development. If we need to provide the `AuthKey` secret for a container, we'll need a way to include that secret in the configuration sources. You may have noticed that when you're running a new container in Docker, you can mount volumes. Mounting a volume is like sharing a folder or file with the container. Technically, we could share a file like the one generated by .NET user secrets, but we'd have to put the file in the user's local folder, which isn't a good approach. Instead, we could add a configuration source that attempts to find a secret from a mounted volume.

A built-in JSON configuration provider can read from a file. To add it, add the line from the following listing to Program.cs.

Listing 13.24 Adding optional file configuration source

```
builder.Configuration.AddJsonFile(          Reads this file
  "/settings/secrets.json",
  optional: true);            OK if file doesn't exist

                                             Adds source
builder.Services.Configure<CosmosDbSettings>(    before binding
  builder.Configuration.GetSection("CosmosDbSettings"));

var app = builder.Build();
```

NOTE Docker allows mounting folders only as volumes. The target folder (the one in the container) should be separate from other folders in the container. When the container host mounts the volume to the target folder, it can overwrite existing files. Listing 13.24 uses a folder called settings, which shouldn't already exist in the container image.

Exercise 3: Mount user-secrets file as a volume
If you open the secrets.json file that the `dotnet user-secrets` command created, you'll see that it's a JSON file using the same format as appsettings.json. Therefore, you can mount this file as a volume in Docker for the container running the EnvTest project we've been working on. First, you need to prepare the EnvTest project for Docker.

(continued)
Add the code to read the secrets.json file from listing 13.24, and test locally. Add the `Microsoft.NET.Build.Containers` package, expose the HTTP port, and give the image a name. Publish the container image to Docker, following the steps earlier in this chapter (section 13.3.1 or 13.3.2, depending on your .NET version).

When creating the container from the image, add a mounted volume in the optional settings. Mount the host folder that contains the secrets.json to the container folder settings. in Windows, the host folder is %APPDATA%\Microsoft\UserSecrets\ <user_secrets_id>\secrets.json; in Linux and macOS, it's ~/.microsoft/usersecrets/ <user_secrets_id>/secrets.json. Then run the application and verify that the `AuthKey` secret is picked up.

Summary

- Containers create a reusable, predictable, and isolated environment in which to run applications.
- Container images are immutable.
- Docker has a multistage build feature that can simplify image creation.
- .NET 7 and later include Docker image creation and publishing in the dotnet CLI.
- ASP.NET Core has built-in configuration capability.
- Configuration is hierarchical and can be represented by using the options pattern.
- Separate secrets from configuration by using mounted volumes.

appendix A
.NET history

.NET is more than 20 years old now. When any complex system gets to this age, information about where things came from can become lost or harder to find. This appendix provides a brief history. None of this information is needed to program with .NET, but it may provide some context on where certain names came from.

A.1 Adoption of .NET Core

.NET Framework 1.0 was released in 2002 and was built to work only in Windows. There were unofficial ports of .NET, at least parts of it, for Linux and Mac (such as Mono), but .NET Framework remained Windows-only. The last version, 4.8, was released in April 2019. The .NET team saw that being Windows-only made .NET less competitive and risked losing developers, so they began working on a new project.

In 2016, Microsoft began releasing a cross-platform alternative to .NET Framework called .NET Core. .NET Core borrowed all the good parts of .NET (and maybe some not-so-good parts). Many new ideas were tried in .NET Core, such as a new build system (replacing MSBuild), scrapping built-in configuration, and splitting libraries into packages instead of one big framework. This approach won favor with innovators and early adopters, but there was a problem. If you're familiar with the technology adoption life cycle, shown in figure A.1 and popularized in Geoffrey Moore's book *Crossing the Chasm,* you'll recognize that the difficulty of gaining widespread adoption of technology is bridging the gap from early adopters to the early majority (crossing the chasm). How did the .NET team get the early majority of .NET Framework developers to move to .NET Core?

One problem to address was compatibility. .NET Core's runtime can execute libraries compiled for .NET Framework because the Common Intermediate Language (CIL) is the same. Those libraries may use .NET Framework-specific APIs, however, causing failures at run time. (See the section on intermediate language in

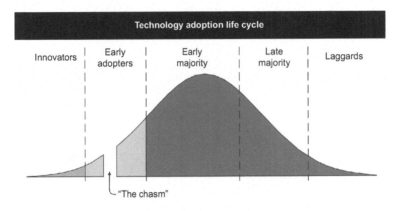

Figure A.1   Technology adoption life cycle

chapter 1.) The obvious solution is to have library builders compile for two different targets. The concept of a target framework was built into .NET early because it's important to know which .NET Framework version the library is targeting. Developers could build for both Framework and Core targets as part of their build process. The NuGet (.NET package manager) package structure already handled multiple target frameworks, so library authors wouldn't need to ship multiple packages.

A problem with the multitargeting approach was that developers were skeptical of Microsoft's commitment to .NET Core as the future. They'd been burned before by Microsoft products (such as Silverlight), and the company's approach to multitargeting seemed to be noncommittal. The answer was to introduce the .NET Standard. Although the .NET Standard was a bit confusing at first, libraries could target the .NET Standard instead of a specific runtime such as Framework or Core. If that version of Core or Framework supported at least that version of the .NET Standard, it could safely use that library. Figure A.2 shows where the .NET Standard fits in this concept.

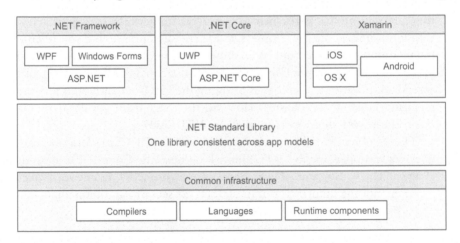

Figure A.2   .NET Standard and runtimes

The .NET Standard addressed only the ease of migrating from Framework to Core. .NET Core also had to offer some must-have features that could persuade Framework developers to move. For many large enterprises at the time, cross-platform wasn't compelling enough yet.

One area that .NET developers cared about was performance. An independent vendor named TechEmpower created a benchmark of as many web frameworks as it could find, and ASP.NET, .NET's web framework, scored embarrassingly low. The ASP.NET team aimed to fix that problem with ASP.NET Core. Their innovations led to improvements across the framework and pushed .NET to the top of the charts.

The performance improvements made for a great adoption story: use your existing in-house .NET expertise, and move to a fast, modern web framework that can deploy via containers to any host (internal data center or cloud). Applications could be migrated piecemeal instead of as full rewrites because of the .NET Standard. Now the early majority was buying into .NET Core.

A.2 .NET 5/6 and the late majority

Although .NET Core connected with the early majority, it left some developers and applications feeling left out. Some organizations can't afford to chase the latest .NET innovations and wait until things are stable. .NET Core didn't offer anything for desktop development. .NET Core was a separate download, whereas .NET Framework was built into Windows and still had support. Also, the terms Core, Standard, and Framework and the choice of version(s) to use were confusing. The .NET team would have to fix these problems to maintain momentum through the late majority.

.NET Framework's last version was 4.8. .NET Core's last version was 3.1. The .NET team decided to drop the terms *Framework* and *Core* and pick the next-highest number to make .NET 5. Desktop development on Windows was added back, including support for Windows Presentation Foundation (WPF) and Universal Windows Platform (UWP), which later changed to WinUI. .NET 5 wasn't a long-term support (LTS) release, so late-majority adopters usually skipped it. But .NET 5 achieved its purpose: making what used to be called .NET Core the official .NET going forward.

The .NET team intends the even-numbered releases to be the ones that the late majority adopts. Support for .NET Framework will continue for the foreseeable future because it ships with Windows and therefore follows the Windows life cycle policy. Developers appreciate this situation because it doesn't enforce a timeline for .NET Framework applications to be converted. Many Framework applications are still out there, even in Microsoft products, but .NET Core has moved well into the late-majority phase.

What happened to the .NET Standard?

The .NET Standard helped standardize APIs across many versions of .NET, such as Framework, Core, Mono, Xamarin, UWP, and Unity. At one time, each .NET implementation was limited to a particular version of the .NET Standard. Most implementations moved to support version 2.0, with the latest Standard version being 2.1.

(continued)
The decision for .NET 5, though, was to stop using the .NET Standard. Reusable librar-
ies would target .NET 5 or 6 instead unless developers needed or wanted to work in
.NET Framework applications or other specialized implementations, such as nano-
Framework. Library authors can still safely target .NET Standard, which has the broad-
est reach. But the .NET Standard won't continue to get new versions.

A.3   *A brief introduction to ASP.NET Core*

ASP has been around since before .NET. The acronym *ASP*, which originally stood for
Active Server Pages, has no substantive meaning in the modern framework. ASP.NET
Core was named to distinguish the product from ASP.NET and ASP, which is why the
Core part of the name remains even though the name *.NET Core* went away with .NET
5. To make things easier, you could think of ASP.NET Core as being the .NET web
framework.

ASP.NET Core isn't only a web framework, however. If not for the ASP.NET team's
desire to improve performance dramatically to compete with the best web frameworks, .NET Core might have never happened. ASP.NET had backward compatibility
all the way back to ASP, before .NET. Many performance problems could be attributed
to back-compat items. Because many performance and back-compat problems ran
deep in the .NET Framework, the team took the bold approach of rewriting from the
ground up, pulling in .NET Framework code only when it was needed and reviewing it
carefully for refactoring.

Rewriting .NET meant modernization: supporting Linux and macOS; embracing
Docker containers; and creating new libraries for dependency injection, logging,
identity, and so on. The ASP.NET team scrutinized memory allocations and performance profiles. They drove changes in the runtime, garbage collector, and compilers.
Before .NET Core, the culture of .NET at Microsoft was to deliver a single massive
framework with everything in it and bundle with Windows. This approach discour-
aged open source and drove developers to other languages and frameworks. The situation changed with .NET Core. The ASP.NET team held regular community standups.
Microsoft distributed packages separately and even took dependencies on existing
open source libraries instead of rewriting them.

Although ASP.NET Core isn't solely responsible for this dramatic change in .NET,
it played a large part. ASP.NET Core continues to innovate and affect change in .NET,
such as the minimal API starting in .NET 6 and the Blazor workload. Other influences
on .NET have contributed to its evolution (such as machine learning) and will do so
going forward. ASP.NET Core heavily shaped .NET into what it is today, and most
readers of this book will work with it, so I've covered the basics.

appendix B
Setting up your
development environment

To follow along with the code samples in this book and to run the code in the supplementary code-samples repo (https://github.com/dmetzgar/dotnet-in-action-code), you need only two things: a .NET SDK (6 or later) and a text editor.

Many editors are available for .NET, including downloadable IDEs and online editors. Because .NET has been around for a long time, some of these editors may not support the latest .NET versions. Unless I'm covering a specific feature, this book sticks to what you can do with only a simple text editor. (Think Notepad or vi.) Investing in a full-featured IDE with a debugger, autocompletion, code analysis tools, and the like will help immensely but isn't required. Here are two free editors to try:

- *Visual Studio 2022 Community edition* (Windows only)—https://visualstudio.microsoft.com
- *Visual Studio Code* (cross-platform)—https://code.visualstudio.com

NOTE For a team of six or more developers, a Visual Studio subscription may be required.

Two great editors are available for purchase:

- *Visual Studio 2022 Professional and Enterprise editions* (Windows only)—https://visualstudio.microsoft.com
- *JetBrains Rider* (cross-platform)—https://www.jetbrains.com/rider

Some editors I don't recommend are

- scriptcs
- Eclipse aCute
- #develop (SharpDevelop)

- Monodevelop (replaced by Visual Studio for Mac)
- Slickedit
- Atom (sunset as of December 2022)

These projects haven't kept up with .NET or were abandoned in favor of writing plugins for Visual Studio Code.

If your editor of choice doesn't come bundled with the latest .NET SDK, go to http://mng.bz/QZv4 to download it. Installation instructions depend on your OS; the .NET site has the most comprehensive and up-to-date information. Be sure to install the full SDK instead of only the runtime.

To verify that you've installed the .NET SDK correctly, run the `dotnet --info` command from a terminal. The command will list the current .NET SDK as well as all the .NET SDKs and runtimes installed.

appendix C
MAUI and Blazor

MAUI and Blazor are two exciting new areas of development in .NET. Much of what you've learned throughout this book applies to MAUI and Blazor. The book doesn't have enough space, however, to explain in depth what these frameworks are and how to use them. In this appendix, you'll learn a bit about how to get started with MAUI and where to find information to get started with Blazor.

C.1   *MAUI*

.NET Multiplatform App UI (MAUI) is a way to create mobile and desktop applications with .NET. If you're familiar with Xamarin, MAUI is an evolution that works with the latest versions of .NET.

One reason why this book doesn't attempt to teach you about MAUI is that it uses eXtensible Application Markup Language (XAML), a declarative language based on XML. XAML is declarative because it declares what goes into a view or control but doesn't have step-by-step instructions for rendering it. If you build a user interface in an imperative language such as C#, you must write all the steps necessary to draw the view or control. Technically, you can build MAUI applications by using C#, but doing so is uncommon. Although the XAML language has only a few constructs, its implementation for creating user interfaces has great depth. XAML is also used for Windows Presentation Foundation (WPF) and WinUI, as well as open source projects like Avalonia, but each language has its own nuances.

If you want to jump into MAUI, Manning has an excellent book called *.NET MAUI in Action*, by Matt Goldman (https://www.manning.com/books/dot-net-maui-in-action). If you're looking to test MAUI to see how it works, you'll need a few things to get started, beginning with Visual Studio or Visual Studio for Mac. Visual Studio Code has some support but is difficult to work with. Running MAUI applications using only the dotnet command-line interface (CLI) isn't possible at this writing. Visual Studio includes tools such as emulators that are required for developing in MAUI.

Fortunately, you can use the free community edition. If you already have Visual Studio installed, run the Visual Studio Installer application to check whether the MAUI workload is installed. If you're installing Visual Studio for the first time, it starts with the installer and has you pick workloads. Figure C.1 shows the workload to enable, which is named .NET Multi-platform App UI development.

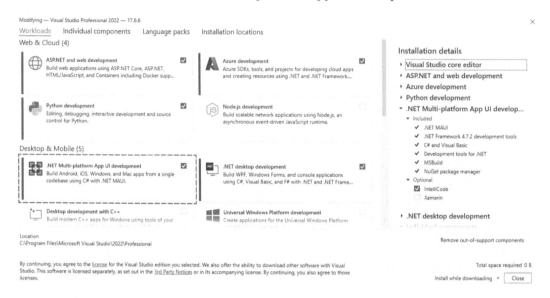

Figure C.1   Visual Studio Installer workload screen with the MAUI workload highlighted

When the workload is installed, run Visual Studio, and create a new MAUI application. When the application is created, you should be able to run it, but you have to pick a target first. If you're running Windows, you need to enable Windows Developer Mode to target Windows. For this exercise, switch to the Android emulator target. To do so, find the Play button that you click to run the application, and choose Android Emulator from the drop-down menu next to it, as shown in figure C.2.

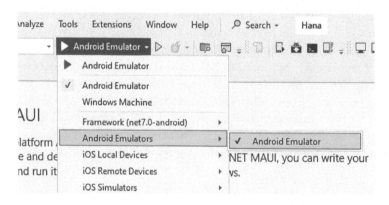

Figure C.2   Choosing the Android emulator target to run the MAUI application

Next, try to run the application using this target. If you've never installed an Android emulator before, Visual Studio will run you through accepting the license agreement and suggesting an emulator. This process brings up the Android Device Manager window, shown in figure C.3.

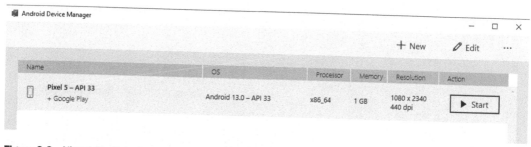

Figure C.3 Visual Studio's Android Device Manager window

When the emulator is downloaded and installed, you can run your application. After booting up, the emulator shows the application's `Hello, World!` screen, which should look like figure C.4.

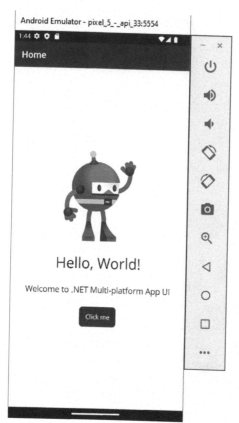

Figure C.4 MAUI application's
`Hello, World!` **screen**

Go back to Visual Studio, and find your Solution Explorer. Open the MainPage.xaml file (the page with the `Hello, World!` message). Notice the button that counts the number of clicks. The following listing shows the code for this button.

Listing C.1   Code for the button that counts clicks in the MAUI application

```
<Button
    x:Name="CounterBtn"
    Text="Click me"
    SemanticProperties.Hint="Counts the number of times you click"
    Clicked="OnCounterClicked"                          ← Refers to a method in the code-behind
    HorizontalOptions="Center" />
```

XAML pages have code-behinds, which we saw in chapter 3 with regard to Razor pages in web applications. Properties on the button can be set to values in the XAML or bound to a model. The button in the template uses an event handler, `Clicked`, to execute a method on the code-behind. Then the method changes the text of the button explicitly. The following listing shows the code-behind.

Listing C.2   `MainPage` code-behind with event handler

```
namespace Hana;                    ← Hana is the name of my app.

public partial class MainPage : ContentPage
{
    int count = 0;

    public MainPage()
    {
        InitializeComponent();
    }
                                                    ┐ Event-handler
    private void OnCounterClicked(object sender, EventArgs e)   ← ┘ method
    {
        count++;

        if (count == 1)                              ┐ Explicit update
            CounterBtn.Text = $"Clicked {count} time";   │ to button text
        else                                         ┘
            CounterBtn.Text = $"Clicked {count} times";

        SemanticScreenReader.Announce(CounterBtn.Text);
    }
}
```

Let's try a small change: binding the text of the button to a property in the code-behind. Normally, you bind to a model class somewhere other than the code-behind, but this exercise is meant to demonstrate XAML data binding. First, make the changes in the MainPage.xaml that are shown in the following listing.

Listing C.3   Binding button text to code-behind property

```xml
<?xml version="1.0" encoding="utf-8" ?>
<ContentPage xmlns="http://schemas.microsoft.com/dotnet/2021/maui"
  xmlns:x="http://schemas.microsoft.com/winfx/2009/xaml"
  x:Class="Hana.MainPage"
  x:Name="MyPage">              ◄──── Add this line.

  <!-- ... -->
```
                                                            Sets binding context
                                                            to this page
```xml
  <Button
    x:Name="CounterBtn"
    BindingContext="{x:Reference Name=MyPage}"  ◄──┘         Binds text to a property
    Text="{Binding CounterBtnText}"             ◄──────
    SemanticProperties.Hint="Counts the number of times you click"
    Clicked="OnCounterClicked"
    HorizontalOptions="Center" />

  <!-- ... -->

</ContentPage>
```

Next, open the MainPage.xaml.cs file, and make the modifications shown in the following listing.

Listing C.4   Notifying that property changed for bound controls

```csharp
namespace Hana;

public partial class MainPage : ContentPage
{
  string _counterBtnText = "Click Me";      ◄──── Adds field for text

  public string CounterBtnText              ◄──── Adds property
  {
    get => _counterBtnText;
    set
    {                                                   Notifies when
      _counterBtnText = value;                          property is changed
      OnPropertyChanged(nameof(CounterBtnText));  ◄──┘
    }
  }

  public MainPage()
  {
    InitializeComponent();
  }

  private void OnCounterClicked(object sender, EventArgs e)
  {
    CounterBtnText = "#" + CounterBtnText + "#";   ◄──── Modifies property
  }
}
```

Run the application and try clicking the button. This action should add a hashtag to the beginning and end of the button text on each click.

This section only scratches the surface of MAUI's capabilities. If you're interested in writing UI applications with XAML, you have other options, such as WPF and WinUI for Windows applications. You can also use XAML to build cross-platform applications for mobile, desktop, and web, using frameworks such as Avalonia and Uno Platform.

C.2   Blazor

Blazor is another workload that requires Visual Studio to develop with. If you've already installed Visual Studio and enabled the ASP.NET and web development workload, you should have access to Blazor new-project templates. Try creating a Blazor server application. Blazor pages use the same Razor syntax that we used in chapter 3, and the layout of the project will look somewhat familiar. Figure C.5 shows the files and folders for a traditional ASP.NET Core Razor-based web application compared with a Blazor server application.

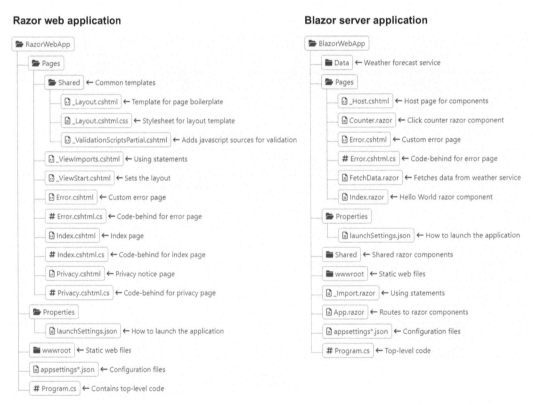

Figure C.5   Side-by-side comparison of the files and folders created by the templates for Razor-based web applications and Blazor server applications

Blazor has a new file extension, .razor, as well as the .cshtml format used by traditional web applications. Both files contain Razor syntax. The difference is that .cshtml is now intended for pages, whereas .razor is for components. The Blazor server template is designed as a single-page application (SPA) with a left bar for navigation among components. The bottom line is that it's not much of a leap to go from ASP.NET Core web applications with Razor to Blazor applications.

What's exciting about Blazor, though, is the fact that it can use WebAssembly. WebAssembly (abbreviated WASM) is a way to run almost any programming language in a web browser. A compiler can take a high-level language such as Go or C# and build a WASM module. You can think of a WASM module as being like a container, but with a restricted instruction set designed for the web. Blazor enables you to run .NET code in a browser by building WASM modules. Try creating a new project by using the Blazor WebAssembly template, and you'll get an application that looks and works much like the server template.

Having both server and WebAssembly support means that Blazor works on both the client side and the server side; it also allows hybrid modes in which some parts run on the client and others run on the server.

Blazor may become the default soon instead of ASP.NET Core for web applications. It gives developers the power of .NET, C#, and Razor to build rich web applications without the need for JavaScript. To learn more about Blazor in a vessel that does it justice, check out *Blazor in Action*, by Chris Sainty (https://www.manning.com/books/blazor-in-action).

appendix D
The async state machine

C# allows running code asynchronously through `Tasks`. Although you can create `Tasks` by hand, the `async` and `await` keywords make this powerful feature accessible. These keywords do a lot of heavy lifting, which can feel like magic.

The C# compiler understands how to turn code using `async` and `await` into a state machine. We'll see how this state machine works by looking at the Common Intermediate Language (CIL; .NET's intermediate language), generated when `async` is used and when it isn't.

You can follow along with the repro steps and see how this process works if you have Visual Studio. Visual Studio comes with a tool called ildasm that we use to view the generated CIL from compiling the code. If you're using JetBrains, the dotPeek application can decompile to CIL.

The first step is creating a new ASP.NET Core Web API application. Use the Visual Studio new-project dialog box or the `dotnet` command-line interface (CLI) to create the project (`dotnet new webapi --name WebApplication1`).

The default webapi template has a `WeatherForecastController` as an example. We'll build a service to time how long the request takes and invoke it via middleware. Create an interface called `ITimerService` with the code from the following listing.

Listing D.1 `ITimerService` interface code

```
namespace WebApplication1;

public interface ITimerService
{
  void StartTimer(string timerName);
  void StopTimer(string timerName);
  void EmitTelemetry();
}
```

We don't need to fill out this interface, but we'll create the middleware. Create a new class called `TimerMiddleware` with the code from the following listing.

Listing D.2 `TimerMiddleware` for timing requests

```
namespace WebApplication1;

public class TimerMiddleware
{
  public const string FullRequest = nameof(FullRequest);
  private readonly RequestDelegate _next;
  private readonly ITimerService _timerService;

  public TimerMiddleware(RequestDelegate next, ITimerService timerService)
  {
    _next = next;
    _timerService = timerService;
  }

  public async Task InvokeAsync(HttpContext httpContext)          ⟵⎯ Signals to create async state machine
  {
    if (!httpContext.Request.Path.StartsWithSegments(
      "/weatherforecast", StringComparison.OrdinalIgnoreCase))
    {
      _timerService.StartTimer(FullRequest);
    }

    try
    {
      await _next(httpContext);          ⟵⎯⎯⎯ Where method logic splits
    }
    finally
    {
      if (!httpContext.Request.Path.StartsWithSegments(
        "/weatherforecast", StringComparison.OrdinalIgnoreCase))
      {
        _timerService.StopTimer(FullRequest);
        _timerService.EmitTelemetry();
      }
    }
  }
}
```

We want this middleware to time calls to the `WeatherForecastController`. We don't need to register the middleware, as we need only compile the project to see the CIL generated for the middleware class. Open a developer command prompt for Visual Studio 20xx, and enter the command `ildasm` (or use `dotPeek` if you have JetBrains Rider). This command should bring up a GUI tool. From the tool, open the new DLL (such as WebApplication1.dll) built for the web application (from the /bin/Debug/net*.0 folder). You can also drag the DLL file to the ildasm application to open it. Find the `TimerMiddleware` class in the tree, which should look like figure D.1.

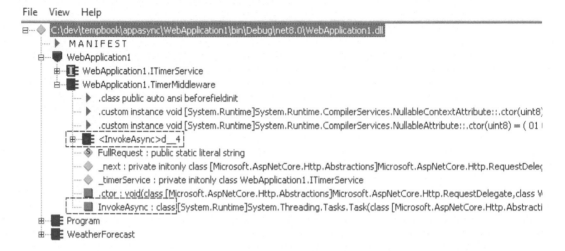

Figure D.1 Image of the `TimerMiddleware` **class in the ildasm tool with the** `InvokeAsync` **method and class highlighted**

Notice that a method called `InvokeAsync` matches the code. But there's also an inner class called `<InvokeAsync>d__4`. If you double-click the `InvokeAsync` method, you'll see the intermediate language, which should contain lines similar to those in figure D.2.

```
WebApplication1.TimerMiddleware::InvokeAsync : class [System.Runtime]System.Threading.Tasks.Task(class [Microsoft.AspNetCore.Http.Abstractions]Micros...   —  □  ×
Find  Find Next
.method public hidebysig instance class [System.Runtime]System.Threading.Tasks.Task
        InvokeAsync(class [Microsoft.AspNetCore.Http.Abstractions]Microsoft.AspNetCore.Http.HttpContext httpContext) cil ma
{
  .custom instance void [System.Runtime]System.Runtime.CompilerServices.AsyncStateMachineAttribute::.ctor(class [System.Run

  .custom instance void [System.Runtime]System.Diagnostics.DebuggerStepThroughAttribute::.ctor() = ( 01 00 00 00 )
  // Code size       63 (0x3F)
  .maxstack  2
  .locals init (class WebApplication1.TimerMiddleware/'<InvokeAsync>d__4' V_0)
  IL_0000:  newobj     instance void WebApplication1.TimerMiddleware/'<InvokeAsync>d__4'::.ctor()
  IL_0005:  stloc.0
  IL_0006:  ldloc.0
  IL_0007:  call       valuetype [System.Runtime]System.Runtime.CompilerServices.AsyncTaskMethodBuilder [System.Runtime]Sys
  IL_000c:  stfld      valuetype [System.Runtime]System.Runtime.CompilerServices.AsyncTaskMethodBuilder WebApplication1.Tim
  IL_0011:  ldloc.0
  IL_0012:  ldarg.0
  IL_0013:  stfld      class WebApplication1.TimerMiddleware WebApplication1.TimerMiddleware/'<InvokeAsync>d__4'::'<>4__thi
  IL_0018:  ldloc.0
  IL_0019:  ldarg.1
  IL_001a:  stfld      class [Microsoft.AspNetCore.Http.Abstractions]Microsoft.AspNetCore.Http.HttpContext WebApplication1.
  IL_001f:  ldloc.0
  IL_0020:  ldc.i4.m1
  IL_0021:  stfld      int32 WebApplication1.TimerMiddleware/'<InvokeAsync>d__4'::'<>1__state'
  IL_0026:  ldloc.0
  IL_0027:  ldflda     valuetype [System.Runtime]System.Runtime.CompilerServices.AsyncTaskMethodBuilder WebApplication1.Tim
  IL_002c:  ldloca.s   V_0
  IL_002e:  call       instance void [System.Runtime]System.Runtime.CompilerServices.AsyncTaskMethodBuilder::Start<class We
  IL_0033:  ldloc.0
  IL_0034:  ldflda     valuetype [System.Runtime]System.Runtime.CompilerServices.AsyncTaskMethodBuilder WebApplication1.Tim
  IL_0039:  call       instance class [System.Runtime]System.Threading.Tasks.Task [System.Runtime]System.Runtime.CompilerSe
  IL_003e:  ret
} // end of method TimerMiddleware::InvokeAsync
```

Figure D.2 CIL disassembly of the `InvokeAsync` **method in** `TimerMiddleware` **that shows how the** async **state machine works**

In the highlighted lines and between them, you can see that a new `<InvokeAsync>d__4` object is being created (newobj). The new-objects fields are populated; then the get_Task method is called. What you won't see is the code that checks the path segments for weatherforecast. The inner class with the strange name implements an interface called IAsyncStateMachine. The async and await keywords are signals to the compiler that it needs to create one of these state machines. The code for the method is contained within the MoveNext method in the state machine.

We can rewrite the middleware code to use only the async state machine when the path segment matches so that any other routes can avoid the state machine. Try rewriting the middleware as follows:

```
namespace WebApplication1;

public class TimerMiddleware
{
  public const string FullRequest = nameof(FullRequest);
  private readonly RequestDelegate _next;
  private readonly ITimerService _timerService;

  public TimerMiddleware(RequestDelegate next, ITimerService timerService)
  {
    _next = next;
    _timerService = timerService;
  }

  public Task InvokeAsync(HttpContext httpContext)          ◁─── No async
  {
    if (!httpContext.Request.Path.StartsWithSegments("/weatherforecast",
    ➥ StringComparison.OrdinalIgnoreCase))
    {
      return _next(httpContext);          ◁─── Returns Task from next middleware
    }

    return TimeRequestAsync(httpContext);          ◁─── Time weather requests only
  }

  private async Task TimeRequestAsync(          ◁─── Splits async to new method
    HttpContext httpContext)
  {
    _timerService.StartTimer(FullRequest);

    try
    {
      await _next(httpContext);          ◁─── Needs async state machine
    }
    finally
    {
      _timerService.StopTimer(FullRequest);
      _timerService.EmitTelemetry();
    }
  }
}
```

Notice that the `InvokeAsync` method isn't marked with the `async` keyword; it returns the `Task` object from other methods. Build the project and load the assembly in ildasm. The middleware class's structure should look similar. The inner class for the `async` state machine will be named after the `TimeRequestAsync` method. The most significant difference is the CIL for the `InvokeAsync` method, as shown in figure D.3.

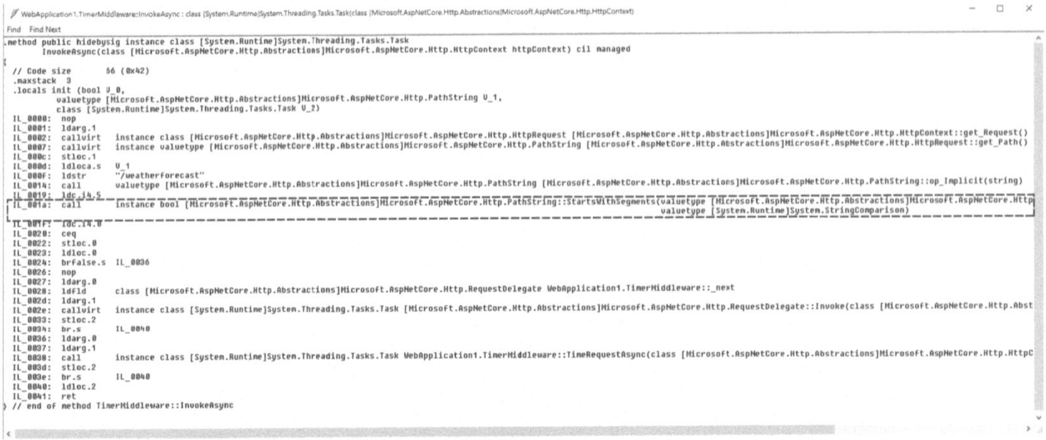

```
WebApplication1.TimerMiddleware::InvokeAsync : class [System.Runtime]System.Threading.Tasks.Task(class [Microsoft.AspNetCore.Http.Abstractions]Microsoft.AspNetCore.Http.HttpContext)
Find  Find Next
.method public hidebysig instance class [System.Runtime]System.Threading.Tasks.Task
        InvokeAsync(class [Microsoft.AspNetCore.Http.Abstractions]Microsoft.AspNetCore.Http.HttpContext httpContext) cil managed
{
  // Code size       66 (0x42)
  .maxstack  3
  .locals init (bool V_0,
           valuetype [Microsoft.AspNetCore.Http.Abstractions]Microsoft.AspNetCore.Http.PathString V_1,
           class [System.Runtime]System.Threading.Tasks.Task V_2)
  IL_0000:  nop
  IL_0001:  ldarg.1
  IL_0002:  callvirt   instance class [Microsoft.AspNetCore.Http.Abstractions]Microsoft.AspNetCore.Http.HttpRequest [Microsoft.AspNetCore.Http.Abstractions]Microsoft.AspNetCore.Http.HttpContext::get_Request()
  IL_0007:  callvirt   instance valuetype [Microsoft.AspNetCore.Http.Abstractions]Microsoft.AspNetCore.Http.PathString [Microsoft.AspNetCore.Http.Abstractions]Microsoft.AspNetCore.Http.HttpRequest::get_Path()
  IL_000c:  stloc.1
  IL_000d:  ldloca.s   V_1
  IL_000f:  ldstr      "/weatherforecast"
  IL_0014:  call       valuetype [Microsoft.AspNetCore.Http.Abstractions]Microsoft.AspNetCore.Http.PathString [Microsoft.AspNetCore.Http.Abstractions]Microsoft.AspNetCore.Http.PathString::op_Implicit(string)
  IL_0019:  ldc.i4.5
  IL_001a:  call       instance bool [Microsoft.AspNetCore.Http.Abstractions]Microsoft.AspNetCore.Http.PathString::StartsWithSegments(valuetype [Microsoft.AspNetCore.Http.Abstractions]Microsoft.AspNetCore.Http
                                                                                     valuetype [System.Runtime]System.StringComparison)
  IL_001f:  ldc.i4.0
  IL_0020:  ceq
  IL_0022:  stloc.0
  IL_0023:  ldloc.0
  IL_0024:  brfalse.s  IL_0036
  IL_0026:  nop
  IL_0027:  ldarg.0
  IL_0028:  ldfld      class [Microsoft.AspNetCore.Http.Abstractions]Microsoft.AspNetCore.Http.RequestDelegate WebApplication1.TimerMiddleware::_next
  IL_002d:  ldarg.1
  IL_002e:  callvirt   instance class [System.Runtime]System.Threading.Tasks.Task [Microsoft.AspNetCore.Http.Abstractions]Microsoft.AspNetCore.Http.RequestDelegate::Invoke(class [Microsoft.AspNetCore.Http.Abst
  IL_0033:  stloc.2
  IL_0034:  br.s       IL_0040
  IL_0036:  ldarg.0
  IL_0037:  ldarg.1
  IL_0038:  call       instance class [System.Runtime]System.Threading.Tasks.Task WebApplication1.TimerMiddleware::TimeRequestAsync(class [Microsoft.AspNetCore.Http.Abstractions]Microsoft.AspNetCore.Http.HttpC
  IL_003d:  stloc.2
  IL_003e:  br.s       IL_0040
  IL_0040:  ldloc.2
  IL_0041:  ret
} // end of method TimerMiddleware::InvokeAsync
```

Figure D.3 CIL disassembly of the `InvokeAsync` method modified to not use the `async` state machine

On the highlighted lines, you see the call to `PathString::StartsWithSegments` to check for `/weatherforecast`. What you don't see is the creation of a new object (`newobj`) in this code. That process happens in the `TimeRequestAsync` method so that it can start the `async` state machine. Because the `InvokeAsync` method doesn't use the `await` keyword and returns the `Task` objects from other method calls, it avoids an allocation and the execution of an `async` state machine if the path segments don't match.

The effect of avoiding a single allocation is small, but the cumulative effect in performance-sensitive areas of your service (such as middleware) can reduce the amount of time spent in garbage collection. More important, I hope that this appendix demystifies how the `async` and `await` keywords work in C# and what the compiler is doing.

appendix E
Testing internal members

This appendix uses the Sudoku solver project from chapter 6. Consider the completed IsValid method. The method is fairly long—more than 60 lines. I could divide it into smaller chunks, which would allow testing of individual methods, but I don't want those methods to be part of the public API. In .NET, you can give tests access to internal (non-public) members and types. The rows, cols, and sqrt variables are used in all the checks, so it would be helpful to make them fields in the Solver, as shown in the following listing. You can get the values for these fields in the constructor with only the validation logic in the IsValid method.

Listing E.1 Moving rows, cols, and sqrt variables to fields in the Solver class

```
public class Solver
{
  private readonly int[,] _board;
  private readonly int _numRows;          ◄──── Renames and makes into a field
  private readonly int _numCols;
  private readonly int _gridSize;         ◄──── Square root is the grid size.

  public Solver(int[,] board)
  {
    _board = board;
    _numRows = _board.GetLength(0);
    _numCols = _board.GetLength(1);       ◄──── We know that there are two dimensions.
    _gridSize = (int)Math.Sqrt(_numRows);  ◄──┐
  }                                           │ Assumes that board
                                              │ is square for now
  public bool IsValid()
  {
    if (_numRows != _numCols || _numRows < 4    ◄──┐
        || (_gridSize * _gridSize) != _numRows)    │ Shortens validation
      return false;                                │ into one expression

    return CheckRows()    ◄──── All must be true to return true.
```

319

```
                && CheckColumns()
                && CheckSubGrids();
    }

    internal bool CheckRows() { }         ┃ Moves logic here with
    internal bool CheckColumns() { }      ┃ return of true at end
    internal bool CheckSubGrids() { }
}
```

The methods CheckRows, CheckColumns, and CheckSubGrids are internal. Because the test project is a separate .NET project, it doesn't have access to internal members in other projects. But we can mark in the SudokuSolver project that we want to expose internal members to the test project. To do so, modify the SudokuSolver.csproj file, and add the section from the following listing.

Listing E.2   Adding the `InternalsVisibleTo` attribute

```
<ItemGroup>
  <AssemblyAttribute
    Include="System.Runtime.CompilerServices.InternalsVisibleTo">
    <_Parameter1>SudokuSolver.UnitTests</_Parameter1>
  </AssemblyAttribute>
</ItemGroup>
```

InternalsVisibleTo is an attribute that applies at the assembly level. You can put this attribute in a class with a statement like [assembly: InternalsVisibleTo("SudokuSolver .UnitTests")] instead of adding it to the project file, which is a matter of preference.

InternalsVisibleTo name matching

In listing E.2, the parameter is set to the name of the unit-test project. Any assembly that has this name will have access to the internals. How great a security concern this is depends on your situation. Anyone can use reflection to examine the private and internal types and members in a library or use a decompiler tool to view the original code. In .NET Framework, it was common practice to sign assemblies and refer to the assembly's full name with a public key in InternalsVisibleTo. But assembly signing has become less common. (The first edition of this book had a section on assembly signing that was removed from this edition.) Even Microsoft projects use only the assembly name. So unless you plan to use an obfuscation tool, you needn't have much concern about doing the same.

Now that the unit tests have access to the internals of the Solver class, we can add tests for individual methods. The following listing adds a new theory to verify the CheckRows method.

Listing E.3   Theory test for the `CheckRows` method exclusively

```
[Theory]
[MemberData(nameof(CheckRowsData))]
public void CheckRows(int[,] board, bool isValid)
```

```
{
  var solver = new Solver(board);
  Assert.Equal(isValid, solver.CheckRows());
}

public static IEnumerable<object[]> CheckRowsData
{
  get
  {
    yield return new object[] { new int[,] {{1,2,3,0,1}}, false };
    yield return new object[] { new int[,] {{1,2,3,0,4}}, true };
    yield return new object[] { new int[,] {{0,0,3}}, true };
    yield return new object[] { new int[,] {{0,2,0,2}}, false };
  }
}
```

> **Calls CheckRows instead of IsValid**

> **No size check, so doesn't have to be square**

Can't create arrays for the board in the InlineData attribute

If you try to use `InlineData` for this theory with an attribute like `[InlineData(new int[,] {{0,0}}, true)]`, the compiler will give you an error message. The first argument initializes an array and therefore isn't a constant expression. Nonconstant expressions require the `MemberData` approach to work.

Exercise: Add tests for the CheckColumns and CheckSubGrids methods

With `CheckRows`, you can test with boards that aren't square or sizes that are perfect squares because the `Solver` uses the number of rows for other calculations. You can't do the same with `CheckColumns`. You could make the `_gridSize` field internal instead of private and set it directly after creating the `Solver` object. Another approach is to use square boards, as in the `CheckRules` theory test. `CheckSubGrids` requires square boards either way.

In the `CheckRows` test, no verification of the board size is required, so you can test boards with single rows of any size. You should also have tests with multiple rows to make sure that the numbers from the preceding row are being cleared.

Black-box vs. white-box testing

When we tested the `IsValid` public API, we were performing black-box testing. How the `IsValid` method works isn't a consideration of the test; we're trying to come up with as many edge cases as possible to make sure that `IsValid` works. Typically, when you start using `InternalsVisibleTo`, you're performing white-box testing. White-box testing is more fragile because the layout and behavior of the internals aren't guaranteed (or are less guaranteed than in a public API). When to use white-box testing is another "it depends" matter in software development. The SudokuSolver tests don't need access to the internals, but in many cases, `InternalsVisibleTo` is useful; it's another tool in your .NET toolbox.

appendix F
xUnit supplement

This appendix contains some other xUnit features that may be useful. You can find the full documentation for xUnit at https://xunit.net/#documentation.

F.1 Traits

Traits allow you to assign any number of properties to a test. You can use traits to organize tests into categories to exercise specific areas of your code. Traits are applied via attributes and can be set on the method, class, or assembly level. You could mark the `ComicFinderTests` class as an integration test and the `ComicRepositoryTests` class as a unit test, for example, as shown in the following listing.

Listing F.1 Distinguishing unit and integration tests with traits

```
[Trait("Category", "Integration")]
public class ComicFinderTests : IDisposable
{
  // ...
}

[Trait("Category", "Unit")]
public class ComicRepositoryTests : IDisposable
{
  // ...
}
```

You make up the name of the trait (first parameter) and the value (second parameter). With the traits set, you can specify command-line parameters to xUnit for the traits you want. So if you want to run only unit tests, you can use the command line in the following listing.

Listing F.2 dotnet CLI command to run tests with the `Category` trait set to `Unit`

```
dotnet test --filter Category=Unit
```

F.2   Collections

xUnit runs some tests in parallel based on certain rules. By default, each test class is its own collection. Only one test per collection can be run at a time. You can configure this default behavior via an assembly-level attribute. The following listing is an example of an assembly-level attribute that you can add to any C# source file in your assembly (but usually put in a dedicated file).

Listing F.3   Assembly-level attribute that controls xUnit's parallelization behavior

```
[assembly: CollectionBehavior(CollectionBehavior.CollectionPerAssembly)]
```

This attribute changes the default behavior from `CollectionPerTest` to `Collection-PerAssembly`. *Collection per assembly* means that only one test method in the assembly can be run at a time.

Some test classes may be able to run in parallel; others may conflict with another specific test class. To keep parallel execution for the rest of the tests, you can add them to the same collection. If you want the `ComicFinderTests` and `ComicRepository-Tests` to use the same underlying database, for example, you can't run them in parallel. What you *can* do is add both test classes to the same collection, as shown in the following listing.

Listing F.4   Putting test classes in the same collection

```
[Collection("UsesSqlite")]
public class ComicFinderTests : IDisposable
{
  // ...
}

[Collection("UsesSqlite")]
public class ComicRepositoryTests : IDisposable
{
  // ...
}
```

TIP   For more options for controlling test parallelization, see the xUnit documentation at https://xunit.net/docs/running-tests-in-parallel.

index